A C

The Family Correspondence of the Parents of
St. Thérèse of the Child Jesus

1863 - 1885

Blessed Zélie and Louis Martin

Translated by Ann Connors Hess
Edited by Dr. Frances Renda

ST PAULS

Photographs with permission of

Carmel de Lisieux
Office Central de Lisieux
Diocese de Séez

Library of Congress Cataloging-in-Publication Data
Martin, Zélie, 1831-1877.
[Correspondence. English. Selections]
  A call to a deeper love: the family correspondence of the parents of St. Thérèse of
the Child Jesus, 1863-1885 / Zélie and Louis Martin : translated by Ann C. Hess ;
edited by Frances Renda.
     p. cm.
  Includes bibliographical references.
  ISBN 978-0-8189-1321-1
  1. Martin, Zélie, 1831-1877—Correspondence. 2. Martin, Louis, 1823-1894–Correspondence. 3. Thérèse, de Lisieux, Saint, 1873-1897–Family. 4. Christian saints–Family
relationships–France–Lisieux. I. Martin, Louis, 1823-1894. II. Title.
  BX4705.M41235A4 2010
  282.092'244—dc22
                                        2010015657

Originally published as *Correspondance familiale (1863-1885)* by
les Éditions du Cerf, Paris, France.

Produced and designed in the United States of America by the
Fathers and Brothers of the Society of St. Paul,
2187 Victory Boulevard, Staten Island, New York 10314-6603
as part of their communications apostolate.

ISBN 10: 0-8189-1321-5
ISBN 13: 978-0-8189-1321-1

Printing Information:

| Current Printing - first digit | 6 | 7 | 8 | 9 | 1 0 |

Year of Current Printing - first year shown

                                                          2021

To
BISHOP PATRICK AHERN
BISHOP GUY GAUCHER, O.C.D.
and
FATHER LINUS RYAN, O.CARM.

Three spiritual guides, who have spent their lives
bringing to the world
the life and spirituality of St. Thérèse of the Child Jesus
and who have furthered the cause of the
life and spirituality of Blessed Louis and Zélie Martin,
the parents of Saint Thérèse.

With deep gratitude
and friendship
we will always treasure.

Internet Resources

For additional information on St. Thérèse and Blessed Louis and Zélie Martin, you may visit the web sites:

- **www.thereseoflisieux.org** featuring a broad range of material on the Martin family
- **www.therese-de-lisieux-catholique.fr** the official site of the *Sanctuaire de Lisieux* [The Sanctuary of Lisieux]
- diocesedeseez.cef.fr/-MAISON-FAMILLE-MARTIN-Maison-.html information about the Martin family home in Alençon
- the web site for the Archives of the Carmelite Monastery in Lisieux, **www.carmeldelisieux.fr** is in development at the time of this printing

For videos relating to St. Thérèse and Blessed Louis and Zélie Martin filmed in Alençon and Lisieux, go to:

- **www.youtube.com** search for "amiedetherese"
- **www.gloria.tv** search for "amiedetherese"

Table of Contents

Acknowledgments

A historical text of this magnitude, translated from French to English, was a joint effort, a collaboration of mind and heart between Ann Hess, the translator, and the editor of this book, Dr. Frances Renda. The decision to add annotated footnotes was to illuminate textual references possibly unfamiliar to English-speaking readers and to add depth and insight to their understanding of the life and spirituality of Blessed Louis and Zélie Martin – a Catholic couple living in 19th century France, whose lives were imbued with their faith and love of God.

First and foremost, this book would not have been possible without the confidence and support of Fr. Edmund Lane, SSP, the Editor of Alba House; we are very grateful. We owe special thanks to Bishop Guy Gaucher, OCD, Dr. Renda's long-time friend and support. His scholarly insights and encouragement were deeply appreciated. We thank Mgr Bernard Lagoutte, Rector of the Basilica of St. Thérèse, for his support. We are grateful to Sister Camille Bessette, OCD, Archivist of the Carmelite Monastery in Lisieux, for her kindness and expertise in providing Dr. Renda with the historical details that will make "The Chronology of the Martin and Guérin Families" a reference source in future Martin family scholarship. We are very grateful to Father Raymond Zambelli, former Rector of the Basilica of St. Thérèse, for the many years of his friendship, support and kindness. We thank the staff of the Pilgrimage Office in Lisieux, Ria Augustijns and Barbara Dziurowicz, with particular thanks to Laurence Panontin for the generous time she spent providing historical data. We thank Father Pascal Marie and Emmanuel Houis for their outstanding exhibitions on the Martin family at the Church of St. Jacques in Lisieux. They provided inspiration and brought to life the life and times of Louis, Zélie and their children. We thank the Sisters of the *Maison Famille Martin* in Alençon, where Louis and Zélie lived much of their married life, for enabling us to experience the presence of the Martin family.

We especially thank Fr. Donald Kinney, OCD, for his expertise in contributing to the reading and critiquing of this manuscript.

Dr. Renda's special appreciation goes to Marianne Dahl for her laborious work in helping to bring this work to fruition. Her commitment and dedication to this project were unwavering.

We're indebted to Susan Ehlert for the indispensable contributions she made from the beginning to the end of this precious work.

This work was accomplished with the generosity of many people who contributed their expertise in the areas of history, medicine, spirituality, and language, doing ancillary translations, helping with research, and providing ongoing support. It would take several pages to describe the contributions of each person, so we will simply list their names below. We are very grateful.

Rev. Peter Martin Batts, OP, Michelle Bontempo, Dr. Kevin Cahill, MD, Rev. Victor Chaupetta, MS, Dominque Chauvel, Sister Helen Coldrick, RDC, Marion Constantine, Laurence Dalbray, Brother Brian Dybowski, FSC, Jean-Louis Fleur, Rev. Benedict Groeschel, CFR, Mary Ellen Hubbard, Rev. Joseph Iyamah, Dr. Craig Katz, MD, Karen Killilea, Catherine Lenz, Rev. Kenneth M. Loughman, Juan Marrero, Brother Samuel Martinez, FSC, Giancarlo Molinari, Sister Grace Therese Murray, SC, Rev. David E. Nolan, Kenneth Nolan, Maureen O'Riordan, Paolo Orlando, Peggy Peet, Dr. Carlos Pizzimbono, MD, Charles Princiotto, Susan Princiotto, Catherine Richie, Father Antonio Sangalli, OCD, Maria Esther Sierra, Judy Turba, Msgr. Desmond Vella, Arnaud de Villeroché, Kathleen Walsh, Brother Gerald Warner, SDB, and Maria Woodman.

We are deeply grateful to the Benedictine Nuns of Abbazia di San Vincenzo al Volturno, Isernia, Italy; the Discalced Carmelite Nuns at the Carmelite Monastery of the Incarnation, Beacon, New York; the Nuns at the Visitation Monastery in Georgetown, Washington, DC; and the Nuns at the Visitation Monastery in Brooklyn, New York. Without the power of their continued prayers and encouragement, this book could not have been completed.

Preface

In 1958, l'Office Central de Lisieux [the Central Office of Lisieux] published *Correspondance familiale (1863-1877)* [Family Correspondence (1863-1877)] of Zélie Martin (*née* Guérin), the mother of Saint Thérèse of the Child Jesus and the Holy Face, with a Foreword by Father Stéphane-Joseph Piat, O.F.M. The work was prepared by Thérèse's sisters, above all by Céline Martin (Sister Geneviève of the Holy Face).

The book was reprinted in 1961 and was subsequently out of print. It was necessary to reissue this book because, after more than fifty years, interest in the parents of Thérèse Martin had not stopped growing in France and around the world. For a long time, they have been prayed to with confidence and, since October 13, 1958, a number of pilgrims in Lisieux, among them many families, have gone to their tombs adjacent to the apse of the basilica to spend time in silent prayer and reflection.

Beginning in February 1958, the *Annales de sainte Thérèse de Lisieux* [The Annals of Saint Thérèse of Lisieux] began to publish the graces and favors attributed to their intercession.

On March 22, 1957, the Ordinary Process concerning Louis Martin was opened in the Diocese of Bayeux. It was closed on February 12, 1960.

At the same time, in the Diocese of Séez, the informative process for Zélie Guérin was opened on October 10, 1957, and taken to Rome on January 21, 1959.

This resulted in an impressive dossier in two volumes entitled *Positio super virtutibus.*[1]

---

[1]   "Position Paper on the Heroic Virtues." *Congregatio de Causis Sanctorum, Canoni-*

After this long and considerable inquiry, in a decree published by the Congregation for the Causes of Saints on March 26, 1994, Pope John Paul II declared Louis Martin and his wife, Marie-Azélie Guérin Martin, "Venerable." This was a step within sight of their beatification. To reach that point, a miracle recognized by the Church after a special process would be necessary.

One understands the interest in republishing the correspondence of Zélie Martin. We added the letters of Louis Martin to fully justify the title *Correspondance familiale* [Family Correspondence].

Unfortunately, we have very few letters written by Thérèse's father, a total of sixteen. We are incorporating them chronologically.

Marie-Azélie Guérin was born December 23, 1831, in Gandelain, a village in Saint-Denis-sur-Sarthon in the Department of Orne. She died of cancer on August 28, 1877, in Alençon, at the age of forty-five years and eight months. She was a prolific letter writer, but only 218 of her letters have survived.

In 1958, 217 letters were published, and later, an original letter was found.[2]

Louis Martin was born August 22, 1823, in Bordeaux and died in the Château de La Musse, near Évreux, on July 29, 1894, less than a month short of his seventy-first birthday.

He wrote few letters. After his marriage on July 13, 1858, in Alençon, he left the letter-writing to his wife and daughters, especially the letters to the Guérin family. Consequently, the number of his letters is very limited.

Taking into account what we say in the "Textual Commentary" (see Appendix II), i.e., that almost all of Zélie's original letters were destroyed by the Martin sisters, we can still attempt a rough sketch of her personality by referring to the existing body of her correspondence.

A Brief Sketch of Zélie Martin

Zélie's spontaneity was expressed throughout her correspondence, as well as her liveliness touched by humor. A sound common

---

zationis servorum Dei Ludovivi Martin et Mariae Azeliae Guerin, [Congregation for the Causes of Saints, "Canonization of the Servants of God Louis Martin and Marie-Azélie Guérin"], Rome, 1991. In total: 2,003 pages. Format 30 x 21 cm.

2   Published in *Vie Thérésienne*, No. 55, July, 1974 (*Archives de famille*, pp. 232-233).

sense that, by its origins, one could describe as down to earth, shows that she had her feet planted firmly on the ground and that she had a deep, selfless sisterly affection that was not afraid of expressing reproaches and advice. She exhibited a strong courage throughout her life, in her exhausting work as a lace maker and especially during her terrible illness. She went to the limits of her strength in her role of wife, mother and educator, her love expressing itself in a thousand subtle ways – worry about her family's health, pride in the qualities of her children, heart wrenching pain in the loss of four of them, and continuous desire for their sanctity. She knew, in many little ways, how to develop her daughters' emotional lives, especially by her vigilant love.

She also knew how to go beyond the narrow framework of her family. She shared in the misfortunes of others, whether they were servants, neighbors, abandoned elderly men, the sick or little Armandine, who was mistreated by two women pretending to be nuns.

Zélie was also a remarkable observer of her time. She writes humorous thumbnail sketches of her circle of acquaintances and comments on events in the light of her convictions. Through these letters, one could put together a little tableau of Alençon society – a few nobles, sometimes impoverished, the upper and lower middle-classes, the newly rich, some notable people, the world of shopkeepers and artisans (in Alençon, the Martins were part of this class), country people, laborers, the poor, the ecclesiastical world and anticlerical people. Let us not forget a brief account of the War of 1870 (the partisans, the German occupation, etc.).

Zélie did not have a happy childhood, being raised by a very strict, rigid mother. Zélie carried the weight of all kinds of suffering in a world where death was very present, and medicine was powerless in the majority of cases. In eighteen years, she experienced eight bereavements, of which four were her children. In the 19th century, infant mortality was still very high. Zélie went through intense periods of overwork, family and professional problems, but she was a very strong woman.

One of her profound joys was motherhood – "As for me, I'm crazy about children, I was born to have them…" (CF 83 - December 15, 1872).

She had an extremely deep faith that expressed itself in many ways – by her persevering prayer, her daily attendance at the earliest morning Mass up until the last days of her life, her trust and abandonment to Divine Providence in spite of frequent worries, the offering up of her numerous sufferings, physical and mental, and her love for the Blessed Mother and the saints, in particular Saint Joseph.

Her sense of the Church dictated rigorous obedience to the rules relating to penance and fasting, and she shared with her husband a scrupulous respect for Sunday (the Day of the Lord) as well as a profound aspiration to sanctity and the Kingdom of God.

We also need to understand the harmony that united the two spouses. They were truly very different, but their qualities complemented each other. If Louis was rather quiet and reserved, Zélie was active and spontaneous. He found his wife too extravagant in outfitting their daughters, but she thought he spoiled them too much. She didn't like meetings, traveling and pilgrimages; Louis frequented the Catholic circles and was always ready to leave for a retreat or a pilgrimage (to Chartres, Lourdes, Soligny, etc.).

Their joy was being together, making each other happy, sharing family intimacies, walks in the country, but also praying together, reciting the rosary, Nocturnal Adoration, and attending Mass.

Both had wanted to consecrate themselves totally to God before their marriage – he as a monk in the Monastery of the Great Saint Bernard, she as a religious in the apostolate of the Sisters of St. Vincent de Paul in the hospital in Alençon. Their desire subsequently did not change, apart from the form. Sanctity – for them and for their children – remained life's absolute ideal.

Zélie's death was a terrible blow for Louis – they were so used to being together and were apart as little as possible.

As for their five daughters, they forever kept a fervent memory of their mother. Little Thérèse, at four and a half, remained profoundly marked and wounded by this death for six years, until the grace of Christmas 1886.

Louis Martin

Let us imagine for a moment that Louis Martin left nothing for posterity except these sixteen letters, extracts and fragments. What image of him would they give us?

We see a father, very attentive to his five daughters, loving each one with tenderness, having an acute sense of family, an even-tempered and considerate traveler, a man of prayer, prompt to admire and to praise God for His creation, always living in His presence.

He places great importance on friendship and has a good sense of humor. He's a generous man, concerned about others.

Everything else we know about him, through the numerous testimonies of others, confirms these impressions. But these remain very superficial. They say only very little of the depth of his personality, his self-sacrifice, his kindness and his generosity, his predilection for silence and meditation, his love of God and the Church, his peace, and his gentleness.

They say nothing of the clockmaker-jeweler whose precision, meticulous attention to detail, and impeccable work over a period of twenty-one years impressed many of his Alençon customers.

Above all, because the published letters stop in the year 1888, they say nothing of "the passion" of Louis Martin – his mental health affected, he was committed to the Hospital of Bon Sauveur in Caen for three years (1889-1892), bearing the number "14,449." The humiliated father lived through this trial surrounded by the prayers of his daughters and the Guérin family. Several doctors have made the retrospective diagnosis of cerebral arteriosclerosis and renal insufficiency, with an enlargement of the prostate leading to uremia.

This word "passion" will be used by Thérèse herself.[3] She knew that her "dear king" had not only given all his daughters to God, but he had offered himself at the altar that he had given to the Cathedral in Lisieux, the parish church attended by the Martin and Guérin families.

There is perhaps no better portrait of these two "Blesseds" than that written by their last daughter, canonized by Pope Pius XI on May 17, 1925, and proclaimed Doctor of the Church by Pope John Paul II on October 19, 1997.

---

[3] *Story of a Soul*, tr. John Clarke, OCD. Washington, DC: ICS Publications, 1996, p. 156.

Thérèse and Her Parents

At the age of four and a half, Thérèse lost her mother. Her memories of her were both indelible and too brief. On the other hand, she lived closely with her father, sharing a deep spiritual bond, from her birth until the day of her entrance into Carmel (April 9, 1888) at the age of fifteen years and three months.

So it is not surprising that in her written work (manuscripts, letters, poetry, etc.) Louis Martin is much more present.

At the end of her brief existence, she had written a broad range of observations of both her parents.

In *Story of a Soul*:

"God granted me the favor of opening my intelligence at an early age and of imprinting childhood recollections so deeply on my memory that it seems the things I'm about to recount happened only yesterday. Jesus in His love willed, perhaps, that I know the matchless Mother He had given me, but whom His hand hastened to crown in heaven.

"God was pleased all through my life to surround me with *love*, and the first memories I have are stamped with smiles and the most tender caresses. But although He placed so much *love* near me, He also sent much love into my little heart, making it warm and affectionate. I loved Mama and Papa very much and showed my tenderness for them in a thousand ways, for I was very expressive."[4]

"What shall I say of the winter evenings at home, especially the Sunday evenings? Ah! how I loved, after the *game of checkers* was over, to sit with Céline on Papa's knees. He used to sing, in his beautiful voice, airs that filled the soul with profound thoughts, or else, rocking us gently, he recited poems that taught the eternal truths. Then we all went upstairs to say our night prayers together and the little Queen was alone near her King, having only to look at him to see how the saints pray."[5]

---

[4] Ibid., pp. 16-17.
[5] Ibid., p. 43.

In a letter to her sister Léonie, dated August 13, 1893:

"...I know this earth is the place of our exile, we are voyagers who are travelling toward our homeland. What does it matter if the route we follow is not the same since the only goal will be heaven. There we shall be reunited never to leave each other, there we shall taste family joys eternally. We shall find our dear Father again, who will be surrounded with glory and honor for his perfect fidelity and especially for the humiliations that were showered upon him; we shall see our good Mother, who will rejoice at the trials that were our lot during life's exile; we shall take delight in her happiness as she contemplates her five religious daughters, and we shall form, along with the four little angels who await us up above, a crown adorning the heads of our dear Parents."[6]

In a letter to her spiritual brother, Father Maurice Bellière, written July 26, 1897, as she suffered in the infirmary of Carmel, she gave a kind of testimonial about her family:

"God gave me a father and a mother more worthy of heaven than of earth; they asked the Lord to give them many children and to take them for Himself. This desire was answered: four little angels flew away to heaven, and five children left in the arena took Jesus for Bridegroom. It was with a heroic courage that my father, like a new Abraham, climbed *three times* the mountain of Carmel to immolate to God what was most dear to him.[7] First, there were his two eldest; then the third of his daughters,[8] on the advice of her director and conducted by our incomparable father, made an attempt in the convent of the Visitation. (God was content with her acceptance, *later she returned to the world where she lives as though in the cloister*). There remained to the Elect of God only two children, one eighteen years old, the other fourteen. The latter, "the Little Thérèse," *asked permission to fly to Carmel, which she obtained from her good father, who pushed his condescension even to taking her first to Bayeux, then to Rome, in order to remove the obstacles which were holding back the im-*

---

6   *Letters of St. Thérèse of Lisieux, Volume II, 1890-1897*, tr. John Clarke, OCD, Letter 148, p. 816. Washington, DC: ICS Publications, 1988. LT 148, p. 816.
7   See Genesis 22:2.
8   Léonie.

molation of her whom he called his queen. When he had brought her to port, he said to the only child who remained with him:[9] "If you want to follow the example of your sisters, I consent to it, do not worry about me." The angel who was to support the old age of such a saint answered that, *after his departure for heaven*, she would also fly to the cloister, which filled with joy him who lived only for God. But such a beautiful life was to be crowned by a trial worthy of it. A short time after my departure, the father whom we cherished with such good reason was seized with an attack of paralysis in his limbs, which was repeated several times, but it could not remain there, the trial would have been too sweet, for the heroic Patriarch had offered himself as a victim to God; so the paralysis, changing its course, settled in the venerable head of the victim whom the Lord had accepted.... I lack the space to give you some touching details. I want only to tell you that we had to drink the chalice to its very dregs and to separate ourselves for three years from our venerated father, entrusting him to religious but strange hands. He accepted this trial, the entire humiliation of which he understood, and he pushed heroism even to not willing that we ask for his cure."[10]

When she was about seven years old, in Les Buissonnets, Thérèse had what she called a "truly extraordinary vision" concerning her father, which had troubled her.[11] Fourteen years later, in 1895, the meaning of this "prophetic vision" was revealed to her:

"It was indeed *Papa* whom I had seen advancing, bent over with age. It was indeed Papa, who was bearing on his venerable countenance and white hair the symbol of his *glorious* trial.[12] Just as the adorable Face of Jesus was veiled during His Passion, so the face of His faithful servant had to be veiled in the days of his sufferings in order that it might shine in the heavenly Fatherland near its Lord, the Eternal Word!

---

[9] Céline.
[10] *Letters of St. Thérèse of Lisieux, Volume II, 1890-1897,* tr. John Clarke, OCD, Letter 261, pp. 1165-1166.
[11] *Story of a Soul,* tr. John Clarke, OCD, pp. 45-46.
[12] The pathology that affected Louis Martin's mental faculties during the last five years of his life and necessitated a stay in the psychiatric hospital.

"It is from the midst of this ineffable glory where he reigns in heaven that our dear Father obtained for us the grace to understand the vision his little Queen had at an age when illusions are not to be feared. It is from the midst of glory he obtained this sweet consolation of understanding that God, ten years before our great trial, was already showing it to us. He was doing this as a Father who gives His children a glimpse of the glorious future He is preparing for them and is pleased to have them consider in advance the priceless riches which will be their heritage."[13]

With hindsight and the discovery of the depth of Trinitarian merciful love, Thérèse found the key to interpreting the life of her father. We noticed that within this text, the word "glory" is repeated three times. This is the ultimate word for this family history, without doubt unique within the more general history of Christian holiness.

Guy Gaucher
Auxiliary Bishop of Bayeux and Lisieux

N.B.: For this edition, we fully benefitted from the work of Sister Cécile de l'Immaculée, O.C.D., and Jacques Lonchampt, essential partners in the *Nouvelle Édition du Centenaire* (Published by Cerf-DDB, 1992).

At the end of this file, we added extracts of Madame Martin's letters copied by Sister Geneviève and recopied by Sister Marie of the Trinity in two school notebooks published in *Vie Thérésienne*. No. 88, October 1982, pp. 310-318, and *Vie Thérésienne*. No. 93, January 1984, pp. 70-80.

---

[13] *Story of a Soul*, tr. John Clarke, OCD, p. 47.

Introduction

to the English Language Edition of the
Family Correspondence of Blessed Louis and Zélie Martin

Louis and Zélie Martin lived ordinary lives in extraordinary times. Their story opened on the Bridge of St. Leonard, which spans the River Sarthe in Alençon, France. As they passed each other walking over the bridge, Zélie heard an interior voice say – "This is the man I have prepared for you." Inspired by the Holy Spirit, their encounter was not accidental. Like any passage over a bridge, which leads from one place to a new destination, their providential encounter, called into being by Divine Love, would lead them from the life they knew to a new life, a married life in Christ. After the formalities of introduction, both Louis and Zélie grew in awareness of their love for one another and they responded to the grace they were given in a work as yet undefined. Both Louis and Zélie understood that their marriage was a call to holiness. Three months later, on July 13, 1858, Louis and Zélie were married in the medieval Church of Notre Dame d'Alençon at midnight, in a candlelight ceremony surrounded by family and friends. Abbé Frédéric Hurel, the Dean of the Church of Saint Leonard and Louis' spiritual director, witnessed their vows. As they stood in mystery and darkness before the majestic High Altar, in the presence of Jesus in the Blessed Sacrament, their love was fused to the flame of LOVE, which would now exist between them, a flame that their children would later be imbued with.

The bridal couple was surrounded by their family and friends, each holding a candle and pledging to support them in their times of darkness, while blazing torches that provided light encircled the entire wedding party. This image gave the impression of a blazing fire – a flame of love in the heart of the Church. A spark from this flame of love from their last child, St. Thérèse of the Child Jesus, would set the world on fire in the 20th century, as she wrote in 1895:

> "I have flames within me,
> And each day I can win
> A great number of souls for Jesus,
> Inflaming them with His love."[14]

And then, in turn, Louis and Zélie promised to be the light of Christ for each other and for everyone that came into their lives. Louis and Zélie's love was a Eucharistic love centered on the Paschal Mystery. They understood the importance of sacrifice for their love to grow and the need to die to oneself in order to live, as Jesus said in John 12:24:

> "Unless a grain of wheat
> falls on the ground and dies,
> it remains only a single grain;
> but if it dies,
> it bears much fruit."

After exchanging their wedding vows, as a sign of his love and commitment, Louis presented Zélie with a silver medallion he had designed and engraved with the images of Sarah and Tobias, two Biblical personages from the Book of Tobit in the Old Testament. Louis' gesture was subtle, although a powerful expression of his inner feelings. As their family and friends looked on, Louis permitted Sarah and Tobias, through this symbolic gesture, to communicate what was in his heart and how he intended to live in marriage with Zélie. This gift was the fruit of his contemplative prayer. He understood through the story of Tobit and his son, Tobias, and his daughter-in-law, Sarah, that God would guide him and Zélie on their marital journey, and

---

14 *The Poetry of Saint Thérèse of Lisieux*, tr. Donald Kinney, OCD, Poem 25, "My Desires Near Jesus Hidden in His Prison of Love," Washington, DC: ICS Publications, 1995, p. 133.

they would receive from God all they needed to be healed of the "blindness and demons" that would afflict them. They were called, through the Sacrament of Marriage, to be like the angel Raphael in this Biblical story, an angel in each other's life, radiating the face of Christ to each other and committed to bringing each other closer to God. Louis also understood through Raphael that God gives us what we need if we ask Him and are open to what He gives us. Louis listened to the command of Raphael to make God a priority in his life and Louis clearly tried to communicate that message to Zélie. Through this story, Louis communicated his intent that charity would be central in his life, and, like Tobit, the father of Tobias, he would feed the poor, clothe the naked, bury the dead and be just to his workers. For him, Christ would be the ultimate focus and priority in his life. And, like Zélie, Louis also gave voice to their deep belief that it was trust, confidence and total resignation to the will of God that would be the pillars of their faith. Thus, their marriage would provide the road for their spiritual journey toward total union with God in love.

Nineteen years later, in a letter to her daughter Pauline (CF 192), Zélie described their wedding day in a visit to her sister Élise (Sister Marie-Dosithée) at the Visitation Monastery in Le Mans. During their visit, Zélie tells us:

> "I went to see her for the first time at the monastery on my wedding day. I can say that on that day I cried all my tears, more than I'd ever cried in my life, and more than I would ever cry again. My poor sister didn't know how to console me.
>
> "And yet it didn't make me sad to see her there. No, on the contrary, I would have liked to be there, too. I compared my life to hers, and I cried even harder. In short, for a very long time, my mind and my heart were only at the Visitation Monastery.... I would have liked to hide my life with hers. You who love your father so much, my Pauline, are you going to think that I was hurting him and that I'd ruined our wedding day for him? No, he understood me and consoled me as best he could because his inclinations were similar to mine. I even think our mutual affection

grew from it. Our feelings were always in accord, and he was always a comfort and a support to me."

So, from the very first day of their marriage, Louis was there for Zélie, understanding, caring and supporting her. Céline comments in the footnote of CF 54 that her father did all he could to alleviate the pressure and stress that Zélie was experiencing. Finally, as an act of love toward Zélie and a total gift of himself, Louis gave up his artisanal business, giving up his artistic expression, the many years of study in Rennes, Strasbourg and Paris, to help Zélie in her lace business, and he became a businessman representing her company in Paris, buying supplies to make lace and selling her artistic work in stores and to private clients. How difficult this must have been for him, to give up the very essence of who he was as an artist and to be on the road and away from his wife and children. Above all, how difficult it must have been when the children were young and very sick, knowing that Zélie was on the road alone, on cold winter mornings and late at night, going to see their sick infant, but he gave and gave generously. This giving of himself was a major part of his Eucharistic spirituality.

You recall that, on their wedding day, Louis had given Zélie the silver medallion engraved with the image of Sarah and Tobias, a young Biblical married couple. In this subtle gesture, he had chosen this image to communicate how he understood his calling in the Sacrament of Marriage.

Throughout their years of marriage, Louis had faithfully lived a complementary relationship with Zélie, and, daily, he was directed by the words of the angel Raphael in the story of Sarah and Tobias. Zélie tells us in her letters that Louis soothed and reassured her throughout their marriage. He supported her as a full partner in the parenting of their children and a full partner in their business. She tells Pauline in CF 192 that Louis "understood" her, and we realize what a significant gift this was for her, since she never had this as a child from her mother and father (CF 15). However, what stands out in bold relief in the letter Zélie wrote to her brother, Isidore, while on her deathbed (CF 216) is what she had needed since her childhood. She writes:

"Finally, I was able to stay in bed as long as I was sitting up. When I began to fall asleep, the imperceptible movement I made no doubt woke up all my sufferings. I had to moan all night. Louis, Marie and the maid stayed by my side. From time to time poor Louis would hold me in his arms like a child."

When Raphael, in the Biblical story, declared his identity as an angel sent by God, he told Tobit and his son, Tobias, "God sent me to heal you and your daughter-in-law, Sarah." (Book of Tobit 12:14) We understand that Louis was like the angel Raphael, sent to heal Zélie by soothing and reassuring her during the many heartaches in their nineteen years together. This was Louis' final gift of love to Zélie as she lay dying (CF 192). In meditating on the captivating image of Louis holding Zélie in his arms like a child as she lay dying, we witness Louis offering Zélie the ultimate gift of loving and cherishing her as she had never been loved or cherished as a child. Louis, whose whole life was focused on rendering Christ present and letting Christ act through him, understood the call of marriage and became the face of Christ for Zélie – loving and cherishing her with Christ's love. Through this letter, we are a witness to Zélie's final journey from his arms to the arms of God's eternal embrace and realize that Louis had responded to the extraordinary graces he was given to fully accomplish his marital commitment.

Louis and Zélie were married for nineteen years in what was both a happy, loved-filled relationship and one filled with extraordinarily stressful and tragically painful times. They had nine children in thirteen years; three died in infancy (Marie-Joseph-Louis at age five months, Marie-Joseph-Jean-Baptiste at age eight months, and Marie-Mélanie-Thérèse at age seven weeks), and one in early childhood (Marie-Hélène, who died at the age of five years, four months). Of the five daughters who did survive, all came very close to death in their infancy or childhood (Marie, Pauline, Léonie, Céline and Thérèse).

The repeated trauma and loss that Zélie and Louis experienced for fourteen years was extraordinarily painful and debilitating. In her letters, Zélie gives voice to her long battle with anxiety and depression, which are characteristic of repeated trauma. Their third child, Léonie, suffered from birth to adulthood and on several occasions came very close to death in the first two years of her life. This "difficult child" suffered from several chronic illnesses; however, her oppositional behavior, uncontrolled outbursts of anger, mood swings, poor peer relationships and inability to function in a school environment caused her and her family much pain and frustration. She was a withdrawn child with poor self-esteem and chronically felt like she didn't belong. With current sophisticated diagnostic instruments and modern psychological evaluation to diagnose her symptomatic behavior, the possibility of abuse would be one important concern to look for given the constellation of symptoms Léonie manifested that are characteristic of either physical or emotional abuse. This was understood five months before Zélie died, when Marie informed her that the maid, Louise Marais, had been abusing Léonie (CF 193).

In their entirety, the 218 letters of Zélie and the 16 letters of Louis are a treasury of rich insights into the lives and spirituality of Louis and Zélie Martin. One has the sense that what we are given are snapshots, as if taken by a camera continuously shooting. The letters give a tone and texture to the basic facts of their lives, and the incidents that Zélie describes are palpable, rendering the reader access to an honesty and intimacy that was not meant for the general public. However, these letters greatly enrich our understanding of this charismatic couple who radiated holiness and brought to life their last child, St. Thérèse of the Child Jesus, the greatest saint of the modern age. They underscore the fact that sainthood is a family project of parents and children immersed in the God of love.

Zélie comes to life in her letters; her strong voice gives witness to a very capable businesswoman, a woman of deep faith and trust in God, a good mother of deep commitment and generosity, a wife who was open to transforming herself from a frightened, immature young bride to the heart and soul of her family and the unexpected gift of love that Louis was given on the bridge over the River Sarthe in Alençon.

Louis, in contrast, wrote only sixteen letters that have survived, casting him in the shadows without a voice and leaving the reader wondering about the role he played in the life of the Martin family. And yet, at a closer reading, we realize that Zélie referred to Louis in

120 letters, bringing him to life and highlighting his relevance as a husband and the father of their family.

Zélie reveals Louis to have many dimensions:

- He was a sensitive and supportive husband and father, full of passion with a wide range of emotions. He was playful and humorous, always patient and understanding of the needs of his wife and children (CF 52, CF 68 and CF 201).
- He was a man who took charge, lending his support and strength in different situations (CF 128, CF 129, CF 146 and CF 157).
- He was a devoted family man to his wife and children, as well as Zélie's family whom he embraced as his own (CF 33, CF 75, and CF 77).
- He was a full partner in parenting their children, constantly present and sensitive to their needs (CF 53, CF 61, CF 91, CF 96 and CF 98).
- He was an astute businessman, who held a significant financial stock portfolio. In addition, he speculated in real estate, with several real estate holdings. All resulting in a man who retired at an early age due to his financial success, establishing his family's financial security while consistently donating a substantial portion to many charities, among those that supported the poor and the foreign missions (CF 114).
- He was a man who loved people. He had several close childhood friends that he associated with. These friendships might have helped to fill the void left in his early childhood by the deaths of both his sisters and his brother. Louis and his friends were part of the Catholic Circle and the Conferences of Saint Vincent de Paul, as well as the Nocturnal Eucharistic Adoration. This group of men and women lived balanced lives, working together in the lay Catholic apostolate to render Christ present, socializing and supporting each other, as well as praying together (CF 172, CF 198 and CF 212).
- He was a man with a deep relationship with God, daily renewing his Eucharistic love and sharing it with his family, friends and the poor. He was a man who lived in the world, but was totally immersed in Christ (CF 116 and CF 175).

Above all, Louis Martin was a man who was extremely generous, and he demonstrated his loving generosity by modeling his life on Christ.

- Louis experienced many losses in his life (see footnote in CF 65), and in the last ten years of their relatively short marriage of 19 years, Louis experienced the excruciating pain of losing half of his family (his wife and four of their children) and the terror and pain of the near loss of all of their remaining children. It was also during this period, in 1868, that he made the decision to send their two older daughters (Pauline and Marie) to boarding school to relieve Zélie of the enormous stress that she was experiencing. Although this was a loss for both of them, Louis made this extreme sacrifice for Zélie despite the pain he experienced from this separation and loss.

- In 1871, sensitive to the enormous burden and anxiety Zélie was suffering, Louis sold his clock and watchmaking business in order to free himself to totally devote his time and business expertise to support Zélie and her lace-making business.

- In 1877, after Zélie's death, Louis, again expressing his selfless love for his children, gave up his life in Alençon to move to Lisieux to live close to Zélie's brother Isidore, his wife, Céline and their children in order to be a part of their family life. This afforded Louis and his children the stability and warmth of an extended family. This sacrifice, which was a gift of self, meant that he would no longer live close to his mother, his family and his friends. He gave up his social and apostolic works, and his friends in religious life who had supported him through prayer and spiritual direction (e.g., The Poor Clares). He gave up his favorite pastime of fishing and walking in the beautiful Normandy pastures and woods, and the hermitage he called the "Pavilion" where he engaged in contemplative prayer.

- Towards the end of his life, in his late 50's and 60's, Louis became more vulnerable, and in 1887, at the age of 63, he experienced his first stroke. During this period, we witness Louis' generosity – of heroic proportions – as he willingly offers each of his daughters to Christ as religious, leaving him without the support he had envisioned and desperately needed in his old age.

In studying the life of Louis Martin, we realize that he ultimately became the Eucharist, repeatedly and totally giving himself as gift – taking up his cross and allowing himself to be crucified – laying down his life for others. Further, it was Louis' transformation of the pain in his life into an energy of love, a spirituality that was given to his children, that greatly influenced Thérèse, his last child. She understood and internalized his spirituality, which was the basis of her spiritual doctrine which she proclaimed for the 20th century, resulting in Pope John Paul II proclaiming her Doctor of the Church on October 19, 1997.

As Louis and Zélie Martin offered themselves to Christ as a couple, they set out to discover the ministry of a man and a woman joined in marriage. They model for us the marital journey to ever deepen our understanding of the Sacrament of Marriage – a call to conversion in Christ – a call to mirror Christ's love – in a word, a call to a deeper love. And they beckon us to join them in the priesthood of the laity, given to us at Baptism, to restore our marriage, our family and the world around us to the God of merciful love, thereby building a Civilization of Love.

Thus, through looking at the marriage of Louis and Zélie Martin, we understand that their marriage was a gift from God to the Church and their love for each other was fruitful far beyond what they could have accomplished through their own sanctity. They call out to us to be attentive and accepting to the God who is present in the everyday events of our lives, however confusing and painful they may be, and to have total trust and confidence in the God of love.

Dr. Frances Renda, Editor
Psychoanalyst

The Historical, Social and Religious Background of 19th Century France in the Time of the Martin Family

To understand the lives of Louis and Zélie Martin, one needs to see them against the backdrop of the times in which they lived. What follows is a brief sketch to help the reader place the events of their lives in a historical context, and to see the contents of the letters as their response to the encounters, struggles and obstacles of their lives.

With the knowledge of 21st century medicine and the insights of modern psychology, to step back in time through the letters of Zélie Martin offers us an understanding of the heroic efforts that were made by this saintly couple with the limited knowledge of their time, always with trust and confidence in the God they loved.

Between Louis and Zélie, they lived 71 years throughout almost three quarters of the 19th century. It was a turbulent time of enormous change. A century of revolutions (1830 and 1848) and counter-revolutions, it was also a time of war, both abroad and at home. It was an age of pandemics and epidemics, of invention, exploration and colonization. It was also a time of economic revolution, which has come to be known as the Industrial Revolution, a major socio-economic shift away from the individual artisan and entrepreneur towards manufacturing, with production as its final goal. The Industrial Revolution would change the very fabric of the world as people had known it.

This economic revolution gave rise to a social revolution, a shift that began to pry the masses away from the rigid, social structures that they had been trapped in for centuries, and opened for them the long process that would eventually give them their God-given right of equality. Louis and Zélie were to witness these historical events, and their last child, Saint Thérèse of the Child Jesus, would eventually incorporate this shift into her spirituality. It was a time of extreme anti-clericalism, and Louis and Zélie witnessed a fierce antagonism against Catholicism, which resulted in mandatory secular education for all children; however, Catholic schools were allowed to function. Also mandated was the closing of some religious communities; and on May 27, 1871, the Archbishop of Paris and 64 priests were assassinated (see footnote in Letter CF 66.)

The 19th century also gave rise to a burst of artistic energy as Chopin's melodies could be heard in Paris, and the first exhibition of the Impressionists was held in Paris on April 15, 1874, one year after Thérèse was born. Renoir, Cezanne, Degas, Monet, Van Gogh, Manet and other Impressionists of the time have been recognized as the century's greatest artists. It was also the time that Victor Hugo wrote *The Hunchback of Notre Dame* and *Les Misérables*, works that addressed the abusive structures of the times and issues that are still relevant in the world today, as their theatrical productions continue to inspire audiences around the world.

This burst of energy not only occurred in France. Tolstoy, Dostoevsky, Tchaikovsky, Dickens, Goethe, Ibsen, Chekhov, Puccini, Verdi, and Johann Strauss were also part of the artistic genius of the 19th century. And in the United States, in 1863, Abraham Lincoln issued the Emancipation Proclamation and freed the slaves.

It was also a time of great inventions. It was during the weeks of June 17-July 2, 1878, almost one year after Zélie's death, that Louis took Marie and Pauline to the World's Fair in Paris. They saw electric lights that had been installed along the Avenue de l'Opera and the Place de l'Opera, flooding the streets in light around the famous Paris Opera House, a phenomenon that the masses had never been able to witness by gaslight. On that night in June 1878, night was forever given a new meaning. They also saw the genius of Thomas Edison's inventions, namely the phonograph, the megaphone to aid the hard of hearing, and the telephone, which was invented by Alexander Graham Bell and improved by Thomas Edison. These inventions would revolutionize mass communication and change the course of history. They saw the urban renewal of Paris, which would transform the dark, old medieval city to a new city with wide boulevards and modern buildings, with magnificent parks and fountains, giving it the well deserved title of the most beautiful city in Europe.

During this time, a series of innovations were introduced, most importantly, the introduction of the railroad in France in the 1820's, which totally transformed French society. It gave people the opportunity to travel, to go on pilgrimage and to transport products great distances, resulting in the expansion of the market for goods. The use of steam was adapted as a source of power and the economy slowly shifted from the individual artisan and entrepreneur who lived in rural areas, to the introduction of mass production in city factories, replacing expensive handmade products with less expensive machine-made items. Machine tools were introduced, as well as the sewing machine, which fostered the mass production of clothing, the typewriter, the camera (which we know Céline used in the convent in the 1890's, creating historical pictures of St. Thérèse), the elevator (which Thérèse used in a Paris department store), and the mechanical saw, which pumped new life into the economy. This opened the way for the rural, poverty-stricken masses that had predominately worked in agriculture to travel to the towns and cities to look for work. This would come to have a significant effect on the distribution of wealth and social power.

However, growth came at a high price. As the masses migrated from the countryside to the medieval towns and cities, the infrastructure could not provide the basic necessities and the municipal authorities could not accommodate them. The mass migration of people from the rural areas to the cities resulted in their living in overcrowded dwellings, with reports of up to 40 to 50 people living in one room. There was very poor ventilation, a candle or oil lamp provided light, and the bathroom area was little more than a receptacle shared by all. This undoubtedly was a breeding ground for disease. Further, there was no running water for bathing, making personal hygiene difficult, and a lack of sewerage caused waste to seep into the ground, resulting in the contamination of the water supply with animal and human feces causing repeated typhoid epidemics. This illness, which was almost always fatal in the 19th century, brought

Marie Martin, Louis and Zélie Martin's oldest daughter, to near death in 1873, after she contracted the disease at school. Beginning in letter CF 91 and continuing through CF 103, Zélie described the anxiety and pain she and Louis experienced as they helplessly watched their daughter ebb closer to death.

Food shortages and poor diets, along with deplorable work conditions in the sweat shops and the six day, 16 to 18 hours a day work-week, left workers exhausted and susceptible to endemic illnesses such as bronchitis, pneumonia, tuberculosis, typhoid and gastroenteritis, as well as major pandemics such as smallpox, cholera and influenza. Poorly ventilated and over-crowded living and working conditions led to the spread of air-borne diseases (whooping cough, measles), the cause of which had not yet been identified by the scientific profession.

Thus, mortality in France increased dramatically, and with the advent of mass railroad transportation, the population, which was highly susceptible and very often infected with contagions, carried diseases as they traveled by train to the textile mills, woolen mills and coal mines in the north, the silk mills in Lyon, as well as to locations where they employed seasonal workers, spreading disease and infecting the mass population along the train route. In 1853, the train was built in Alençon, and the mass migration traveling along the train route that passed through Alençon would have a great impact on the Martin family.

Infant mortality in the towns and cities reached the point of crisis. Infant mortality was very high, particularly where women, who found work in factories, left their infants with a wet nurse. The concept of screening a wet nurse for her competence and the ongoing supervision by the medical profession and governmental agencies was non-existent. The rate of infant mortality resulting from infants left with a wet nurse was extraordinarily high. Further, as the demand grew for wet nurses, the available nurses could not fill the growing demand, and good nurses became scarcer. This gives us a window into the crisis Louis and Zélie experienced when they were in need of a wet nurse. In CF 61 we see Louis leaving at four in the morning and walking to Héloup, a small town 7.6 kilometers (4.7 miles) southwest of Alençon, in search of a wet nurse to no avail. In CF 60 and 61,

Zélie described the tragic death of their infant daughter, Mélanie-Thérèse, who died because of criminal neglect and starvation by an alcoholic wet nurse in Alençon. Further, in the footnote in CF 48, Céline described her near death as an infant at the hands of another alcoholic wet nurse until her father rescued her.

As the cities became more populated, the shortage of wet nurses resulted in a crisis in France. It's incredible to think that with the resources that Louis and Zélie had, they were unable to find a competent wet nurse in Alençon, and had to rely on Rose Taillé, a good and responsible woman, who lived about 8 kilometers (5 miles) from Alençon. This resulted in their infants having to be sent away to be nursed, and the emotional trauma that the infant and Zélie experienced in the separation. In CF 21, we see both Louis and Zélie leaving Alençon for Semallé by foot, at three in the morning in the freezing cold, in the snow and slippery ice, after they had been awakened and informed that the wet nurse was fearful that their four-month-old son, Marie-Joseph-Louis was dying. Again, in CF 32, Zélie described leaving her home twice each day, at five in the morning and eight at night, walking about 32 kilometers (20 miles) each day, to be with her five-month-old son, Joseph-Jean Baptiste, who was gravely ill. And in CF 89, Zélie described leaving at daybreak, as Thérèse lay dying, to persuade Rose Taillé in Semallé to take on the position of wet nurse for Thérèse. Zélie described a frightening encounter on a dark deserted road when she came across two men who caused her concern. These incidents highlight the difficulties both Zélie and Louis encountered because of the shortage of wet nurses. Zélie's idea of employing a wet nurse to live with them to care for their newborn was not possible considering this shortage.

Bacteriological medicine and isolating those who were seriously ill, as well as concern for hygiene, and efforts to reduce the possibility of infection, were basically unknown. Doctors in the 19th century had very little knowledge of the connection between microorganisms and gastro-intestinal disorders. It would be years before Louis Pasteur in France and Robert Koch in Germany would develop a "germ theory" that would contain and manage the illnesses brought on by bacteria that plagued the masses and caused the illnesses and deaths of at least three of the four Martin children, and the near death of four of the five surviving children. The origins of the bacteria that caused most diseases were only identified in the late 1880's, and only then were the first medications developed. Thus, a high rate of infant mortality continued until pasteurization began in the 1880's.

However, this period was also marked by an extraordinary burst of spiritual energy between July 18, 1830, and January 17, 1871, a span of 41 years, in which the Blessed Mother appeared in France in five different locations:

July 18, 1830 - Our Lady of the Miraculous Medal, Paris
November 27, 1830 - Our Lady of the Miraculous Medal, Paris
1836 - Our Lady of Victories, Paris (locution)
September 19, 1846 - Our Lady of La Salette
February 11-July 16, 1858 - Our Lady of Lourdes (16 apparitions)
January 17, 1871 - Our Lady of Pontmain

What stands out in bold relief is that the lives and marriage of this saintly couple were framed in the apparitions of Mary. In the 20 apparitions and one locution during this period, Mary implored her children to pray and to transform their lives, as she went about healing their broken bodies and wounded souls. In these apparitions, Mary reassured them of her care and protection. It was Mary's requests and direction that formed part of the spirituality of Louis and Zélie.

During the mid 19th century, the time that the Martin family lived in Alençon, the consequences of the French Revolution and the Revolutions of 1830 and 1848 still had a great effect on the Church. These revolutions had unleashed a fierce wave of anti-clericalism which polarized the Church and State in France. The Church was viewed as an institution that took away freedom and fostered superstition.

The Revolution had devastated the Church, stripping it of its influence and good works. Vocations to the priesthood and religious life dropped radically, and the growth of religious orders were determined by the government. Three thousand schools operated by religious teaching orders were closed.

However, by the mid-19th century, a major attempt was made by the Church to reawaken the spirit of the Catholic faith and counter religious indifference. Religious vocations began to increase, and the Church worked hard to improve and enrich the quality of pastoral care for parishioners. In Alençon, the Church fostered public expressions of faith, sponsoring public processions, e.g., the annual Corpus Christi procession that the Martin family participated in. A procession was held to honor Joan of Arc and another to honor St. Catherine of Alexandria (CF 146), Patroness of young girls and of lace-makers. The Church took advantage of the new railroad and sponsored mass national pilgrimages to Lourdes and La Salette, and during the last decade of the 19th century, 500,000 pilgrims visited Lourdes alone. Spiritual retreats (CF 135) and parish missions (CF 51) were held to enrich the faithful. Louis and Zélie participated in these spiritual exercises. In 1854, Pope Pius IX proclaimed the dogma of the Immaculate Conception, which fostered a new growth in Marian devotions.

The parish priests were also supported by organizations of lay people who helped the priests to enrich the spiritual life of the Church. Among them were:

- The Works of the Twelve Apostles, which encouraged religious vocations,
- The Conferences of Saint Vincent de Paul, whose members visited the poor in their homes and attended to their physical and spiritual needs (Louis Martin was an active and committed member),
- The Apostolate of Prayer, encouraging a spirituality dedicated to the Sacred Heart,
- The Confraternity of the Rosary, an association committed to Marian devotions and the recitation of the rosary,
- The Confraternity of the Scapular, whose members were committed to wearing the scapular of Our Lady and participating in Marian devotions,
- Adorers of the Blessed Sacrament, committed to Eucharistic spirituality and Nocturnal Eucharistic Adoration (Both Louis Martin and Isidore Guérin were active members),
- The Society of Saint Vincent de Paul, committed to the care of the poor,
- The Catholic Association for French Youth, committed to the spiritual and social well being of young people,

- The Catholic Circle, a social group committed to young Catholics, fostering an outlet to socialize, enrich their spiritual life and participate in Catholic social action. (Louis Martin was an active member),
- The Children of Mary, committed to fostering Marian devotion for young girls. (It has been noted that Marie, Pauline and Thérèse were members),
- The Archconfraternity of Christian Mothers, a lay group of women committed to praying for the spiritual life of their children and their husbands, and strengthening the vital role of the mother in the Christian family. (Zélie was a committed member of this group),
- The Confraternity of Children of Mary Immaculate was linked to the Daughters of Charity, and its goal was to provide a means to continue the good influence of their Catholic education on children who had gone to Catholic school,
- *The Little Messenger of the Heart of Mary*, a religious magazine.
- And lastly, the Third Order Franciscans (Zélie Martin was a member), and the Third Order Carmelites (Isidore Guérin was a member).

All of these factors – historical, social, technological, political, spiritual, medical and artistic – had a profound impact on the lives of both Louis and Zélie Martin and their family. Through these letters, one witnesses the joys and hardships they endured, and the trust and confidence in the God of Love that opened them to the Divine Energy that moved through and supported them. They understood that the events that had an impact on their lives as a married couple were the very things that would bring them to a deeper and more enduring Love, and thus could lead them to the heights of sanctity, recognized by the Church on October 19, 2008, as Blessed Louis and Zélie Martin, a couple that radiated Christ's love.

Dr. Frances Renda, Editor
Psychoanalyst

Translator's Notes

It was a great privilege to be asked to be the "English voice" of Blessed Zélie and Louis Martin. It provided me with the opportunity to enter their world in a very personal and concrete way and to see their holiness lived in the everyday.

The meanings of many French words have evolved since the 19th century when Blessed Zélie and Louis Martin wrote these letters. The University of Chicago's ARTFL Project (The Project for American and French Research on the Treasury of the French Language), in which French dictionaries from the 16th, 17th, 18th and 19th centuries are available online, was an invaluable resource in researching the correct translations for the period (http://artfl-project.uchicago.edu).

In keeping with other English translations of books relating to St. Thérèse and her family, we have kept the prefix "CF" (for *Correspondence familiale*) in identifying the letters by number.

To provide a broader historical and cultural context for the English-speaking reader, some of the original footnotes from *Correspondence familiale* were expanded and a significant number of footnotes added. In addition, we have included more information in the "Biographical Guide of Proper Names" and added two appendices: a detailed chronology of the Guérin and Martin families from 1777 to 2008 and letters written by Marie Martin to her aunt and uncle, Céline and Isidore Guérin, during the final stages of Blessed Zélie's illness. This historical research has built a framework within which the letters of Blessed Zélie and Louis Martin can be more fully appreciated.

I am deeply grateful to Dr. Frances Renda, who edited this

work. She brought great psychological and spiritual insights to the process. Her profound knowledge and understanding of St. Thérèse's life and spirituality, as well as the extensive research she did for the additional footnotes and the Chronology of the Guérin and Martin families, added tremendous depth to the completed work. I was very honored to collaborate with her on this book.

Above all, I thank my husband, Robert Hess, for his intelligent insights and unwavering support throughout this project.

Ann Connors Hess

A CALL TO A DEEPER LOVE

PART ONE

The Letters of Zélie Martin

1863

All the letters written by Zélie in the year 1863 are addressed to her brother, Isidore Guérin, then twenty-two years old, who was studying medicine in Paris. Zélie, his sister, was very alarmed at seeing him exposed to the "dangers of the Capital" and not having a sound piety to sustain him. There is one letter to Zélie from Louis Martin (CF 2-a) written while he was traveling on business.

CF 1   Alençon[15]
                                                          January 1, 1863
My dear brother,[16]

I wish you a happy New Year and desire with all my heart that you do well in your studies. I'm sure you'll succeed if you want to, this depends only on you. God protects all who trust in Him. Not a single person has ever been abandoned by Him.

When I think of what God has done for me and my husband, God, in whom I've put all my trust and in whose hands I've put the care of my whole life, I don't doubt that His Divine Providence

---

[15] Given that most of the letters written by Zélie Martin were dated from Alençon, the place of origin will only be indicated if it varies.

[16] At the time this letter was written, Zélie was thirty-two years old writing to her younger brother. After the death of Zélie's mother in 1859, Zélie assumed the maternal role since their older sister Élise was in the convent. At times the tone of her letters to Isidore is maternal, and at other times they are playful and even critical when she felt that Isidore was insensitive or exhibiting bad judgment.

watches over His children with special care.

My dear friend, I'm very concerned about you.[17] Every day my husband makes sad predictions. He knows Paris, and he tells me that you'll be up against temptations that you'll find hard to resist because you're not religious enough. He told me what temptations he had and the courage he needed to overcome his struggles. If you only knew what ordeals he went through.... I beg you, my dear Isidore, do as he did; *pray*, and you will not let yourself be carried away by the torrent. If you give in once, you're lost. On the path of evil as well as that of goodness, the first step is the hardest, and, after that first step, you'll be swept away by the current.

If you want to give me a New Year's gift[18] and would agree to this one request I'm asking of you, I'd be happier than if you sent me all of Paris. Here it is: you live very close to Notre-Dame des Victoires.[19] Well! Go there just once a day and say a Hail Mary to the Blessed Mother. You'll see that she'll protect you in a very special way, and that she'll help you succeed in this world and give you eternal happiness. What I'm saying to you is not exaggerated piety and unfounded on my part. I have reason to have trust in the Blessed Mother, I've received favors from her that only I know.[20]

You well know that life is not long. You and I will soon be at the end, and we'll be very grateful that we lived in a manner that doesn't make our last hour too bitter.

Now, if you have an unkind heart, you'll laugh at me, but if you're kindhearted, you'll say I'm right.

---

[17] Since December 10 or 15, 1862, Isidore was enrolled in the School of Pharmacy in Paris.

[18] Exchanging gifts on New Year's Day was a custom dating from the early Roman times extending a wish for good luck for the New Year. The custom ended at the close of the 19th century with the commercialization of Christmas.

[19] Notre-Dame des Victoires (The Church of Our Lady of Victories) was a Parisian sanctuary founded by Louis XIII in 1629. In 1836, after the Blessed Mother appeared to Father Charles Desgenettes (1778-1860), he designated this shrine as a place of prayer for the conversion of the world. Notre-Dame des Victoires then became a great center of Marian pilgrimage. It played an important role in the life of the Martin family, in particular, that of Thérèse. At the time of this letter, Isidore Guérin was living in the Hotel Sarlés, 15 rue Saint-Hyacinthe-Saint-Michel.

[20] An allusion to graces received through the intercession of the Blessed Mother on December 8, 1851, and later. (See footnote in CF 16.) See Père Stéphane-Joseph Piat, OFM, *La Vierge du Sourire et sainte Thérèse de l'Enfant-Jésus* [*The Virgin of the Smile and Saint Thérèse of the Child Jesus*]. Lisieux, France: Office Central de Lisieux, 1951, p. 17. (Not translated.)

When you write to me, don't mention what I said regarding Louis' thoughts about your situation because he wouldn't like it. I'm always so happy with him, he makes my life very pleasant. What a holy man my husband is. I wish the same for all women; that's my wish for them for the New Year.

Tuesday I'll send you some potted goose and jars of jam.

My little girls[21] are very cute. Your goddaughter doesn't want to walk by herself anymore. She fell and became so fearful that nothing in the world can persuade her to take a step without support; she goes for a walk along the chairs and the furniture. You can't imagine how good and affectionate she is. She hugs us every minute without our telling her to do so, and she sends kisses to Jesus. She doesn't talk, but she understands everything. In other words, she's an ideal child....

CF 2   *April 5, 1863*

...Marie is always the same; she's doing very well and speaks to us of her uncle in Paris.

Little Pauline walks very well now, and she almost never falls. She's very cute and is beginning to talk well. Her health is delicate, but she's coming along little by little. She knows everything or almost everything by its name. Right now she's sitting next to me on the desk and doesn't want to leave me alone, so what I'm writing is all crooked.

Believe me, she already loves to dress up. When we tell her that we're going out, she runs quickly to the closet where her most beautiful dress is and extends her little face saying, "Wash me." I find all this marvelous, as if it weren't perfectly natural....

---

[21] Marie-Louise (called Marie), born February 22, 1860, and Marie-Pauline (called Pauline), born September 7, 1861. Marie's godfather was her maternal grandfather, Isidore Guérin, Sr. (July 6, 1789-September 3, 1868) and her godmother was her paternal grandmother, Marie-Anne Fanie Boureau Martin (January 12, 1800-April 8, 1883). Pauline's godfather was Isidore Guérin, Zélie's brother, and her godmother was Pauline Romet, sister of Vital, Hortense and Pierre Romet, friends of Louis Martin. Both girls were born at 15 rue du Pont-Neuf, the house Louis bought on November 9, 1850, and were baptized by Father Lebouc in the parish church, St. Pierre de Montsort, in Alençon. After the baptismal ceremony of each of his nine children, Louis engraved their names and birth dates on the inside of his watch case.

CF 2-a[22]   To Zélie Martin
                                                        October 8, 1863

My dear Friend,

I won't be able to arrive in Alençon until Monday. It seems like a long time to me, and I'm longing to be with you.

Needless to say, your letter made me very happy, except I see that you've tired yourself out far too much. So I strongly recommend calm and moderation, above all in your work. I have some orders from the *Compagnie Lyonnaise*;[23] once again, don't worry so much. We'll manage, with God's help, to build a good little company.

I had the happiness of receiving Communion at Notre-Dame des Victoires, which is like a little heaven on earth. I also lit a candle for the intention of our entire family.

I kiss you with all my heart, while waiting for the happiness of being with you again. I hope that Marie and Pauline are being very good!

                              Your husband and true friend, who loves you for life.
                                                        (Louis Martin)

CF 3   *November 12, 1863*

You can't imagine the joy I felt when I received your telegram.[24] I cried from happiness for the first time in my life. You know, I contributed a little to your success because I asked the Poor Clares in Alençon to pray for you Wednesday and Thursday at 10:00 in the morning, thinking that was the time of your exams. Then I received Communion for you. I hope you're a little appreciative for all I've done.

Louis was very happy as well. In your honor we bought a goose on Saturday and celebrated on Sunday. We were all very sorry that you weren't here to share in the feast and have fun with us!

I don't have enough time to write any longer and, besides, the more I say to you the more you'll tease me about my style; I'm certain of it.... I did, however, win first prize in style in the past. Out of eleven

---

[22] Louis was on a business trip to Paris for the Alençon lace.
[23] Company of Lyon.
[24] Isidore had just received a Bachelor of Science degree.

compositions, I won first prize ten times, and then I was in the first division and in the upper class.[25] So judge the ability of the others!

1864

All the letters written in the year 1864 are addressed to her brother.

CF 4   *January 5, 1864*

We received your letter yesterday. It was a little late in coming; we were hoping it would arrive for the 1st of January. I was beginning to be very annoyed with you, and I felt you were ungrateful.

Everyone is well. Louis sends you his kindest regards. Little Pauline is always cute and boisterous at the same time. Little Léonie[26] is not coming along very well; however, she's not sick. Marie is above average and already she's beginning to spell moderately well. She received, along with her sisters, beautiful gifts from the young ladies X[27] who are always very pleasant, but they hardly think of you! So much for their opinion!

I wish you, my dear Isidore, good health, a happy life and paradise at the end of your days.

CF 5   *January 17, 1864*

It seems you weren't happy with my letter of the first of the year. What did you want me to say? If I had complimented you, you would have made fun of me. If I had preached to you, you would have laughed at it. So I wrote what was going through my mind at the moment. But that doesn't stop me from loving you, and I'd give

---

[25] Zélie and her older sister Élise were students in the School of the Religious of the Sacred Hearts of Jesus and Mary in Alençon.

[26] Marie-Léonie (called Léonie), was born at 15 rue du Pont-Neuf on June 3, 1863. She was baptized on June 4, the feast of Corpus Christi, by Father Lebouc in the parish church, St. Pierre de Montsort, in Alençon. She was named Léonie after her godmother, Madame Léonie Gilbert Tifenne, a friend of Louis Martin. Her godfather was Adolphe Leriche, Louis Martin's nephew. (See footnote in CF 54.)

[27] Prior to publication of Zélie Martin's letters in 1941, some people were identified only by initial(s) in order to protect their identity.

all I have rather than abandon you, even though you might forget me and do the most foolish things.

As you had planned, come soon if you can. We'll have a good time together. We'll argue a little, as we always do, but that will be a diversion. It's a little way to pass the time!…

I would say much more, but Louis is waiting for my letter to add it to my father's,[28] and he's ready to go so I must finish.

CF 6   *March 11, 1864*

If we hadn't received your letter yesterday, you would've received one from me the following morning, because I was at the point of writing to you to find out if you were dead or alive. We were beginning to believe you had thrown yourself into the Seine!

You asked me to write you a long letter. Unfortunately, I have to send out an order of lace[29] tonight, and it's difficult for me to do as you asked.

The little girls are well enough. Pauline is the brightest and most robust. She amuses my father very much with her curious remarks, but she doesn't speak of her uncle anymore; she's forgotten him!

Marie is not doing well. She's not been in class for six weeks[30]

---

[28] Isidore Guérin, Sr., born July 6, 1789, was a soldier during the Napoleonic Wars. In December 1866 he moved back to the house at 36 rue Saint-Blaise (later the number of the house was changed to 42 and is currently number 50), the house he had bought on February 9, 1843, and into which he and his family moved on September 10, 1844. He died there on September 3, 1868. It was in this house that Saint Thérèse was born on January 2, 1873. When this letter was written, Louis and Zélie Martin lived at 15 rue du Pont-Neuf.

In the 16th century, at the top of the rue Saint-Blaise, there was a chapel dedicated to St. Blaise, who was revered in the Middle Ages as the patron saint of ploughmen, of hemp and wool workers and the protector of herds and the healer of sore throats and snake bites. During the 19th century the street was lined with expensive apartments and houses. On feast days, the street was decorated with flowers and garlands as people made their way to the fair grounds. Pierre-Marie Gautier, *Alençon dans l'Orne.* Alençon, France: de l'Ornal Editions, 2008, p. 88.

[29] During the Industrial Exposition which was held in Alençon in June 1858, "Zélie received special praise from the jury for 'the beauty' of her lace, 'the richness of her designs,' and 'her intelligent direction.' She was recognized for her ability on June 20, 1858, one month before her marriage to Louis Martin." Conrad DeMeester, OCD, editor, *St. Thérèse of Lisieux: Her Life, Times, and Teaching.* Washington, DC: ICS Publications, 1997, p. 14.

[30] Marie was a day student at the School of the Providence. The school was founded by the Sisters of Providence, a local religious community. The school was located

and she's taken an intense dislike to school. This is unfortunate because she was learning very easily, but I fear making her completely sick by forcing her in this way.

Little Léonie is over nine months old, and she can barely hold herself up on her legs as Marie was doing at three months old. This poor child is so weak. She has a kind of chronic whooping cough,[31] fortunately not as strong as the attack Pauline had, as she wouldn't be able to survive it, and God only gives us what we can endure.

Would you like to make me happy? When you go to Madame D's house, go into Notre-Dame des Victoires and light a candle for me; this would be a help to me. Don't be ashamed of this. Besides, nobody knows you in this church.

Above all, don't go so long without writing; that makes us anxious.

CF 7   *March 28, 1864*

I'm opening my father's letter to send you a few words and to give you some news from Alençon which perhaps, might interest you, although my father doesn't want it to affect you.

I don't know if you knew Monsieur Ch, who owned the big mill and was married to a sister of Madame L. Well! This Monsieur Ch and his wife were having a magnificent house built directly across from the Renaissance Café. They took great delight in this house even before they moved in. They were supposed to move into it on Saint John's Day and were to live in it for the rest of their days. The wife especially felt such great joy in living there that she would say to everyone, "My God! Oh, how happy I am! I lack nothing. I have my health, I have wealth, I can buy all that I desire, and I don't have any children to disturb my rest. In short, I don't know anyone as well off as I am."

I've always heard it said, "Misfortune, three times misfortune, to those who talk like that." And my dear friend, I'm so convinced

---

near the Church of Notre-Dame d'Alençon. At present, the Sisters are no longer in charge of the school.

[31] Pertussis, also known as whooping cough, is a highly contagious bacterial disease spread by coughs and sneezes. The bacteria releases toxins that inflame the lining of the lungs. It was a feared child-killer before antibiotics and vaccines.

of the truth of this saying, that at certain times in my life, when I said I was happy, I couldn't think of it without trembling because it's certain and proven by experience that happiness is not on earth.... No, happiness can't be found here below, and it's a bad sign when all goes well. In His wisdom, God wanted it this way to make us remember that the world is not our true home.

Finally we return to our story:

Monsieur and Madame Ch went out about six o'clock in the evening, on Saturday, to visit their magnificent residence and to spend the evening with their relatives at the Renaissance Café.[32] About 8:30, the gentleman said to his wife, "I have a letter to mail and it's already late, come with me." They left immediately and, upon returning, said to themselves, "To save time, let's take a shortcut by going through our garden." In fact, their garden does face that place, ending just in front of the café where their relatives were waiting for them. But at the end of the garden a ditch was under construction, and they had to go around it on some boards. Since they couldn't see very clearly, the gentleman got too close to the ditch and fell in. His wife fell in after him and knocked loose a rock as she fell; it hit her husband and he was killed by the blow. She cried for help, and her cries were heard. She was seriously injured. They brought her to her sister's house, and she died ten minutes later.

Around 9:30, I heard several footsteps in front of the house and people speaking loudly. I looked outside, and people were carrying the two bodies on stretchers. So here is the terrible story of this "happy couple!"

Little Pauline is becoming cuter and cuter. In a month, I'll take her to Le Mans. She knows her aunt[33] well because on Good Friday, while she was in church and looking at a little paper doll dressed in a Visitation habit that Élise had sent me, she took it, raised it above her head and shouted with all her might, "Here's my aunt!" That made all the people around her laugh.

---

[32] "The *Grand Café de la Renaissance* was built in 1839 on the rue Saint-Blaise. It had a rich decor and a lively atmosphere. It attracted business people, tourists and the local population." Pierre-Marie Gautier, *Alençon dans l'Orne*, p. 89.

[33] Sister Marie-Dosithée, Zélie's sister, Marie-Louise-Pétronille Guérin, also called Élise, a religious of the Visitation Monastery of Le Mans. (See the Biographical Guide of Proper Names in the Appendix.)

You tell me that our aunt in Paris[35] should come this week. That makes us very happy, and we're already rejoicing. Marie does nothing but talk about it. She asks me if we'll put on the tablecloth, if we'll eat cake, if we'll drink wine and liqueurs; all of this interests her very much.

You say she'll spend only one day at our house. We'll see when she's with us. I'd like her to stay much longer. But if you can persuade her not to come until next week, I'd be much happier for the following reason: Wednesday, Friday and Saturday are the fast days of *Quatre-Temps*.[36] You know that Louis is a strict observer of the Precepts of the Church – he would neither want nor eat meat, nor would he not fast for all the riches in the world, and I doubt my aunt would be as faithful to her duty. When Monsieur D came this Lent, you couldn't believe how uncomfortable we were. Louis fasted alone, since I find myself exempt from fasting for the moment. He watched us eat good things while he took nothing but his light meal. And I could serve only lean meat. So, try then to arrange it for the following week and tell us the day and the hour. We'll wait for our good aunt at the station.

My father has almost made up his mind to spend a few days in Paris. I believe he'll go with my aunt.

I know of nothing new in Alençon. I expect that you'll have a little nephew – or niece – in the month of October. This baby will go to a wet nurse, unfortunately, since I'm unable to nurse the baby myself anymore.[37] It's in God's hands.[38]

---

[34] The address of this letter has been preserved: "Monsieur Isidore Guérin, Pharmacien Interne, hospice de la Vieillesse homme, à Bicêtre, près Paris."

[35] Madame Ambroise Guérin, sister-in-law of Monsieur Guérin, Sr.

[36] During this period, the Liturgical Calendar included the *Quatre-Temps*, which was a time of fasting at the beginning of each of the four seasons.

[37] The announcement of the birth of Marie-Hélène, who was born October 13, 1864.

[38] "At each new birth, she used to make the following prayer: 'Lord, grant me the grace that this child may be consecrated to You, and that nothing may tarnish the purity of its soul. If ever it would be lost, I prefer that You should take it without delay.' Her union with God and the fervor of her prayers, during her months of pregnancy, were so great that she was astonished not to see these pious dispositions manifesting themselves in her children from the dawn of their intelligence." Céline Martin (Sister Geneviève of the Holy Face), *The Mother of the Little Flower*, tr. Fr. Michael Collins, SMA. Charlotte, North Carolina: TAN Books and Publishers, Inc., 1957, p. 7.

Little Léonie is not doing well. She doesn't seem to want to walk. She's by no means big and fat. However, she's not sick; she's just very frail and small. She just got over the measles[39] and was very sick; she had very strong convulsions.

Pauline is always the same. She's very funny and very mischievous. I think I'll take her to Le Mans tomorrow to see my sister. Marie will not go; one will be enough to pester me! The other day I was praying the Marian devotions for the month of May with her, and I told her to pray to God for you. She interrupted her prayer, crying because she wanted to see her uncle!

CF 9   *June 21, 1864[40]*

I think my father and my aunt arrived last night[41] in good health. I'd very much like to have some news. I'm asking you because my father wouldn't want to write. Above all, don't tire him too much by running around. Ask him to bring us back his portrait and yours, but done by the hand of a master, so it doesn't have to be done again. He can give us this little gift.

He forgot to take the package that Monsieur R[42] had given him. I saw that it was a number of small boxes containing all sorts of lozenges, so I thought it was for you when you have a cold; so I'll keep it until further notice. Tell me what I should do with it and if I can give some to my three little girls to try. Otherwise, we won't touch it anymore, and we'll treat it as if it were a relic!

I have nothing new to tell you. I expect my father will tell you all that he knows. Remind him to light a candle for himself and for me in Notre-Dame des Victoires.[43] He promised me he would.

Your loving sister, Z. Martin.[44]

---

39 The measles is an acute illness caused by a highly contagious airborne virus usually spread by coughing and sneezing. High fever, runny nose and body rash are symptoms; a high mortality rate resulted from this disease. A measles vaccine became available in 1963.

40 The first three lines of the original letter, written on blue paper, were preserved.

41 In Paris.

42 Probably Monsieur Vital Romet, a friend of Louis Martin, and a pharmacist in Alençon. (See the Biographical Guide of Proper Names in the Appendix.)

43 Note the constant devotion of Zélie to Our Lady of Victories.

44 This line and the signature have been preserved from the original letter.

I received your letter and it made me very happy. I'm very glad you're coming in September. You'll be here for the baptism of your little niece Marie-Hélène. Here, already, is her name even before she's born. Marie will be godmother with Monsieur J as the godfather; he is 45 years old.

I have my father's portrait and yours above the mantelpiece. They came out perfectly and, above all, they're a good likeness. Pauline, though, doesn't recognize you. She says, "There's Grandpa and the other one, he's a priest." That's what she calls you. If only that were true! I would willingly give up my share of the inheritance for you to be a good priest, but that will never be. Oh well, we've seen such great miracles, but none would be greater!

It seems you're still thinking of Mademoiselle X? I think you're foolish.... I can't stop thinking about it. You're going to hurt yourself, either with her or with someone else, because you only consider the superficial things, beauty and wealth, without worrying about the qualities that make a husband happy or the faults that cause him grief and ruin. You know all that glitters is not gold. The main thing is to look for a good woman whose interests center on the home, who is not afraid of dirtying her hands with work, who devotes time to her appearance only as much as she has to, and who knows how to raise children to work and be holy. A woman like that would scare you; she would not be brilliant enough in the eyes of the world. But sensible people would love her better even if she had nothing, rather than another woman with a dowry of fifty thousand francs and who lacked these qualities. Oh well, we'll speak of that later.

1865

All the letters written in the year 1865 are addressed to her brother.

I wrote you a five-page letter two weeks before the first of the year, but you probably didn't receive it since you haven't mentioned it. That upset me a little.

The entire family is well. I thought that the little girls were getting the measles, but it was only a bad cold. Little Léonie is walking by herself at last. Little Hélène[45] is doing very well, and she's as beautiful as an angel. I went to see her at the first of the year, and, I want you to know, I miss her terribly. I think of her all the time. She has a good, healthy wet nurse.[46]

Marie, Pauline and Léonie received beautiful New Year's gifts. The Mademoiselles X spoiled them and are always very kind to us. Mademoiselle Pauline R[47] gave her goddaughter a pretty doll. My little Pauline is always very funny. She likes to tease Marie. Every day she points to your portrait while saying, "That's my godfather. He's handsome, my godfather. Look, Marie, he has hair on his head and yours doesn't." She says this because her grandfather is bald.[48]

I don't know what else to tell you because I'm too distracted. I hear everyone talking at the same time.

Louis asked me to send you his compliments. He just reprimanded me for not answering your letter sooner. I would have written to you, but you see, I wasn't very happy. You hadn't said one word to me about my letter, me, who stayed up so late to write it and who was so tired.

---

[45] Marie-Hélène (called Hélène), was born at 15 rue du Pont-Neuf on October 13, 1864. She was baptized in the parish church, St. Pierre de Montsort, in Alençon. Her godmother was Marie, her oldest sister, and her godfather "Monsieur J," was 45 years old.

[46] For the first time, Zélie had to entrust her baby to a wet nurse. In the memoirs of Sister Marie of the Sacred Heart (Marie), written in 1909 at the request of Mother Agnès of Jesus (Pauline), she wrote: "One of the childhood memories that I really remember is when we went to see little Hélène at the nurse. I was only five and a half but it seems that I remember it as if it were now. First of all, Hélène was with the nurse near Chene, a farm that belonged to our relatives four or five leagues from Alençon. That seemed fine. I thought it was rather sad to have such a nice little sister so far away from our house. I can still see Mama kissing little Hélène before leaving. And I said to myself, 'How much it pains me to leave my little sister! How unhappy Mama must be! Poor Mama! But why doesn't she take her with us?' I thought that the woman who took care of my little sister was very happy and I couldn't understand such a mystery. So, I thought for the first time that life was filled with sacrifices. But I didn't say anything of my feelings as it was impossible for me to express them." *Thérèse de Lisieux*, "Marie, L'Intrépide" [Marie, the Intrepid], Lisieux, France: Pelerinage Sainte Thérèse, February 2010, p 5.

[47] Pauline-Rose-Marie Romet. (See the Biographical Guide of Proper Names in the Appendix.)

[48] Monsieur Guérin, Sr., was Marie's godfather.

I wish you a happy New Year, good health and Heaven as late as possible, because I believe that you'll only enter it willingly when you have no other choice....

CF 12   *March 5, 1865*

You must be very mad at me for having taken so long to respond to your letter, which, however, amused us a lot. Louis laughed with all his heart at your comparison of Father Loth. As for me, I didn't laugh; I must be getting old and I didn't find it amusing. Nevertheless, I comfort myself by thinking that you're not a prophet.

I should have written to you last Sunday, but Madame X came to invite me to spend the evening at her house with my husband, which we did reluctantly and simply not to be unfriendly towards them. These are the people who attended the party: me, in the front line!, my husband, Monsieur D, a curate at the Church of Notre-Dame, a master pianist from Sées,[49] teacher of the young ladies, Monsieur Guérin, Sr., (Monsieur Guérin, Jr., being absent, made it necessary that his father replace him,) Madame X, her father, her daughters and her aunt, and finally, their little dog, whose name I can't recall. They all sang from eight o'clock until a quarter to eleven, and then everyone went to bed.

Now, let's speak of something else. For the last two months, my little Léonie has had a kind of purulent eczema[50] on her entire body, and the illness is getting worse every day. I'm very upset, and the doctor doesn't know how to treat it. He told me to give her some antiscorbutic[51] syrup, which I did, but the ravages of the illness didn't lessen. It seems that these kinds of illnesses are almost incurable. Please, give me your advice and tell me what I should do. Perhaps you know some famous specialists who will be able to give you some effective remedies. You wouldn't believe how much I suffer seeing my

---

[49] The town of Sées (formerly known as Séez), approximately 25 kilometers (15.5 miles) northeast of Alençon. The diocese still maintains the traditional spelling, i.e., Séez.

[50] Purulent eczema is a chronic disease of the skin characterized by rashes, swelling, itching and dryness, crusting, flaking and blistering with an oozing of pus and blood.

[51] A remedy to counteract scurvy.

poor little daughter in this state. I've just written to our sister Élise asking that she say a novena for her.[52] I'm not asking you for your prayers, I don't have enough confidence in you.

Last Tuesday I went to see my little Hélène. I left alone[53] at seven o'clock in the morning, through the rain and the wind that took me there and brought me back home. Imagine how tired I was as I walked along the road, but what kept me going was the thought that I would soon hold in my arms the object of my love. There's no prettier jewel than little Hélène. She's ravishing.

I don't know what else to tell you. If you saw, however, the letter I wrote to my sister in Le Mans, you'd be jealous, it was five pages long.[54] But I tell her things I don't tell you. We talk to each other about a mysterious, angelic world, and, to you, I must speak of earthly things. Nevertheless, I know of a beautiful incident. Should I tell you? I hesitate. It's a lost pearl. Oh well, let's risk it.

Recently a religious of the Poor Clares was buried, and the gravedigger, while digging her grave, came across a coffin that he had broken. It belonged to a Sister who had been dead for thirty-six years, and she was perfectly preserved. In giving a blow to the coffin with the pickaxe, he cut into an arm. Blood flowed from the arm in great abundance since the earth he dug up was soaked in this blood. I didn't see it, but I found out about it from a trustworthy person. But they don't want these facts made known. Now believe it if you wish. As for me, I believe it as if I'd seen it, because I know that, among these nuns, there are true saints.

CF 13   *April 23, 1865*

Hastily, I'm writing you a few words, because I'm unable to write you a long letter. I have a violent headache[55] and I'm up against constant aggravation. Moreover, we have my father-in-law[56] who is

---

52 Sister Marie-Dosithée, Zélie's sister, a nun at the Visitation Monastery in Le Mans.
53 Louis Martin was working alone in his jewelry and watch making shop.
54 This letter was not preserved.
55 Zélie suffered from migraine headaches.
56 Captain Pierre-François Martin, Louis' father, was eighty-eight years old. (See the Biographical Guide of Proper Names in the Appendix.)

near death; I don't think he'll live another two weeks. He's dying of old age; already half his body is paralyzed.

We received your letter. I don't remember at all what it contained. I know that you succeeded in your exams, that you received the money we sent you, that our uncle and aunt are doing well and that my father must go to Paris, which he won't do. Last week his leg was swollen, and he couldn't go out for several days. He's doing better now, but his leg is still stiff. I'm in constant fear that he'll have an attack of paralysis. He saw the doctor who told him to put himself on a light diet, which he has no desire to do because he has a good appetite. His nephew, G. Guérin's son,[57] stayed at his house for a few days. He's a little "tripotot,"[58] who rather looks more like a cleaning woman than a student.

Little Léonie is doing well now, as well as the other three. Two weeks ago I went to see Hélène, the one who is with the wet nurse. I can't remember ever having felt such an intense feeling of happiness as at the moment when I took her in my arms and she smiled at me so graciously. I believed I was looking at an angel. Oh well, I can't express it. I believe we've never seen, nor will ever see, a little girl so charming. My little Hélène, when will I have the happiness of possessing her completely? I can't imagine that I have the honor of being the mother of such a delightful creature!… Oh! I admit I don't regret being married. If you had seen the two older ones today, how pretty they looked, everyone was admiring them and could not take their eyes off of them. And me, I was there beaming. I said to myself, "They're mine! I have two others who are not here, one beautiful and one less beautiful that I love as much as the others, but she won't honor me as much."

Let's speak of more serious things. You know that when I was a young girl, I hit my breast on the corner of a table. We didn't think anything of it then, but today I have a gland in my breast that worries me, especially since it started to be a little painful. However, when I touch it, it doesn't hurt, although I feel some numbness several times a day, every day. Well, I don't know what else to say about it, but

---

[57] Isidore Guérin, Sr., had six brothers and sisters. One of his brothers was named Grégoire. Nothing is known about this son.

[58] The precise meaning of this word is not known.

what's certain is that it's making me suffer.[59]

What can I do about it? I'm quite confused. I'm not afraid of an operation, no, I'm completely willing to have it, but I don't have complete confidence in the doctors here. I would like to take advantage of your stay in Paris, because you could help me a lot in this situation. There's only one thing that holds me back, how will my husband manage during this time? I know nothing about the surgery. Be kind enough to tell me your thoughts on this subject as soon as possible.

Louis sends you his kindest regards, and, since you don't want to pursue your studies for a doctorate, he would like you to have a pharmacy like that of Monsieur R,[60] and that very one if it were possible.

There's nothing else new to tell you, but this is already enough; I, who was only going to write you a few lines.

CF 14   *June 27, 1865*

My father-in-law died yesterday at one o'clock in the afternoon. He received the sacraments last Thursday. He died like a saint; as he lived, he died. I would never have believed that this could have such an effect on me. I'm shattered.

My poor mother-in-law spent her nights taking care of him over the last two and a half months, without accepting help from anyone. It is she who prepared him for burial and watched over him day and night. In other words, she has extraordinary courage and very beautiful qualities.

I confess, death terrifies me. I just came from seeing my father-in-law. His arms are so stiff and his face so cold! And to think that I will see my family like that or that they will see me!… You may be accustomed to seeing death, for me, I'd never seen it so close.

Something's been bothering Louis for some time, and I don't

---

[59] Zélie reports for the first time that she is worried regarding symptoms in her breast and her fear of a breast tumor. She will not mention it again until October 20, 1876, in CF 168.

[60] Monsieur Vital Romet (See the Biographical Guide of Proper Names in the Appendix.)

know what it is. He does nothing but talk about you. He would like you to come; he feels he needs to see you.[61] I admit (between you and me) that this surprises me. If he were sick, I'd believe he was dying; but, thank God, he's not there yet if he lives as long as his father. So write to us as soon as possible and tell us when you will come to satisfy Louis and all of us.

Pauline was in the procession on Sunday, dressed in white, as well as Marie. Both of them had their hair curled with a wreath on their head. Pauline was as beautiful as an angel and had such refined manners! She is liked more than her sister; she has every admirable quality. Marie is pretty but too shy, and this hurts her because she's not at all naughty, and she has a great fear of offending God. She's like my sister in Le Mans who, when she was very little, would cry when we spoke to her of marriage. Marie would do the same.

Léonie is very cute and rather strong. It's an absolute fact that she's never been sick since my sister made the novena to Blessed Margaret Mary, who was beatified in September.[62] When Madame D came, she was in a pathetic state and had been since her birth. She had continual heart palpitations and an inflammation of the intestines that started when she was born. In short, I saw her hover between life and death for sixteen months.

I remember that during that time I wanted to stand her up on her feet and I was unable to do it successfully. Immediately after the novena she could run like a little rabbit. She's incredibly agile.

My father is doing well, as well as little Hélène. Again, I tell you, she's a beautiful child, but by no means fat; at seven months she only weighed fourteen pounds. This doesn't prevent her from doing well, and she's as fresh as a morning rose.

I went to see the holy girl[63] a week ago. She told me beautiful things that did my heart good. When you write to her, send her some stamps for the letters she writes to you; I give her mine. She asked me

---

61 Louis probably wanted to speak with his brother-in-law, who was a pharmacist, about his wife's health.

62 Saint Margaret Mary Alacoque (1647-1690) was a nun of the Visitation at Paray-le-Monial. Jesus revealed the love of His Sacred Heart to her in 1673 and 1675. The feast of the Sacred Heart was celebrated for the first time in Paray-le-Monial in 1686. She was beatified in 1864 and canonized in 1920.

63 Her sister at the Visitation Monastery in Le Mans, Sister Marie-Dosithée.

for some money to buy flowers for her St. Joseph. I gave it to her with great pleasure, and I'll give her more whenever she wants.

I send warm regards from me and the entire family to our uncle and aunt. My father has almost made up his mind to go to Paris and to bring Marie with him. As for me, I don't want to burden him with such a young child. I'd be afraid that he would regret it after he left.

CF 15   *November 7, 1865*

My father has shared your letter with us, and he's hurrying to send you the money you need (which is enclosed) so you won't go to Monsieur D,[64] who is, we know, very financially embarrassed again despite the 3,000 francs we lent him. Business has not been good these past three months, and, if it continues, he'll have to abandon his profession!

You'll have your box of linen within two weeks. The finest worker in the city has worked on it. I'm sorry to see that you need them so badly. If I had known, you would have received them much sooner. It's a little my fault and a little yours, as well. I'll tell you frankly that we were not happy with you. You did not deign to write to us, and we were a little mortified by that. I thought you didn't care much for us.

Let's speak of something else. I'm completely disillusioned. I used to see you in Le Mans[65] and I eagerly looked forward to paying you a little visit from time to time. That was a bright spot in my so monotonous and laborious existence.

But what you want makes it necessary to give up everything. I never had much joy in my life, no, never what one would call joy. My childhood, my youth, was as sad as a shroud because, if my mother spoiled you, as you know, she was too strict with me. She, though so good, didn't know how to treat me, so my heart suffered greatly.

---

[64] Monsieur and Madame D were lace merchants in Paris and would place their orders with the manufacturers. Zélie had business dealings with them for Alençon lace.

[65] Isidore was attempting to buy a pharmacy in Lisieux belonging to the Fournet family. He will marry their daughter, Élisa-Céline Fournet (known as Céline), on September 11, 1866. (See footnote in CF 18.)

Now, I'm not unhappy. I admit I'm happier than I was. However, I have many problems that other women in my situation don't have. It's this awful Alençon lace that makes life difficult. When I have too many orders, I'm a slave to the worst kind of slavery. When it's not going well and I find myself liable for 20,000 francs out of my own account, and I have to send to other firms the workers who were so hard to find,[66] this gives me reason to worry, as well as nightmares! Oh well, what can I do? I must accept it and come to terms with it as bravely as possible.

But here is another reason to be sad: you want to move seventy leagues[67] from here![68]... So, I'll say goodbye to you forever; we'll hardly see each other until the next world because, never in my poor life, which, I believe, will not be long, will I have the time to go see you. As for you, you won't have any more time than I'll have. We'll only speak to each other by letter, and when I want to see you, I'll look at your portrait, which is a very poor consolation.

If, by chance, you can get away for two days to come and see us, there will be, on both sides, as much pain as pleasure. When the distance that separates you is so great, the separation is very painful. On the other hand, if you lived in Le Mans, all you would have to say is, "If I want, I can see her in two hours!" This would be enough to calm you. And how much our poor sister in Le Mans wanted this! I even dreamed of a happiness that perhaps will never be realized. I would say to myself, "Maybe Louis will want to move to Le Mans after we retire."

Oh well, this shouldn't make you take the wrong road. You must go where you believe you can build a good business. You'll have a wife and children who will fill the void and who'll make you forget everyone else... up to a point. If I didn't have my husband and

---

[66] Zélie employed lace makers who worked at home. Every Thursday they would bring their completed pieces of lace to Zélie and she would assemble them into the master design.

[67] 170 miles or 274 kilometers (one French league equaled 2.422 miles).

[68] Zélie is devastated at the loss of her brother who will not return home from Paris but will relocate to another city to open a pharmacy. Her brother had abruptly decided not to pursue a medical degree but to become a pharmacist. Since 1858, Zélie lost her sister Élise, her mother and her father-in-law, and now faces the possibility of losing her brother. That will leave her with no family except her father close by to be of support.

children, it wouldn't matter that you go far – if you went to Africa, I would follow you there. My father would come also, and I would keep house for you the best I could. I'm going to say a prayer to the Blessed Mother and Saint Joseph that the pharmacist in Le Mans decides in your favor, if it's for your happiness.

I finish my letter with a heart filled with sadness.

My father is well, as are all of us, except for little Hélène, who has had a fever for several days.

CF 16   *December 3, 1865*

If you could light a candle for me at Notre-Dame des Victoires next Friday, the Feast of the Immaculate Conception, I would be very grateful. I'm making a novena so my two little girls, Léonie and Hélène, will get well. Please, do not refuse me this! Try to find a moment during the day. But no, you won't want to; you look at it as nothing. If you knew what a memorable day December 8 is for me! Twice I received great graces on that day.[69] I hope that you'll do as I wish.

CF 17   *December 10, 1865*

We received your letter which made us very, very happy. I didn't think you were so good, so I dreamed impossible dreams that I don't dare tell you here because you'd make fun of me! I'll tell them to you if they come true.

I would never have suspected that my father was so sensitive. My husband gave him your letter to read and he cried. We pretended not to notice so we wouldn't embarrass him. Finally, we were all excited, our hearts overflowing with affection for one another.

As you know, for a long time my father has intended to leave the house near us where he's living to move into his own house on

---

69 On December 8, 1851, Zélie heard an interior voice that urged her to "make Alençon lace." Later she prayed that she would have a second daughter; this will be Pauline, who was born on September 7, 1861.

the rue Saint-Blaise.[70] I'm very concerned about this because my poor father doesn't know how to manage on his own. It's necessary that I look after him in order to prolong his days. Otherwise, I would be constantly worried.

Probably, he already told his landlord because yesterday some people came to see the house. It was going to be rented, and I didn't have a single moment to lose. But what could I do? Unfortunately, the one on the rue Saint-Blaise is vacant, and I had no hope of being able to convince him to take on two houses. However, I've prayed to the Blessed Mother that he'll stay here.

When I talked to him about this he was furious, but I pointed out that I couldn't do without him and that he was a great help to me. In other words, I begged him to stay. My husband joined me. He eventually left and didn't say anything more. I had finally convinced him. Imagine, seeing him alone until the end of his days in that house on the rue Saint-Blaise, far from all that he needs! Did I not do the right thing?

I discussed something else with him. I hope you won't be upset. Well, I told him that we'd take responsibility for the rent of his current house for this year and that we'd each pay half when you're established. But he wanted none of it. Finally, worn out and overcome by my deluge of words, he left. I followed him every step of the way to his house. I wanted his consent. He didn't raise his voice, all he did was say weakly, "Leave me in peace," and he smiled.

I didn't ask for anything more, and I went to renew the lease for three years. Now, I'm happy, my mind is at ease. You wouldn't believe the burden that's been lifted from my shoulders! But I'm going to write "the saint of Le Mans"[71] to ask her to pray to God so that the house on the rue Saint-Blaise will be rented, because my father would worry a great deal if it were not. I'm going to post it throughout the city.

My little Hélène no longer has a fever, and Léonie is also much better.

---

70   See footnote in CF 5.
71   Her sister, Sister Marie-Dosithée.

1866

All the letters written in the year 1866 are addressed to her brother.

CF 18   *April 22, 1866* [72]

Today I learned from Monsieur Vital Romet, [73] whom you had told, of your decision to buy the pharmacy in Lisieux. [74] I didn't write to you on Thursday because I was very confused by what I should say to you. I didn't want to advise you, not knowing enough about the matter. On the other hand, I wouldn't have wanted to deter you. I entrusted it all to the will and the grace of God. Now, all is decided and, good or bad, we mustn't worry about it anymore; that would not get us anywhere.

I feel very sorry for you, my poor friend. You're going to enter into real life, full of misery, worries and work. You truly must have courage and patience, because you're not finished struggling. You'll work as much as the Trappists and the reward will be much less grand. I assure you that I was very upset all day thinking of you. I'd like to see you happy, and it seems to me that that's not going to happen soon. If only you were lucky enough to meet a woman like the one I wish for you. She would make you happy, but they're very rare, and I hardly know any. Only God could put her hand in yours, to give her to you.

I was very surprised that you hadn't let our sister in Le Mans know. I believed you had more faith, and I thought you would have commended yourself to her prayers for something like this, on which your future depends. I wrote her on Thursday so that she would pray for you, and I told her that you were about to buy a pharmacy. Poor Élise had written to me two weeks ago asking for news about you,

---

[72] The original address was preserved: "Pharmacien Interne à l'hospice de Bicêtre-Hospice de la Vieillesse homme, Paris."

[73] Vital Romet, a close childhood friend of Louis Martin who will be Céline's godfather. He was a pharmacist in Alençon. (See the Biographical Guide of Proper Names.)

[74] Isidore bought a pharmacy at the corner of Place Thiers and Grand-Rue (today Place St. Pierre) from Monsieur Pierre Fournet. Isidore married Monsieur Fournet's daughter, Céline, on September 11, 1866, at their parish church, the Cathedral of St. Pierre in Lisieux, and they lived above the pharmacy after their marriage.

complaining that she had not received any news directly from you.

I see nothing more to add. My heart is not very cheerful, so I don't feel up to speaking about anyone else and enjoying myself laughing.

CF 19   *November 18, 1866*

I received your letter, which kept us waiting a long time. My husband was sorry that you didn't write. As for me, I find, as you do, that it's better to wait until you have something new to tell us.

It hurts me that you're still thinking of the little squabbles that you and I have had. They're nothing, and I forgot them long ago. I've known you for a long time, and I know you love me and that you have a good heart. If I needed you, I'm sure you wouldn't let me down. Our friendship is sincere. It doesn't consist of fine words, it's true, but it's not any less solid, and it's built on stone. Neither time, nor man, nor even death will ever destroy it.

Marriage must not put a distance between our hearts, and I'm quite convinced that your affection for me is still the same.[75]

As for my affection, it's doubled. I still love you very much and my dear sister-in-law as much as you. You don't know how happy I am to think that you made such a good choice. Before your marriage, as I've said to you many times, I was very anxious about your future. Now, I find that your happiness is assured. As our dear sister in Le Mans has told you many times, I think that you've always been lucky and that God has unceasingly protected you in a visible way.

---

[75] Zélie was unable to attend her brother's wedding because she was expecting the birth of her fifth child. After the birth, Isidore and Céline visited Alençon, and Zélie and Louis held a reception in their honor. In a letter from the bridegroom to his sister, written in November, 1866 upon his return from the trip to Alençon, he thanks her: "You were expecting news, perhaps, much sooner, but what would we have told you? That we spend a great part of the day with our heads in the clouds, that the "honeymoon" still shines at its brightest! All things which you know very well. We left Alençon with regret, especially after such a full week, and the gracious and cordial receptions that everyone gave us. The one that gave me the most pleasure is still yours, because I know your customs, which, besides, are the same as those of all our family and in which we were raised. I know your dislike for ceremony, and I saw with what enthusiasm, what warmth you received us. Thank you again for your reception. Thank you for my good old father, who was so happy to see such a pretty little daughter-in-law and who, in his abundant joy, made us enter the church to thank God for it."

I wonder if my plan to go to see you will ever be realized. I encounter so many obstacles that I dream about them at night. For example, one time I dreamed that I left, and I saw my husband make a long face, saying that I was leaving him in a predicament. The next day, I told him about my dream, and he said that I had dreamed the truth. He didn't need to tell me; I know him well. It's also true that it isn't easy for me to be away, above all because of my lace business. And then, when it's necessary to leave four children for two weeks, it's a little long. However, I really want to get away, but I don't know how to do it. If I were able to go and return in the same day, I would have done it already.

I just came back from seeing my little Joseph.[76] Oh! My beautiful little boy, he's so big and strong! It's impossible to wish for better. I never had a child who did so well, except for Marie. Ah! If you knew how I love my little Joseph! I believe my fortune is made!

Kiss my sister-in-law for me. Tell her that I truly love her. A little letter as soon as possible would make me so happy!

CF 20   *December 23, 1866*

My father is content and happy to see that he is loved and wanted in your home, so he's hurrying to pack his bag in order to leave Wednesday on the 8:00 train.[77] He will arrive in Lisieux at noon, accompanied by... a goose "recommended and fattened" especially for you!

Here's the advice that I ask you to give my father: first, could you tell him that it is urgent that his house be shown. He doesn't want to do it because it's rented to an officer, but the officer could leave any day now. Then, suggest to him not to take on a servant and to come

---

[76] Marie-Joseph-Louis (called Joseph), was born at 15, rue du Pont-Neuf on September 20, 1866. He was baptized in the parish church, St. Pierre de Montsort, in Alençon. He was the Martin's fifth child and the first boy. At the time this letter was written, he was with a wet nurse, Rose Taillé, née Rosalie Cosnard (January 5, 1836-May 17, 1908) who lived in Semallé, 8 kilometers (5 miles) from Alençon. She will also be the wet nurse for two of Zélie's other children, Marie-Joseph-Jean-Baptiste and Marie-Françoise-Thérèse (St. Thérèse). Rose, who was called "Little Rose," and her husband, Louis-Moïse Taillé, had four children: Rose, born in 1861, Auguste in 1863, Marie in 1866 and Eugène in 1871.

[77] The railroad was built in Alençon in 1853.

live with us, because you wouldn't believe the problems I'm having in finding him reliable and devoted people. My husband supports this arrangement. You wouldn't find one in a hundred who would be as good as he is towards a father-in-law.

You know him, our father is a very good man, but he's developed certain little habits of old age. His children must put up with them, and I'm completely determined to do so. If you lived here, he would live with you because he loves you more than me. But he won't move to a different part of the country, so he'll have to stay at our house until the end of his days. Once again, advise him to do so.

You must have a lot of frustrations having so many people working for you. I feel deeply sorry for you. Do as much on your side and pity me, as well. I have a lot of trouble with this wretched Alençon lace which gives me the hardest time. I earn a little money, that's true, but, my God, it costs me so much!… It's at the price of my life because I believe that it's shortening my days, and, if God doesn't protect me in a special way, it seems to me that I'll not live long. I could easily be consoled by that if I didn't have any children to raise. I would greet death with joy, "like one greets the sweet, pure dawn of a beautiful day."

I often think of my holy sister, of her calm and tranquil life. She works, to be sure, not to earn perishable wealth; she only stores up treasures for Heaven, towards which all her longings go. And me, I see myself here, bent towards the earth, going to great trouble to accumulate gold that I can't take with me and that I have no desire to take. What would I do with it up above!

Sometimes, I find myself regretting that I haven't done as she did;[78] but quickly I tell myself, "I wouldn't have my four little girls, my charming little Joseph…. No. It's better that I struggle where I am and that they are here. As long as I reach Heaven with my dear Louis and see them all there far better placed than I, I will be happy enough like this. I don't ask for anything more."

Please, my dear friend, don't read this letter to your wife. She

---

[78] In 1850, Zélie sought admission to the Congregation of the Daughters of Charity at the Hôtel-Dieu in Alençon, but she was not accepted. In the 18th and 19th centuries, the Hôtel-Dieu was a refuge that housed about 200 of the poor and sick of Alençon. It was situated on the rue de Sarthe and was served by the Daughters of Charity. Pierre-Marie Gautier, *Alençon dans l'Orne*, p. 48.

would find me fanciful because I see that I went wherever my thoughts led me. But this is how I write to my sister. It doesn't embarrass me with her, and I'm not afraid of telling her all that comes to my mind. And yet your little wife is so good that I'm sure she would forgive me.

Tell her that I love her with all my heart and that I eagerly await the day when I'll be able to see her again. I wish her a calmer life than mine, and, in the coming year, a beautiful little boy who will make you both very happy, that you live together on earth for a long time and that you'll be reunited in Heaven, never to be separated again.

I end in offering you my wishes for a very prosperous New Year and embrace you both with affection.

1867

CF 21 To her sister-in-law, Madame Guérin
January 13, 1867

My dear sister,

I was so touched by your kind letter. What you confided to me, was it not that you already hope to become a mother? Now the little worries will come, but in the midst of all that, there will also be many joys. I learned from my father that you've been sick. I also was sick with my first little girl. I believed that all was lost and I cried, I who so wanted a baby! But that didn't prevent the little one from being born at the proper time, and she was very strong.

Thank you for the lovely presents you sent my little girls. I can't tell you how happy you made them. Upon opening the suitcase, there were such cries of joy that my poor father was stunned. After the cries of joy came the tears, and all four of them cried, which was the most amazing thing. The little ones wanted what the big ones had. We had a very hard time making peace. Grandpa had to get angry and threaten to take away all these beautiful toys, but they told him that he was not the one who gave them, that it was their aunt who gave them the toys, and he couldn't take them away.

I enjoyed myself like a child playing a game of Patience, and I paid for my childishness. I had to make a very urgent order of lace, and, to make up for lost time, I stayed up until one o'clock in the morning.

The white wide-brimmed hat fits little Joseph perfectly. But I'm truly annoyed, my dear sister, that you spent so much money on my children. If I had just one or two, I wouldn't say anything, but five, it's too much. If it were necessary to give New Year's presents to each one, it would never end. The older ones now have enough toys to last their entire childhood. They take good care of their belongings because I don't give them to them to misuse. So please, let it end there.

I had the happiness of seeing my little Joseph the first of the year. For his New Year's gift, I dressed him like a prince. If you only knew how beautiful he was, how heartily he laughed! My husband said, "You carry him around like a wooden statue of a saint." I showed him off, in fact, like a novelty. But… oh, the vanity of the joys of this world! The next day, at three o'clock in the morning, we heard a loud knock at the door. We got up and went to open the door. Someone said, "Come quickly, your little boy is very sick, and we're afraid he's going to die."

As you can imagine, I didn't take long to dress and found myself on the road to the country[79] on the coldest night, in spite of snow and slippery ice. I didn't ask my husband to come with me, I wasn't afraid, I would have crossed a forest alone, but he didn't want to let me leave without him.

The poor little boy had a bad case of erysipelas[80] and his face was in a pitiful state. The doctor told me that he was in very grave danger;[81] in other words, I saw him already dead!… But God didn't

---

[79] Zélie and Louis left for Semallé to see their baby at Rose Taillé's house. (See footnote in CF 19.)

[80] Erysipelas, also called St. Anthony's Fire, is an acute streptococcus bacterial infection of the skin resulting in inflammation and a painful rash and typically involves the lymphatic system. The infection can spread to other parts of the body. Prior to the use of antibiotics, it was a feared disease that led to very high infant mortality.

[81] Marie-Joseph-Louis died a month later, on February 14, 1867, from erysipelas and enteritis. (See footnote in CF 48.) He was five months old. We see here an important gap in the correspondence of Zélie and Isidore. It's due, again like the others, to the later revision made by Isidore who, before giving his sister's letters to his nieces, wanted to omit those he judged having details or confidences that were too intimate. The older daughters of Madame Martin had heard their mother, holding the first little Joseph on her knees, say to their father with pride, "Look how well made his little hands are! How beautiful they will be when he raises them at the altar or when he preaches!" And later, the happy mother planned to make an alb of Alençon lace for her priest….

make me wait so long for a little boy to take him from me so soon. He wants to leave him with me, and he's now thriving. But, would you believe that they blamed me for what happened because I made him come to Alençon in weather that was too cold. As you see, I paid very dearly for my pleasure on New Year's Day, but I won't do it again.

CF 22
To her brother
May 3, 1867 [82]

It's impossible for me to leave Monday for Lisieux. I must postpone my trip for a week because I have 25 meters of Alençon lace to send out at the end of next week. It will be very difficult to manage to do it, although I have as much help as possible. But by using the lamp to lengthen the days, I hope to succeed.

You mustn't worry if you're delayed at the pharmacy when I come to Lisieux. My intention is not to go here and there. If this was my only reason for coming, I wouldn't be looking forward to it so much; my reason is to be with you.

First, I don't like going out. You mention Trouville,[83] but I care little for the sea. However, I'm very grateful for your thoughtfulness. You spare no expense to make me happy, it's too much! Later, when the girls are grown, we'll see; then we'll take many little trips together to the countryside. In the meantime, we'll simply visit Lisieux. Don't be afraid that I'll be bored; there's no danger of that!

Thank my sister-in-law for her kindness in wanting me to bring the girls,[84] but I prefer to wait until next year. They're still very young to get up so early. It's true we could leave on the eight o'clock train, but I'll already have too little time because it's impossible for me to stay more than two days. I must absolutely return on Wednesday.

So count on me for Monday at eight. I'll only write you if I have an unforeseen difficulty, something I don't expect and greatly fear.

---

[82] The original mailing address was preserved.
[83] Trouville is on the northern coast of Normandy, 27 kilometers (16.7 miles) from Lisieux. It was a popular seaside resort.
[84] Léonie, three years and eleven months old, and Hélène, two years and seven months old.

28

CF 23

On Thursday, the 19th, at ten-fifteen in the morning, my little Marie-Joseph-Jean-Baptiste was born.[86] He's very strong and quite lively, but I had a terrible time and the baby was in the greatest danger. For four hours I suffered the most severe pain I've ever felt. The poor little one was almost asphyxiated, and the doctor baptized him before his birth. Now, I'm perfectly fine. I got up for a little while, and I'm taking advantage of it by writing to you. I wish with all my heart, my dear sister, that you'll be happier than I am. I ask God that it be so and that He give you a beautiful baby.

I won't write any more now; soon I'll send you a longer letter.

My little one just left with the wet nurse. I'm afraid he won't be easy to raise. He cried from Thursday night until this morning, that is, thirty-six hours non-stop. The wet nurse did not undress for two nights. Last night I was so sorry to see the poor little one writhing in pain that I didn't sleep. I was crying, as was the wet nurse, who didn't want to take him with her because she was too afraid that he would die at her house. This morning, the doctor reassured us. The baby was very calm all morning long, all he did was sleep, and he was sleeping when he left this afternoon.

1868

CF 24

Yesterday I received news of my little Joseph. He's quite cute, and they have to wake him up to make him drink. He's always sleeping and hardly ever cries. I'm longing to see him very much because I'm in constant fear ever since the tragedy of his little brother. However, I believe that God will leave this one with me.

---

[85] The original mailing address was preserved.

[86] Marie-Joseph-Jean-Baptiste (called Joseph), was born at 15, rue du Pont-Neuf on December 19, 1867, at 10:15 a.m. He was baptized in the parish church, St. Pierre de Montsort, in Alençon. His godmother was his sister Pauline. Two days after his birth, he was placed with Rose Taillé, the wet nurse living in Semallé. (See footnote in CF 19.)

CF 25

To her sister-in-law
January 12, 1868

I received your letter as well as the box containing the New Year's gifts for the children. I begin by scolding you and I have the right, I'm the older sister. Thus I will tell you, as I did last year, that you shouldn't spend money like that; it upsets me, I assure you. You must be more reasonable in the future.

When I saw all that was being unpacked, I didn't laugh, I murmured my objections. But there were four here who didn't do as I did. They were laughing very hard and were quite surprised to see that I wasn't happy, especially Marie and Pauline who found you so rich, so rich that they can't get over it. They haven't stopped talking about your fortune since Thursday!

Today we had a lot to do with all these beautiful things. There was an exhibition of the games and a complete doll's tea set made of pretty porcelain to use for the first time; this lasted close to two hours. The children have never had so much fun. Pauline said this evening, "Oh! What a pity today is over. I'd like it to be this morning again!" I didn't completely agree with her because I've had a tough battle. For three days, I've been alone with these little ones because the maid is with her family. Along with this, I have a terrible cold and a fever, and I can barely stand up. Fortunately, I have my father's housekeeper who's helping me a little. My little Joseph is growing like a mushroom.

CF 26

To her brother
February 14, 1868

Your last letter made me happy. However, I would like your business to do even better, and I won't be happy until you can tell me that each year you put 8 to 10,000 francs aside. So, try to write me soon that you're able to do this. In the meantime, you must take heart and not worry. I was like you when I began my Alençon lace business, and I made myself sick over it. Now, I'm much more reasonable. I worry much less and resign myself to all the unfortunate events that happen to me, and may happen to me. I tell myself that God allows it, and then I don't think about it anymore.

You ask me if I'll visit you at Easter. I can't say because I don't know what I'll have to do then. Unforeseen things happen so often that I can't give you an answer. What is certain and what I can promise you is that, if you're unable to come the month of September because of the baby or for any other reason, I will come during the holidays with my two oldest girls. It's rare that I can't find a little free time during that period. However, it's up to you to come this year, but I don't see you coming soon.

I'm very concerned about my sister-in-law regarding the dear baby she's expecting. I'm worrying much more about her than I do about myself when it's my turn, because then I don't even think about it. I hope she's like me and lets others worry about her. When I speak to my husband about my fears on this subject, he tells me that he doesn't understand me, that all will be for the best. I hope so, but meanwhile I'd like it all to be over. This month seems long to me.

I'm happy to see that no one's forgotten the layette for little Jeanne. (My husband says the baby will be a boy, a little Jean.) I also thought of her; nearly two months ago I bought her a silver rattle. As for trinkets, I know nothing about them.

Today I saw little Joseph. He was sick for almost two weeks. He's doing much better, but he's lost a lot of weight and so is not very strong. He's as pretty as a little bouquet, and he laughs heartily and joyfully until he chokes! I'd like very much for God to leave him with me. I pray and beg Him for this every day. If, however, He doesn't wish it, I'll have to resign myself. The wet nurse always says to me that he's going to die, that he's like the other little Joseph. I have to go and console her, but I don't see him dying, thank God!

Louis sends his kindest regards to both of you, as well as our little girls, who all, except Marie, want Pauline's godfather to be their godfather.[87] When we bring out the games, they're always from him. And, as for their aunt, they also want her to be their godmother!

---

[87] Her uncle, Isidore Guérin.

CF 27 To her brother
February 24, 1868

I'm sure you must be overjoyed at the birth of your little Jeanne.[88] You must have been very anxious because you often worry quite a lot about less important things. I beg you, don't keep me in suspense. Write me immediately after the baptism. Tell me if the little one is pretty, if she cries a lot, I must know everything. My father made a face when he heard it was a girl; he wanted a boy. That will be for another time.

My dear friend, I want to go and see you so badly that I can't stand it any longer. I could have cried this evening when I saw all the preparations my father was making for his trip while I was making none. I love your wife as much as you; she's so good, so affectionate. And the little dear, how I love her already! So it's unfortunate that we're so far away; we would have such a good time together. But no, our visits must be far apart and our time together too short.

I'm ending my letter because I'm in no mood to write this evening.

When I received your telegram it filled me with such emotion that I felt it all evening. It's midnight, and I'm still not myself.

My eye has been really hurting me for a month. It's not red, and we can't see anything. It's a nerve that's affected. If you have any medicine to relieve it, send it to me. I'm anxious about it, and I'm afraid of not being able to work.

Tell me if your wife is pleased with the new maid and if your pharmacy student has returned, so that I'm sure you're not in a predicament.

---

88 Jeanne-Marie-Élisa (called Jeanne), was born February 24, 1868, in Lisieux, to Isidore and Céline Guérin. She was the first of three children: Jeanne (February 24, 1868-April 25, 1938), Marie-Louise-Hélène, known as Marie (August 22, 1870-April 14, 1905) and Paul (stillborn on October 16, 1871). Jeanne and Marie were first cousins and playmates of the Martin children. Marie will enter the Carmelite Monastery in Lisieux on August 15, 1895, and will receive the name Sister Marie of the Eucharist. Her novice mistress will be her cousin, Sister Thérèse, later known as St. Thérèse. (See the Biographical Guide of Proper Names in the Appendix.)

My dear sister,

We received the telegram about nine o'clock this evening. Here, at last, is the little Jeanne so longed for! May God keep her with you and may she be your joy! You wouldn't believe how happy I'd be if I could leave with my father to go give you both a hug. I find him so privileged. I envy him, but I have to resign myself to staying because there's no way of doing otherwise.

When I told him the good news, my father was peacefully seated in the corner by the fire smoking his pipe. He wasn't at all determined to leave so quickly. It took all the energy I had to sway him. Finally, I succeeded, and my husband immediately went to inform my father's maid.

I assume the baptism will take place tomorrow? Isidore must write me Wednesday morning to give me your news and that of the charming little Jeanne. As soon as you recover, I'm expecting a letter from you because you'll give me so many more details than my brother. He doesn't tell me half of what he should, and his letters are always too short.

CF 29

Tell my father that we're eagerly awaiting his arrival, above all little Hélène, who, every time she returns from class, asks if her grandpa has arrived. Léonie is very worried about her little cousin. She made our lives miserable yesterday. All morning long she had it in her head to leave for Lisieux, and she wouldn't stop crying. We had no peace until her father got angry and told her she couldn't go. The two oldest girls pester me every day, wanting to know how much time remains until summer vacation, when we go to see you....

If you're satisfied with the maid I sent you, try to keep her because it's very difficult to find a good one. It's not always high wages that assure the loyalty of household help; they need to feel that we love them. We must be friendly towards them and not too formal. When people are good-hearted, one is sure they'll serve with affection and devotion. You know that I can be very sharp; however, all the household help I've ever had loved me, and I've kept them as long as I wanted.

The one I have at the moment would be sick if she had to go away. I'm sure if she were offered 200 francs more she still wouldn't want to leave. It's true that I don't treat my servants any differently than my children.

If I tell you this, it's not to offer myself as an example. I assure you, I'm not thinking that, because everybody tells me I don't know how to treat servants. Madame X, in particular, but what do you want, I could never act like her, and I won't even try.

CF 30   To her brother
March 23, 1868

I was happy to hear that little Jeanne is doing well and that she's so good and easy to care for. My little boy is very good as well. He's the picture of my first little boy; I've never had children who look so much alike. Let's hope they're not alike to the very end! I'm always afraid that this little one will fly away like his brother. He's very strong, but he doesn't look very well, like my first boy, and I don't like that at all.

I hope good Saint Joseph will let me keep this one. It's enough that he already has one. He had the kindness to send me another son right after I gave him the first. Surely, I owe this last one only to his special intercession. Last year I made a novena during his month, and I finished it on his feast day. Nine months later, to the day, he answered me. As you see, he couldn't have done any better. Perhaps you'll laugh at what I've written, but I don't laugh at it, I take it literally.

CF 31   To her sister-in-law
April 14, 1868[89]

Your last letter made me very happy. I was so eager to hear from you, and I still am because I'd like to know how little Jeanne is doing, as well as all of you.

---

[89] Original address preserved on blue quadrille paper.

34

I see you've already had many concerns about your dear little girl. But, my dear sister, you mustn't worry unnecessarily; children always have a few problems. I'm so used to it with mine that I just accept it.

However, I've had plenty of reasons to be anxious over the youngest one, who was very sick three weeks ago. The wet nurse arrived, sobbing, to tell me that there was no hope, that he was sick exactly like his little brother. The fear of seeing him die in her home frightened her so much that she wanted to return him to me. The doctor went there right away and saw he had bronchitis. We took care of him as best we could, and now he's completely cured.

We went to see him today. He smiled at his father and me as if he knew us. I feel so deprived not having him with us, and I'm longing for the moment when he returns, although I already fear the extra problems his return will bring us because we're so overworked here. If I had three times less work, I'd still have so much that I'd rarely have a free moment. But it's such sweet work to take care of little children! If I only had that to do, it seems to me I'd be the happiest of women. But it's quite necessary that their father and I work to earn money for their dowries.[90] Otherwise, when they're grown, they won't be very happy with us!

---

[90] Throughout her correspondence, Zélie often appears driven and overly stressed regarding her work. Céline (Sister Geneviève of the Holy Face) in her book entitled *The Father of the Little Flower*, cited in a footnote in CF 54, stated that Louis insisted that Zélie hire additional workers or even close the business in order to relieve her of the stress she was under. In several letters, her brother Isidore also advised her to limit the intake of new orders. However, she did not act on their advice.

In an attempt to understand one of Zélie's underlying motivations, one might consider an experience in Zélie's later adolescence. The Guérin family lived on Zélie's father's military retirement pension, and their financial situation was strained. Her parents decided to open a café and billiards room in their home on the ground floor of the rue Saint-Blaise. It was decided that Zélie's mother would run the business. However, she drove the customers away by her rigid and arrogant personality, oftentimes highly moralistic, resulting in the closure of their business. This left her parents in a precarious financial situation and unable to provide for both the college tuition of their son Isidore and the dowries of their two daughters, Élise and Zélie.

After she was refused admittance into the Convent of the Daughters of Charity, Zélie understood the need to generate money for her own dowry, since without an adequate dowry, the choice of a suitable marital partner would be compromised. On the feast of the Immaculate Conception, Zélie prayed to the Blessed Mother for guidance and heard an inner voice tell her, "See to the making of Alençon lace." Consequently she enrolled in a lace-making school in Alençon and became a master lace maker of *Point d'Alençon*. She opened her own business and was very successful.

Zélie's realization that she was not able to trust or depend on her parents to adequately

In my last letter, I forgot to thank you for the beautiful box of candy you sent home to us with my father. He gave us a charming account of little Jeanne's baptism. He was truly impressed.

Everyone here is in good health, but my poor Léonie took a bad fall and has two very large and deep cuts on her forehead. This is the third time she has cut her forehead, and the marks from the first two times are very noticeable. I'm sorry about that. But on the other hand she has the best nature you could imagine. She and Pauline are charming; little Hélène is very cute as well. Marie has a very special and determined nature. She is the prettiest, but I'd like her to be more obedient. When you write to me, don't mention what I say to you about this child, other than being so gifted. My husband wouldn't be happy; she's his favorite!

I hope to receive news from you soon. Will you tell me if the pharmacy is doing well, if my brother still worries and if he's sad? I'd like you all to be happy, but true happiness is not of this world. We waste our time looking for it here.

CF 32   To her sister-in-law
                                                          May 1868

I was so happy to hear the good news about your little Jeanne. You must be happy to have such a good little girl. I was very happy also when I was taking care of my first child; she was so healthy. I was too proud. God didn't want that to last. All the other children I had afterwards were difficult to raise and have given me a lot of problems.

The youngest, little Joseph, is still among them; he's always sick. Three months ago he came down with bronchitis, which put him in a sad state. Last week we thought he was going to die. The doctor put a vesicant[91] between his shoulders, and he left it there for

---

provide for her could possibly have resulted in one of the reasons for her drive to succeed. This emotional scar may be one of the reasons for Zélie being a highly guarded person, experiencing herself as needing to be extremely independent because she was frightened to depend on others. This was in spite of the realities that both Zélie and Louis were financially very well off.

[91] A pharmaceutical or plant substance applied to the skin with steam that caused blistering from which blood, presumably bad blood, could be released.

several days. Imagine how our little boy had to suffer! And with all of that, a continuous cough and pressure that was suffocating him. I went to see him twice a day. In the morning I left at five o'clock and in the evening at eight o'clock, and I always returned with a heart filled with anguish.[92]

He's been doing better since Saturday. He's beginning to take a little nourishment, and he coughs less, but he's far from being cured. I'm sure your little one is much more resilient than he is because there's nothing left of him, and he has no strength. I would, though, have been quite happy to have had a very vigorous little boy. Without doubt, it's not meant for me to be happy now; maybe that's in store for later, I console myself with this hope.

I'm happy you've decided to come to Alençon this year; it's about time after not seeing you here for two years! Since I'll have the pleasure of having you here, I won't go to Lisieux as I'd been thinking. I need to be reasonable. If you knew how much I was needed at home and how difficult it is when I'm away. I can't rely on my father's servant. I can only compare her to the one I sent you. One is no more serious than the other. They're only maids who spend their time looking at the people passing by, and they set a bad example for the children.

I'm delighted that your business is going well, that reassures me. Mine is going badly, completely badly, it couldn't go any worse. I positively believe that I'm at the end of my reign. It is, however, against my will because I would have wanted to work until my last child. We already have five, without counting those who may come, because I haven't lost hope of having three or four more!

My father's been sick for several days. He was suffering yesterday, and he was complaining a lot about all of his limbs. He believes he's going to die. It saddens me very much to see him like this. He doesn't want to consult a doctor, but if this continues, I'm going to ask the doctor to come.

---

[92] Zélie had therefore walked 32 kilometers (20 miles) that day.

To her brother
                                                June 8, 1868[93]

My father is very, very sick. Yesterday, Sunday, I didn't know
what to do. I was determined to write you to tell you to come quickly,
but my husband preferred that I wait until today. The doctor came
Wednesday and Friday. Every time my poor father wants to sleep, he
starts gasping for air, and at night we have to open the windows. Last
night, he suffered as he never had before and couldn't lie down on his
bed; we had to sit him up in his armchair. What's more, he's suffering
very much from a bedsore, but the weakness still continues. Yesterday
he told me that he was finished, that he was going to die.

Don't worry, I'm constantly at his side; in other words, I never
leave him. I'm the one who dresses his wound twice a day. I give him
all that I think is best for him, but he has no appetite, and when it's
necessary to make him take something, it's truly torture for him
and for me. He can neither move himself nor sit up in his bed. My
husband has to come help us, and if this continues, we'll need two
men to lift him. We feel so deeply sorry for my poor dear father; he
endures all with a great deal of patience.

I've had enough problems. All of a sudden business has woken
up. I received some urgent orders, very urgent. If I don't fill these
orders, I'll lose a lot. I'd like to fill them all, and I don't know how
to do it. Only a moment ago, I received a letter with an order I have
to deliver on the 18th. I don't know which way to turn anymore. I'm
up from four-thirty in the morning until eleven o'clock at night. All
my time should be for my father, and I shouldn't have anything else
on my mind.

Our dear patient speaks about you to everyone; your ears must
be burning. All his discussions with Doctor Prévost revolve around
you.

I worry whether or not I should ask a priest to come right away;
this torments me. The doctor told me the illness is not serious, that

---

[93] A letter dated June 14, 1868, was destroyed. The original envelope was preserved.
The same for a letter dated July 2, 1868, the original square blue envelope was
preserved.

he sees nothing worrisome apart from his 79 years. But I find it hard to convince myself of that and everybody would think the opposite, that it wouldn't be difficult for me to believe the doctor.

CF 34

Little Joseph has been home for a month. With the wet nurse caring for her mother who's in poor health, I saw that she had too much to do, and I preferred to bring him home. He's always sick, and six weeks ago he came down with an intestinal illness.[94] His limbs are no bigger than those of a three-month old. I'm full of sorrow and have all kinds of trials and tribulations.

Tell me the exact time you're coming. The children are on vacation, so it would have to be the beginning of September or the end of this month, the sooner the better. It will be some consolation, and I need it very much, right away.

I'm eagerly looking forward to seeing your wife and your little girl, who must be much stronger than my little Joseph. This will make me utter deep sighs. It will not be from jealousy, please believe me, because it would make me very sad to see you as unhappy as I am and, especially, burdened with a difficult business and five little children to raise. But God, who is a good Father and who never gives His children more than they can bear, has lightened the burden, the Alençon lace business is slowing down. I assure you that it's almost a relief for me at this point because I don't know how I would cope if it were necessary for me to fill orders at this time.

Just this minute I received your letter, so I await with happiness your arrival on the 30th. Make sure that there are no unforeseen difficulties because if you miss this time, we'll be upset, very upset! The children are all around me, dancing with joy.

---

[94] Enteritis. (See footnote in CF 48.)

CF 35   To her brother
August 23, 1868[95]

I think we're again going to have the tragedy of losing little Joseph; he's very near death. This morning Louis assured me that it would take a miracle to save him, everyone tells me as much. He's been so much worse since Tuesday. Until then, his condition was not serious and didn't prevent him from sleeping or eating. He even seemed not to suffer because he was very cheerful and never cried, only he didn't thrive. For the last five days he's been throwing up everything he eats.

I saw two doctors; one prescribed nothing and the other not much. I believe they don't have any hope of saving him. I'm truly disheartened, and I don't even have the strength to take care of him. It tears my heart out to see a little person suffer so much. He only has a mournful cry. For forty-eight hours he hasn't closed his eyes. He's doubled over with pain. When you receive this letter, he will probably be dead.

So, my dear friends, if you come, you see the joy that awaits you. However, I always hope. I can't imagine that God will not leave my dear little boy with me.

I'll write you in two or three days. If the baby is doing better, you must come as we agreed. Otherwise, postpone your trip for a week because we wouldn't be in any condition to receive you.

CF 36   To her brother
August 24, 1868

My dear Isidore,

My dear little Joseph died this morning at 7 o'clock.[96] I was alone with him. He had a night of cruel suffering, and tearfully I

95 The original address is preserved on a square blue envelope.

96 Marie-Joseph-Jean-Baptiste died August 24, 1868, at 7:00 a.m., from enteritis (see footnote in CF 48) and bronchitis. He was eight months old. In Céline's biographical reflections of her mother, she states, "Concerning the death of the second little Joseph, I often heard it said that my mother placed a crown of white roses on his head, and she kept close to his tiny coffin up to the last moment. 'My God,' she would sigh from time to time, 'how hard it is to put him into the grave, but since You will it so, may Your holy will be done.'" Céline Martin (Sister Geneviève of the Holy Face), *The Mother of the Little Flower*, p. 79.

asked for his deliverance. My heart was relieved when I saw him utter his last sigh.

We'll expect you on Sunday.[97] I'm sorry I won't be able to entertain you as I had hoped.

I am, for life, your loving and very unhappy sister.

CF 37

To her sister-in-law
August 29, 1868

My brother asked me to give you an account of what happened today. He's tired, and I sent him to rest.

This morning, at seven o'clock, we both said the prayers for the dying at my father's bedside. At ten o'clock, he began to feel better. This improvement continued throughout the day, and we hope to save him. He speaks much more freely and is interested in everything. This evening he's a little worse, the fever returned. I'm afraid of what will happen during the night.

Goodbye, my dear sister. As you see, I'm in great pain. This is a sad week for me. My dear little angel, who was so beautiful, had to leave us.

I wish with all my heart that you'll never know such sorrow. And my poor father, I'm so afraid of losing him, too.

In the memoirs of Sister Marie of the Sacred Heart (Marie), written in 1909 at the request of Mother Agnès of Jesus (Pauline), she spoke of her memories of little Joseph: "I also remember very well my little brothers, especially the second. To make him laugh, I danced with you [Pauline] and with Léonie and Hélène too I believe, on a bed across from his cradle. We broke the bed frame. He had bursts of laughter which amused me to see that he was beginning to understand us at five to six months even. He was really very intelligent. When I said to him, 'He was naughty, that little Joseph,' immediately he stuck out his lower lip and without a sound, big tears formed in his angel eyes. Then I would say quickly, 'No, no, he's nice!' He would start to smile. I never saw such a jewel. Mama said looking at his fingers, 'He has the well-formed hands of my future little priest.' ...I still see his little coffin in the office. Mama had put a crown of white roses on him and she said looking at him, 'My God, must he be put in the ground?!! But since You want it, may Your will be done.' What courage! What faith! I was eight and this sight was profoundly engraved in my heart. She didn't cry, she couldn't cry under the circumstances and her amazing energy caused everyone to say that she didn't suffer from the death of her children, that her faith was so great that she was happy to give them to God. Poor little Mother! Happily He who sees into hearts saw all her anguish." *Thérèse de Lisieux*, "Marie, L'Intrépide" [Marie, the Intrepid], February 2010, p. 5.

97 Only Isidore Guérin could come. He was urgently called to be with his dying father.

You know the latest loss we have suffered. This morning, at five o'clock, our good father offered up his soul into the hands of God. Last night the fever returned. He had been feeling better all day, and the doctor hoped to save him. I stayed to take care of him until midnight. Our poor dear father suffered horribly, and I shudder just thinking about it. Each breath was an effort. However, I had seen him this bad before, and I hesitated a long time before calling my brother, who so needed his rest. I believed our good father was going to get better, as he had done so many times before. Finally, I couldn't bear it any longer, and I went to look for Isidore. He told me that he didn't seem any worse, and he made me go lie down. But around four o'clock, I got up. My brother told me to go back, that our dear patient was doing better, and there was nothing to fear at the moment. He'd had the maid come, so he himself could rest a little in the armchair, because he couldn't keep his eyes open.

And then, at five o'clock, the servant called him to tell him that my father's eyes were lifeless and that he had died. There was still time. They came to look for me, and I was barely able to see his last sigh. I'd been well expecting that the end was quite near, but my heart was broken in sorrow and, at the same time, full of heavenly consolation.

If you knew, my dear sister, with what holiness he prepared for death. At three o'clock, he made the sign of the cross. I have the hope, and even the conviction, that our dear father was well received by God. I want my death to be like his. We've already had three Masses said for him. We intend to request a great number of them so that, if he has anything to atone for, he'll quickly be delivered from Purgatory. His grave will be very near that of my two little Josephs.[98]

Good-bye, my dear sister, I embrace you, as well as your little Jeanne. But each time I intend to speak of her, my heart aches to

---

[98] Isidore Guérin, Sr., was buried in the Cemetery of Our Lady of Alençon. In 1894, his remains were transferred to the cemetery in Lisieux in the Martin family vault. (See the Biographical Guide of Proper Names in the Appendix and the footnote in CF 5.) Note that Zélie and Louis lost little Marie-Joseph-Jean-Baptiste on August 24 at the age of eight months, and, ten days later, on September 3, Zélie lost her father as well, at the age of 79.

think of my little Joseph, who was such a handsome and sweet little boy! I had eagerly looked forward to showing him to you, but what can you do. I'm used to sorrow....

CF 39

I'm truly touched by the very affectionate concern you showed me, and I'm very grateful to you for it. I'm sorry that poor Isidore is sick, but he has to be reasonable and resign himself to the will of God.

I preach to others, and I'm hardly reasonable myself. Saturday I looked everywhere for my father, it seemed to me that I was going to find him. I couldn't imagine that I was going to be separated from him forever. Yesterday, I went to the cemetery. To see me, one would have said, "Here is the most indifferent person in the world." I was kneeling at the foot of his grave, and I couldn't pray. A few steps away I knelt by that of my two little angels, the same apparent indifference....

I walked along a path I had taken five weeks ago with my little baby and my father. I couldn't tell you all I was feeling. I didn't pay attention to anything happening around me. I looked at the places where my father had sat, and I stood there, almost without thinking. Never in my life had I felt such heartache. When I arrived home, I couldn't eat. It seemed as if I would now be indifferent to any misfortune that happened to me.

If you knew, my dear sister, how much I loved my father! He was always with me, I never left him; he would help me as much as he could.

This morning I received a letter from Élise. She told me that, at first, she cried so much that she lost her voice, but now her soul rejoices in thinking of the grace God gave us in the holy death of our father. Apparently, within the Community, they're making the Stations of the Cross and offering their Communion for the repose of his soul. I intend to request one hundred and fifty Masses right away for my father and mother. Since I know well that in the years I still have left to live I won't have peace of mind if I don't arrange for more to be celebrated, I intend to come back to this later. Finally, if my brother wants more, we can make the arrangements together.

CF 40   To her brother
                                                October 9, 1868[99]

Wednesday I took my two oldest girls to the boarding school at the Visitation Monastery of Le Mans.[100] I'm sad that I don't have them with me anymore, but it's best to accept this sacrifice.[101] My sister's health is good.

CF 41   To her brother
                                                October 1868

I've just come from the cemetery. That's where I walk every Sunday. My father follows me everywhere; I seem to see him suffering. I offered up all the sacrifices I could make during my life and all my sufferings for him. I even made the "heroic vow"[102] for his benefit. As for me, when I'm in Purgatory, I'll serve my time.

So, I think the violent toothache that I've been suffering from

---

[99] Original address preserved.

[100] "In her personal notes, Marie related: 'When mother accompanied Pauline and me to the Visitation School at Mans, as the train was passing the cemetery she used to rise and look out towards the grave of her little angels. When no stranger was in the carriage, she would prayerfully speak to them out loud.'" Céline Martin (Sister Geneviève of the Holy Face), *The Mother of the Little Flower*, p. 60.

[101] Marie was age eight and a half and Pauline age seven. It was Louis who made the decision to send their two daughters, Marie and Pauline, to boarding school, despite the deep pain he felt when they were separated from the family. "His intention in this was to lessen the work of his wife, whose health had not ceased to make him anxious." He also felt reassured that his sister-in-law, Sister Marie-Dosithée, Zélie's sister, and a nun at the Visitation Monastery, would be there to oversee their care and education. Stephane-Joseph Piat, OFM, *Story of a Family*. Charlotte, North Carolina: TAN Books and Publishers, Inc., 1994, p. 84.

[102] During that time, the expression "heroic act" referred to a spontaneous offering of all the praiseworthy works of one's life for the benefit of the souls in Purgatory. As Céline noted in her biographical reflections of her mother: "In his old age, she took her father into her own home. He was hard to please, but she took care of him with tireless devotedness, doing everything in her power to comfort him in his last days. She wished even to go to Purgatory in his place, and had made *The Heroic Act* for his sake." Céline Martin (Sister Geneviève of the Holy Face), *The Mother of the Little Flower*, p. 66.

for several days is going to relieve him. My God! Yet I'm so bored with suffering! I don't have a penny's worth of courage. I get impatient with everybody; So much for my beautiful sacrificial acts for my dear father!

I'm overwhelmed with work at the moment. I sold some beautiful lace, and I've received orders for more than forty meters. I have, among others, an order for twenty meters of lace that is very difficult to make, a pattern that costs one hundred and eighty francs per meter, to be delivered by December 25.

Since my maid is sick, I had to hire someone to replace her. This person has been here for five days. She stole from me, and I dismissed her this evening. So, I was very disturbed. (She's the nineteen year old girl that I wanted to send you. It's a good thing I tried her first.) I'm going to be all alone for a week, that is, without a servant. Mine is going to her parents' home to rest. I think I'll have to choose another one. This upsets me. Reliable people are so rare, including my maid who doesn't have every quality I would like. Oh well, I hope she gets better!

I'm very much afraid that all these details won't be very interesting to you, nor is there any reason for them to be. But they concern me, and that's why I'm mentioning them to you.

When you write to me, you'll make me happy, very happy. For me, it's one of the greatest joys on earth. I've lost some of those I love, and now, the ones who live far away and whom I can only talk to through letters, console me by sharing their news.[103]

Did you take the picture that my sister had sent to my father two weeks before his death, the one on which she had written, "Dear Father, death is sleep"?[104] If you took it, don't be embarrassed. I've

---

[103] In a letter to Isidore Guérin dated October 25, 1868, Sister Marie-Dosithée wrote: "Poor Zélie is not easily consoled for the many losses she has undergone this last year. She goes back in memory over the happy evenings she had formerly with all her children; while the good grandfather, seated beside the fire, joined in with the fun of the little ones. Now, they are all passed away, the dear old father and the babies.... I am afraid that eventually the health of the mother will not withstand so many shocks. However, what gives me some confidence is her spirit of faith and her truly prodigious courage. What a valiant woman! She is not defeated by adversity, nor elated by prosperity. She is admirable!" Ibid., p. 80.

[104] The complete text written by Sister Marie-Dosithée on this picture was, "Dear Father, death is sleep, it is the end of the day when the soul goes to receive the prize for his work, it is the end of the exile where the child finds a Father tenderly loved."

looked for it everywhere, so let me know. If you have it, keep it or send me half of it! If you don't have it, tell me so I can continue looking for it.

CF 42   To her brother
                                        November 1, 1868

I'd like you to come on the 15th, but I see that won't be. You'll probably wait for the baptism of another baby because, whatever you say, we're going to have another child! That's certain, unless something terrible happens beforehand.[105] But if God still wants to take him from me, I pray that he doesn't die without being baptized, so at least I'll have the consolation of having three angels in heaven. I hope this will be the case, because I have a feeling I won't raise this baby any more than the other two....

I'm not as sad as last Sunday. I'm not suffering as much, although I continue to have a sore throat, a headache and a constant toothache, but it's quite bearable. My appetite is good, only I don't sleep well. I suffer the most at night. Blood rushes to my head, and I have, one could say, a frightening appearance. Many people believe that I don't have long to live. I hope they're wrong because I don't have time to die; I have too much work at the moment.

I asked the Poor Clares[106] to pray for my father.

I'm leaving my letter to go to the cemetery, and I'll finish it when I return. The stone should have been put in place this week. I didn't buy a wreath; there are many graves that don't have one. If you think it's necessary to place one there, tell me. As for me, I would prefer to have more Masses said.

---

[105] Zélie was three months pregnant with Marie-Céline, who was born April 28, 1869.

[106] The Monastery of the Poor Clares was founded in Alençon in 1501. A quiet, prayerful presence for over five hundred years, the nuns have lived the spirituality of St. Francis and St. Clare and have been present to the spiritual needs of the people of Alençon. For Louis and Zélie, the nuns were a symbol of their highest aspirations, a source of encouragement, and a powerhouse of prayer in their times of difficulty. Louis often brought them his catch of fish, and Zélie met there monthly for meetings of the Archconfraternity of Christian Mothers. She was a Third Order Franciscan, attending monthly meetings on Franciscan spirituality; she had made her profession at this Monastery. They supported Louis and Zélie during each of the crises of their four dying children, offering their prayers and sharing their grief. They counseled Zélie regarding Léonie and often made a novena for her transformation.

I often wish you were here so I could speak to you of my father. What a holy death he had, my poor father!… Remember when he grasped our hand, the day before he died? How saintly he was! If God listened to me, He would welcome him in Heaven today. If it were me, I would definitely let him in! My good father was not used to suffering. As for me, I'm not afraid of going to Purgatory; suffering seems completely natural to me. If God wanted it, I would immediately make a deal to do my father's penance in Purgatory as well as mine. I would be so content to know that he was happy!

I just returned from the cemetery. The gravestone is ready. It was done well, but the cross on top, for which we paid more, is not what I had in mind. It's much less beautiful than the one we'd gotten for my little Joseph. It was a waste of money.

1869

CF 43   To her brother and sister-in-law
January 1869

I went to Le Mans[107] to pick up the children. I found my sister[108] in a pitiful state. She had such a hard time breathing that she was barely able to talk to me. She always gets bronchitis, one attack after another, and that will end up taking her to her grave. I see this with the greatest pain. In losing her, I'll lose everything. She is so dear to me and so helpful to my children. My heart is broken thinking about it. When she's no longer there and I have to return to the Visitation Monastery, I won't have the courage.

She got up to receive me. She had a vesicant[109] on her chest and could only speak to me in a whisper, so I left at two o'clock instead of three to let her rest. This may be the last time I'll see her. However, she's not dying. All last winter she was like this, and she recovered in August.

---

[107] Thursday, December 31, 1868.
[108] Sister Marie-Dosithée.
[109] See footnote in CF 32.

I found the little girls[110] very good and very strong, especially Marie, who has become even prettier. She's made a great deal of progress, as has Pauline. They're delighted by Pauline's charming nature, and everyone loves her, but she has an extraordinary liveliness that prevented her, for nearly six weeks, from receiving the award called the "Rosette" and being the "Child of Jesus" at Christmas.

Marie doesn't have such a happy nature, but she tries. Her aunt and her teachers are very satisfied with her. Yesterday, my sister told me that Marie had to have several large bad teeth pulled, and she pledged to suffer without saying anything, offering it up for the repose of the soul of her grandpapa. At eight o'clock this morning I took her to the dentist. She asked me if this was truly going to relieve the pain of "her poor grandpa." After I answered yes, she didn't whisper a word, so that the dentist told me he'd never seen such a determined child.

However, he didn't want to extract the bad baby teeth, which never made her suffer anyway, and he explained the reason to me. Well! She said to me as we were leaving, "It's too bad, poor grandpa wouldn't be in Purgatory anymore."

On arriving home with the little girls, we opened the box containing the toys. All four of them were around the table, filled with joy. Marie and Pauline were delighted. There was more than enough to make the two little ones happy. I thank you a thousand times, although I'm annoyed that you always spend far too much.

I, as well as my husband, wish you all the happiness you desire in this world. A thousand kisses to little Jeanne, whom I think of so often. I talked about her a lot with my sister, and she said to me, "I hope to see her next year." She seemed to want that very much.

Your letters are too short; you don't tell me if your business is going well and a great many other things that interest me.

CF 44   To her brother
                                                     February 3, 1869

I'm happy that you're doing well and your sales are going up. As for me, I'm not too sure how my business is doing. I make lace

---

[110] Marie and Pauline were enrolled in the boarding school at the Visitation Monastery of Le Mans. (See footnote in CF 40.)

to sell without knowing if it will sell well. I'm always hopeful when I work without worrying too much, since God has allowed that we have enough money now to live in peace.

As for my health, it's not bad, nor is that of the whole family. It's been nearly two weeks since I received news from the little girls in Le Mans, and I'm very annoyed. I miss seeing them very much.

Don't worry that your little Jeanne is too lively. That won't keep her from being an excellent child later on and from being a comfort to you. I remember that Pauline was the same way until the age of two. I was very upset about it, and now, she's my best child. I must tell you that I didn't spoil her, and, as little as she was, I didn't let her get away with anything, yet without making a martyr out of her, but she had to obey.

I believe your little girl will soon be walking on her own. If she weren't so lively, she would do it sooner. However, you who were as clever as a devil, you were running like a rabbit at nine months!

Where did you get the idea that I told you I wanted to receive something for the baby I'm expecting? On the contrary, I'd told you that if you put yourselves out it would make me very unhappy because I have all I need, and I promise you, the baby will be well dressed. I chose a very good godfather and a very good godmother[111] so half the things are already made.

The baby is due April 20. We'll baptize him privately as soon as possible because, unfortunately, the baptism in the church won't be able to take place before the month of August or September.

CF 45   To her sister-in-law
                                            February 28, 1869

I'm annoyed with you. You bought cloth in Lisieux that was much more expensive than what I would have gotten for you. I found some here that's so good it's like nothing I've ever had. It's worth twice what I used before. You must have really thought it was an oversight on my part not to have answered your question, and you shouldn't have assumed that it bothered me in any way. I'm happy and satis-

---

[111] Vital Romet will be the godfather and Céline Guérin, Zélie's sister-in-law, will be the godmother.

fied only when I'm given the opportunity to help you in some way. The next time I forget to answer a question you've asked me, please remind me of it, and above all, don't buy any cloth; I'll get it for you first hand.

Today I took charge of looking for a cook for you. I've already found ten of them, if you don't insist that they know how to cook perfectly. There are as many ordinary servants as drops of water in the river, but the capable ones are very sought after and difficult to find. It's truly sad to be forced to serve other people. I have such a great fear of sending you a bad servant that it bothers me more than I can say. I'm asking the Blessed Mother to put her hand on a perfect one. Don't be impatient; I'm going to devote so much time to it that I'll end up succeeding.

Now let's speak of something else. The day I received the news that my little girls were admitted to the Congregation of the "Children of Jesus,"[112] both of them arrived that evening with Monsieur Vital.[113] That was two weeks ago Thursday; they're still here, and I don't know when they'll go back. It's because an older student came down with typhoid fever.[114] They thought it prudent to return the boarders to their families until the sick girl herself was well enough to return to her parents' home. I was quite upset by this because they won't have any vacation at Easter. Now, I'm waiting from day to day for a letter telling us they can return to school. Both of them were sick, especially Marie, who was very sick to her stomach and had a bad cold.

I'm happy to see, my dear sister, that your little girl is your pride and joy. I, too, was so happy with my first child. To my eyes, there had never been a child like her. I hoped that it would go as easily for all the others. I was mistaken. That will teach me for next time not to dream of lasting happiness, something quite impossible here below!

---

[112] A pious association for children.

[113] Vital and Pauline Romet had a brother who lived in Le Mans. They went there often, picking up Marie and Pauline from the boarding school and bringing them back to Alençon.

[114] An acute infectious disease of the digestive tract and occasionally in the bloodstream caused by *bacterium salmonella typhi* and usually contracted through water or food contaminated with feces from an infected person. Symptoms include sustained fever as high as 104 degrees Fahrenheit (40 degrees Celsius), profuse sweating, gastroenteritis, non-bloody diarrhea, and a severe rash. It was one of the deadliest diseases of the 19th century.

So, you can't imagine how frightened I am of the future, about this little person that I'm expecting.[115] It seems to me that the fate of the last two children will be his fate, and it's a never-ending nightmare for me. I believe the dread is worse than the misfortune. When misfortunes come, I resign myself well enough, but the fear, for me, is torture. This morning, during Mass, I had such dark thoughts about this that I was very deeply moved. The best thing to do is to put everything in the hands of God and await the outcome in peace and abandonment to His will. That's what I'm going to try very hard to do.

CF 46   To Louis Martin, on a business trip
                                                                      1869
My dear Louis,

    This morning I received your letter, which I was waiting for with great eagerness. How surprised I was to see that, against all hope, you were able to do some business.[116] It is Notre-Dame des Victoires[117] who protected you.

    I saw little Céline on Sunday. She's very strong and robust – if you saw how she kicks her legs; she's gained a pound and a half in the last month.

    You don't need to worry about the children. Sadly, I don't think I'll ever have any more. I had always hoped, though, to have a little boy, but if God doesn't want it, I resign myself to His will.

    Everyone probably knows that you're not here because I don't see anyone. I haven't caught sight of any thieves yet. I watch over the shop, and I don't dare go upstairs. Friday evening I stayed up until one o'clock in the morning.

    When you receive this letter, I'll be busy organizing your workbench for you. Don't get upset, I won't lose a thing, not even an old square, not the end of a spring, in short, nothing. Then it will be tidy from top to bottom! You won't say, "I only moved the dust" because there won't be any left.

---

[115] Marie-Céline was born April 28, 1869.
[116] Louis Martin was in Paris dealing with some orders of Alençon lace.
[117] Our Lady of Victories.

I told the little girls that you were in Paris and had passed through Lisieux and will return Thursday morning, but that you wouldn't be able to see them in Le Mans, even though you really wanted to go.

I kiss you with all my heart. I'm so happy today at the thought of seeing you again that I can't work.

Your wife who loves you more than her life.

CF 47   To her sister-in-law
July 11, 1869

I'm very happy that Marie has made her First Communion, despite her young age.[118] If you knew how well-prepared she was; she looked like a little saint. The chaplain told me he was very satisfied with her. He awarded her the first prize for Catechism.

The two days I spent in Le Mans were the most beautiful days of my life. I've rarely felt such happiness. My sister was feeling better. Marie told me that she prayed so much for her aunt that she was sure God would answer her prayers.[119]

I noticed that our poor sister didn't realize her condition at all. Mother Superior came to speak to me and sent me several times to reassure her and lead her to believe that she's not dangerously ill. I asked the Sisters what they thought about it. From what I noticed and what the chaplain told me, there are grave fears. She has a very diseased lung.[120] However, the doctor doesn't despair completely. He

---

[118] Marie made her First Communion on July 2, 1869, at the Visitation Monastery in Le Mans. It was because of the alarming state of her aunt's health that little Marie's First Communion was moved forward; she was nine and a half years old. Sister Marie-Dosithée prepared Marie for her First Communion. "During this time, [Zélie] wrote her child a series of letters so beautifully expressed and filled with such deep spirituality, that the nuns themselves learnt of them and read them with pious eagerness. Marie considered this collection as her greatest treasure and, refusing to leave it behind, took it home with her in the holidays. Alas, one day she found, to her distress, that the precious package had disappeared. Louise, the maid, without looking at it closely, had used it to light the fire!" Stéphane-Joseph Piat, OFM, *Story of a Family*, pp. 85-86.

[119] Sister Marie-Dosithée's health was rapidly restored. Later she said to Marie, "'It is to you that I owe seven years of my life.' The little girl gave all the credit to St. Joseph, and in token of her gratitude took 'Josephine' as her Confirmation name." Ibid., p. 87.

[120] In 1853, prior to entering the Visitation Monastery, Sister Marie-Dosithée was diagnosed with slow developing consumption (tuberculosis).

thinks that with a lot of care she might get better.

I'm longing to see you again, as well as little Jeanne. I'll do my best to find ways for you to relax. We're going to the country. Count on staying with us for at least two weeks. But I'd very much like my dear Isidore to come also. If he doesn't, that will hurt me very much.

Little Céline is doing wonderfully. She's beginning to babble, she's already very advanced. I haven't seen her for two weeks because she's with the wet nurse. I'm about to go see her. However, it's very hot, but I've never gone so long without seeing her.

CF 48   To her brother and sister-in-law
August 29, 1869

We're expecting you Saturday night without fail. Monsieur Romet was notified, and all the invitations are finished. I'll do my best to make it a beautiful celebration and see that everyone has a good time.

I think it will be completely unnecessary to bring me a baptismal cape for the baby;[121] it's too hot. We're overjoyed to see you again, and the children speak of nothing else. I won't write any more since we'll see you at the end of the week.

However, I must tell you that little Céline is with her third wet nurse. Seeing how difficult it is to find a good one,[122] I wanted to try

---

[121] Marie-Céline (called Céline), was born at 15, rue du Pont-Neuf on April 28, 1869, and privately baptized the same day. She was given the Complementary Rites of Baptism in the parish church of St. Pierre de Montsort in Alençon on September 5, 1869. Her godmother was Céline Guérin, the wife of Zélie's brother Isidore, and her godfather was Louis' friend, Vital Romet.

[122] Prior to Madame Georges, her third wet nurse, Céline was in the care of a wet nurse in Alençon which proved disastrous. She reported: "As I was born after the death of my two little brothers, I was confided to a nurse in Alençon itself, in order to keep me as near as possible to our home. My foster mother was remarkable for her orderliness and cleanliness. In spite of that Papa was very anxious, and purposely used to walk up and down in front of her house. I was only a few weeks old when one day he heard me crying convulsively. He entered and found me in the cradle all alone. He searched around the house and inquired from the neighbors; the nurse had gone – for a drink! He learned then that she was often drunk, and did not nourish me sufficiently. Already puny I was dying of neglect. I was therefore taken away from there and was sent to the country, this time to be nursed by a good, decent woman. It was only after a thousand mishaps that I gradually grew strong." Céline Martin (Sister

again to keep the baby at home. She was doing very well, but after four days she came down with a fever and enteritis.[123] We hurried to go find her a wet nurse in Semallé. This time, I think she's in the right place.[124] I went to see her on Wednesday, and she seemed on the right road to recovery.

I've already gone through many ordeals with this child. I feel I'm wearing myself out, and I have the impression that I won't live long. During the six days I was taking care of the little one, I had a fever every day. This was not so much from fatigue as from anxiety. I feared what did, in fact, happen, that she would have to go back to the wet nurse.

CF 49   To her sister-in-law
                                  October 1869 and January 1869[125]

My children speak to me often of your little Jeanne, and they ask me if she's coming back soon. Léonie calls her "the little boy Jeanne." We're having a hard time making her understand that Jeanne's a little girl and not a boy. She understands things so slowly, but she's always been sickly, and I hope she'll develop later on.

Hélène had the measles[126] and was very sick. For three days I was worried; now, she's doing very well except for sore eyes, left over from her illness. However, she won't be going out too soon; she stayed

---

Geneviève of the Holy Face), *The Father of the Little Flower. Louis Martin 1823-1894.* tr. Fr. Michael Collins, SMA, Charlotte, North Carolina: TAN Books and Publishers, 2005, pp. 40-41.

[123] Enteritis is an acute abdominal disease caused by drinking substances that are contaminated by the bacteria *e-coli*, *listeria*, and *salmonella*. The bacteria settles in the small intestines, causing inflammation and swelling, which leads to abdominal pain, cramping, diarrhea, fever and dehydration. This gastro-intestinal illness was responsible for more infant deaths than any other disease.

[124] The wet nurse, Madame Georges, lived not far from Rose Taillé, the wet nurse for Zélie's two sons and, in 1873, the wet nurse for Marie-Françoise-Thérèse (St. Thérèse). Madame Georges died in 1875, when Céline was six years old.

[125] This letter seems to result from the combining of two letters: paragraphs 1 and 6 would be from October 1869 and the rest of the letter, by its contents, would find its more natural chronological place in January 1869. This letter by Zélie Martin would then have crossed in the mail with that of her sister-in-law, Céline Guérin (letter 94). The destruction of Zélie Martin's original letters prevents verification of this hypothesis, which, however, offers great credibility.

[126] See footnote in CF 8.

in bed for a week and inside the house for three weeks. Léonie had the measles at the same time as her sister, and for the third time. She went through it without staying in bed and almost didn't suffer.

Marie and Pauline went back to the Visitation Monastery on the 8th of this month. They like it there a lot and love their aunt very much, but they like being with their mama even better. Marie shed so many tears when she had to leave, and I did also. I miss them very much, and I'm making a great sacrifice in sending them far away from me.

My oldest daughter is becoming very reasonable. We see that she tries very hard to correct herself of her little faults, but she's so loving! When she sees that it hurts me, she bursts into tears. Pauline is very cute and wins everyone's heart, but she has an exuberance without equal. It's stronger than she is, so her aunt criticizes me for it.

Last Thursday I received a letter from my sister giving me better news about her health. This doesn't keep me from worrying, I'm afraid we'll not keep her with us for long. She'll be delighted about it because she looks upon death with joy, but for all of us, it will be a great sorrow and a true misfortune for my children.

I'm doing very well at the moment. I'm too happy for it to last because neither on one side nor the other do I have any big problems. My business is neither going well nor poorly, and I wish it were always that way. Oh well, for the moment, the only thing I'm lacking is trouble!

1870

CF 50

To her brother
February 8, 1870

I wasn't surprised to learn your news.[127] I'd be very happy to be the godmother, and I'm quite ready to help you as much as possible. But I think you'll have the dilemma of having to baptize the baby privately because I probably won't be able to come to Lisieux then for

---

[127] Isidore and Céline Guérin are expecting another baby.

I, too, am expecting a baby in August.[128] You won't be the godfather of this one. I'll try to find a little boy among our acquaintances who will have this honor, and Pauline will be the godmother.

So my trip will be delayed, and I won't go to see you at Easter. The little girls will be very surprised, but they'll come with me in September.

Little Céline is growing like a mushroom. She's never sick, has a very good appetite and eats whatever we want to give her. As for Hélène, she's very delicate and has had a fever for two days, something that happens rather frequently. She learns very easily and reads fluently.

The two older girls in Le Mans are doing very well. Marie received the Cross of Excellence, the Ribbon of Diligence, the Cross of the Order and the Ribbon of Manual Work. Louis is going to see them on Mardi Gras.[129]

Their holy aunt is also feeling very well. She spent only four days in the infirmary this winter. She wrote to me on Sunday and spoke about you regarding a thank you letter I received from Issoudun, for the "Little Work of the Sacred Heart."[130] She told me she was very hurt that you withdrew from it, all the more because you had admitted to her that you don't have many opportunities to give alms, and yet we have to give alms in order to go to Heaven.

I see that your little girl is still very good and very advanced, and you can be sure that this will continue, and she'll be very intelligent. The only disadvantage I find is that this may make her proud. More than others, children who are idolized by everyone have to overcome this fault, if it's not suppressed by their parents.

You didn't tell me, do you still have the maid you've had since you came to Alençon?

I'm upset that you don't have the Hospice as a customer because you need to earn money. Everything is so expensive in Lisieux and now children are coming. If you have as many as I do, this will

---

128 Marie-Mélanie-Thérèse was born August 16, 1870.
129 The Tuesday before Ash Wednesday.
130 A free school for poor children that was part of the Little Work of the Sacred Heart founded by Father Chavalier and Father Vandel. It was attached to the Sanctuary of Our Lady of the Sacred Heart in Issoudun, in the center of France, approximately 315 kilometers (195 miles) from Alençon.

require much self-sacrifice and the desire to enrich Heaven with new chosen ones.

I received Marie's handkerchief. It's too beautiful, not like what I had expected. I resolved never to say what I want, because I'm never given what I want, it's always more beautiful by half! It's like little Céline's dress, I'm trembling about it already. They sell some very pretty ones in Alençon for 10 or 12 francs, in trimmed cotton piqué, which I'm sure are double the price in Lisieux. Let me buy this dress as I think best. That will be one less thing for your wife to do, who already has too many problems, and one less postage to pay. You'll reimburse me. Tell me, does this work for you?

Give a big hug to your dear little wife for me and assure her that I'll be delighted to be godmother to a big boy or a beautiful little girl. Until then, I very much want her to get better. I won't be at ease until she herself writes to me.

A thousand kisses to little Jeanne. Tell her that her aunt in Alençon loves her with all her heart. My husband sends a thousand kind regards to you all.

CF 51
To her sister-in-law
February 12, 1870

I'm sorry to hear that you're sick. It's quite tedious for you to have to stay in bed, but take heart; it's only a few weeks to get through. You must be careful and not tire yourself because you're not at all strong.

Neither am I, and I'm not doing very well either. For the last six weeks I've often had a fever. However, it hasn't stopped me. I do my work as usual. For over two weeks I even got up at five-thirty every morning to go to the Church of Saint Léonard[131] to hear the

---

[131] Located on the rue St. Léonard, St. Marguerite de Lorraine (1463-1521) oversaw the construction of a number of famous churches in Alençon including the Church of Saint Léonard which was the first church built in Alençon in 1489. Destroyed by the Huguenots in 1560, it was subsequently rebuilt, fell into ruin and was rebuilt in 1836. In 1498, St. Marguerite also founded the Monastery of the Poor Clares in Alençon. She was canonized in 1921. Pierre-Marie Gautier. *Alençon dans l'Orne*, pp. 16 and 50.

Capuchins preach a mission. It ended today, but I don't mind because it's very cold.

I'm rejoicing, my dear sister, to think that next August we'll each have a little boy, at least I hope so. But, girl or boy, we must accept with gratitude whatever God gives us because He knows what we need better than we do. What troubles me is to think of having to put my baby with a wet nurse again. It's so difficult to find good people! I would also like to have the wet nurse live at our house, but that's impossible; I already have enough people! In the end, I think God will help me. He knows well that it's not laziness that keeps me from nursing my children because I'm not afraid of the effort.

I spoke about you yesterday with Madame Y. She finds you very happy and told me that she would like to be in your place. There are some people who advise her to go on a trip to Lourdes[132] to obtain the grace of having children, but she declares that she doesn't want to because she'd be afraid of having too many. As she loves her pleasure immensely, she prefers not to have any at all rather than be a slave. Her sister-in-law has been dangerously ill for several weeks, and they're extremely worried about her.

So you see, my dear sister, everyone has troubles. The happiest

---

[132] Bernadette Soubirous, a fourteen year old poor shepherdess, had gone to the Massabielle (today known as the Grotto of Lourdes), within walking distance from her home, with her sister, Antoinette, and her friend, Jeanne, on a cold winter morning to gather firewood to help heat her poor family's freezing one-room dwelling. The Blessed Mother, today known the world over as Our Lady of Lourdes, appeared to Bernadette for the first time on February 11, 1858. She appeared eighteen times in total, the last apparition occurring on July 16, 1858. The Blessed Mother prayed the Rosary with Bernadette and, during the following apparitions, told Bernadette, "to go and drink at the spring and wash yourself there." In another apparition, Bernadette was given the heart of the spirituality of Our Lady of Lourdes when the Blessed Mother said: "Penance, penance, penance…. Pray to God for sinners." In the thirteenth apparition, Our Lady told Bernadette to "Go and tell the priests to build a chapel…" and "go tell the priests people should come here in procession." In the sixteenth apparition, she identified herself to Bernadette by saying, "I am the Immaculate Conception." Since 1858, millions of people have come to the Grotto of Lourdes to immerse themselves in the healing waters and ask to be cured. Zélie went to Lourdes to ask the Blessed Mother for a miraculous healing, and to pray for the strength to respond to what God was asking of her. The message Our Lady gave in her apparitions to Bernadette is that we need to pray for ourselves, we who are sinners, and to do penance. This means to pray for us to see and acknowledge our broken selves – to pray for a conversion, meaning a healing of the wounds of our broken lives, physical, spiritual and psychological, so we might change from our present life of brokenness to a more virtuous and holy life.

are only those who are less unhappy. The wisest and simplest thing to do in all this is to resign oneself to the will of God and to prepare oneself to be ready to carry one's cross as courageously as possible.

I'm going to write to the Visitation Monastery and ask my sister and my little girls to pray for you so that everything will turn out for the best. I'd like to be helpful to you and console you, but unfortunately I can't do that. Well, I'll pray for you that God will cure you and give you a child that will be your joy, like your little Jeanne.

I'll be waiting for news from you towards the end of this week. Please, tell Isidore he must write to me and above all answer everything that I asked him in last week's letter. He always forgets half of it....

My little Hélène is neither worse nor better.

CF 52   To her brother and sister-in-law
                                                              February 24, 1870
My dear and beloved family,

Your letter did me good. I'm truly grateful for all your concern for me, and I thank you for it. I'm resigning myself to the will of God, although it's very hard to lose such a pretty little girl.[133] But what I regret the most and what I can't console myself for, is not having better understood her condition. I didn't think she was seriously ill. For a long time, I had been accustomed to seeing her suffer. I took care of her the best I could, giving her the tonics recommended to me by the doctor.

When I saw her come down with a little fever again, two weeks ago, at first I thought it was a cold, and I wasn't worried about it. After five days, I had the doctor come. He told me that he didn't find a full blown illness and that he didn't see the need to come back, unless she got worse. And I was so blind I couldn't see that the poor little thing was noticeably getting worse.

Saturday night she still came downstairs to be with us. We always gave her meat broth with a little vermicelli[134] and barley water.

---

[133] Little Hélène died February 22, 1870, at the age of five years and four months; the cause of death is unknown. She died on her older sister Marie's tenth birthday.
[134] A type of pasta in long, very thin strands.

She was so tired of it that the maid said to me, Friday night, that it would be better to give her a light bread soup. I listened to her. The little one ate some twice on Saturday, and she liked it so much that I gave her some again on Sunday, at noon. That's what I regret and what I will regret my entire life. However, I don't think that was the cause of her death because she passed away from weakness.

Sunday night she had trouble breathing, and I sent for the doctor right away. He wasn't there and didn't come until Monday morning. He told me the child had a mucous fever[135] with congested lungs, that she was in very great danger and that I shouldn't give her anything but broth. However, he gave me permission to add a little vermicelli or semolina[136] when I told him that she didn't want to drink clear broth.

After he left, I looked at her sadly; her eyes were dull, there wasn't any more life in them, and I began to cry. Then she put her two little arms around me and consoled me the best she could. All day she had been saying to me, "My poor little mother's been crying!" I spent the night with her, a very difficult night. In the morning, we asked her if she wanted to take some broth. She said yes, but she couldn't swallow it. However, she made a supreme effort, saying to me, "If I eat it, are you going to love me better?"

Then she took it all, but afterwards she suffered terribly, and I didn't know what was happening. She looked at a bottle of medicine the doctor had prescribed and wanted to drink it, saying that when she had drank it all, she would be cured. Then, around a quarter to ten, she said to me, "Yes, in a moment, I'm going to be cured, yes, soon...." At that moment, while I was holding her, her little head fell onto my shoulder, her eyes closed; then five minutes later she didn't exist anymore....

That made an impression on me I'll never forget. I didn't expect such a sudden end, nor did my husband. When he came home and saw his poor little daughter dead, he began to sob, crying, "My little Hélène! My little Hélène!" Then together we offered her to God.

---

[135] "La fièvre muqueuse." Emile Littré, *Dictionnaire de la langue française (1872-1877)*, [Dictionary of the French Language]. Mucous fever was defined as an indefinable fever, sometimes with an irritation of the digestive and lung mucous membranes.
[136] The finest wheat flour.

And now I'm left with the bitter remorse of having given her something to eat. My dear brother, do you think that this made her die? I beg you, tell me what you think, and although I was very uncertain what to do, I was afraid that she would get too weak.

Two weeks ago today our maid's father came to our house. The little one had been suffering for three days. He said to his daughter, "You won't be taking care of her long. She's a child who's going to die of weakness." He was right, and I saw nothing! Sometimes I gave her roasts cooked in wine to sustain her. She loved this so much, but perhaps this wasn't good for her. I blame myself completely.

Before the burial, I spent the night next to the poor darling. She was even more beautiful dead than alive. I was the one who dressed her and put her in the coffin. I thought I was going to die, but I didn't want anyone else to touch her. The church was full of people at her funeral. Her grave is next to that of her grandpa.[137]

I'm very sad; write me if you can, to console me.

CF 53   To her brother
                                                        March 6, 1870

I received your last letter, and I promise I'll put into practice all the good advice you gave me.

I'm even more inclined to constantly blame myself for my little Hélène's death, but I never for a moment thought it would end like that. I'd seen Pauline and Léonie so gravely ill when they were little and then recover very well, that I was no longer afraid of childhood illnesses. But now it will be completely the opposite, and I'm afraid my fear will go too far as soon as I see the slightest thing.

You tell me to change doctors, but which one should I use? I tried Doctor P for Léonie, seeing that Monsieur D didn't prescribe anything. He gave me a new prescription every day, and the more the child took his medicines, the worse she got. He had to give up on her. I tried the first doctor again who told me to stop all the medicines because the child was too young and there was nothing to be done, apart from not giving her food that's too rich. I believe he was right.

---

[137] Her maternal grandfather.

I also had such contradictory experiences with my second little boy. In the end, I have nothing to blame Doctor D for in my little girl's illness. My dear friend, I'll be crying for my little Hélène for the rest of my life!

Now Léonie has had a problem with her eyes for almost two years. If you know a remedy for this, please let me know. God willing, it will be more effective than those I've tried so far! This poor child concerns me because she has an undisciplined character and a limited ability to understand.

As for me, I'm not strong. For two weeks straight, I've had a fever. Thursday night I was so sick that I thought I was finished. I thought I had the same illness as my little Hélène.

Louis went to Le Mans on Tuesday to see the children. I'd promised them so long ago that he would come. He didn't want to travel because of the death of our little darling, but I persuaded him. They would have been too sad. They've cried a lot for their little sister.

In April I'm going to bring Céline home from the wet nurse. Having her here will comfort us a little because in the summer I won't have the courage to go anywhere but the cemetery. Besides, I can't imagine seeing myself on the street without a child by my side. Give me your advice about Céline. She'll be one year old on April 28. I don't think it will hurt her to wean her, all the more because the wet nurse makes her eat everything, and she's doing very well.

I hug all three of you with all my heart.

CF 54   To her sister-in-law
                                                            March 27, 1870

I was happy to receive your news. We waited so long for it. I grumbled about my brother, and I think that if he'd known how much time I'd lost watching for the postman over the last two weeks, and the disappointment I felt, he would have hurried a little more than he did!

I was worried about you. I'd like to know you've completely recovered. If you want to make me very happy, write me immediately that you're no longer in bed because I don't like you there. I believe you dislike it there just as much....

As for me, I'm not confined to my bed, but I'm not doing well at all. I often have a fever, or, more accurately, I have a fever every day. I'm not suffering very much, but I have a constant headache and a general weakness. I have no more energy. I have no stamina for work, and I don't have the heart for it. Sometimes I imagine that I'll go away as gently as my little Hélène. I assure you that I barely care for my own life. Ever since I lost this child, I feel a burning desire to see her again. However, those that remain need me, and, because of them, I ask God to leave me on this earth a few more years.

I deeply regretted the loss of my two little boys, but I grieve even more for the loss of her. I was beginning to enjoy her. She was so pretty, so affectionate, so advanced for her age! There isn't one minute of the day when I don't think of her. The Sister who taught her class told me (and it was well said) that children like her don't live long. Well, she's in Heaven, much happier than here below. But for me, I feel that all my happiness has flown away.

We've had an event in our lives that's created a little diversion. My husband's nephew[138] has inherited a sum of money, and he's decided to buy our watchmaker business.[139]

The deal should be closed in three or four days, and, if all goes as arranged, he'll take possession of the shop this week.

We still don't know where we're going to live. If we don't find

---

[138] Adolphe Leriche (January 7, 1844-December 7, 1884) was the only son of François-Adolphe Leriche (died May 25, 1873) and Louis Martin's sister Anne-Françoise-Fanny Martin (March 10, 1826-October 9, 1853). After the death of his mother in 1853, Adolphe (age 9) went to live with his maternal grandparents (Pierre-François Martin and Marie-Anne-Fanie Boureau) and his uncle, Louis Martin, at 15 rue du Pont-Neuf. Later, he became a watchmaker in Paris, and in 1871, he bought Louis' watchmaking business in Alençon. On June 4, 1863, he became baptismal godfather of Léonie Martin. Adolphe married Marie Nanteau and they had two children.

[139] "My mother had a very active temperament. She was always busy. Her household duties, in addition to the overseeing of her lace-making enterprise, absorbed her, sometimes even to excess. Father helped her in every way he could, and she was astonished at his success in business matters. When he saw her over-tiring herself beyond measure, he insisted that she should take on more workers, and even went so far as to suggest that she might be obliged to give up the whole undertaking. But when anyone tried to moderate her zeal, either concerning her work or her cares as a mother, she would not easily listen to reason. Papa was often obliged to let her go ahead. However, to be able to give up more of his time to her lace-making enterprise and to lighten her work of correspondence, etc., he sold out his own jewelry shop." Céline Martin (Sister Geneviève of the Holy Face), *The Father of the Little Flower*, pp. 30-31.

anything, we'll stay here until the house on the rue Saint-Blaise is available. However, I wouldn't want to settle there. The garden is too small. Even if it means we retire from business, I would prefer a house with a big garden. I don't miss the jewelry shop, we have more than enough to live on and raise our children. Besides, I'll continue with the Alençon lace.

They brought little Céline to me two weeks ago. She's coming along very well and is very good, but you never know. I won't take her back before the month of July. She'll be too difficult to take care of, and I believe she won't walk on her own for three or four months. She always has to be in someone's arms. I'm not strong enough and neither is my maid because I have the luck of being burdened with an invalid, she's always sick. I'm sorry about that.

Something else, to amuse you a little – there will be a big festival in Alençon on Easter Monday, a formal procession. There was a fundraiser that brought in 10,600 francs. Madame Y is making all kinds of preparations for the grand ball that will be held at City Hall for this occasion. I know many young women who have their heads on backwards over this. There are those (would you believe it?) who are bringing in workers from Le Mans to make their dresses for fear that the workers in Alençon will reveal their secret before the celebrated day of the event. Isn't all this laughable?

I received a letter this morning from my sister and the little girls. All is well, and they're very much looking forward to coming home at Easter.

CF 55   To her sister-in-law
                                                   May 1, 1870

...I'm bringing little Céline home the 21st of this month. I went to see her the Tuesday of Easter week, and I noticed the wet nurse is hardly breast-feeding her any more. She's giving her food that is too coarse. She's boiling a big piece of bread in milk. The poor little one took two or three spoonfuls of this in front of me, and she couldn't swallow it.

Well, there's nothing better to do, I believe, than bring her home as quickly as possible. What misery to have to send one's children to the country. So I don't want to hear about it anymore. I've definitely decided to care for the baby who's coming in August.[140] What upsets me is that I've gone so long without seeing you, and this will keep me from being godmother. I've been looking forward to that so much.

Thank you a thousand times for the beautiful dress you sent me for little Céline. I'm going to make her a little matching hat. She'll be as beautiful as a love.

I took my little girls back to Le Mans on Friday; their aunt is doing very well. She wanted to know all about you and asked me to give you her kindest regards. Marie received the Cross of Excellence again this term. I've really been deprived of my two oldest girls. You can't imagine what it costs me to send them away, but we have to learn to make sacrifices for their happiness.

CF 56   To her sister-in-law
                                         June 10, 1870

Little Céline seems very intelligent, but I have to spend three quarters of my day taking care of her. She's in excellent health and walks very well on her own. It's so funny to see this tiny little girl walking so easily that, on the street, people stop to look at her. She's no bigger than a six-month old and hardly speaks. Her father loves her very much because she always wants to go to him, so he often takes her for a walk.

I'm frightened at the thought of caring at home for the little one I'm expecting. Sometimes I waver in my resolution. I could get sick over it because I already have more work than I can handle. If I find a good wet nurse, I think I'd decide to entrust the baby to her.

On this subject, I must tell you that I have a godfather and a godmother for the baby. The godfather is my husband's cousin, Monsieur de Lacauve,[141] a battalion commander, and the godmother is Mademoiselle X. She's the one who arranged all this. She wanted to be godmother and told me this a long time ago, but I didn't have a

---

[140] Marie-Mélanie-Thérèse, Zélie's eighth child, was born August 16, 1870.

[141] Henry Charles de Lacauve, born in Paris on September 1, 1826. He was the son of Sophie Boureau, Louis Martin's maternal aunt, and Louis-Henry de Lacauve. He was the first cousin of Louis Martin. (See footnote in CF 59.)

godfather distinguished enough to please her. I didn't want to say anything. Finally, I thought of the handsome cousin who had previously refused to be a godfather, but this time he accepted wholeheartedly.

From what I told him of the young lady, he's dreaming of marriage, despite his 43 years. It's true he doesn't look his age. Mademoiselle X asked me how old he was. She thought a moment and said, "That's a little old." I wouldn't be surprised if it were to happen. He's from the nobility, and decorated – a decoration he earned at the point of a sword. He also has, or should have, a nice fortune from his family, unless he lost it. He inherited it nearly 30 years ago. If he's put aside the income, it should have given him one hundred thousand francs, but I doubt it. I'm very happy to have Mademoiselle X as godmother. However, I would have preferred to do things more simply.

Goodbye, my dear sister, I don't have time to write more. I began this letter two days ago. I have to look after my Céline. I'm the one who makes her eat, and she eats everything, but a little at a time. She truly has a special preference for her father. When he's there, no one else can hold her. She shouts with all her might to go to him, and when we want to take her from him, we have to pull her away by force.

From what I see, little Jeanne will become quite a scholar. She already writes rather well. Kiss her for me and tell her that her aunt loves her with all her heart.

CF 57   To her sister-in-law
                                                July 19, 1870

I was in Le Mans on July 2 for Marie's Second Solemn Communion.[142] How happy I was to see my dear oldest daughters! Both of them have changed quite a bit. Their teachers are very pleased with them. When the new school year starts, I'd like to send Léonie with them, but I had the misfortune of speaking of the little one's character in a letter, and the Mother Superior doesn't want her anymore. In a

---

[142] The Second Solemn Communion was a renewal of the gift of the Holy Eucharist received at First Communion. During the period between First and Second Communion a person was encouraged and guided to deepen his or her relationship to the Eucharistic Lord.

way, I'm not upset because I don't think they would have kept her. It's better to wait another year so she can develop more. She's very sweet at heart, but in spite of this, we have difficulty making her obey.

Little Céline has been very uncomfortable for the last two weeks because of her teeth. Two have broken through, and the others are ready to come out. Except for that, she's doing well and running around like a little rabbit. It's funny to see her take all her little precautions in order not to fall. She's very cute and very intelligent.

On the Feast of Corpus Christi, she wore, for the first time, the charming dress her godmother gave her. If you knew how good it looked on her! Everyone was admiring her, and I assure you, I was proud of my daughter. She wore a pretty white-feathered hat with it. In a word, everything was beautiful. We've taken to dressing her in white. She doesn't go out anymore unless she's wearing a white dress, very simple, but she's so beautiful that way! I never dressed my other children so well.

I believe I'm going to find myself without a godfather. Mademoiselle X is preoccupied with this. The poor godfather is going to fight in the war. I'm truly afraid for him. The young lady has already chosen Monsieur T in the event that there's an accident, but that needn't concern her. She's going to order a blue silk dress made especially for the baptism. As a gift, she'd like to give her godchild a white cashmere baptismal cape, but I anticipated it and quickly bought the cape, which I showed her, so she doesn't have to give anything. I believe this settles it very well, as does mama X!

I'm sure that in Lisieux, as in Alençon, people are talking about the draftees leaving for the army.[143] Monsieur Pierre Romet[144] has

---

[143] The Franco-Prussian War had just begun. Provoked by Otto von Bismarck, the chancellor of Prussia, the French Emperor Napoleon III ordered the mobilization of army reserves on July 14, 1870, and, on July 19, France declared war on Prussia. Bismarck planned to create a united German Empire with King Wilhelm I of Prussia as its sovereign, and Bismarck saw war with France as a way to unite Germany. The German military was superior to that of the French, and, after several defeats and heavy losses, Napoleon III surrendered at Sedan on September 2, 1870. He and 83,000 soldiers were taken prisoner. The war continued. Under Bismarck's protection, elections for a national assembly were held in French and German-occupied France to form a government with which Bismarck could negotiate. A provisional peace treaty was signed February 26, 1871, and on May 10, a formal treaty ending the war was signed. The terms of surrender stipulated that France cede the regions of Alsace and part of Lorraine to Germany and pay an indemnity of 5 billion francs. The consequences of the war were far-reaching; the balance of power in Europe

twelve employees who are going. I'm afraid you'll be inconvenienced because of your young people. Do you have enough of them? Be kind enough to write me back right away because I'm eager to hear your news! I don't have time to write to you. This morning I got up at four-thirty to write this letter. What concerns me most is knowing if you have a maid. I'm afraid you may have a problem.

Isidore shouldn't worry about my father's estate. He'll be given the amount he wants in January or at the end of December, and there will be no further payment. This will be quite enough to generate an income when he has the money. I don't like it as it is, that you pay me an income.

CF 58   To her sister-in-law
                                                         August 17, 1870

My dear sister,

My little Marie-Mélanie-Thérèse[145] was born yesterday, Tuesday, at eleven o'clock in the evening. She's very lively, very good, but not fat. She only weighs four pounds two hundred grams. I hesitate to give her to a wet nurse. I still don't know exactly what I'm going to do. I only had one solid hour of labor. I eagerly await your news. I would want this time to be over for you. Goodbye, soon I'll send you a longer letter. I hug you with all my heart, as well as my brother and little Jeanne.

Your loving sister

---

shifted from France to a unified German Empire and, in 1870, the Italian army was able to annex the Papal State of Rome, which at that time was independent of Italy, when the French garrison stationed in Rome was recalled to France, thus no longer protecting the pope. Geoffrey Wawro, *The Franco-Prussian War: The German Conquest of France in 1870-1871*. Cambridge, England: Cambridge University Press, 2003.

[144] Pierre Romet was a brother of Vital, Pauline, Hortense, Augustin Adrien and Adrien Romet, friends of the Martin family. (See the Biographical Guide to Proper Names.)

[145] Marie-Mélanie-Thérèse (called Thérèse), was born at 15 rue du Pont-Neuf on August 16, 1870, at eleven o'clock in the evening. She was given the Complementary Rites of Baptism in the parish church of St. Pierre de Montsort in Alençon on September 5, 1870.

To her sister-in-law
August 23, 1870

I just received a letter from my brother announcing the happy birth of your little girl.[146] I would have wanted you to have a boy; you would have been happier. But if you're like me, you're not distressed by it, because I never had one moment of sadness over it.

I'm upset now for not having agreed to be the baby's godmother because my little Marie-Mélanie-Thérèse (we call her Thérèse) is with a wet nurse. I kept her with me for four days and tried to breastfeed her. Unfortunately, this wasn't sufficient and we had to make her drink from a bottle. The third day she came down with such an upset stomach that the doctor told me we didn't have an hour to lose, that we had to find her a wet nurse right away.

I knew one in Alençon, about whom I had very good information. I gave the baby to her Saturday night.[147] The very next day the child was doing well, but I'm not happy to have placed her with a wet nurse. I wanted to raise her, hiring a maid to help me. I think I would have done much better if the Alençon lace was dead and buried a long time ago.

Isidore asks me what plans he has to make for the baptism. However, I already told him that my husband put him in charge of it. Let him do things as they need to be done without sparing anything. He needs to imagine that he's the godfather and act accordingly. We'll approve wholeheartedly all that he's done.

He still asks me if I've found a godfather and a godmother. So, he doesn't make the effort to read my letters! However, I've spoken to you enough of Mademoiselle X and Major de Lacauve! I don't know how he could forget that. As for the godfather, he's away at war. Will he return? Only God knows, not me![148]

---

[146] Marie-Louise-Hélène (called Marie), was born August 22, 1870, in Lisieux and baptized privately the same day. She was given the Complementary Rites of Baptism in their parish church, the Cathedral of St. Pierre, on September 14, with Louis Martin as her godfather. On August 15, 1895, a week before her twenty-fifth birthday, she entered the Carmelite Monastery in Lisieux and joined her cousins Marie, Pauline, Thérèse and Céline. She was known as Sister Marie of the Eucharist.

[147] The wet nurse lived on the rue de la Barre in Alençon.

[148] The day after Marie-Mélanie-Thérèse was born, Major Henry Charles de Lacauve was wounded at the Battle of Privat and was taken as a prisoner of war. He had a distinguished career, served in several African campaigns, and retired as an officer of the Legion of Honor with the rank of major. He died in Versailles on May 20, 1889. (See footnote in CF 56.)

I'm fully recovered now. On Saturday I got up at six o'clock to help the woman I had hired to look after me and the baby. The maid, who had slept perfectly, didn't get up and this woman was in a quandary with little Céline and little Thérèse, both of them crying. I went back to bed at nine o'clock, got up at noon, and so on all day. Sunday, I was busy almost the whole time with the children. Monday, I made a shipment of lace and didn't have one minute of rest. So tell me again I'm not strong! Soon, I hope, I'm going to see my little girl.

Goodbye, my dear sister, write me as soon as possible; it will give me so much joy to hear from you! Isidore could very well do it, but he's like my husband, very lazy about writing. It's no use asking him. It's as if I didn't say a thing.

Marie and Pauline were quite delighted this morning after receiving your letter that assured them they're going to Lisieux.

I hug you, as well as your two little daughters and Isidore.

Your loving sister.

CF 60 To her sister-in-law
October 8, 1870[149]

...My little Thérèse died today,[150] Saturday, at one o'clock in the afternoon.[151] Last Sunday, I believed she was saved. She was much

---

[149] The original address has been preserved.

[150] Marie-Mélanie-Thérèse was seven weeks and four days old.

[151] According to research done by the *Institut National d'Études Démographiques* [National Institute of Demographic Studies] in France, as cited in the article entitled *"Évolution de la Mortalité Infantile Endogène en France dans la Deuxième Moitié du XIXe Siècle 1855-1913"* ["The Evolution of Endogenous Infant Mortality in France in the Second Half of the 19th Century 1855-1913"] by Robert Nadot, the following information is pertinent for the infant mortality rate (under the age of one year) for the years of the Martin children's deaths.

Name	Died	Infant Deaths Per Thousand	Percentage of Population
Marie-Joseph-Louis	1867	171/1,000	17.1%
Marie-Joseph-Jean-Baptiste	1868	192/1,000	19.2%
Marie-Mélanie-Thérèse	1870	170/1,000	17.0%

(*Population.* Volume 25, No. 1, 1970, p. 55.)

Please note that the fourth Martin child, Marie-Hélène, who died when she was five years and four months old, is not included in this table as she was not an infant at the time of her death.

better and had gained three hundred grams during the week. The same day, towards evening, she began to throw up everything she'd eaten. Wednesday she was worse; Thursday she seemed better, and she laughed as she never had before. It was a very good night, but Friday morning, after using the doctor's prescription, she was dying. At noon, it was finished!

Her death agony began this morning, at ten-thirty. You couldn't imagine how she suffered! I'm heartbroken. I loved this child so much. With each new loss, it always seems to me that I love the child I'm losing more than the others. She was as sweet as a bouquet, and then I looked after her all by myself. Oh! I would like to die, too! I've been completely exhausted for two days. I've had almost nothing to eat, and I was on my feet all night, in mortal anguish. On Wednesday I brought my little girls to the Visitation Monastery. Their aunt asked me to tell you that she won't be able to write to you until after the Feast of the Presentation.

CF 61

To her brother
October 1870

I received your letter when I returned from Le Mans. My little one was already very sick. I was out of my mind. If you knew what happened to my poor little Thérèse. It was her disgraceful wet nurse who made her die of starvation.

I found out, too late, that my child wasn't being fed by her.[152]

---

[152] "...Marie was very intuitive, and at the age of ten, during her visit to the wet nurse to see Marie-Mélanie-Thérèse, she realized that the little one was insufficiently fed and literally being starved. She informed her mother but it was too late. The child was taken back to the family home, but died soon after." (See footnote in CF 193.) Stéphane-Joseph Piat, OFM *Une âme libre: Marie, Soeur Aînée et Marraine de Sainte Thérèse de L'Enfant-Jésus.* [A Free Soul: Marie, Oldest Sister and Godmother of Saint Thérèse of the Child Jesus], Lisieux, France: Office Central de Lisieux, 1967, p. 28. (Not translated.)
In the memoirs of Sister Marie of the Sacred Heart (Marie), written in 1909 at the request of Mother Agnès of Jesus (Pauline), she wrote: "I also remember very well the birth of the first little Thérèse (Marie-Mélanie-Thérèse). She was ravishing. Again we were obliged to place her with a nurse but in Alençon. We went to see her often when Mama couldn't. Louise, our maid, went with us. I always went with her to see my little sister because I loved my little brothers and little sisters a lot. I can say it was one of the joys of my childhood. I was however only 10 years old, but that nurse whose cleanliness was perfect and her house well kept didn't inspire any confidence

As soon as she'd been taken away from the wet nurse the doctor told me. You could have counted her bones, and yet she wasn't sick at her house, except for three days before I brought her home. Then she recovered a little. I thought she was saved; we saw her getting bigger, but she was too impaired and too weak to overcome it.

She was such a pretty little girl. She had eyes like you never see in babies her age and such fine features! And to think she was allowed to starve to death! Isn't that appalling? You don't know how much I was looking forward to raising this little one myself! I was as happy to have her as if she were my first child....

Now I'd like God to give me another child. I don't want a little boy, but a little Thérèse who will look like her and who won't go to be with a wet nurse (because this time I'll have the wet nurse live in my home). No, if God grants me more children, they'll never leave this house. Perhaps if my poor darling had continued to be breastfed she would have been able to get better, but I looked everywhere and found no one to help me. My husband went to Héloup[153] at four o'clock in the morning the day after we brought the little one home in order to bring back a wet nurse by ten o'clock. We still had some hope that we could find one, but as it happened the one we'd been

_____

in me. I didn't find that she had an honest look and when we arrived she nursed the little one who threw herself on the breast with such quickness that it seemed to me that it was like a little starving baby who was dying of hunger. I didn't say anything at age ten. What could I have said? But when we left I mentioned my thoughts to Louise, I told her I was sure that my little sister wasn't taken care of well by that woman and that I would tell Mama that she threw herself on the nurse like someone who is dying of hunger, etc.... Louise told me I didn't know anything, that it wasn't worth the bother of worrying our poor little mother, that she had enough trouble without that, etc.... But one day unable to keep it to myself any longer, I said looking at the bread, 'Ah, if that poor little Thérèse only had a little morsel at least she wouldn't be dying of hunger.' Louise looked at me stupefied, sensing what was about to happen. Indeed, Mama questioned us and from the next morning on the poor little one was at our house. Alas! it was already too late, she was too weak to recover and soon she went to join the two little angels who had preceded her in Heaven. Mama had so much pain over her death that whenever we were out for walks with her, she avoided walking on the side of the 'rue de la Barre' where little Thérèse had been with the nurse. She could never look at that street again. As for me, I had a pain in my heart for reproaching myself about not having said sooner what I thought and for fear of Louise, having caused the death of my little sister. Now I am very happy that all these angels have arrived at port, sheltered from the shipwrecks in this stormy sea of life." *Thérèse de Lisieux*, "Marie, L'Intrépide" [Marie, the Intrepid], February, 2010, p. 5.

[153] A small village 7.6 kilometers (4.7 miles) southwest of Alençon.

counting on had fallen ill. Tell me that we didn't have misfortune! Finally, it's over, there's nothing else we can do. The best thing to do is to resign myself. My child is happy and that consoles me.

I'm very glad your wife has recovered. I was worried. See how happy you are. You weaned your little girl, and she didn't notice it, and mine died after I watched her dying on my knees for two and a half hours....

Good-bye. Write to me soon. I tell you again, it makes me so happy.

Little Céline is very affectionate; she's beginning to talk sweetly. Every day I would bemoan the death of my little Thérèse, and I would say, "My poor little girl!" Right away, Céline would come and hang on me, thinking that she was the one I was talking about. She looks everywhere for her little sister and asks for her "sissy."[154]

To console me, several people have said to the maid that Céline won't live a long time! It's true she doesn't look very well at the moment. Nevertheless, she's stronger than Jeanne was when I saw her a year ago, but she's small in size.

Good-bye. Once again, I hug both of you with all my heart. A thousand kisses for Jeanne and Marie.

CF 62

To her sister-in-law
November 30, 1870

On the 22nd of this month we had a real alarm in Alençon. We were expecting the Prussians the next day and nearly half the population of the town had left. I'd never seen such desolation. Everyone hid their valuables. A gentleman who lives near us hid them so well that he himself couldn't find them again. It took three people, digging all morning, to find the hiding place!

I wasn't very afraid. Nothing frightens me anymore. If I'd wanted to flee, I would have gone straight to your house. But my husband would have been very upset all alone, and I would have been very anxious. It was best to stay.

The Prussians went to Bellême[155] and the surrounding villages

---

[154] Céline would say *"sesoeur,"* a childish pronunciation of the word *"soeur"* (sister).
[155] Bellême is 48.5 kilometers (30 miles) from Alençon.

and made quite a lot of requisitions, but one of them turned into a comedy. As it happens, they took the pig of a poor fellow who defended his beast with unprecedented courage. Had it been his child, he could not have fought harder. When the pig was tied to a horse, the man began to pull the horse's tail with all his might. He had to be satisfied with this because, to make him let go, the soldier struck it a blow with his saber so that the tail remained in the hand of the farmer!

In leaving Bellême to go to Alençon, they passed by Mamers,[156] and then they turned off and went towards Le Mans. There were twenty thousand of them.

I'm very worried about my two little girls. People were saying there was heavy fighting being waged in Le Mans, and there was no way to go get them. The railroad was requisitioned by the troops, and we couldn't go by road because it was blocked off by the enemy.

Saturday morning I received a letter from my sister telling me not to be alarmed, that the children were safer there than at home because the Prussians would never enter the convents. She said many women in the town had come to ask the nuns to take in their young girls.

But the Prussians didn't stop in Le Mans. They want to head for Paris. What worried me most was that the authorities had decided that the town should put itself in a state of defense, and they called up the National Guard. They sent some scouts into the forest. My husband went there Saturday morning and was to spend the night, but since there was no more danger they made him relieve his post that night, so he returned around midnight.

I'm worried and upset. However, I don't have as much reason to be, as do many others, because, in all probability, Louis won't leave, and my brother is even surer yet of staying.[157] I thank God for that, but it's still quite possible that they'll make men between the ages of forty and fifty go. I'm almost expecting it. My husband is not worried about this at all. He would not ask for any preferential

---

[156] Mamers is 25.3 kilometers (15.7 miles) from Alençon.

[157] Louis Martin was then forty-seven years old and the head of the family. Isidore was twenty-nine but his pharmacy had been considered a priority for the townspeople. Both their fathers had been soldiers.

treatment and often says that, if he were free, he would soon join the *francs-tireurs*.[158]

My brother is asking if we would have any money available if he needs it? The time is past when I earned eight to ten thousand francs a year and my husband also made a profit from the watchmakers shop. Now we can't even get money to live on. No one wants to pay their debts. I truly don't know what we'll do if this continues. We haven't touched the income from *Crédit Foncier*, nor that of the Railroads,[159] and all the people who owe us money say they can't pay. We're supposed to receive seven thousand francs in January from the sale of our houses on the rue des Tisons. I'm still afraid that the woman who has to come up with these funds won't be able to pay us. We're counting on this money to help you.

If we could only have the eight thousand francs that are owed us from Paris, but I look upon this sum as lost! Madame D also owes us a thousand francs, and we'll never get it; she's destitute. She's been living in Le Mans for three months. I invited her to come see us, and she replied that she doesn't have the means to make the journey.

CF 63

To her sister-in-law
December 30, 1870

My dear sister,

Today I went to Le Mans to bring back Marie and Pauline. When I returned, I found your letter. You were sick again? As you say, this has been a bad year for you, and it's a blessing that the year is coming to an end. We've all had our share because one sees nothing

---

[158] The *francs-tireurs* was the name given to bands of armed French civilians created as a guerilla force to monitor the movement of the enemy during the Franco-Prussian War (1870-1871).

[159] Louis and Zélie supplemented their work earnings with financial investments in the stock market and real estate speculation. They invested in a company that focused on the expansion of the railroads and *Crédit Foncier*, a mortgage bank that invested in urban renewal. It was during this period that *Crédit Foncier* invested in the reconstruction of Paris. Charity was a priority for the Martins. They consistently donated a percentage of their total earnings to charity, e.g., the poor and other charitable works, with a large portion going to The Society for the Propagation of the Faith (i.e., the missions). In the family account book, there, in detail, is a record of the generous amount set aside for this purpose. Louis labeled this offering as "God's Portion."

but sadness and devastation. I'm heartbroken over it. We have never been so unfortunate.

But there is still nothing in our towns. You would have to go to Le Mans to get an idea of the desolation that this sad war is leading to. My sister told me things that make my heart bleed. The poor sick people are dying by the thousands. At the Hospice of Le Mans alone, they're burying up to eighty people a day, and there are mobile hospitals everywhere. The secondary school and all the religious communities are obliged to take people in.

Fifteen minutes before I arrived at the Visitation Monastery, the municipal authorities came to tell the nuns that they were going to send them thirty patients.

Imagine the difficulty of those poor sisters, they who had promised to live a cloistered life! The entire Community was very upset. They went to find the Bishop so that he would plead on their behalf, but I believe there will be no way of escaping it. They're going to have to break through the walls and block the doors leading to where the Community lives in order to preserve their enclosure.

They had decided not to return the children to their parents, so they could say they were their boarding students. Just as I arrived my sister was writing to tell me not to come and get my children, and she didn't want me to take them home. You had to see how my daughters and I were crying. Marie could no longer go down the stairs. She was leaning on the banister sobbing profusely.

Finally, they let me take them, but I was so struck by all this I'm still saddened by it. I wasn't able to hug the children until we were settled in the coach. We ran away from the Visitation Monastery as if we were being pursued by bandits! They didn't decide to let us leave until three o'clock. The trunks weren't ready, and we had to be at the station at three-forty! When we arrived, the train was packed. They had to reattach a car for us, and we had the luck of finding ourselves alone in the car for the entire trip. So here was our return, but you see it wasn't easy!

In addition to the forced mobile hospitals in Le Mans, you see the Red Cross on every street. Almost all the rich people have patients in their homes, to the extent that Madame D took in a soldier dying of dysentery. Smallpox also reigns on all sides.

At the Visitation Monastery, they had up to sixteen soldiers to house and feed in a private house. The thirty patients being sent to them will also be at their expense. Last week, thirty patients were also sent to the Carmelite Monastery. As these poor sisters couldn't house them, the authorities left them at their door, saying, "Let them die there, if you want!" So they had to take them in.

They're saying there's a lot of ill will towards the measures being taken by the municipal authorities, who do the worst things to disturb the religious houses. Really, shouldn't they make an exception for them? How can they force poor cloistered nuns to house servicemen? I would find it more just if they forced me to take in sick people rather than send them to the Poor Clares,[160] but at the moment, they want them in the convents.

I don't think the children are going to return to the boarding school soon. That's the opinion of my sister, also. I'm certainly going to keep them at home for the duration of the war.

My little Céline has a rash on her face. She's suffering a great deal, and we must be with her constantly. She's hardly able to open her mouth. Doesn't my brother know of any remedy that will help? If he does, I'd be very grateful if he would let me know.

I'm sending you very modest things for my two little nieces' New Year's gifts: two little silver eggcups. But this year is not about New Year's gifts.

1871

CF 64

To her sister-in-law
January 17, 1871

My dear sister,

I'm not sure if you know that the Prussians have been in our home since Monday morning, at seven o'clock. They marched in front of the house until one o'clock in the afternoon. There were twenty-five

---

[160] The Monastery of the Poor Clares in Alençon is on rue Demi-Lune. (See footnote in CF 42.)

thousand of them. I couldn't describe our anxieties. Saturday night, the Prefect assembled the National Guard. He wanted them to defend the town. During the night, on his order, they began preparations to blow up the three bridges, but a petition was made to prevent them from continuing. About eleven o'clock in the morning, they were, fortunately, made to stop the work.

All the townspeople are appalled. Our poor soldiers went to fight against the Prussians, who were a league[161] from the village. We heard the cannon on three different roads, the Mamers road, the Aunay road and the road to Le Mans, until six o'clock in the evening.

It was pitiful to see our poor soldiers returning, some without feet, others without hands. I saw one with his face covered in blood. In the end, many of them were injured, and all the mobile hospitals were full. We don't know how many are dead. Among them, there are a number of *francs-tireurs*.[162]

Does it make sense, when we have so few men to fight against the enemy, to send them to the slaughter like that, against an army like this one we've seen with our own eyes?

No one imagined what it would be like. The Prussians have a powerful war machine. It's very ominous seeing their battalions with black flags and a skull on their helmets. How can it be that everyone does not recognize that this war is a punishment?

Monday, around three o'clock, all the doors were marked with the number of enemy soldiers to be housed. A big sergeant came to ask us to inspect the house. I took him up to the first floor while telling him we have four children. Fortunately for us, he didn't try to go up to the second floor. Finally, they made us take in nine of them, and we can't complain. In our part of town, small shopkeepers who have only two apartments are taking in fifteen, twenty, and even twenty-five. Those we have are neither mean nor looters, but they love to eat like I have never seen. They eat everything without bread! This morning they asked for cheese. I bought a big one for them, and they ate a quarter of it without even a mouthful of bread! They swallow mutton stew as if it were soup.

---

[161] One French league equaled 2.422 miles or 3.898 kilometers.
[162] See footnote in CF 62.

I'm not bothered by them. When they ask me for too much, I tell them that it's impossible. This morning they brought enough meat to feed thirty people, and we're in the process of having it cooked for them.

We've had to let them have the entire first floor and move to the ground floor. If I told you everything, I'd have to write a book.

The town refused to pay the amount they demanded, and we've been threatened by reprisals. Finally, the Duke of Mecklembourg was happy with three hundred thousand francs for an enormous amount of material. All the livestock in the surrounding area were taken. Now there's no more milk anywhere. What will my little Céline do? She drinks a liter a day! And what are the poor mothers who have only small children going to do? Nor is there any meat in the butcher shops. In short, the town is in desolation. Everyone is crying except me.

My husband is sad. He can neither eat nor sleep. I believe he's going to get sick.

I forgot to tell you that, at the beginning, during the bombing of the town, there was a wooden building site and many houses which were burned down. Shrapnel fell even on our street. A projectile smashed a storefront very close to us. We had to go down into the cellar.

But I must stop telling you all these horrors. I'm very afraid, my dear sister, that your town has the same fate. May God protect you from it! It truly makes one shudder. We've received no news from Le Mans.[163] All the lines are cut, as well as the telegraph.

I thank you a thousand times for the beautiful New Year's gifts you sent to the children. It's far too much for such an unfortunate year. Little Céline was filled with wonder by her doll and her box. This was perfect because, for the last four days, she's been quite sick with red blotches over her entire body and a terrible fever. I didn't sleep for two nights. I didn't know what was going to happen to this poor little girl any more. Finally, thank God, she's doing better, and the blotches appear to be gone.

Marie and Pauline were coloring pictures all day, and they argued quite a bit over your famous box of paints. One would say, "It's

---

[163] The French were defeated at the Battle of Le Mans between January 10-12, 1871.

mine." The other would answer, "It's mine, too. My aunt said I can use them." But Pauline, who is so lively, lost the brushes and put on too many colors. To finish it, I collected the box until further notice.

Pauline's white book is too beautiful. She's enchanted with it. But will this poor girl use it this year?

I'm very afraid that she'll not be able to make her First Communion[164] because I don't know when they'll be able to return to the Visitation Monastery.

Please, write me as soon as possible. I'm worried about you because of the occupation of the country.

CF 65   To her sister-in-law[165]
May 5, 1871[166]

...I'm very happy you're satisfied with the maid I sent you. I'd very much like to have one like her myself, but, unfortunately, you don't often find them. She'd promised to write me within three weeks, and she hasn't kept her word. Tell her that I'll be the one who'll probably bring her Madame S's little package. I've wanted to come see you for a long time. I'll never be freer than I am now, so I'd like to take advantage of it by spending a few days with you.

I'm glad my brother insisted on this in his last letter. This persuades my husband, who doesn't like to see me leave.[167] I prefer to go now rather than during summer vacation. This will not be a trip for the older girls, but for Léonie and Céline. Imagine that I'm dreaming of taking both of them. The little one is so good that I find it hard to part from her. I'd only have to take her out for walks and take care of

---

[164] Pauline made her First Communion on July 2, 1872, at the Visitation Monastery in Le Mans.

[165] Some original fragments of this letter were preserved.

[166] The Franco-Prussian armistice was signed January 28, 1871.

[167] At the time this letter was written, Louis, who was 48 years old, had experienced the death of thirteen immediate family members: his father, his older brother, three sisters, two brothers-in-law, his father-in-law, his mother-in-law and four of his children. For Louis, one might think that further loss would be frightening, and what he regarded as unnecessary separation might have been considered threatening and dangerous. Consequently, Louis would have been resistant to his wife and children leaving their home for any period of time unless it was necessary.

her with your little Jeanne. We'll go to the *Le Jardin de l'Étoile*.[168]In other words, I'm looking forward to it as if I were a child.

Louis tells me it's crazy to bring the little one. I think he's right, and I may regret it. She's really not difficult to care for, but usually a 25-month old child is hardly reasonable. Nevertheless, if you knew how very cute she is. I've never had a child so attached to me. No matter what she wants to do, if I tell her that it hurts me, she stops that moment.

When we dress her to go out, she's very happy. Above all, it's her beautiful white hat that she's taken with. But at the moment she's leaving, if I say to her with a sad expression, "So, you're going to leave me?" she immediately leaves the maid, comes to my side and embraces me with all her might. "No, no, not leave you, Mama, go away...." Then when I speak to her happily about her leaving, she looks me in the eyes to see if it's really true and that I'm not hurt anymore, and she starts to jump for joy.

She had the measles three weeks ago.[169] She was very sick for five days, and I was very afraid I might lose her. Several children here are dying of it. Now she's cured, but she still coughs a little, and she doesn't look so well. Marie and Pauline also had the same illness at the Visitation Monastery. When they returned there, on April 10, Marie had already had a bad cold for two days. I said to their father, "Believe me, let's not send them back. Marie has a bad cold, and she'll be put in the infirmary as soon as she arrives." All the same, he wanted them to leave, saying that it was nothing.

Monsieur Romet had taken responsibility for going with them to Le Mans. I only went as far as the train station in Alençon. When I returned, I noticed my little Céline already had some measles spots, and I thought, "Here's what Marie is going to have, and it will be quite a problem at the Visitation." I wasn't wrong. On arriving,

---

[168] *Le Jardin de l'Étoile* (The Garden of the Star) is a park in Lisieux a short distance from Les Buissonnets, the home of Louis Martin and his children. They moved there after the death of Zélie. The park was developed by a private individual in 1778 on the road to Pont-l'Évêque. It was bought in 1824 by a group of shareholders who rented its access to some travelers. It became one of Thérèse's favorite spots to walk with her father. Monsieur Pierre Fournet, Céline Guérin's father, was the president of the society in charge of the garden.

[169] See footnote in CF 8.

Marie had a fever, and they put her to bed. She was very sick for three days. The doctor was called, and he determined it was only a rash, a poorly developed case of measles, like she had once before, six years ago. Finally, by Friday, she was cured, and she soon started her studies again.

Sunday, my sister wrote me that they were at the point of dismissing the entire boarding school. Five students came down with the measles, as well as Pauline, and it was Marie, supposedly, who gave it to the others. Pauline was barely sick with it. That didn't keep her from spending three weeks in the infirmary, and they regret not doing the same for Marie. One other thing, their father, who is sorry about what happened, won't send them back to school again with a cold!

I see, my dear sister, that you're expecting a child again.[170] I'm worried about your health. Well, God never gives us more than we can bear. Many times I've seen my husband worry about my health, when I couldn't be any calmer. I would say to him, "Don't be afraid, God is with us." I was, however, overwhelmed with work and problems of all kinds, but I had the firm confidence of being supported from on high.

Hearing me speak this way, a friend said to me, "God surely sees that you could never cope with raising so many children, and He took four of them to Paradise." But to tell the truth, that's not how I understand it. In the end, God is the Master, and He doesn't have to ask for my permission. On the other hand, until now, I've very well endured all the hard work of motherhood, entrusting myself to His Providence. Besides, what do you want? We're not on this earth for our enjoyment. Those who expect to enjoy life are very wrong and remarkably disappointed in their expectations. We see this every day and, sometimes, in a very striking way.

Last week, a little eleven-year-old boy who lived on our street died. He was the happiness of his parents. He was charming in body and spirit. Their remaining child, a good little girl who is twelve years old, is going to have the same fate. She is close to death. These are very rich people, who have just bought a beautiful house in order to retire from business. What's the point, now that their lives are broken?

---

[170] The Guérins are expecting their third child; Paul Guérin was delivered stillborn on October 16, 1871.

Perhaps this is barely going to interest you, my dear sister, but I love to speak with you of what strikes me.

I end by hugging you with all my heart, as well as your two beautiful little girls.

CF 66

To her sister-in-law
May 29, 1871

When I received your letter last week, I was in bed with violent headaches that lasted two days.[171] It was impossible for me to stand up. I was happy not to be on my way to Lisieux. What would you have done with me? Finally, now I'm very well in body, but not in spirit, especially this morning. Everything that's happening in Paris fills my soul with sadness. I just learned of the death of the Archbishop and sixty-four priests who were shot yesterday by the Communards.[172] I'm very, very distressed by it.

---

[171] See footnote in CF 13.

[172] The Communards were members of the short-lived 1871 Paris Commune formed in the wake of the Franco-Prussian War, the result of an uprising after France was defeated. They were in power from March 26 through May 28. The widespread discontent was due to military failure, food shortages, the gap between the rich and the poor and the Prussian siege of Paris. Hundreds of thousands of Parisians became part of a citizens' militia, under the leadership of the Communards, to help defend Paris. A formal government was formed; the majority of Communards were revolutionists. The National Assembly's army crushed the Paris Commune. During the *Semaine Sanglante* ("Bloody Week"), May 21 through May 28, approximately 20,000 Communards and supporters were executed and 7,500 were jailed or deported. The Archbishop of Paris, Georges Darboy, and sixty-four priests were shot along with other hostages on May 27, 1871. Just before he was shot, Archbishop Darboy blessed his executioners. As Céline noted in her biographical reflections of her mother: "Mother had a veritable cult for the Church, for the Pope, and for the priesthood in general. It was a source of grief for her that the Holy Father was exposed to persecution, and that he was virtually a prisoner within the Vatican. On account of her love for the Church, she was completely overcome when the reports published the excesses of the Paris Commune, with the massacre of the hostages. Her prayers for the welfare of the Church and of France were, at that time, most fervent. Never would our mother criticize the clergy. In our home it never occurred to us to refer to the defects of priests." Céline Martin (Sister Geneviève of the Holy Face), *The Mother of the Little Flower*, p. 57.

In addition to Archbishop Darboy, two other Archbishops of Paris were killed during Louis and Zélie's lifetime:

Archbishop Denis-Auguste Affre, Archbishop of Paris (1840-1848) was shot to death on June 27, 1848, at the entrance to the Faubourg-Saint Antoine, a suburb of Paris, while attempting to restore peace between the workers and the government troops during the Revolution of 1848.

I'm also worried about my brother. It even causes me heartache. It's like a nightmare that follows me everywhere. I see he's pushing himself too hard for his drug business[173] and working like a slave without earning anything. This worries me terribly. I want so much to see you happy. You have so many expenses in your home! It seems to me that if I had to manage a house like yours, I'd lose my head over it, and what's more, another child is on the way! God has gone to the wrong house because I, who lost my last little girl, would be so happy to have another child. But no, I won't have any more! Now it's useless to wish for it. I'll never get over the death of my little Thérèse.[174] Quite often it keeps me awake at night.

How I regret not being able to lend you money right now. We're not receiving one cent in income from the Railroad and *Crédit Foncier* stocks.[175] Regarding the last one, my husband went to see Monsieur Lindet[176] who told him to kiss it goodbye, that due to recent events it was pretty much lost. Oh well, what can you do? When this storm has passed, we'll pick up the pieces that are left and find a way to live with less.

If my brother can take out a loan for a year, it's almost certain that we'll be in a position to loan him money then. It won't be long before we receive seven thousand francs from a company, and perhaps we'll receive more. I'm still making a little Alençon lace. We receive orders for weddings from all over. There are – and always will be – rich people. It's because of these that, if we are ruined, I hope to still be able to earn my living in the lace business.

CF 67 To her sister-in-law
June 21, 1871

...Monday I went to Le Mans, and the little girls were very happy, as you can imagine. We went for a walk a large part of the

---

Archbishop Marie-Dominique-Auguste Sibour, Archbishop of Paris (1848-1857) was assassinated in Paris on January 3, 1857, by Jean-Louis Verger, a priest who had been suspended because of his outspoken views against Church dogma.
[173] In May 1870 Isidore added a wholesale drug business to the pharmacy.
[174] Marie-Mélanie-Thérèse, who was born August 16, 1870, died October 8, 1870.
[175] Due to the Franco-Prussian War, shares fell on the stock exchange. Louis and Zélie sustained heavy losses in their investments. (See footnote in CF 62.)
[176] A banker who lived on the rue Saint-Blaise.

time despite the rain. In the end, we had a very good day, and I didn't leave until eight o'clock.

I told my sister about my problem regarding Léonie's studies. She thought about it and said, "I have to try." She found the Mother Superior and asked to take the little girl and look after her until the vacation. So Léonie has been at the Visitation Monastery for several days with her sisters. She was delighted to go. I hope they'll be able to keep her. Since I know that she's in such good hands and, on my side, I see myself so calm, it seems like I'm in Heaven.

CF 68

To her sister-in-law
July 30, 1871[177]

...I had a hard week! We've moved.[178] I had enough people. However, we had to put everything in its place. I was so tired in the evenings I couldn't sleep, and, with that, I had to take care of little Céline.

I don't have a maid anymore. A month ago my maid came down with rheumatoid arthritis. I took care of her for three weeks. We had to watch over her day and night. I had someone from her village come who stayed two weeks, but she didn't work out. Finally, last Monday, I had my patient transported on a bed by carriage. Her mother is going to take care of her. I think she'll still be with her for some time, but since I know she's not going to die from it, I'll wait for her. I'm very fond of her and she of me. For the time being, I have a cleaning woman.

I leave Tuesday[179] for Le Mans to pick up my little girls. While it's a great joy, it's also a lot more work.

I tormented my husband so much that he decided to sell part of his *Crédit Foncier* stock, with a loss of thirteen hundred francs

---

[177] The original address was preserved.

[178] The family left the house on the rue du Pont-Neuf and moved into 36, rue Saint-Blaise (later the number was changed to 42 and it is currently number 50) across from the Prefecture. (See footnote in CF 5.) The Prefecture is the building that contains the administrative offices that represent and administer, on a local level, the affairs of the French Republic, and, at the time this letter was written, was the residence of the Prefect and his family.

[179] August 1.

out of eleven thousand francs that it brought in. If my brother needs money and asks for it right away and he tells me it's necessary to sell the rest, Louis won't be pleased to lose so much.

I don't have time to write more, I have so much to do at home. Above all, it's little Céline who gives me trouble. She's becoming temperamental. We've spoiled her too much.

We've settled in perfectly. My husband had the house arranged exactly as I like it. You'll see the beautiful bedroom that we'll give you when you come, but unfortunately that time is still far away. Oh well, I hope it will be next year, with the three babies.... Also, you must be honest and tell me what I need to give my little goddaughter or godson, but I think it's going to be a goddaughter, by the fear I have over it because of you!

My husband hasn't forgotten his little goddaughter, Marie. He bought her a gold chain for her neck, with a cross.

Goodbye, my dear sister, I look forward to hearing from you. Hug my brother and my two little nieces for me.

CF 69   To her brother
                                        September 5, 1871[180]

It's been such a long time since you've written. I'm worried about you, especially about your wife. How is she? And the children? And you, are you still working as much? Is your business going well? Mine wouldn't go too badly if I dared to throw myself into it, but I'm always afraid. However, I did sell three thousand francs worth of Alençon lace last month.

My children are wondering a great deal if I'm going to be a godmother soon and if it will be during the holidays, so I can bring them to the baptism?

Yesterday we went for a carriage ride six leagues[181] from Alençon. We didn't have much luck because it rained almost the entire afternoon. Marie was very upset that we spent our money and didn't have a good time!

I'm already accustomed to the house on the rue Saint-Blaise.

---

[180] Original address preserved.
[181] 14.5 miles or 23 kilometers (one French league equaled 2.422 miles).

Icon of the Martin Family authored by Paolo Orlando.
With permission from Father Antonio Sangalli, OCD.

Pierre-François Martin (1777-1865).
Louis Martin's father.

Marie-Anne-Fanie Boureau Martin
(1800-1883). Louis Martin's mother.

Isidore Guérin, Sr. (1789-1868).
Zélie Martin's father.

Left to right, Zélie, Isidore and Élise (Sister Marie-Dosithée) Guérin in 1857.

The bridge over the River Sarthe where Zélie first encountered Louis.

Zélie Guérin in 1857, the year before her marriage.

Louis Martin in a photo taken around 1863.

The interior of the Basilica of Notre Dame in Alençon.

The exterior of the Basilica of Notre Dame in Alençon.

Louis and Zélie Martin's Marriage Certificate issued by the Church (now Basilica) of Notre Dame in Alençon.

The silver medallion with the images of Sarah and Tobias designed and engraved by Louis Martin and given to Zélie on their wedding day.

Louis Martin's watchmaker and jewelry shop at 15 rue du Pont Neuf. It was here that Louis and Zélie lived after their marriage. Eight of their children were born in this house. It was also the home of Louis Martin's parents.

A clock repaired by Louis Martin.

The house on the rue Saint-Blaise.

Zélie and Louis Martin's bedroom in the house on the rue Saint-Blaise. The birthplace of Saint Thérèse.

The Prefecture, situated across the street from the house on the rue Saint-Blaise.

An unpublished, unretouched photo of Zélie Martin. Although the photo was taken after the death of Joseph-Jean-Baptiste (August 25, 1868), Zélie is holding in her arms Joseph-Louis (died February 14, 1867), painted by Céline directly onto the photo.

Céline

Pauline and Marie in 1865.

Hélène at the age of four and a half.

A holy card made by St. Thérèse in remembrance of her siblings who had died. On the left is Marie-Joseph-Jean-Baptiste, who died August 24, 1868, at the age of eight months; on top Marie-Hélène, who died on February 22, 1870, at the age of five and a half; on the right Marie-Joseph-Louis, who died February 14, 1867, at the age of five months. On the bottom, representing Marie-Mélanie-Thérèse, is a picture of an angel carrying a baby to heaven. Mélanie died October 8, 1870 at the age of seven weeks, and there were no photos of her.

The students at the Abbey of Notre-Dame-du-Pré in 1880. In the second row from the front, counting from left to right, the fifth child is Marie Guérin, the seventh is Céline Martin and the last is Jeanne Guérin. In the fifth row, the fifth child is Léonie.

Léonie as a boarding student at the Abbey of Notre-Dame-du-Pré in Lisieux.
She entered school in January 1878 and left in October 1881.

Marie

Pauline

If you knew how much I long for you to come and see us here! So when will you bring the three little girls? You mustn't let my prediction frighten you because I've noticed that things always turn out the opposite from what I think will happen. So I don't trust myself and my ideas, above all when they're about important things.

What's taking place at the moment is that I'm having a discussion with Louis regarding a business matter that I'd like to share with you. You know that he sold his *Crédit Foncier* stock because I pleaded with him. Now it happens that we were too impatient. The stock rebounded quite a bit. If we'd waited until now, we would have lost twelve hundred francs less. Well, it's done. But what bothers my husband the most is to have our money doing nothing.

This morning, while reading the newspaper from the Stock Exchange, I saw Pontifical bonds. Right away I thought that these should be excellent later on because I firmly believe in the imminent victory and restoration of the Holy Father to his States.[182] If this happens, it seems to me that this would be a very good investment. So tell me, please, what you think about it. Louis is undecided on the matter. I press him continually. I know I could make him decide, but I wouldn't want him to have only my advice. He doesn't know that I'm consulting you on this. However, he has great trust in you and will do what you recommend.

CF 70

To her sister-in-law
October 1, 1871

I'm very sorry to hear that you need to stay in bed all day and that you're dying of boredom. No one understands better than I, since

---

[182] Vatican Council I had been interrupted by the occupation of Rome by the Italians. Pope Pius IX had excommunicated King Victor-Emmanuel II on November 2, 1870. On March 27, 1861, the Italian Parliament declared Rome the capital of the Kingdom of Italy, in the final step in the unification of Italy. However, the Italian government could not be established in Rome because the French, under Napoleon III, had posted their troops there to protect Pope Pius IX, who was determined to retain his temporal powers. In August 1870, due to the heavy losses France sustained in the Franco-Prussian War, it withdrew its army from Rome, leaving the pope vulnerable. The pope refused the peaceful take-over of Rome offered to him by King Victor-Emmanuel II. Consequently, on September 20, 1870, the Italian Army entered Rome and began its occupation, which lasted until the signing of the Concordat of 1929. In this agreement, the Church relinquished its claims over most of the city of Rome in return for Italy's recognition of the independent sovereignty of the Vatican State.

I can't stand spending two days in bed. How much I admire your patience! You tell me, however, that I have courage. It's true I don't pamper myself, but if I knew I had to be inactive for several months, I don't know what I would do. I don't believe God would allow me to have such a calamity. It would be too much for me. So you see, my dear sister, I don't have as much courage as you think.

I remember when my last little girl was born. I was busy with my lace business until nine thirty in the evening, took care of Céline and sang her to sleep, and Mélanie-Thérèse was born before eleven o'clock. I said to myself, "I'm so lucky!" But I wasn't always lucky, and many times I would have preferred to be afflicted as you are and to keep my little girl.

I had said to God, "You know well that I don't have time to be sick." I was answered beyond all hope, and I gloried in it a little. Then God seemed to say to me, "Since you don't have time to be sick, perhaps you'll have time to suffer a lot of pain?" And I haven't been spared, I assure you!

You see, in this world, that's what it's like. We have to carry our cross in one way or another. We say to God, "I don't want that one." Often our prayer is answered, but often also to our misfortune. It's better to patiently accept what happens to us. There's always joy alongside the pain. That's what will happen to you, my dear sister.

Next Thursday, the children go back to the Visitation Monastery, but to my great regret, my Léonie won't be returning there. She's not able to keep up with the others, and at the moment, they don't have a teacher to give her private lessons. What's more, my sister's health is so fragile during the winter that the Mother Superior wants to spare her the fatigue of keeping an eye on this child.

Céline is very strong; she talks like a magpie, and she's charming and spiritual. She knows her uncle and aunt well, and little Jeanne, too. She says their names while pointing to their pictures. She learns everything she wants to. Her sisters only have to sing a little song four or five times, and we hear Céline repeat it in the same pitch. But as soon as she realizes we're listening to her, she stops.

To her brother
October 17, 1871

...I'm grief-stricken, my heart is as broken as when I lost my own children. I see you all in tears, next to your little loved one, who died under such distressing conditions.[183] And yet God has still granted you a great grace, since he had time to be baptized. So, my dear friend, you have to have courage, and I don't think you lack it. You have enough strength and faith to endure the afflictions of life.

I received your letter just as I was sitting down at the table with company because we had people over. I assure you, what I ate didn't hurt me. I could eat nothing. My heart was so shattered, I couldn't breathe. If I could only cry when I'm like this, but no, this relief is denied me. When I'm in great pain, I can't cry.

I was supposed to be the godmother, and I was rejoicing so much over that! Well! It's destined that all my celebrations turn out this way....

I don't know why, but I had a vague premonition of some misfortune. Saturday night, on receiving the dress that I'd had made for the occasion, I said to myself, "I'm rejoicing too much, something terrible could very well happen."

I wasn't wrong. If the child had died after several days, I would feel less pain, but given the way things took place, I imagine that it was the doctor's fault.

As you see, my dear friend, I'm giving you peculiar consolations, but I don't know what I'm doing anymore. I can't console you because I myself need to be consoled. When I saw our guests, during lunch, enjoying themselves as if nothing upsetting had happened, I felt a lot of bitterness. Don't think, however, that Louis was one of them, because he was very sensitive to your pain and speaks of it constantly.

---

[183] Paul Guérin was delivered stillborn on October 16, 1871. According to research done by the *Institut National d'Études Démographiques* [National Institute of Demographic Studies] in France, as cited in the article entitled, *"Évolution de la Mortalité Infantile Endogène en France dans la Deuxième Moitié du XIXe Siècle 1855-1913"* ["The Evolution of Endogenous Infant Mortality in France in the Second Half of the 19th Century 1855-1913"] by Robert Nadot, the stillbirth rate in 1871 was 43/1000 or 4.3% of the total population of France. *Population,* Volume 25, No. 1, 1970, p. 55.

We're going over in our minds all the suffering and all the troubles your poor wife has had to endure the last six months, and we're bemoaning the sad ending. Yes, this is very hard. However, my dear friend, let's not complain, God is the Master. For our own good, He may allow us to suffer a great deal, but never without His help and His grace.

Yesterday I received, at the same time, a letter from our aunt, Madame Frédéric Guérin, announcing the death of her husband[184] who was struck down by a stroke[185] last Tuesday. She invited us to the service that will take place on Thursday. She didn't give me any details. I don't know if he had time to see a priest. This saddened me, but not nearly as much as the news you gave me.

If you can write once before I come to see you, you would make me happy. Tell me, above all, if the child was alive when he was baptized. The doctor should really have baptized him before his birth. When they see a child in danger, it's always there that they should begin.

While waiting for a letter from you, I hug you with all my heart.

CF 72   To her sister-in-law
October 17, 1871

The tragedy you've just suffered saddens me deeply. You are truly being tested. This is one of your first sorrows, my poor dear sister! May God grant you resignation to His holy will. Your dear little baby is at His side. He sees you, he loves you, and you will see him again one day. That is a great consolation I've felt and still feel.

When I closed the eyes of my dear little children and when I buried them, I felt great pain, but it was always with resignation. I didn't regret the sorrows and the problems that I had endured for them. Several people said to me, "It would be much better never to have had them." I can't bear that kind of talk. I don't think the sorrows and problems could be weighed against the eternal happiness

---

[184] Zélie is referring to their uncle Frédéric, the brother of their father, Isidore, Sr.
[185] A stroke is caused by a rupture or obstruction of an artery of the brain.

of my children. So they weren't lost forever. Life is short and full of misery. We'll see them again in Heaven.

Above all, it was on the death of my first child that I felt more deeply the happiness of having a child in Heaven, for God showed me in a noticeable way that He accepted my sacrifice. Through the intercession of my little angel, I received a very extraordinary grace.

My little Hélène, who, since then, has gone to join him, was suffering from an earache for six months, and this illness kept getting worse. I had consulted several doctors and other people who, supposedly, were very knowledgeable, but nothing was working. It got to the point that she was wearing a bandage, and the pus, which gave off an unbearable odor, would seep through the bandage in less than two hours. Finally, the poor little girl couldn't hear any more on the side she had the earache.

One day, while returning from taking her to the doctor, who didn't have anything good to say, and seeing the helplessness of everyone, the inspiration came to me to turn to my little Joseph, who had died five weeks earlier. So I took the child and asked her to say a prayer to her little brother. The next morning her ear was completely cured. The discharge had stopped all of a sudden, and the little one never again felt any pain. I've also received several other graces, but less notable than this one.

You see, my dear sister, it's a very good thing to have little angels in Heaven, but it's no less painful to lose them. These are the great sorrows of our life.

How I wish I were near you to console you! If I listened to what I'd like to do, I'd arrive in Lisieux next Sunday. But I'm afraid of tiring you out, considering how weak you are. So I'm resigned to wait.

A moment ago I was saying to my husband that I would leave the Sunday before All Saints' Day and return on Wednesday, but unfortunately, the feast day falls on that Wednesday. I'd have to move up my return in order not to travel on a holy day, so I prefer to postpone my trip until the following week. For a long time I've felt the need to see you all. I would have wanted it to be for a happy occasion, but since God did not allow it, we must accept it.

CF 73   To her sister-in-law
                                                    November 5, 1871

...My brother's last letter made me feel much better, because I couldn't overcome the sadness I was feeling. I saw that both of you are resigned to the will of God, who deprived you of your dear little angel in order to place him without delay among the ranks of the blessed. No doubt you're in pain to have lost a beautiful baby here on earth, but you're happy to have an angel in Heaven. These are two feelings: sorrow and joy; I often feel both at the same time. We know that life is short, and soon we'll see them again.

As for me, I'm afraid that this will be sooner than I would like, because I've felt very tired for some time. Despite the strong desire I have to see my four little angels again, I prefer to be deprived of them longer, knowing that they don't need me. I would rather stay with the four who remain with me and, it seems to me, to whom I can still be useful.

The bells for Vespers are ringing. Goodbye, my dear sister. While waiting to hear from you, I hug you with all my heart.

CF 74   To her brother
                                                    November 26, 1871[186]

I'll take the train to Lisieux on Sunday, at three-thirty in the morning. I tried to make different arrangements, but I didn't see anything better. It's impossible for me to leave on Saturday this time, and on Sunday, I can't travel all morning. That would be against my principles because I believe that we have to be very careful not to contribute to work on Sunday. However, I'll have to return Tuesday morning. I won't be able to stay any longer. I always have orders that are urgent, and I can't get away from them. I didn't want to continue my business at the moment, and I'm so forced to because they plead with me. Oh well, the main thing is that we'll see each other. We'll still have two days to talk.

So I'm going to finish my letter right away. I want to keep all I

---

[186] Original address preserved.

have to tell you until next week.

I still find it hard to believe I'm leaving. There might be some new unforeseen difficulties. I won't believe I'm on my way until I'm on the train. I hope, though, that there won't be any obstacles because if I don't take advantage of this moment of rest, my departure will be postponed until I don't know when. In order to be able to leave on Sunday, for the last week I've been working until midnight. So I plan to ship my piece of Alençon lace on Friday night.

I'm asking you not to give extravagant New Year's presents. I would be very upset over it! I know you'd only be doing it to make me happy. Your motive would be enough because I know you're usually too generous.

It upsets me to have made you hold a promissory note for seven thousand francs. You already have too many financial obligations. So I've definitely decided not to accept any interest on this amount.

CF 75

To her brother
December 25, 1871[187]

I'm truly sorry that your poor wife is still sick, but she has a calmness and patience that are very rare.

Since I've returned from Lisieux, you've been on my mind constantly. I'm sorry that the happy moments I spent with you are over. It seems to me that now we'll have to go so long without seeing each other. It feels like an eternity. I'm already counting the months until summer vacation, but I hope that, in the meantime, you'll shorten the time we have to wait.

Louis is going to take care of the matter concerning your drug business. He's already started looking for a manager, but I have doubts he'll find one. However, you have good friends in Alençon. I was happy with Monsieur Y's behavior towards you. I didn't expect it. I've had so many disappointments in my life that I hardly believe in true friends any more.

And I who had the weakness to make fun of Madame Y; I'll regret it forever. I don't know why I don't like her. She's never been

---

[187] Original address preserved.

anything but helpful and nice to me. I hate ungrateful people. So I have to hate myself because I'm nothing but a true ingrate. Thus I want to change completely for the good. I've already started because for some time I've been taking every opportunity to speak well of this woman. This is even easier because she's a very good person who deserves more than all those who make fun of her, beginning with me!

Your loving sister.

CF 76

To her brother
December 28, 1871

Yesterday I received the box containing your New Year's gifts. I can't tell you I was happy because I'd be lying. I found that you'd spent at least double what was necessary. Oh well, you're incorrigible, and I wish with all my heart that the giving of New Year's gifts was no longer the custom. This wouldn't prevent the giving of gifts, but at least it wouldn't be at a fixed time. It would be when we want to.

However, Léonie doesn't agree with me. If you could have seen her yesterday, she was wild with joy. She was trembling with it. Little Céline opened her eyes wide. She was completely dumbfounded. She stayed that way for a long time, amazed, hugging her bunny. When we told her it was her godmother who had sent it, as well as her beautiful dress, she replied in a tone of regret, "I don't know her, my godmother.... She's kind, you say?"

I sent for the dressmaker this morning. She's coming Tuesday to make the dress. If you were the one who chose this fabric, I congratulate you. You have very good taste. It's very pretty.

My husband went to find Monsieur Leconte, Director of the Hospice Pharmacy, to give him your letter. He said that he hadn't had the time to examine your current prices and that he couldn't change suppliers if he didn't see any benefit in it. Finally, he said he'd do what he thought possible, but he had enough stock for two months.

Louis was disillusioned and I even more so. However, he hasn't decided to let it go. If you don't do business with this man, it's because there will be no way to do it. But I tell myself that it's impossible for you to supply him at the same price, since you buy at the same price they do. Your drug business worries me as much as you. I've never looked upon it with joy. God willing, it will turn out better than I think!

I'm sorry that your poor dear wife has gotten to the point where she can't move. But I think this will only be temporary. When will all her troubles end? Give her a big hug for me, and tell her that I thank her a thousand times for the pretty dress she sent to Céline. She is too good, the beautiful little rabbit was more than enough. But finally, there's nothing to say except thank you.

I wish you all the blessings of Heaven. If God answers my prayer, you will be the happiest of men, in this world and the next....

1872

CF 77

To her brother
January 6, 1872[188]

Friday I went to Le Mans to bring back my daughters. Their aunt and their teachers are very pleased with them. Marie is an excellent student, and Pauline learns everything she wants and applies herself very much. She's the most advanced child in her age group. She's only eleven years old, and there are some who are fourteen years old and below her. One day when Marie was talking to her while they were studying, she said to her, "Don't waste our time because this costs Papa and Mama money." Both of them are a credit to us.

Yesterday I saw Madame Tifenne,[189] who was very kind. She spoke about you a lot and seems to take a very big interest in you. She was supposed to come to see me today and bring Léonie's New Year's gifts because she knows how much I dislike going to her house this time of year, as if I'm looking for them. So I didn't bring Léonie to her house.

---

[188] Original address preserved.
[189] Léonie Tifenne, née Gilbert (June 4, 1843-June 9, 1930), was Léonie's godmother. The Tifenne house was near the Martin's on the Place de Plénître. She married Jacques Tifenne, a pharmacist and friend of Louis Martin and Isidore Guérin.

My sister is terribly sad because of you. Your wife has gone through so much with her health that it saddens all of us.

I'd spoken to you of the balance my father owed on the house he had built. We thought the contractor didn't want it because we'd asked him about it many times and never received an answer. My father had refused to pay him, saying that the contractor had charged him too much and he wanted to have an appraisal done beforehand.

Well! Two weeks ago that man came to ask for the money. Of course, we paid it, as well as the interest on this amount that hadn't been paid for eight years. My husband said to me, "I insist that Isidore not pay his share of it. He's been far too good to you." I'm telling you this to show you how good Louis is.[190]

CF 78 To her sister-in-law
April 24, 1872[191]

I'm happy to learn of your complete recovery. I was sure that the good weather would make you feel completely better, but my brother was right to insist that you go to Trouville;[192] you need the sea air to restore your strength.

Now, I'm in absolute slavery due to orders coming in one after the other that don't allow me a moment's rest. I have almost a hundred meters of Alençon lace to make. Last week I received more orders, totaling more than fifteen thousand francs.[193]

Yesterday I received a letter in the mail from my two little girls

---

[190] From Céline's biographical reflections of her mother: "I said that there was perfect understanding between our parents, even if at first their views might differ on some particular point. Mamma had as much admiration for father as she had affection for him; she allowed him to exercise an authority which was really patriarchal. My sisters have affirmed many times that their union was never clouded by any misunderstanding; my mother's correspondence is filled with this testimony." Céline Martin (Sister Geneviève of the Holy Face), *The Mother of the Little Flower,* p. 9.

[191] The original address of a letter dated April 3, 1872, has been preserved. The letter itself was destroyed.

[192] Trouville and Deauville are seaside resorts on the northern French coast approximately 28 to 30 kilometers (17 to 19 miles) from Lisieux. The Guérins often went there on vacation, staying in various houses.

[193] After the Franco-Prussian War, the economy recovered and there was an increase in the sale of luxury items; Zélie's lace business was flourishing.

and my sister. She really took me to task because I had written to her that I didn't think the Easter vacation was long enough. My poor sister has a very difficult time with us. I'm not happy, and, on the other side, the children can't get used to school. Every time they go back, there's nothing but tears and lamentations. She has to threaten to expel them in order to calm them down. I'm hardly more reasonable than they are. It's difficult for me to do without my little girls. If it weren't for their own good, I wouldn't have the courage to be apart from them.

You mentioned the collection they made in Lisieux for the war indemnity.[194] There was also one in Alençon a month ago, with a cavalcade and a masked ball. This was not very edifying, especially during Lent, but our residents of Alençon don't look at it so closely. It seems that they're taking a liking to it and want to do it again soon.

You must, my dear sister, send me your lace. I'm going to have it whitened like new for you, and I'll mend it if it's missing anything. It will be a real pleasure to do this little thing for you. I'd like to have the chance to do bigger things.

CF 79

To her brother
May 1872

I'd very much like to know what you think of the terrible events predicted for this year, since it's just the opposite of what we expected: the government is more assured than ever, everything seems to be going for the best, and it's impossible to believe that anything tragic will happen, unless one is a prophet. Oh well, I'd like, though, to have a little idea of what to make of these things. I'm making enormous sacrifices to make sure I receive payment for my goods by the end of June.

Next Tuesday I'm going to send a flounce of lace[195] costing three thousand francs to a very good company, but I won't be paid until

---

[194] In accordance with the Peace Treaty signed on May 10, 1871, the French agreed to pay the Prussians five billion francs in war reparations. (See footnote in CF 57.)
[195] A strip of lace attached by one edge used as a ruffle on dresses, shawls, veils, etc.

the end of July. If I ask for payment next month, I must give a 5% discount, which results in quite a noticeable loss. But what I dislike most is looking like we're having financial difficulties because, if we act like that, we'll be seen as a business without credit. You understand, then, that one can't imagine my fear of a revolution.

However, my husband isn't reassured, and I saw today that he wouldn't mind hearing your opinion and knowing what you would do in our place. If then, you can write me a short note for Sunday, you'll make me very happy. If you can write a long letter, it will make me feel even better.

Tuesday morning at five o'clock Louis left to go on a pilgrimage to Chartres[196] with six men from here. They've been back since yesterday. There were nearly twenty thousand people at the feet of the Madonna. Apparently it was magnificent, but there weren't enough beds for everyone. They had to sleep on straw or in the church. Louis spent the night in the underground chapel, where Masses were said from midnight until noon the following day. He ate dinner with the priests from Alençon and those from the Pilgrimage. He told me they all seemed to believe that things would be settled amicably, with neither broken heads nor burned down houses. One of them claimed to know, from a completely reliable source, that the Church would soon triumph. May he be speaking the truth!

CF 80   To her brother and sister-in-law
                                                       July 21, 1872

I received the letter with the picture of your little Marie, which we all found charming. She has the sensible expression of a big girl and seems much stronger than when I saw her. I sent the photograph

---

[196] Chartres is approximately 120 kilometers (75 miles) from Alençon. After the Franco-Prussian War, there was a big increase in the number of pilgrimages in France, e.g., to Chartres, Lourdes, Paray-le-Monial, etc. The Catholic Church was afraid of another uprising following the bloodshed associated with the Paris Commune. (See footnote in CF 66.) Louis joined a pilgrimage of 20,000 people to Chartres to pray for peace, to ward off another revolution, and to plead with the Blessed Mother to intercede in the anticlerical movement that swept through France during the time between 1870 and 1890.

to my sister the same day. At the Visitation, the school vacation begins August 5.

I'm fully expecting all of you to come next month. The troubles didn't happen as had been predicted. Now I don't believe it any more for this year, and I'm quite determined not to rely on any prophet, nor on any prophecy. I'm beginning to become quite an unbeliever. I say that only God knows the day and the hour. Others think they see something there, and they see nothing. So then I expect all of you. You'll let me know, of course, a week in advance.

I must share with you an event that will probably take place at the end of the year, but which is of hardly any interest to anyone but me at the moment and still doesn't delight anyone else. However, I would be happy over it if I knew I could raise this poor little person who is coming to live in our home, who will not leave it as long as he and I are alive.[197]

I'm feeling better than the last time. I have a good appetite and never have a fever. I hope this child does well. Misfortune isn't always at the same door. Oh well, may God's will be done!

Madame Z had a little girl last month. I haven't gone to see her, and I've hardly any desire to do so. After her marriage, she seems to not want to look at me anymore. I, who loved her so much, this hurts me.

Before her marriage, she couldn't do enough for me. I think now that she wasn't very sincere and expected me to be the intermediary for her marriage to Lacauve's cousin, which she wanted so much. But now she probably finds herself too far above me. So she often comes to see the doctor's wife, who lives quite near here, but there's no danger of her entering our house!

This world is so strange! So, the woman Madame Z visits makes fun of her as much as she can; I know this from the maid. And as for Madame Z, she can't stand her, but these are people who are drawn to each other by their ideas and their tastes. All of this makes me more and more detached from this world that's so false. I don't want to become attached to anyone except God and my family.

---

[197] The first mention of the existence of Marie-Françoise-Thérèse Martin (St. Thérèse). Zélie is four months pregnant.

CF 81 To her brother
July 1872

If you only knew how happy your letter made me, yet not without a touch of sadness. I'd like to see your drug business prosper. It's so painful to go to all that trouble for nothing. You can say you know the problems and the anxieties.

Yes, I understand that you worry even more about Monsieur M[198] than about yourself. These are two crosses you bear, but I have the firm hope that all this will not last a long time because it's impossible that God would abandon you.

I was struck by what you told me about some words of Holy Scripture you found by chance, but it's not in vain, nor by chance, that one discovers something so appropriate to our needs of the moment. No, your ordeal can't last. I have a reason to believe this that I don't want to share with you. I even have several of them, and I'm as impatient as you are to see them come true. I'd be twice as happy because I take almost as much of an interest in Monsieur M as you do. I find that this is such a good family,[199] so connected to you that your interests are the same. You couldn't be happy one without the other. It's very beautiful to live in harmony this way.

My sister spoke to me a lot about your business. She thinks that you could have a representative in several towns. As for me, I think this would be almost as difficult as catching the moon with your teeth!

I told her not to wrack her brains over all this, that there was only one thing to do: to pray to God because neither she nor I can help you in any other way. But He, who is not at a loss, will get us out of this when He finds that we've suffered enough. And then you'll recognize that it's neither your abilities nor your intelligence which you owe your success to, but to God alone, like me, with my Alençon lace. This conviction is very helpful, I've tested it myself.

---

[198] Monsieur Césard Maudelonde was married to Céline Guérin's sister, Marie-Rosalie Fournet, on July 7, 1861. They had five children: Céline, Ernest, Hélène, Henry and Marguerite-Marie. He entered into a business partnership with his brother-in-law, Isidore Guérin, on February 15, 1873. He was to manage the newly-opened wholesale drug business, but it was destroyed in a fire on March 27, 1873. (See footnote in CF 90.) (See the Biographical Guide of Proper Names in the Appendix.)
[199] The Martin and Maudelonde children were very close.

You know that we're all given to pride, and I often notice that those who have made their fortune are, for the most part, unbearably arrogant. I'm not saying that I've reached that point, or you either, but we've been more or less marred by this pride. It's certain then that constant prosperity takes us away from God. Never has He led His chosen ones down that road. They have passed through the crucible of suffering beforehand to be purified.

You're going to say that I'm preaching; however, that's not my intention. I think about these things very often, and I'm telling them to you. Now call this a sermon if you want!

I'm very happy with Marie, who's truly my consolation. Her tastes are not at all worldly. She's even too unsociable, too shy. If this doesn't change, she'll never get married because her inclinations are quite the opposite.

I only have one sorrow, not seeing my poor Léonie like her. What's more, I can't analyze her character; the most learned would be baffled by it. However, I hope the good seed will one day sprout up from the earth. If I see this, I'll sing my *Nunc Dimittis*,[200] but my sister tells me that I'll probably not see it. She probably thinks that I don't have much longer to live. However, for the moment, it doesn't look like I'll be going so soon because I'm feeling very well.

Good-bye, my dear friend. Yes, you are my friend. I don't have any others, apart from my Louis, who is so good. I also love you with all my heart, as well as your wife, and I'd very much like to see you happy.

---

[200] *Nunc Dimittis* is the beginning of the Latin translation of Simeon's Canticle: *"Nunc dimittis servum tuum, Domine; Secundum verbum tuum in pace"* ("Master, now you are dismissing your servant in peace, according to your word.") found in Luke 2:25-32: "Now there was a man in Jerusalem whose name was Simeon. This man was righteous and devout, awaiting the consolation of Israel and the Holy Spirit was upon him. It had been revealed to him by the Holy Spirit that he should not see death before he had seen the Messiah of the Lord. He came in the Spirit into the temple; and when the parents brought in the Child Jesus to perform the custom of the law in regard to Him, he took Him into his arms and blessed God saying: 'Now, Master, you may let your servant go in peace, according to your word, for my eyes have seen your salvation, which you prepared in sight of all the peoples, a light for revelation to the Gentiles, and glory for your people Israel.'" This refers to the fulfillment of a revelation made by the Holy Spirit to Simeon. Simeon states that now that he has seen the fulfillment of God's revelation, he can die in peace. Zélie is referring to her wish to see the transformation of Léonie, so she too, can die in peace.

CF 82 To her sister-in-law
September 29, 1872

We're finally at the end of the summer vacation. It's time that Marie sent you the letter she promised you. The children were supposed to return to school October 2, but I received word from my sister that it was delayed until the 9th because of repairs that aren't finished at the boarding school. As you can well imagine, this didn't make them cry.

You asked me if we went on some nice outings during the holidays? We went to the Butte de Chaumont,[201] where I was quite bored. To tell you the truth, I only enjoy myself when I'm seated at my window assembling my Alençon lace.

We didn't go to Madame L's house. She was supposed to come look for us, but thank God she forgot her promise, and I assure you I was very happy about that. I had no desire to go waste my time at her home. I had other things to do for the time being.

I'm asking my brother not to forget the two kilos of good quality candy that I need for the baptism of "the little Thérèse."[202] Let him send me, at the same time, 50 pounds of chocolate and tapioca in small quantities. He can put it in a basket, and I'll return it to him with a goose inside when it's time.

I'm already thinking about the end of the year because of the child who's coming as my New Year's gift. How will I raise her? I have nightmares about it every night. Oh well, I have to hope that I'll come through it better than I think and that I'll never know the pain of losing her.

---

[201] La Butte Chaumont is a small, privately owned mountain approximately 15 kilometers (9.3 miles) northwest of Alençon, near La Roche-Mabile. In the 12th century, a hermitage was founded on the summit by Benedictine monks from the Abbey of Saint Martin of Sées. There, a chapel dedicated to Saint Martin was built, later destroyed at the beginning of the 18th century. A stone cross dedicated to St. James still survives. Hermits lived there from the Middle Ages through the 18th century. For many years it was the site of a very popular pilgrimage on May 1, the feast day of Saint Philip and Saint James, for which people would pray for the healing of fevers. Zélie states in CF 97 that, at La Butte Chaumont, "they honor[ed] a saintly man who cured fevers." Jean-Marie Foubert, *ÉCOUVES – La belle au bois normand* [ÉCOUVES – The beauty of the Norman Woods], Cully, France: Orep Éditions, 2008, pp. 38, 39 and 48.

[202] Note that Thérèse is going to "succeed" the little Marie-Mélanie-Thérèse who died almost two years before at the age of seven weeks (born August 16, 1870, she died October 8, 1870).

CF 83

To her sister-in-law
December 15, 1872

I'm expecting my little angel any day now, and I'm very much at a loss because I still haven't found a wet nurse.

I've seen several of them, but they didn't suit me perfectly, and my husband has never been able to make up his mind and choose one. It's not because of the cost. It's because we're afraid of bringing someone into our home who's not very suitable, as are generally all the wet nurses today.

As for hiring a second maid who would put me through a lot of trouble and not take care of my child as I would like, I prefer to remain silent. If God gives me the grace of being able to nurse my child, it will be nothing but a pleasure to raise her. As for me, I'm crazy about children, I was born to have them, but it will soon be time for that to be over. I'll be forty-one years old the twenty-third of this month, old enough to be a grandmother.

I probably won't write you before the birth of my baby. I hope this will take place around Christmas, and I fully expect to be the one who'll announce the news to you.

1873

CF 84

To her sister-in-law
January 3, 1873

My little girl was born last night, Thursday, at eleven-thirty.[203] She's very strong and in very good health. They tell me she weighs eight

---

[203] Marie-Françoise-Thérèse (called Thérèse), was born at 36, rue Saint-Blaise (later the number was changed to 42 and is currently number 50) on January 2, 1873, at eleven-thirty in the evening. She was baptized by Father Lucien Dumaine in the Church of Notre-Dame, their parish church, in Alençon on the afternoon of January 4, 1873. Father Dumaine was a personal friend of Louis Martin and later gave witness at the process of beatification for St. Thérèse. The baptism was delayed because her parents were waiting for the arrival of the godfather. According to Pauline, who was at the baptism, the delay worried Zélie because she was convinced the baby was in danger. Her godmother was her sister, Marie, and her godfather Paul-Albert Boul, who was born on November 29, 1863 and died on February 17, 1883, at the age of

pounds. Let's say six, which is still not bad. She seems very sweet.

I'm very happy. However, at first I was surprised. I was so sure I was having a boy. I'd been imagining this for two months because I could feel she was much stronger than my other children.

I barely suffered a half hour. What I felt before was practically nothing. She'll be baptized tomorrow, Saturday. The only thing missing to make the celebration complete is all of you. Marie is going to be the godmother, and a little boy close to her age will be the godfather.

I received your letter, as well as the box containing the New Year's gifts. I don't know if I should scold you. I want to very much, and yet I also want to thank you, but everything is too beautiful and too expensive. Céline wore her beautiful fur and muff for the first time on the first day of the year.

I wish all of you a happy New Year. Please remember me to Monsieur and Madame Fournet and Monsieur and Madame Maudelonde.[204]

I look forward to sending you a longer letter. I can't write a long one today.

Marie and Pauline have been on vacation since Tuesday evening. They'll stay with me until Monday or Tuesday.

---

nineteen, the son of a friend of Louis Martin. Soon after the birth of Thérèse, a little boy appeared at the Martin home on the rue Saint-Blaise and handed them a note. Inscribed in it was the following poem:

"Smile and grow up quickly.
Everything calls you to happiness,
Tender care, tender love.
Yes, smile at the dawn,
Bud that has just bloomed,
You will be a rose one day."

"It was the graceful gesture of the father of a family, whom M. [Louis] Martin had one day met with his wife and son, famished, turned out of doors, sheltering in the porch of the Prefecture. Moved by such 'shamefaced poverty,' for the family had known better days, his wife [Zélie] had brought them in, fed them, gained their confidence, whilst he [Louis] exerted himself to find a lucrative position for the unfortunate unemployed father. The letter that day expressed his gratitude in a particularly touching way." Stéphane-Joseph Piat, OFM, *The Story of a Family*, pp. 124-125.

[204] Pierre-Célestin and Élisa-Ernestine Fournet, Céline Guérin's parents, and Césard-Alexandre and Marie-Rosalie Fournet Maudelonde, her brother-in-law, and sister.

To her sister-in-law
January 16, 1873[205]

I'm completely recovered now. The little one is also doing well. She promises to be very strong, but nevertheless, I don't dare count on it. I'm always afraid of enteritis.[206]

I had begun to breastfeed her, and, fearing that this was not enough, I wanted to help by giving her a bottle. This worked very well until Sunday, but the famous bottle spoiled everything. It was impossible to make her go back to breastfeeding. I tried everything. I let her fast, but she cried so pitifully I had to give in.

She drinks perfectly. We give her half water in which we boiled some bread and half milk. That's all she eats. I've decided not to give her anything else for three or four months, despite all the advice I've been given, because everyone disagrees with me, including the doctor who wants me to give her a cup of chocolate every morning! Just tell me if such a young child has the strength to endure that kind of diet. Under these conditions, it wouldn't take long to give her the illness I dread so much. When I try to make her eat, I'll ask you to tell me what food you gave your children to start with.

My little one is not at all difficult during the day, but at night she often makes us pay dearly for her good day. Last night I held her until eleven thirty. I was exhausted, and I couldn't do it anymore. Fortunately, afterwards she didn't do anything but sleep.

This child is named Thérèse, like my last little girl. Everybody tells me that she'll be beautiful. She already laughs. I saw this for the first time on Tuesday. I thought I was mistaken, but yesterday it was impossible to doubt it any longer. She looked at me very carefully, and then gave me a delightful smile.

While I was carrying her, I noticed something that never happened with my other children – when I sang, she would sing with me.... I'm confiding this to you. No one would believe it.

---

[205] Original address preserved.
[206] See footnote in CF 48.

To her brother
                                                      January 17, 1873

...I'm extremely worried about my little Thérèse. I'm afraid she has an intestinal illness. I notice the same alarming symptoms as those of my other children who died. Must I lose this one, too?

Tell me how I should feed her, if the bread water with half milk is suitable. All she's been doing is sleeping since three-thirty this morning. We make her drink while sleeping, so she's taken almost nothing.

I don't know if it's the weakness that causes this sleepiness, and I'm very anxious. As for me, I barely sleep more than two hours because I'm almost constantly around the little one, who for some time has been very restless a good part of the night.

If you can write me and encourage me with your advice, that would make me very happy because I need it so much.

To her brother
                                                       March 1, 1873

After you left Alençon, my little Thérèse was perfectly fine. She was growing stronger before my very eyes, and I was very proud of myself. But today, things are very different. She's very sick, and I don't have any hope at all of saving her. This poor little girl has been suffering horribly since yesterday. It's heartbreaking to see her. However, she's sleeping well. Last night I picked her up only once. She drank and then slept until ten o'clock this morning. But now, here she is up until ten o'clock at night.

The doctor is leaving here. I don't know why, but I have no confidence in his remedies.

Now I have to tell you a story. It dates from my little one's first illness. The night you arrived, I'd just mailed a letter to my sister in Le Mans telling her that little Thérèse was dying and that she didn't have more than two days to live.

So there's my sister, who begins to pray to Saint Francis de Sales with extraordinary fervor and makes a vow that, if the little girl is cured, we'll call her by her second name, Françoise. The vow made, she goes to find Marie and Pauline, who were very despondent, and says to them, "Don't cry anymore. Your little sister is not going to die." And she announces to them what she has just done. The Superior adds, "You must write to your sister right away so she begins to call her Françoise."

When I received this famous letter, I was dumbfounded. My sister told me that she'd made this vow, being sure that I would confirm it, and that she had said to Saint Francis that if I didn't agree to call this child by his name, he was free to take her back. In that case, she added, I had nothing to do except to have a coffin made.

This made an impression on me in spite of myself, and yet I haven't decided to give a name to my little girl that I don't like. So I wrote to Le Mans that Saint Francis hadn't cured her because she was already much better before my letter had arrived. And this is true, because if you remember, from Sunday morning the baby was cured, so to speak, and did nothing but sleep all day, though Saint Francis hadn't been prayed to yet.

Oh well, what do you say about all this? Was I guilty? Should I have called her Françoise?[207] I hadn't been the instigator of this vow, and besides, what would it matter to Saint Francis de Sales whether I called her by one name or another? My refusal couldn't be a reason for him to make her die!

If I hadn't had the misfortune of giving her, among her names, the name of Françoise, my sister wouldn't have had this idea. Even before the baby was born, she'd already written to me believing that it would be a boy, so I wouldn't give him the name Joseph, but Francis, as if she suspected good Saint Joseph of having taken my children!

I told her that he would die from it or not die from it, but I would call him Joseph because I would not agree to give him a name that I didn't like.

However, I'm confiding to you that a vague concern remains with me over "this coffin that I had to have made if I didn't want to agree with my sister's vow." Please write me by return mail, because if you delay, my little Thérèse will probably be dead. I prefer to call her Françoise or any other name and not to have to make a coffin. It makes me tremble just to think about it!

---

[207] "Françoise" is the feminine French version of "Francis."

You'll write me a long letter and tell me what I should call her so that she doesn't die. If anyone sees this letter, they'll think I've lost my mind! I'd like my sister not to know about what I've written you because I wouldn't want to hurt her. She's so good, and she loves us so much! But this time, she surprises me.

I often think of the mothers who have the joy of feeding their children themselves. As for me, I have to see them all die one after the other!

CF 88   To her sister-in-law
March 9, 1873

I'm taking advantage of a quiet moment to answer your last letter. For two weeks I've been so busy and so unhappy that I've had no rest either day or night. My little girl is sick. She has enteritis[208] and I'm afraid of losing her.

However, she's always happy. As soon as she has a little moment of relief, she laughs heartily. In spite of this, her face has changed. Since Thursday, I find her very pale, and yet she's not lost weight.

I'd have a lot of things to tell you if I had a little more time, but I'm all alone looking after the little one who's sleeping at the moment, so I'm hurrying as much as possible.

I want, though, to amuse you by telling you about a costume ball given by Madame Y... and that made quite a stir in Alençon. Everybody is talking about it. It was magnificent, admirable, without equal! Ever since Alençon has existed, no one has seen anything like it.

Madame Y was Queen and had a gold crown with a veil studded with stars. Madame O represented *la Folie*.[209] She wore a dress of yellow Indian fabric that was too tight and made her look completely ridiculous. When she saw herself in this getup and noticed the richness of the other women's costumes, she didn't know where to hide herself.

---

208 See footnote in CF 48.
209 *La Folie* is a fictitious character who, in 19th century France, was represented by the figure of a woman and who exhibited a lively cheerfulness and extravagance. Historically, this figure's actions were meant to entertain.

I know all these details through some people who attended the much talked about ball, which lasted until five o'clock in the morning. To end it, there was a splendid dinner, after which all the guests went to bed.

They had to shore up the floor of the drawing rooms, or else the dancers would have fallen into the room below. I forgot to tell you that these drawing rooms were decorated with garlands of flowers and branches of ivy. It's a shame to go to so much trouble and spend so much money to make a laughingstock of yourself.

I leave you now, my dear sister. I haven't time to write anymore. I wanted to cheer you up a little, and yet my heart is barely up to it, I assure you.

Pray to God that He keeps my little Thérèse for me. I still have a little hope because she's not so sick as to not be cured. Tell Jeanne and Marie to pray for their little cousin. God hears the prayers of children.

CF 89   To her sister-in-law
March 1873

Since I wrote to you, I've had so much trouble. My little girl became worse and worse. Last Monday I sent for another doctor, Dr. Belloc. He came around five o'clock in the evening. After examining the baby, he asked me what I had been giving her. I told him what I'd been doing. He thought that this was good but not enough to nourish her in the weak state that she was in.

He thinks that one can feed a baby without milk for two or three days, but not more. And for two weeks she didn't take anything but barley water almost without milk and for two days gruel water without milk. Finally, he said to me, "This child must be breastfed right away. That's the only thing that can save her."

I didn't know what to do because I couldn't think of feeding her myself, and I didn't have any wet nurse in mind. I explained my dilemma to him, and he gave me a prescription. Twice a day I had to give her a spoonful of rice water and one of lime water in two spoonfuls of milk.

When I saw the prescription I said to myself, "My little girl is lost. She won't be able to tolerate two-thirds milk in the state she's in." Madame Leriche[210] came to see her that night. She was so shaken that she went to bed without eating dinner and could only cry. She looked at her child and said, "If he were in that state, I would die!"

Finally, that night I was looking for a way to find a wet nurse at all costs when I remembered a woman I know very well and who suits me in every respect.[211] But her child is exactly one year older than mine, and I thought the milk was too old.

It was 7 o'clock, and I left to go to the doctor's house. I spoke to him about the wet nurse who's been nursing her child for one year. He thought about it a little and said to me, "You must hire her right away. She's the only option we have now to save your baby, and if this doesn't save her, at least you'll have nothing to reproach yourself for."

If it hadn't been so late, I would have left that moment to go and get the wet nurse. The night seemed long to me. My little one almost didn't want to drink. All the gravest signs that preceded the deaths of my other little angels were present, and I was very sad, convinced that the poor darling wouldn't take the breast given her weak state.

So at daybreak I left to go to the wet nurse who lives in Semallé, almost two leagues from Alençon. My husband was away, and I didn't want to entrust the success of my mission to anyone else. On a deserted country road I met two men who frightened me, but I said to myself, "Even if they killed me, it wouldn't matter." I had death in my soul.

---

[210] Madame Marie Leriche (née Nanteau), the wife of Louis' nephew, Adolphe Leriche, who purchased Louis' watchmaker shop. Adolphe was the son of Louis' sister, Anne-Françoise-Fanny Martin. It was Madame Leriche who took care of Céline and Thérèse in the final weeks before Zélie died. In *Story of a Soul*, Thérèse wrote, "Céline and I were like two poor little exiles, for every morning Mme. Leriche came to get us and brought us to her home where we spent the day. One morning we didn't have time to say our prayers and during the trip Céline whispered: 'Should we tell her we didn't say our prayers?' 'Oh! Yes,' I answered. So very timidly Céline told Mme. Leriche, who said: 'Well, my little girls, you will say them,' and placing us both in a large room, she left. Céline looked at me and we said: 'Oh! this is not like Mama! She always had us say our prayers with her.'" *Story of a Soul*, tr. John Clarke, OCD, p. 33.

[211] She's referring to Rose Taillé, who had been the wet nurse for Marie-Joseph-Louis, born on September 20, 1866, the Martin's fifth child and the first boy. He died on February 14, 1867. She was also the wet nurse for Marie-Joseph-Jean-Baptiste, born on December 19, 1867, and died on August 24, 1868. Thérèse was entrusted to Rose from March 15 or 16, 1873, to April 2, 1874. During Thérèse's stay the ages of Little Rose's children were: Rose, 12, Auguste, 10, Marie, 7, and Eugène, 1. Rose lived in the village of Semallé, in the countryside about 5 miles (8 kilometers) from Alençon. (See footnote in CF 19.)

Finally, I arrived at the wet nurse's house and asked her if she would come with me right away to live with us full time. She told me she couldn't leave her children and her house, but she would stay with us a week and then take the little one home with her. I agreed, knowing that my baby would do very well in her home. This woman had already cared for one of my children.[212]

We left together after a half-hour, and we arrived home at ten-thirty. The maid said to me, "I wasn't able to make her drink. She didn't want to take anything." The wet nurse looked at the child and shook her head with an expression that seemed to say, "I made this trip for nothing!"

I quickly went upstairs to my room. I knelt at the feet of Saint Joseph and asked him for mercy, that the little one be cured, resigning myself completely to the will of God if He wanted to take her. I don't cry often, but I cried while I was praying.

I didn't know if I should go downstairs... finally, I decided to go. And what did I see? The child was suckling with all her heart. She didn't let go of her hold until about one o'clock in the afternoon. She threw up a few mouthfuls and fell against her wet nurse as if she were dead.

There were five of us around her. We were all stunned. There was a worker who was crying. As for me, my blood froze. The child had no visible breath. We bent down to try and find some sign of life, but it was no use. We saw nothing, but she was so calm, so peaceful, that I thanked God for having let her die so gently.

Finally, a quarter of an hour passed. My little Thérèse opened her eyes and began to smile. From that moment on, she was completely cured. Her healthy appearance returned as well as her cheerfulness. Since then, everything is better.

But my poor little one has left. It's very sad to have raised a child for two months and then to have to entrust her to strangers' hands. What consoles me is knowing that God wants it this way, since I did everything I could to raise her myself. So I have nothing to reproach myself for in this regard.

I would really have preferred to keep the wet nurse at my house,

---

[212] In fact, Rose Taillé was the wet nurse for two of Zélie's children. See previous footnote.

as would my husband. He didn't want the others, but he very much wanted this one. He knows her to be an excellent woman.

Although I have a lot of confidence in my brother, I think he was mistaken in telling me to only feed the child water with gum syrup in it because the doctor told me I shouldn't go from one extreme to the other. The child needed nourishing food, but on the other hand this food could cause her death. Oh well, to die either way, she wasn't going to die of hunger.

You'll think of this what you want, but I hope with all my heart that you never have a child in this state. You don't know what to do or how to handle it. You're afraid of not giving her the right thing. It's a continual death. You'd have to go through it to know what a torture it is. I don't know if Purgatory is worse than this. Well, here's another hard trial that's over.

CF 90   To her sister-in-law
March 30, 1873

My dear sister, I'm sorry to hear of the fire you told me about.[213] When I think of all the trouble my brother went through to organize his drug business and, in an instant, to see all his efforts lost. One must have a great deal of faith and resignation to accept this setback without complaint and with submission to God's will.

As for me, I feel the consequences of this misfortune. This, joined with the tribulations I already have, has taken away my courage. I just wrote a letter to my little girls that is hardly going to delight them. I just spoke to them about your disaster and the troubles of this world. It's true that each person has a cross to bear, but there are some for whom it is heavier than others. My dear sister, you've already begun to see that life is not a bed of roses. God wills this to detach us from the world and raise our thoughts toward Heaven.

Yesterday, while going with the doctor to see my little Thérèse, who is very sick, I noticed a beautiful château and some magnificent

---

[213] On March 27, there was a fire at Isidore Guérin's wholesale drug business, located across the street from his pharmacy. The business was destroyed but it was later reopened. It was liquidated in 1883.

properties.[214] I said to myself that all of that is nothing. We'll only be happy when all of us, we and our children, are reunited in Heaven, and I offered up my child to God.[215]

Ever since she's been with the wet nurse, she's always well. She's even gained a lot of weight, but the intestinal irritation was only dormant. Since Friday it's moved back up to her throat and her chest. When the doctor saw her, she had a very high fever. However, he told me he didn't believe she was in danger.

Today she's doing better, but I have some serious fears. I believe we'll not be able to raise her. My first little boy was like this. He was coming along very well, but he had a stubborn case of enteritis[216] and couldn't get over it.

Oh well, I did everything I could to save her life. Now, if God wills otherwise, I'll try to endure the ordeal as patiently as possible. Truly, I often need to restore my courage. I've already had to suffer so much in my life. My dear friends, I'd so like you to be happier than I am, and I see with sorrow that adversity comes to visit you, too.[217]

I hope, my dear sister, that you won't be long in giving me the details of your accident and telling me how you're going to set up business again. I know you put your confidence in God. That makes me believe that you'll come through this bad time much better than you think.

Madame Tifenne seems much happier than you. She lives only for luxury and pleasure. She gives balls in mid-Lent. And yet would you believe that I prefer to see you with your adversity than to suppose that you, like her, are forgetting Heaven for the brief pleasures of the world. Goodbye, my dear sister, give a big hug to your dear little girls for me. Tell my brother that I'm going to ask the Poor Clares[218] to say a novena so that the disaster will be repaired quickly and do you the least possible harm. In other words, for all that you need.[219]

---

[214] Probably the Château of Aché in Valframbert, which is 5.6 kilometers (3.5 miles) from Alençon.

[215] This fragment of the original letter was preserved.

[216] See footnote in CF 48.

[217] This fragment of the original letter was preserved.

[218] See footnote in CF 42.

[219] These last two paragraphs are preserved from the original letter.

To her sister-in-law

Every day I've been thinking of telling you about Marie's illness. I was resolved to wait until Sunday, assuming that you already had enough worries without this one.

So I'm going to tell you that Marie arrived Saturday evening[220] with Monsieur Vital Romet. She was only in the boarding school's infirmary since Thursday, but for four days prior to that, she was suffering without complaining. The doctor for the Visitation Monastery in Le Mans believed that it would be nothing and said it wasn't necessary to make her leave, but my sister thought it more prudent to send her home Saturday.

If she had waited one day longer, Marie wouldn't have been able to withstand the journey. The very next day at eight o'clock I saw the doctor, who immediately feared it was typhoid fever.[221]

I gave my little patient some broth that she found difficult to get down. She had a very bad night. She was delirious until three o'clock in the morning. She asked me to take away a ball that was on her pillow. Then she came to her senses again and said to me, "I'm mistaking my head for a ball, it seems to me that I have a head made out of wood." Afterwards, she was calm enough, and she slept a lot. When the fever broke, she had the look of death. She could neither stand nor get out of bed.

Although she wasn't very bad Saturday night, when she arrived I felt a blow to my heart. I couldn't shake off the feeling that she was going to die. For a long time I've been worried about her future. She's a child with an extraordinarily tender heart. She couldn't get used to the boarding school again, and she couldn't suffer the deprivation of not seeing us. She told me some things about this that broke my heart.

I'm doing all I can to console her and make her hope for a quick recovery. Yesterday I told her that she will be the one who will take care of the house and raise her little sisters when I'm dead. It was very unfortunate that I spoke to her about this; she did nothing but cry.

---

[220] On April 5, Marie was sent home from the Visitation Monastery boarding school because she was sick. She was then thirteen years old.
[221] See footnote in CF 45.

She couldn't bear the idea that I would die before her. I'm very afraid that God will grant her wish.

It was agreed that Pauline would not come home for Easter vacation. I asked the doctor what he thought about it. He told me I could have her here on the condition that I not let her go into her sister's room and that there wouldn't be any danger that way. In any case, she has to come. Marie couldn't get over knowing her sister would be there all alone. As long as there was a question of Pauline staying at the convent, there were constant tears.

Now, she's moaning because "little Paulin," as her father often calls her, will return without her, and she's convinced that this will cause her very great sorrow.

I said to her the day before yesterday, "Since you can't get used to the Visitation Monastery, you won't go back there." She responded immediately, "Oh! I want to go back there; my poor aunt would feel too sad." So we hope that God won't allow so great a trial as to lose this child. My husband is devastated, and he never leaves the house. He played nurse this morning because, today being Thursday, I had to receive my workers all morning, and he replaced me. But it makes him sick to hear her moan and takes away all his courage.[222]

Goodbye, my dear friend, pray for us so that if God requires such a sacrifice, we'll have the strength to bear it.

Marie made her Easter Duty[223] Tuesday morning. She received Communion at five-thirty, with perfect devotion and an angelic expression.

---

[222] "It is sufficient to read my mother's letters to realize how much my father had at heart the desire to help her in all her anxieties, whether it was to set out at 4:00 in the morning to find a wet nurse for a sick baby, or on another occasion to accompany her a distance of six miles from Alençon on a freezing cold night to the cradle of their dying little Joseph. Again he watched for days and weeks as a sick nurse beside their eldest daughter, Marie, who at the age of thirteen was suffering from typhoid fever." Céline Martin (Sister Geneviève of the Holy Face), *The Father of the Little Flower*, p. 41.

[223] All Catholics who have made their First Communion are required to take part in the Sacrament of Reconciliation and receive Holy Communion during the Easter season.

CF 92   To her daughter Pauline, a boarding student at
                         the Visitation Monastery in Le Mans[224]
                                                        April 11(?), 1873

My dear little Pauline,

Despite any hope I'd given you, I'm very sad to have to tell you that you'll not be leaving school for Easter vacation because, you see, it's impossible. Marie has typhoid fever, and it would be dangerous.

I know that I couldn't prevent you from seeing your sister. I wouldn't have that kind of courage, nor would Marie. She can't insist more as it is. She speaks of her "Little Paulin" all day long. She would want to see you, but you would catch the illness. So this is what's been decided:

You will come spend a week in Alençon as soon as Marie is recuperating. This is not going to be long. The doctor said the illness couldn't last longer than twenty-one days, and he's counting the beginning from the Sunday she felt sick. So a week from Saturday, it will be finished. We'll wait another week to be cautious, and then your father will come to get you. Take heart, you don't have to wait more than two weeks.

I assure you, my little Pauline, you won't be sorry. You'll be so much happier than if you came now. If you knew what little enjoyment you would have! I'm sad and always at Marie's side. I don't even take the time to eat. What's going to worry me is the fear that you may be sad. If I know that you aren't, I'll be happy. I'll write you every two days until you come.

This evening I have a Sister[225] watching over Marie who's looking after her very well. She tells me that her patient is in absolutely no danger. However, she's quite sick, our poor Marie! She continually prays to God that He'll cure her because she's afraid of losing her prizes. At her suggestion, I'm sending you her paint box so you can play with it. I'm enclosing a piece of thick green parchment. You trace on it and I'll use it. I'm putting in some cotton to use as a lining. You

---

[224] Pauline was then almost twelve years old.

[225] In 1818, Abbé Bazin founded the Sisters of Mercy, a community of nuns devoted to nursing the sick in their homes. They originated in the Diocese of Séez.

need to use a number 2 needle just right for sewing "the track."[226] I'll try to send it to you tomorrow morning. I know you really enjoy making the track for Alençon lace.

If you don't like this, don't do it. If you prefer to knit, ask your aunt to have some nice blue and white wool bought for you. You can make some stockings for Thérèse. And if this doesn't interest you either, buy tapestry wool and make a beautiful little footstool cover or whatever you would like, or else two pictures for my desk. I need them.

Will you write me a little letter and tell me if you're sad? If you are, it's better for you to come, and we'll do what we can to keep you from seeing Marie.

Your father sends you a big hug. He's also very afraid that you'll be upset.

My little Pauline, I'm telling you again that I'm sending you some chocolate so they'll make you a cup every morning and also so that you can eat some when you have your snack. Marie is better; soon she'll be cured and then you'll come. We'll all go to see your little sister[227] as soon as Marie is able to withstand the carriage ride.

If you come now, you'll go back without seeing Marie or little Thérèse and almost nothing of your mama. You'd have to speak in a low voice. We have to have Céline stay at Mademoiselle Philomène's[228] house all day because she makes too much noise. So you would be very unhappy.

I'll write you a letter on Easter Sunday, and you'll have it Monday morning.

I recommend, my Pauline, that you prepare for your Easter Duty, and be sure to pray for your sister.

---

226 To make Alençon lace, first one makes "the track" (an outline) of the work on green parchment lined with fabric perforated along the design to be reproduced. The various stitches (*points*) of the design are then executed over the outline.

227 Thérèse, who was living with her wet nurse, Rose Taillé, in Semallé. (See footnote in CF 89.)

228 Mademoiselle Philomène Tessier, a friend of the family, lived with her parents in the Prefecture across the street from the Martin home on the rue Saint-Blaise where her father was an employee.

To her sister-in-law
April 13, 1873[229]

Since the day I wrote you, the illness has gotten worse. Marie was absorbed by her illness during the day, and at night the delirium hardly left her. Last night was better, and today she's feeling much better. She told me right away that she wasn't suffering at all anymore. However, she's so weak that she can barely turn over in bed.

This morning the doctor said again that it was definitely typhoid fever that she has, but a less serious case. The Sister[230] that's taking care of her assures us the same thing. However, it's such a treacherous illness that we don't know exactly what it could do.

Please thank all your family for me for taking so much interest in my dear Marie. Don't forget me either to the ladies of the P family.[231] It makes me happy to see that they're so interested in my Marie. There are also many people in Alençon who are worried about her. Sometimes they bother me, but still we're pleased.[232] As for the beautiful Madame Y, who gives balls to make the entire town spin, she hasn't asked about Marie once!

Oh well, the important thing is that Marie gets better quickly. I'm beginning to have hope. Yesterday it was different. I was alarmed, as was everyone else in the house.

From Friday night to Saturday morning, I spent the cruelest night imaginable. It was sinister. My little patient called me in a muffled and mysterious voice to tell me things that made no sense. One time she said to me, "I took a Host. I'm going to the prison. It's for the poor prisoners. They're going to be so happy!" Usually every other night is not as bad, but we fear the next night. I'm the one who has to stay with her because I only have the Sisters every two nights, but one Sister promised me she would come back tonight. I'm very relieved.

Despite what I wrote in my last letter, I made my little Pauline sacrifice her Easter vacation. But now I'm sad she stayed at the Visitation Monastery since the doctor told me that I could have had her

---

[229] Easter Sunday.
[230] See footnote in CF 92.
[231] Josephine and Clémence Pigeon, friends of the Guérin family.
[232] These three lines are preserved from the original letter.

come, that there was no danger as long as I didn't let her go in her sister's room.

I passed this opinion on to Le Mans, secretly hoping that they would send my little girl home to me. But they didn't want to give her to Monsieur Romet yesterday, who would have brought her to me. It seems that the entire convent was in turmoil over such carelessness! Monsieur Romet and his sister, Mademoiselle Pauline, didn't agree with this opinion either, and they did everything they could so that she wouldn't come.

As for me, I'm not as afraid as they are, and I don't believe you can catch this so easily. If anyone were going to catch it, it would certainly be me, or poor Louis, because we never leave the patient and stay on our feet all night, close to her. I'm sure, under these conditions, it would take the grace of God not to succumb. Yesterday afternoon I had a very high fever, but it was due to exhaustion. It seems to be gone now.

Your loving sister.

CF 94

To her sister-in-law
April 20, 1873

Since Wednesday, there's a noticeable improvement. Marie is no longer delirious. However, she still has a fever. She's still eating nothing but broth. She's very weak and sleeps a lot. We hope that soon her convalescence will start. I'm waiting for it very impatiently. The wet nurse brought our little Thérèse today, who's in good health and very strong.

I thought I wouldn't have time to write you. I'm taking advantage of a moment of rest. I hope to hear from you soon, and I'll write to you again as soon as Marie is a little better.

CF 95

To her daughter Pauline
April 1873

Marie does nothing but talk about you. If she says two words, one of them is for her "Little Paulin." She's always asking me what time it is, and then she tells me what you're doing.

She was so happy with your little letter that she sang this morning. We thought she was cured, but unfortunately she's not. She still has a fever, and we don't know exactly when it will be over. This illness is very long, and my poor Marie has a great need for patience. She eats nothing and drinks only broth every two hours. The doctor let her have some vermicelli[233] and I made some for her, but she couldn't eat it. Her father went to catch some fish for her. She wanted some very much, but was only able to try a mouthful. Deep down, I was happy about this because I was afraid it would make her sick.

I'm very upset to see my Marie sick for such a long time and then also to be deprived of my little Pauline, because I don't think you'll be able to come for three or four weeks. But, be brave, four weeks will pass quickly. Then, all of us will be so happy. Your father is very pleased with you, and he says you're very sensible.

Marie asks that you take all the letters that are in her cabinet for the second course and give them to your aunt. Also, cover her atlas, put it in her cabinet and be as careful as possible, as well as the pictures that are in her style notebook. She also wants you to help yourself to her notebook to write down your expenses, but nothing else. She asks for her "tatting"[234] cotton and her crochet hook. Send these to me by Monsieur Romet. Finally, she wants me to tell you that tomorrow we're going to make you a pretty black hat decorated with moiré ribbon and a pretty feather.

There, I think I've given you all her messages. But no, she still insists that I ask you if you still have the same place in the refectory and in the dormitory? I'm at her side while I'm writing you. She has an endless number of things to tell you! Though I must finish.... If I listened to her, I'd be here writing all night!

Goodbye, my "Little Paulin," I'll see you soon.

CF 96	To her sister-in-law
	April 27, 1873

I was happy to learn that you've found a suitable place to reestablish your drug business. With all my heart, I want you to

---

[233] See footnote in CF 52.
[234] A type of lace that is made with little shuttles.

succeed better than you have in the past with this famous enterprise that's already given my brother so many problems. Oh well, I have confidence in the future. You are good Christians, and I can't help believing that, if God tested you, He'll fully make it up to you by making you prosper beyond all expectations.

Marie is not doing well. She still has a fever, and along with this, she suffers a lot of foot pain. From what Monsieur Vital told me, she'll have it still for a long time. They assure me that if I get away with her having it for only a month, I'll have nothing to complain about. There's a fine consolation! Oh well, we hope that all these people are false prophets....

Goodbye, my dear sister. Give your little girls a big hug for me. Tell Isidore to write me when he can and tell me how much the estimate of the merchandise has gone up. My husband would like to know, and I want to know how much they value his losses.

CF 97   To her brother, Grand-Rue 74[235]
May 4, 1873

I don't know how to find the time to write you because, like you, I'm in a great dilemma. There's only me to take care of Marie day and night, and yet I have many other things to do. I'm up and down the stairs constantly. You're going to say to me, "Get help," but Marie doesn't want anyone else to touch her but me. Last Thursday I had to stay at my desk to receive the workers, and I had to leave all of them to go to her. The maid came to say to me, "Mademoiselle Marie wants it to be 'Mama.'"

When all is said and done, she's not doing better.[236] We're devastated. She's wasting away before our very eyes, and if this continues any longer, I fear another illness will come along and steal her from us.

Monsieur Vital and Mademoiselle Pauline just left this minute. They hadn't seen her for a week. They seemed worried and found

---

[235] Original address preserved.

[236] At the time this letter was written, what would be called the pre-antibiotic era, good care and nutrition were the only methods used to stabilize the patient and ward off death (often to no avail). Currently, there are highly effective vaccines for prevention and a number of antibiotics for treatment and cure.

her sicker than last week. And yet her condition is still more or less the same. The fever hasn't gone up or down, but the longer it lasts, the weaker she gets.

I don't know when this illness will end, and if it continues, I believe that it will be my turn to get sick, from fatigue and sorrow. Tomorrow, Monday, Louis leaves on a pilgrimage on foot while fasting, some leagues from Alençon, where they honor a saintly man who cures fevers.[237] Let's hope....

CF 98   To her daughter Pauline
                                                            May 5, 1873

My dear Pauline,

I don't have good news to tell you. Marie is not at all better. We're all sorry to see that this illness continues to go on like this.

Our patient cried a lot on Friday. She was upset while saying, "I want to see my 'Little Paulin.' I love her so much!" I found it very difficult to console her, as did your father. He's often at her side to distract her, and she's so happy when he's there. Little by little, she's getting better! She's lost a lot of weight, and it will take a long time for her to gain it back.

Her father leaves this morning for Butte de Chaumont[238] on a pilgrimage for Marie. He'll leave fasting and wants to return the same way. He insists on doing penance so that God will grant his prayer. He has to walk six leagues[239] on foot. I'll write you on Thursday to tell you if he obtained the grace. Mademoiselle Pauline[240] will bring you my letter. She's going to the Second Communion[241] of her niece, and her intention is to take you with her for this celebration, if they let you go.

Marie wants me to tell you that little Thérèse came to see us yesterday. We weren't expecting her. The wet nurse arrived with her four children at eleven thirty, just as we were sitting down at the table. She put the baby in our arms and left immediately for Mass.

---

237 In CF 98 Zélie puts this pilgrimage at La Butte Chaumont. (See footnote in CF 82.)
238 See footnote in CF 82.
239 14.5 miles or 23 kilometers (a French league equaled 2.422 miles).
240 Romet.
241 See footnote in CF 57.

Yes, but the little one didn't want this. She cried almost to the point of passing out![242] Her father left almost without eating. The entire house was in disarray. I had to send Louise[243] to tell the wet nurse to come immediately after the Mass because she was supposed to go buy shoes for her children. The wet nurse left halfway through the Mass and came running. I was annoyed over this. The little one wouldn't have died from crying. Oh well, she was instantly consoled. She's very strong, and everybody's surprised. I walked her and shook her so much to make her stop crying that I got a backache from it that lasted the entire day. We don't find her as beautiful as little Céline. She is, however, very pretty. In other words, it's Céline who, for the moment, has the first prize for beauty, but we can't judge Thérèse yet. She's too little; a tiny baby of four months hasn't blossomed.

Every day Marie talks about the party we'll have when you're here, when we go to see little Thérèse. It's agreed that I'll bring a lot of bread because she says she'll be very hungry.

As she's deprived of all food at the moment, for a sick person

---

[242] This is the first indication that Thérèse suffered from separation anxiety.

[243] Louise Marais (Madame LeGendre) (1849-1923) was the servant to the Martin family. She lived with and worked for them in Alençon from 1865 until the death of Zélie in 1877. She was an important witness to the daily occurrences of the Martin family. She was present for the birth of the last five children and was there when four of the Martin children died. It was Louise who carried Thérèse and accompanied the family to the parish church of Notre Dame on the day Thérèse was baptized. She was a witness to all the family events and commented, for example, on Zélie reading spiritual biographies, her charitable works, and her financial donation to the victims of a severe flood in Lisieux. It was Louise, on the day of Zélie's funeral, who looked sadly at the two youngest children and said: "Poor little ones, you have no mother!" Céline rushed into Marie's arms and said, "Well then you will be my mother!" Then Thérèse ran to Pauline and said, "Very well! Pauline will be my mother." Louise was faithful until death. However, she was an extremely insensitive, domineering and controlling woman. She found fault with everything, nagging constantly and tyrannical in her authority. Tragically, it was Louise who was found to have emotionally and physically abused Léonie. Zélie requested that after her death, Louise was to be discharged from working for the Martin family and that was accomplished. On July 22, 1923, months before she died, Louise testified at the process of beatification of St. Thérèse and revealed important information about Louis and Zélie Martin. She said, "In my acute suffering, I invoke the aid of little Thérèse and, at the same time, of her good and saintly Mamma. If little Thérèse is a saint, I believe that her mother is also a great saint. She had a great many trials during her life, and she accepted them all with resignation. And how eager she was to sacrifice herself constantly!" Céline Martin (Sr. Geneviève of the Holy Face), *The Mother of the Little Flower*, p. 113.

Louise Marais also confessed her guilt and sorrow regarding her treatment of Léonie and said the pain of regret never left her for the rest of her life.

she has incredible cravings. She wants a three-pound loaf of bread all for herself when we on our outing, without counting the cake with jam. She seriously believes that she'll eat her three-pound loaf and says to the maid, "Louise, Mama is going to bring a loaf of bread just for me." Louise responds, "It's a penny loaf of bread, no doubt?" But Marie gets angry when she hears her speak of a penny loaf of bread. She says to me, "Yes, I'll carry one in my pocket to eat along the way, but that won't keep me from eating my three-pound loaf of bread and again black bread at the wet nurse's house."

Goodbye, my Pauline. Don't worry. I'd very much like Marie to be able to eat her three-pound loaf of bread, but unfortunately she's not there yet. Oh well, we hope that she'll be cured soon. Pray a lot to the Blessed Mother for this.

Your father sends you a thousand kisses, and as for me, I hug you with all my heart.

CF 99   To her daughter Pauline
·   *May 1873*[244]

My dear Pauline,

Marie was much better Monday and Tuesday, but yesterday, Wednesday, she had a bad day, and her fever came back worse than before.

Last night was a very good night. I only had to get up once to give her something to drink. She no longer has[245] a headache, and she almost isn't deaf anymore. The doctor found her much better, and I think she's on the road to recovery.

She's bored to death of always being in bed and regrets above all her compositions and the prizes she's going to lose. To console her, I tell her that I'm going to buy her some books, but that's not what she needs. It's not my books she wants!

I try every way possible to lift her spirits. Tuesday evening I made a list of everything she'll do when she's cured. This made her very happy, but I had the misfortune of saying, "You'll be much happier than Pauline." At that very moment, she covered her face with

---

[244] Original address preserved.
[245] The fragment, "I only had to get up... she no longer has," was preserved from the original letter.

her blanket and began to sob. I could no longer console her. As soon as she thinks of you, the same thing happens....

She pestered us all day so that I'd send you your hat. I didn't find this very helpful, but to make her happy, I asked Mademoiselle Pauline Romet if she could take care of bringing it to you. When you receive it, write to Marie that you like it a lot. I hope now that she's going to get better and better. If I can see my little Pauline at the end of May, I'll be very happy.

Céline is eagerly looking forward to seeing you. She speaks of it every day and says that she wants to sit next to you at the table. She sings pretty little songs that Mademoiselle Philomène[246] teaches her. She's very intelligent.[247] She learned all her letters in two weeks, and she'd know how to read now if Marie hadn't been sick. But for five weeks I haven't made her spell once. However, she likes it a lot and often goes to get her book.

Tell your aunt that I don't have time to write her because today is Thursday, and I have a lot of work. All morning I have to take care of Marie and receive my workers.

Goodbye, my dear Pauline. I hug you with all my heart.

CF 100   To her sister-in-law
                                                     May 13, 1873[248]

I regret not having written to you on Sunday to tell you about Marie. However, I'm very busy today, but I'm upset for having neglected you. I'm putting everything aside to tell you that our patient is much better. She's beginning to recover. At noon, she ate a piece of meat without bread, and it didn't hurt her.

She still had a slight fever in the afternoon, but very slight. I hope that a week from now she'll be up part of the day. It's a shame I'm in such a hurry; I've had so much to tell you. This morning I received a letter from my sister who speaks about you a lot.

Goodbye, my dear sister. Hug your little ones for me and big Isidore as well!

---

[246] Philomène Tessier. (See footnote in CF 92.)
[247] Three lines preserved from the original letter. In the French edition of the letters, *Correspondance familiale,* the spelling was corrected.
[248] Original address preserved.

To her daughter Pauline
May 14, 1873

My dear little Pauline,

You'll be very happy to learn that Marie got up and came to the table with us today. She ate a good little piece of steak, and she would have eaten much more if we'd listened to her. But I don't give her anything to eat without trembling. I have such a great fear of a relapse that could kill her! Your father isn't as sensible as I am. I very often have to stop him from giving her what she asks for.

She was up for four hours. We sat her in a big armchair in the garden. Then we put her back to bed, but she wanted to get up again to have a late supper with us. I was very much against her doing it, but she started to cry, and papa gave in!

I didn't want her to eat anything other than her vermicelli[249] either, but she got a good look at the dishes on the table, which made her want them. Her father gave her two mouthfuls of cheese, then this and that....

We just took her up to her room. We help her walk by supporting her under the arms, like we do with her little sister Thérèse. Oh well, I hope she'll be walking soon without support. I only fear carelessness now. She still has a fever this afternoon. I even find she has a slightly higher one today than she did yesterday. I think it's the fatigue of having been up such a long time. But her fever doesn't keep her from being very hungry and we put her to bed hungry.

Yesterday we received all your little letters, and Marie was so happy with them! Mademoiselle Pauline[250] brought them to us at seven thirty in the morning. She came in to see our patient with her sister, Madame Benoît. They stayed a long time to explain all that you'd said about Marie, who was very happy to see you love her so much. But now she wants you to be delighted at the thought that you're coming home soon, because it's agreed your godmother[251] will come get you May 31.

So we still have two weeks to wait. It's quite a long time, and we

---

[249] See footnote in CF 52.
[250] Mademoiselle Pauline Romet.
[251] Pauline Romet was Pauline's baptismal godmother.

all want to see you very much. As for me, I can't stand it anymore; I have to give you a kiss no matter what.

It's wonderful that Mademoiselle Pauline happens to be going to Le Mans on that date. As a matter of fact, I wanted you to come home that day. If you come home earlier, you won't have a good time because Marie will still be too sick, and you won't be able to go for a walk with her.

I'm hoping she'll go out for the first time on the Feast of the Ascension[252] to go to the eight o'clock Mass. So, my Pauline, see how happy we'll be and how you did the right thing by agreeing not to come for the Easter holidays. We'll make it up to you, I promise you.

Yesterday Marie spent her morning reading the letters and looking at her beautiful pictures. She asks you to thank her friends for her and especially Sister Marie-Paula.[253] She's very happy to have the Ribbon of Honor, but she doesn't know if she really deserves it, and this casts a shadow on her happiness. She also asks me to tell her aunt that she loves her with all her heart.

CF 102   To her daughter Pauline
                                                  May 22, 1873

My dear Pauline,

Today is the beautiful Feast of the Ascension and I'm taking the opportunity to write to you. This will be the last time I write before you leave since Mademoiselle Pauline will bring you home May 31. We only have to go eight more days without seeing each other. Marie talks about it nonstop, but she's ready to cry when she thinks of you going back to school. However, we must resign ourselves to it. Happiness can't last forever.

Your vacation comes just at the right time. At the moment, they're getting ready for some big celebrations in Alençon for the occasion of an Exposition. They'll begin on Pentecost Sunday, that is, the day after your arrival. There will be fireworks, balloons, a torchlight procession every night for a week, and a thousand other

---

[252] Thursday, May 22.
[253] The headmistress of the boarding school at the Visitation Monastery of Le Mans.

things that I don't have time to tell you. You've never seen anything like it in Alençon. As for me, all this doesn't amuse me, but for you it will be different.

Marie went to the eight o'clock Mass this morning. She was a little tired when she returned. I just made her lie down. Now we don't prevent her from eating anymore. However, we mustn't move too quickly yet. She stays up almost all day.

The whole family is celebrating your arrival. We make Céline do everything we want her to do by saying to her, "If you do this, Pauline will come."

A week from Monday we'll go by carriage to see little Thérèse. She's very strong now. I saw her last Thursday. Her wet nurse brought her, but she no longer wants to stay with us. She let out piercing screams when she didn't see the wet nurse any more.[254] So Louise had to take her to the market where "little Rose" was selling her butter. There was no other way of handling it.

As soon as she saw her wet nurse, she looked at her and started laughing. Then she didn't breathe another word. She stayed like that, selling butter with all the good women, until noon! As for me, I can't hold her for a long time without getting very tired; she weighs fourteen pounds. She'll be very good and even very pretty later on.

Your father leaves Tuesday on a pilgrimage to Chartres.[255] He won't be back until Wednesday during the night.

Goodbye, my dear Pauline, I hug you with all my heart.

CF 102-a   Louis Martin to his daughter Pauline
                                                    May 1873[256]

My dear Pauline,

Your mother tells me that you want very much to receive a letter from me, even if it's only a few lines, and I want to please you.

Pray a lot, my dear little girl, for the success of the pilgrimage

---

[254] Again, a symptom that Thérèse is suffering from separation anxiety. (See footnote in CF 98.)

[255] This pilgrimage took place May 27-28. (See footnote in CF 79.)

[256] It's possible this letter was written May 22 and sent with Zélie's letter written the same day.

to Chartres in which I will be participating. It will bring together many pilgrims from all over our beautiful France to the feet of the Blessed Mother to receive the graces our country needs so much in order to prove itself worthy of its past.

I'll think of you, my Pauline, and of your dear Visitation Monastery, in that privileged sanctuary of the Queen of Heaven.

Let me add this: it's fully agreed that we're all expecting our "Little Paulin" at the end of the month without fail.

Your father who loves you.

CF 103

…Marie has made a complete recovery. She goes out every day now and her strength is coming back before our very eyes, although she's still very thin. I don't expect to send her back to Le Mans before the end of the summer vacation. She must rest and build up her strength.

Pauline, who didn't have an Easter vacation, will arrive Saturday evening to spend a week with us. The timing is perfect because we're going to have great celebrations in Alençon as part of an Exposition. They begin Sunday and end June 8.

I'm writing to ask you if it's possible for you to come spend this time with us. You see that I'm leaving it to the last minute, just like people who send out an invitation late in order to receive a refusal! I assure you that's not what I'm thinking. You know I would be happy to see all of you, but I don't dare hope for this happiness. Oh well, if it's possible, I'd be so happy!

I hope you're in good health, as well as your dear little girls. Everyone here is doing well. Little Thérèse is growing before our very eyes. She weighs close to fifteen pounds. The wet nurse began making her eat only a week ago. I'm very satisfied with this woman. You rarely find one like her. I hope Céline Maudelonde is also doing well? I would like you to tell me about her, as well as my little Marguerite[257] whom I love very much because she resembles my little Hélène.

---

[257] Céline Maudelonde (February 25, 1873-June 1, 1949) and her sister Marguerite (February 24, 1867-April 30, 1966) were the children of Céline Guérin's sister Marie-

My dear little Pauline,

Saturday evening I went to your godmother's house to let her know the ceremony for your Second Communion[259] will be postponed. I don't know if you'll be able to go out on Thursday, but you'll soon be on summer vacation which lasts more than one day. Now you should do nothing but prepare yourself well for the Renewal of your First Communion. Pray especially for Léonie so that she'll be able to go to the Visitation Monastery when school begins again. She wants to very much and promises to be very well-behaved.

Thursday the wet nurse brought little Thérèse. She did nothing but laugh. She especially liked little Céline, who made her scream with laughter. You could say she already wants to play. That will come soon. She holds herself up on her little legs, stiff as a post, and I think she's going to start walking early.

Now she's eating well, and I assure you she finds my porridge good! I made a lot on Thursday so little Céline could also have some, but Thérèse didn't think it was too much. All that was left was the part stuck to the pot.

We decided that we won't go to see her until next month when you're here. We don't want to have that pleasure without Pauline.... I wouldn't be able to go so long without seeing the baby, but the wet nurse brings her to me on Thursdays.

Rosalie and her husband Césard Maudelonde. They were first cousins of the Guérin children, Jeanne and Marie. The Maudelonde family spent a great deal of time at the Guérin home in Lisieux and vacationed with them in Trouville. When the Martin children moved to Lisieux after the death of Zélie, the five Maudelonde children became their playmates. (See footnote in CF 81.)

[258] Thérèse quotes this letter in *Story of a Soul,* dating it July 10 and in a different version. We quote: "The nurse brought little Thérèse here on Thursday. The little one did nothing but laugh. Céline pleased her especially and she went into peals of laughter with her. One would say she already wants to play, so that will come soon. She holds herself up on her two little legs straight as a post. I believe she will walk very early and she will be very good. She appears very intelligent and has the face of a little cherub." *Story of a Soul,* tr. John Clarke, OCD, pp. 21-22. Note that this is the same version as in the 1958 French edition of *Correspondance familiale, 1863-1877.* Lisieux: France. Office Central de Lisieux, 1958. It is slightly different than the version of Sister Marie of the Trinity.

[259] See footnote in CF 57.

Your father just told me to give you a big hug for him. He's leaving to go fishing, his favorite pastime.

Goodbye, my Pauline. I also hug you with all my heart.

Your loving mother.

CF 105

To her daughter Pauline
July 9, 1873

My dear Pauline,

Since I can't go to your Second Communion,[260] I wanted you to receive a letter to console you a little in my absence and to console myself, because I'm deeply sorry that I'm unable to attend.

I would be so happy to see my dear Pauline take part in this beautiful ceremony! But I'm with you, at least, in spirit and unite my heart to yours.

I was very upset to learn that Monsieur Vital Romet hadn't given you my letter until a week later. This is the second time this has happened, so I won't give him anything again. I don't want to make you cry anymore. I don't know if Mademoiselle Pauline Romet told you that her nieces won't be returning to the boarding school in Le Mans. You might not be happy about this, because you won't be able to go out on the first Thursday of the month anymore. Your godmother was only going to Le Mans because of her nieces. As for me, I'm not upset about it, especially if Léonie goes to the Visitation Monastery when school begins again. I would have been afraid of bothering this kind young lady too much.

Céline is learning to read very well, but she's becoming as clever as a little devil! I have to say she's only four years old and, thank God, I manage her easily. For example, here's an amusing story. Last evening she said to me, "I don't like poor people!" I told her that the good Jesus wasn't very happy, and He wouldn't love her any more.

She answered, "I love the good Jesus very much, but I won't love poor people, never in my life. Anyway, I don't want to love them! What does it matter to Jesus? He's definitely the master, but I'm also the mistress."

---

[260] Ibid.

You can't imagine how upset she was, and nobody could make her see reason. But there's an explanation for her hatred of poor people.

Several days ago she was standing in the doorway with a little friend when a poor child who was passing by looked at her in a defiant and mocking way. Céline didn't like this and said to the little girl, "You! Go away." Furious, before the little girl left, she gave Céline a good slap. She still had the red mark on her face an hour later!

I'd encouraged her to forgive the poor child, but she hasn't forgotten the incident and declared to me yesterday, "Mama, you want me to love the poor people who come to slap me, so that my whole cheek burns? No, no, I won't love them!"

But she slept on it and the first thing she said to me the next morning was that "she had a beautiful bouquet that was for the Blessed Mother and the good Jesus." Then she added, "I love poor people very much now!"

Goodbye, my dear Pauline. I'll see you again soon. If you're counting the days, I'm counting them too, because I'm longing to see you and hug you whenever I want. Your father told me to give you a big hug for him as well, and he asks that you say a little prayer today for him.

CF 106   To her sister-in-law
                                            July 20, 1873

I'm taking advantage of Monsieur Adrien Romet's[261] visit to send you a few words. Besides, I wanted to write to you today but Marie, who had intended to do the same thing, asked me to wait until tomorrow. Her letter is postponed until another time.

She's doing as well as possible now and is taller than me! We intend to go to Lisieux in September, and I can't go away before then. I must love you a lot to decide to leave the house because traveling doesn't appeal to me.

I'm going to Le Mans to pick up Pauline on August 4th. She's

---

[261] Brother of Vital, Pauline, Pierre, Hortense and Augustin Adrien Romet.

extremely bored without Marie. It's incredible how sad she was during her sister's illness. She's also grown a lot this year. There's only Léonie who doesn't change. She's like an eight-year-old child. She should go to the Visitation Monastery in October as long as her aunt doesn't ask that I keep her home another year.

Céline is big for her age, but she's not strong. I'm always afraid she'll fall ill like little Hélène. Thérèse is a big baby, tanned by the sun. Her wet nurse takes her into the fields, carrying her in a wheelbarrow on top of a load of grass. She almost never cries. "Little Rose" says that you could never see a cuter baby. So as you see, my dear sister, all is going well. The beginning of the year was sad for me, but apparently the end of the year will be better.

CF 107

I had decided to leave for Lisieux sometime during the last two weeks of September, but since it's more convenient for you, we'll move our trip up to the 30th of this month. We'll take the eleven o'clock train. I would have liked to see all your family and I'm sorry about the setback that's come up, because it's impossible for me to leave earlier because of an order of lace I have to make.

The children are very sad to think they'll not see Marguerite Maudelonde. They're begging me to leave Saturday, but I can't. Wouldn't it be possible to rejoin your parents in the country instead of going to Trouville as you intend to do? As for me, I'd quite gladly sacrifice the pleasure of seeing the sea in order to visit with your family.

So, it's settled. We'll go spend a day in the country if it doesn't bother anyone. Pauline absolutely wants Marguerite to be her cousin. She declares that, since Jeanne is her first cousin as well as Marguerite's first cousin, it's impossible that Marguerite is nothing to her. So it's agreed that Marguerite is everybody's cousin!

On the feast of the Assumption we had a pilgrimage in Alençon. The three parishes were combined, as well as three parishes from the area. There were five to six hundred young girls dressed in white. The pilgrimage went to the *Chapelle de Notre-Dame de Lorette*[262] at the gates of the city. Quite a lot was said about this. They claim it was to obtain the restoration of Henri V.[263]

In the meantime, I saw some men pass by pushing the crowd aside and with a threat on their lips, saying, "We're going to save France, we are!"

Goodbye, my dear sister. Soon we'll have the happiness of seeing each other again.

CF 108   To Louis Martin
Lisieux, August 31, 1873

My dear Louis,

We arrived yesterday afternoon at four thirty. My brother was waiting for us at the station and was delighted to see us. He and his wife are doing everything they can to entertain us. This evening, Sunday, there's a beautiful reception in their home in our honor. Tomorrow, Monday, we're going to Trouville. Tuesday there will be a big dinner at the home of Madame Maudelonde and, perhaps, a drive to the country house of Madame Fournet.[264] The children are thrilled and if the weather were good, they'd be ecstatic.

As for me, I'm finding it hard to relax! None of that interests me! I'm absolutely like the fish you pull out of the water. They're no longer in their element and they have to perish! This would have the

---

[262] The Chapel of Our Lady of Loretto, founded in the late 17th century, is on the rue du Mans in the Montsort quarter of Alençon. It was near here that the Circle Vital Romet met. Louis belonged to this group of Catholic men who met in friendship. Their focus was to deepen their faith through prayer and works for the poor. They also sponsored social activities, e.g., dances, plays, lectures. It was here that Louis Martin, an excellent player, enjoyed playing pool. See footnote #389 in CF 154.

[263] Some echoes of political conflicts: certain Catholics hostile to the Republic wished for the return of the monarchy with Henri de Bourbon, Count of Chambord (1820-1883). Posthumous son of the Duke de Berry, he became the legitimist pretender ("Henri V") to the throne of France after the death of Charles X. But in 1873, he rejected the tricolor flag as the national emblem of France and vowed not to become the "legitimate king of the revolution." Frederick Brown, *For the Soul of France: Culture Wars in the Age of Dreyfus*. New York, NY: Alfred A. Knopf, 2010, p. 46.

[264] This was the country home of Céline Guérin's parents in the village of Saint-Ouen-le-Pin, 10.7 kilometers (6.6 miles) from Lisieux. It was at this house that Thérèse visited and played with her cousins Jeanne and Marie and the Maudelonde children.

same effect on me if I had to stay a lot longer. I feel uncomfortable, I'm out of sorts. This is affecting me physically, and it's almost making me sick. However, I'm reasoning with myself and trying to gain the upper hand. I'm with you in spirit all day, and I say to myself, "Now he must be doing such and such a thing."

I'm longing to be near you, my dear Louis. I love you with all my heart, and I feel my affection so much more when you're not here with me. It would be impossible for me to live apart from you.

This morning I attended three Masses. I went to the one at six o'clock, made my thanksgiving and said my prayers during the seven o'clock Mass, and returned for the high Mass.

My brother is not unhappy with his business. It's going well enough.

Tell Léonie and Céline that I kiss them tenderly and will bring them a souvenir from Lisieux.

I'll try to write you tomorrow, if possible, but I don't know what time we'll return from Trouville. I'm hurrying because they're waiting for me to go visiting. We return Wednesday evening at seven thirty. How long that seems to me!

I kiss you with all my love. The little girls want me to tell you that they're very happy to have come to Lisieux and they send you big hugs.

CF 109   To her brother and sister-in-law
                                                    October 27, 1873

This morning I received your letter, and it made me very happy. I've already read it many times because I always read your letters several times to make the pleasure last as long as I can.

I see that you're afraid of the future. It's certain it won't be wonderful and, sooner or later, we'll have to pass through a terrible ordeal. As for me, I didn't believe for one moment that Henri V[265] could come to the throne at the present time. Nor do I believe in that disgraceful slander that he would have compromised his convictions to adopt the principles of the revolution. I'll believe it only when he sends out a proclamation to that effect. But it would still be possible

---

[265] See footnote in CF 107.

for the revolution not to break out right away. Oh well, no one knows how all this will get sorted out.

In the meantime, I'm quite worried because I have orders worth six thousand francs to deliver the first two weeks of November, and I'm very concerned about this. My husband doesn't want me to make these deliveries, based on the advice he received from a reliable gentleman who foresees very serious events in the near future. This advice must be the best because it comes from someone who isn't in the habit of giving his opinion so categorically.

Oh well, I'll do what I can. I have to send the most urgent order and I started it today. It's in God's hands. If we lose money, I've resigned myself to not having it. I've already waited so long, based on a lot of predictions which all deceived me, that now I don't believe anything anymore if I don't see it with my own eyes. It's true that I'm like everyone else in this respect, I see clearly after events have unfolded. I confess, I wouldn't be sorry if they had already unfolded.

I brought the children back to Le Mans on the 8th of this month. Léonie still hasn't started school there yet. I pushed that back until the first of the year. If it weren't so important to me that her aunt prepare her for First Communion, she'd never go to the Visitation Monastery, but I want to see if our sister manages to change her, as I hope.

Céline doesn't go to class. I'm teaching her to read myself. She's such a delicate child that I have to keep her near me. In spite of all my care, I'm very afraid I won't be able to raise her. She's almost always burning with fever. She's a little girl who's turning out exactly like her sister Hélène.

Thérèse is still doing very well. She's very big and strong. She holds herself up leaning against the chairs, and I think she'll be walking by her first birthday. My husband went to Lourdes[266] on a diocesan pilgrimage and brought us back two little stones broken off from a rock a few meters from the Grotto of the Apparition. There was a good woman hitting it with a hammer, but her hitting did no good, and nothing was happening. Louis took it from her and skillfully succeeded in getting a piece. Everyone gathered around him, wanting a piece of it!

However, a security guard threatened to go get the police cap-

---

[266] See footnote in CF 51.

tain, and when he arrived, the fellow said to him while pointing to Louis, "It's that tall one there, Captain." But they didn't say anything to him.

He didn't see any miracles. He was there when a paralyzed woman was lowered into the bath. A good elderly pilgrim was seated on a bench, very close to the spring. Seeing that the patient wasn't being cured, he said naively, "Well, hurry up, my good Blessed Mother, let's go, you're not doing anything!" It didn't do any good; the woman wasn't cured.

When the pilgrims returned to Alençon there was an enormous crowd around the station and all along the road. I was unable to go meet Louis, and it was fortunate! One would have said I suspected what was going to happen. The travelers were wearing all the badges from the pilgrimage.

My husband left first, with a little red cross attached to his chest. Several people heckled him, and others laughed. But that was nothing compared to what happened next. When they saw most of the pilgrims wearing rosaries around their necks with beads as big as chestnuts, they insulted them in every way. Several were brought to the police station. However, they didn't return in a procession because the town council had forbidden it.[267]

My dear Isidore, you say goodbye to me. I don't like that word. So you think we'll never see each other again? As for me, I say, until we meet again, I'll see you soon. Soon I'll send you a nice beautiful goose.

CF 110   To her daughters, Marie and Pauline
                                            November 1, 1873
My dear little daughters,

I received your letters last Wednesday and I was anxious to get them. I'm very happy that Marie has adjusted well to being back at school again and has such good intentions of doing well. I hope you'll receive Communion today, All Saints' Day, and that you'll do so again tomorrow, All Souls' Day.

There was a beautiful ceremony here for the feast. The Bishop

_____
[267] An example of the quarrels between Catholics and anticlerical people in the 1870s.

of Autun officiated. Every evening, for nine days, we'll have Solemn Benediction of the Most Blessed Sacrament for the intention of France.

Your aunt and uncle in Lisieux wrote to me this week. Your uncle spoke of an enormous red comet[268] that's moving toward us and is still visible at four o'clock in the morning. It was reported in the newspapers and soon we'll see it. In the meantime, we must serve God and His Saints, my dear little girls, and try to deserve to one day be among the saints whose feast we celebrate today.[269]

I haven't seen little Thérèse since the day we all went together to Semallé, and I miss her very much. And yet I have to make up my mind to go there, but it's very hard for me. It's so far away! Fortunately, she won't have to stay there much longer.

Your father went to Nocturnal Adoration last night, although he was very tired when he left us at nine o'clock in the evening.[270]

While all the worshippers were in front of the Blessed Sacrament to say the usual prayers, Monsieur Tessier[271] went to light the stove in the room above the sacristy where the gentlemen take turns resting. After the prayers were said, they went to the sacristy to draw their hours of adoration.

As sometimes happens, your father asked Monsieur de Morel to draw for him because he was very tired. He then went upstairs to rest a while, but when he got to the room, he smelled suffocating smoke which prevented him from going any farther. He shouted, "Fire!" They all left their lottery and rushed into the apartment. There were two beds on fire. They hurried to throw the mattresses out the windows. Finally, they managed to put out the fire.

If your father hadn't gone up so early, they wouldn't have been able to control the fire. There were about thirty beds there and all made of wood. The sacristy was burned, and perhaps the fire would have reached the church. Consequently, the gentlemen looked upon this as providential and, every hour, each worshipper said an Our

---

268 Among the comets visible in France during the year 1873, we point out as possible candidates: Tempel 1 (9P/1873 G1), Tempel 2 (10P/1873 N1), and Brorsen (5D). (With our thanks to Gilbert Javaux.)

269 Sentence preserved from the original letter.

270 Louis was very diligent in attending Nocturnal Adoration with a group of friends from Alençon.

271 See footnote in CF 92.

Father and a Hail Mary to thank God for this protection.

Monsieur Tessier hadn't noticed that two beds were touching the stove, and that was how the fire started.

I'm sending you a letter (?) from Céline. She's beginning to write and draws some lines. We'll soon make a scholar out of her! It was the maid who made her write her letter. I wanted to read it, but I couldn't decipher these hieroglyphics!

The other day the poor little one had a bad toothache. To distract her, Louise gave her Marie's beautiful porcelain tea set, but she was suffering so much she couldn't play. The toy remained against the garden windows when, in the afternoon, she kicked it while running and everything overturned. I let out a cry, and the little one got so frightened she ran off I don't know where.

I collected the tea set and checked to see if anything was broken. Fortunately, there was no damage. Then I set out in search of Céline, since she didn't come back.

I saw her heading for the side of the shed. I went there, nothing.... Then I began to get worried, and I called her name.... No answer! Finally, I returned to the garden. For the third time, I looked under the shed. I saw her nestled between two small groups of branches, in such a small corner that I wondered how she was able to get in there. There was just enough room for a cat! We had a very hard time making her come out. I assure you she didn't make any noise!

My dear little daughters, I must go to Vespers to pray for the intention of our dear late relatives. There will come a day when you will go there for me, but I have to see to it that I won't have too much need of your prayers. I want to become a saint, and that won't be easy. There's a lot of wood to chop and the wood is as hard as rock. It would have been better if I'd tried earlier, while it was less difficult. Oh well, "better late than never."

I hope Marie is going to be very sensible. Anyway my children, get used to speaking well. I would truly be very sad if you let yourselves go on this point, as you did during your last vacation, after having spent so many years in boarding school. I also hope that Marie becomes a Child of Mary this year, but, above all, it's absolutely necessary that she try hard to deserve this beautiful title.

Your father asks me to send you his love a thousand times and, as for me, I hug you with all my love.

Your letter arrived as we were sitting at the table with Monsieur Maudelonde. You needn't worry, there's no danger of talking about prophecies with him, or even anyone else, because I have little confidence in them, and I don't dwell on any of them. And yet I always have Marie Lataste[272] in my head, and if the fourth year of the Holy Father's captivity passes without his release, I'll be very surprised, but I've already been surprised many times, so I don't get flustered anymore.[273]

I have more patience than ever, and now I act as if nothing has to be done right away. I'm taking care of the big orders, and I take my time delivering my merchandise. I'm tired, very tired of the fears that paralyzed me and did me considerable harm. I wasn't surprised by the results of these political affairs; from the beginning, I was expecting what happened.

Little Thérèse is still growing remarkably well. I'm bringing her home from the wet nurse on March 11. I'd promised she would stay a year, and it's best that I keep my promise. Otherwise, I would bring her home two months earlier. Céline is also getting stronger.

Pauline is not well. Her aunt wrote me asking that I send her some wine to build her up. They're very happy with Marie. She's a charming girl, and her aunt is delighted with her.

I'm having a young lady with an advanced diploma give Léonie lessons. The child is having a very hard time learning, but finally she's beginning to learn a little. She's definitely leaving for the Visitation Monastery the first of the year. We're in the process of putting together her wardrobe. I think it's a waste of money, but, more than anything, it's the trouble she's going to give her aunt that worries me. However, my duty forces me to try once again. If she doesn't succeed, I'll have nothing to reproach myself for.

My dear sister in Le Mans is still doing reasonably well. She's much better than she was last winter, and we don't understand that

---

272 Sister Marie Lataste (1822-1847), a French religious of the Congregation of the Sacred Heart. Zélie is referring to a vague prophecy made by Sister Marie Lataste referring to restoring the pope to his rightful authority and ridding the Vatican of its enemies.
273 See footnote in CF 69.

at all. I've gotten the idea that God is leaving her with me so she can transform my Léonie, because she's the only person who has any influence over her. Also, when we ask my poor little girl what she wants to be when she grows up, her answer is always the same, "Me, I'll be a nun at the Visitation Monastery, with my aunt." God willing, this will be so, but it's too beautiful, and I don't dare hope for it.

As for the two oldest girls, here are their thoughts: Marie doesn't want to hear a word about the convent, and she wants to remain an old maid. Pauline wants neither the convent, nor marriage, nor to remain an old maid – and I don't know how she'll be able to manage that!

It seems that your little Jeanne is fearless, according to what Monsieur Maudelonde told me, and that she wants to be the best at everything, at all costs? If this continues, with her intelligence you'll make her famous....

CF 112   To her daughters, Marie and Pauline
November 30, 1873

My dear little girls,

Mademoiselle Pauline[274] isn't going to Le Mans, so I had to trust Monsieur Vital with the little package. I wouldn't have done so if it weren't the ball of cotton for the hat to be crocheted. This famous ball of cotton has given me enough trouble! It would have been much better for you to have bought it in Le Mans the day you went out with Mademoiselle Pauline. You would have found some just as easily as in Alençon, and it would have been no more expensive and perhaps less. I hope this time it will be fine enough; it's the best there is.

I don't know if Léonie will be able to enter the Visitation the first of the year. She has eczema and it's still spreading. Your aunt has to tell me if I have to wait until she's recovered.

I saw Thérèse Thursday despite the bad weather, and she behaved better than the last time. However Louise wasn't very happy. The little one neither wanted to look at her nor go to her, and I was very embarrassed. Workers were coming to see me the entire time, and I gave her to them one after the other. She wanted to go to them, even

---

[274] Romet.

more willingly than to me, and she kissed them several times. Country women dressed like her wet nurse, this is the world she needs.

Madame T arrived while one of the workers was holding her. As soon as I saw her, I said to her, "Let's see if the baby wants to go to you." Very surprised, she replied, "Why not? Oh well, let's try!..." She held out her arms to the little one, but Thérèse hid herself while letting out a cry as if she'd been burned. She didn't even want Madame T looking at her. We had a good laugh over this. In short, she's afraid of people who are fashionably dressed!

I'm hoping she'll be walking on her own in five or six weeks. All we have to do is place her standing near a chair, and she holds onto it very well and never falls. She takes her little precautions against falling and seems very intelligent. I believe she'll be good-natured; she smiles continually and has a predestined expression.

And now I must tell you something else, although the end of the story isn't very nice and testifies to a very bad attitude among the people.

So, recently something peculiar happened to a woman whose carriage was parked across from our house in front of the Prefecture. The coachman was dressed in magnificent livery, completely trimmed with fur. A badly dressed man carrying a cloth bag in his hand happened to be passing by. He stopped a moment to look at the coachman, then the woman in the coach. He headed for the open door of the coach, untied his bag and emptied the contents onto the woman's lap.

Immediately, she began to let out terrible screams. The coachman quickly came to help her, and passersby came running. They saw this woman doubled over in a panic and, on top of her, about twenty frogs. She even had them on her head. In other words, she was covered with them!

The malicious man watched her struggle. When the police commissioner came and asked him why he would do such a thing, he said calmly, "I just caught these frogs to sell, but seeing this 'aristocrat' with her coachman all covered in fur, I preferred to give her a good fright rather than sell my frogs." They took him to jail, and he certainly deserved it!

I'm sure you're going to say, "If anyone did such a thing to Mama, she would die!" That could very well be because you know my irrational fear of frogs!

I'm expecting a letter from you this week. I hope it will be a good one, that is to say it will bring me good news. I'm counting on you both to receive Communion on December 8, the Feast of the Immaculate Conception. Don't forget to pray for Léonie.

Soon we'll only have four weeks until the January vacation, so be happy and try to make the best of the little time you have left. On Thursday your father said he's looking forward to bringing you home from school. But he cares less about bringing you back to school because he doesn't like to see you cry.

Little Thérèse won't come back until New Year's Day, but she'll definitely come that day because of you.

CF 113   To her brother and sister-in-law
                                                      December 13, 1873

Today you're going to receive a little package containing the New Year's gifts for Jeanne and Marie. I'm sending Jeanne a purse for her watch and change, an accordion, and a book entitled *Les petites filles modèles*[275] by Madame de Ségur. For Marie, two boxes of toys that weren't worth sending! and a book of ABCs.

A week ago I was just about to write you to ask what gifts you

---

[275] *The Model Little Girls* by the Countess Sophie de Ségur, née Rostopchine (1799-1874), a French writer of children's books whose books were often read in the Martin home. *The Model Little Girls* was the first part of a trilogy of novels for children written by Countess de Ségur in 1858 and 1859. Her goal was to "educate and entertain children at the same time." Her wish was to promote and foster values in the lives of children. In the novel entitled, *The Model Little Girls*, Ségur presents four little girls: Camille and Madeleine de Fleurville and their friend Marguerite Rosbourg who are the model good girls. In Chapter 7, Sophie Fichini is presented as a foil to the three good girls. She is constantly being reprimanded and beaten by her stepmother. Sophie is an anxious and nervous child, often angry and selfish and, at times, dishonest. She continually acts out, and she struggles to correct her faults. The "model children" try to model patience and kindness; however, they find her difficult to be with. The story gives the young reader an opportunity to think about good and evil, good and bad intentions, and the alternative motivations for moral judgments. The author also focuses on the abuse Sophie sustained (a subject that was close to the author, since she also was a victim of child abuse). Claire-Lise Malarte Feldman, "La Comtesse de Ségur, A Witness of Her Time," *Children's Literature Association Quarterly*, Vol. 20, No 3, Fall 1995, The Johns Hopkins University Press, pp. 135-139. Of interest, this book was in the Martin house and read by the children, at the same time Léonie was being abused and victimized by the servant, Louise Marais. One notes that the character of Sophie and Léonie Martin, both children who were abused, manifest similar symptoms of the abused child syndrome.

would suggest for your children, but I thought you wouldn't want to tell me. And yet, among family, one shouldn't stand on ceremony, and I assure you that you'd make me happy if you didn't do so from now on. As for me, I don't stand on ceremony, and I'm going to tell you frankly what I want.

Céline would like a little carriage for her doll, that is, a little basket on wheels that one pushes in front of oneself. I promised her that her godmother would send her one, and every day she asks me if tomorrow is New Year's Day! So you would fill her with joy by giving her the toy of her dreams. For Thérèse, she's still with the wet nurse, so let's wait for next year.

As for Léonie, she's entering the school at the Visitation Monastery in January. Don't send her stationary or a workbox because she has all that, it would be a waste of money. Send her only a book on piety, either an *Imitation*[276] or a *Manuel du Chrétien.*[277]

If you want to satisfy Pauline's wishes, give her an *Imitation* as well, but with prayers and practices for each chapter. Above all, the books shouldn't be valuable. It would be as if they had received nothing because they wouldn't use them until they're more careful.

Léonie wears out a Catechism in a month, without knowing anything at the end!

Marie is out of favor, and if you send her any New Year's gifts you'll make me very unhappy. I'm counting on your kindness not to want to upset me.

I have nothing new to tell you except that the Count de Curial's château burned down the day before yesterday in the middle of the night. It was impossible to put out the fire and it's completely destroyed. One more thing – the newspaper *Le Progrès,* in Alençon, is being threatened with suspension, and for the moment it's forbidden to be sold in public places. That's not going to suit poor P who's not too rich as it is!

Also, my little Thérèse is almost walking on her own. She still only has two teeth, and she's very cheerful and very cute.

I finish by wishing you a good year-end and that you're satisfied

---

[276] *The Imitation of Christ* by Thomas à Kempis (1380-1471), a German monk and mystic.
[277] *A Christian Manual.*

with your inventory and that next year will be happier for you than this one was.

My husband asks that I give you all his best wishes.

1874

CF 114 To her brother and sister-in-law
January 11, 1874

...Last Monday I took the children back to the Visitation Monastery. Léonie was delighted to go. If she likes it there and they're able to educate her, I'll let her be a boarding student for a good many years.

There's a rumor in Alençon that grave events will take place next month. I don't believe any of these threats. I'm receiving letters from all over. The big merchants in Paris are begging me to make Alençon lace. I've never seen anything like it! They're not even worried about the work being well made, it's unbelievable!

Yesterday I saw one of the biggest shopkeepers in the capital. My husband asked him if foreigners were the reason luxury shops were doing so well. He said it was France alone and, since the war, luxury had become bigger than ever!

But how can I want to run a business like this when I have to pull the work out of the workers and take care of my children? It's too much. With all my heart I want this to change and very quickly. I'd prefer to be less rich and have a little rest.

My little Thérèse has been walking on her own since Thursday. She's as gentle and cute as a little angel. Already we see that she has a delightful nature, and she has such a sweet smile. I'm longing to have her home with us.

I received a letter from our cousin Alphonsine[278] who asked me to send you this funeral card. I believe you'd said that her sister had

---

[278] Alphonsine Macé, a first cousin of Zélie and Isidore on their mother's side. Her sister, Constance, a religious, was born June 10, 1846 and had died September 8, 1873 in Garches. She had another sister, Mother Marguerite, who was the Superior General of the Auxiliary Sisters of the Immaculate Conception. She died in Paris on January 14, 1927.

died and that she'd had some extraordinary honors at her funeral. The mayor approved three thousand francs to erect a monument. It seems she was very revered, and she did a lot of good. She taught little children and cared for the sick with a remarkable devotion.

CF 115   To her daughters Marie and Pauline
March 1874

I saw the wet nurse's husband today. He told me Thérèse is coming on Thursday, and now I'd like to have her with me right now. I already have a sky-blue dress in mind for her, with little blue shoes, a blue belt and a pretty white coat. It will be charming. I'm already rejoicing in dressing this little doll. I wouldn't be so happy if it needed thirteen meters of fabric like it would for Marie!

I'll write you again on Sunday to give you news about Thérèse. Mademoiselle Pauline is going to Le Mans on Monday, and she'll bring you my letter. I would like her not to take you out because it upsets me that Monsieur Vital keeps you out until eight o'clock at night. You must tell him that your aunt doesn't want you staying out so late, and she recommends you return by two o'clock. Truly, one hardly ever sees friends like this. In all my life I've rarely met such good people.

CF 116   To her brother
March 29, 1874[279]

Your letter is very brief. I would have liked to have had more details about the death of your poor friend, Paul D. I'd taken his salvation to heart. I prayed as best as I could and diligently said a novena for him. I was hoping Saint Joseph would convert him, which is why I'm very happy that he ended up a good Christian.

I congratulate you on the letter you wrote to his father, which he read in front of me. You have a special talent. It was remarkably said! I imagined he'd been quite distraught thinking of all the suffering his unfortunate son had endured, and I was very surprised to

---
[279] Sister Marie of the Trinity's copy of this letter is dated March 19.

see him continue making the same comments against him because of sixteen thousand francs his son had spent. Constantly, he wants to be forgiven for having abandoned him and letting him die in misery. I couldn't manage to get a word in so I finished by cutting the conversation short and leaving.

He asked me many times to justify his actions to you and asked me if I'd done so. You see that I'm conscientiously carrying out my promise to justify him! I feel bad, but I've written it, I can't do anything more there.

I'm happy to see that you're well regarded in Lisieux.[280] You're going to become a man of merit, and I'm very happy about that, but what I want above all is that you become a saint. However, before wanting sanctity for others, I would very well have to take that road myself, something I'm not doing. Oh well, we must hope that will come.

I'm writing to you today because I don't know when I'll have time for it later. Little Thérèse definitely arrives Thursday.[281] She's a delightful child, very sweet and very advanced for her age.

Monday I leave to get the other children. A week ago I received bad news about the child her aunt calls "the predestined one."[282] If they send her back to me, all is lost. The only hope I have is leaving

---

[280] In 1874, in Lisieux, Isidore took part in the foundation of the Conferences of Saint Vincent de Paul and the Catholic Circle. The Conferences of St. Vincent de Paul was a lay apostolate for men founded by Frederick Ozanam in April 1833. The primary focus was to visit the homes of the poor and bring Jesus' love to them. They were concerned and committed for the needs of the poor on all levels, emotional, physical, and spiritual. They ministered in many areas, one important focus was ministering to soldiers. Both Louis Martin and Isidore Guérin were active members of the Conferences of Saint Vincent de Paul. An important part of their ministry was participating in the Nocturnal Eucharistic Adoration. Louis Martin and Isidore Guérin were important figures in both Alençon and Lisieux in the founding of, and participation in, the Nocturnal Eucharistic Adoration. Isidore also became a member of the *Conseil de fabrique*, an advisory board of prominent people, at Saint Peter's Cathedral, his parish church.

[281] Thursday, April 2, 1874, after a year's absence. Thérèse was fifteen months old.

[282] She is referring to Léonie. Her beginnings at the boarding school were satisfying enough, according to the details given by her aunt, Sister Marie-Dosithée, to Monsieur and Madame Guérin a month before, February 8: "You would like me to give you some news about Léonie [...] as you know, this poor child had many faults. The first month, I would scold her when she didn't do well, and this happened so frequently that I hardly did anything else.... I could see that I was going to make this little girl unhappy, and that's not what I wanted to do, I wanted to be God's Providence with regard to her. [...] So I began to treat her with the greatest gentleness, avoiding scolding her and telling her that I saw that she wanted to be good and to please me, that I had faith in her [...]. This had a magical effect on her, not only temporary but

her there for many years. You who are beginning to become a saint, I beg you, pray that she remains at the Visitation Monastery.

Kiss your wife and your charming little girls for me.

I forgot to tell you that Louis expressly asked that I send you his best wishes.

CF 117 — To her sister-in-law
June 1, 1874

I know you've learned from her aunt in Le Mans of my poor Léonie's departure from the boarding school.[283] As you can imagine, this upsets me greatly. That doesn't say it enough. This has caused me profound sorrow which still continues. My sister was my only hope to reform this child, and I was convinced they would keep her. But it wasn't possible, in spite of their best good will, or else they would have had to separate her from the other children. As soon as she found herself in their company, she couldn't control herself and displayed a lack of discipline without equal.

Finally, I believe that only a miracle could change her nature. It's true, I don't deserve a miracle, and yet I hope against all hope. The more I see her being difficult, the more I convince myself that God will not permit her to remain that way. I'll pray so much that He'll let Himself be swayed. At the age of eighteen months she was cured of an illness that could have killed her. Why would God have

---

long lasting, because it's reasonable and I find her quite gentle [...]. She comes to me with innocence to tell me her misdeeds and I told her that I wanted it this way. She's very obedient [...]. I hope God will bless our efforts and that she'll become very good, because all is not yet done, and it will still be necessary, more than once, to season the gentleness with firmness."

[283] Léonie, eleven years old, returned permanently to Alençon on Easter Monday, April 6. Sister Marie-Dosithée wrote the following to Monsieur and Madame Guérin on April 5, 1874: "I'm expecting Zélie tomorrow. This is not going to be a happy visit, I assure you, because she has to take her poor Léonie home with her. What can one do? What a cross! How I pity my poor dear sister! How I would like to be able to help her, but I can do nothing, nothing at all. Nevertheless I hope in the Lord, yes, and with all my strength, I have such great trust in Him...." On Friday, April 10, her aunt, Sister Marie-Dosithée, continued her unfinished letter: "I saw Zélie, she was quite resigned. She indeed thinks that when our children are not like the others, it's the parents' problem. But in the meantime, she doesn't know what to do so she's going to keep her at home. Her pain is great because she had so much confidence that the gentleness and kindness of the Visitation Monastery would change her daughter."

saved her from death and not plan to show her mercy?

I would have liked to take her on the pilgrimage to Paray-le-Monial, which leaves June 25, because it was through the intercession of Blessed Margaret Mary[284] that she was cured before, but I can't go away at that time. On the other hand, I'm intending to take her, every year, to Notre-Dame de Séez[285] on the Feast of the Immaculate Conception.

I would lose my mind over it, but, thank God, I'm consoled by other things. Marie and Pauline are as well as possible. Céline and Thérèse show a lot of promise. There's only one thing that worries me about Céline; she's terribly thin. She's growing a lot. I'm always afraid she'll become like my little Hélène.

As for my big Thérèse, it's not the same. I've never had[286] such a strong child, except for the first. She seems very intelligent. I'm very happy to have her, and I think she'll be the last. She'll be beautiful, she's already graceful. I love her little mouth, which the wet nurse used to tell me was "as big as an eye!"

I hug you with all my heart, as well as my brother.

Your affectionate sister,
Z. Martin

CF 118

To her sister-in-law
June 24, 1874

I received your letter a little too late, just a half-hour before Monsieur Maudelonde arrived, and this bothered me because I was alone. The maid and the children were at the funeral of a fifteen-year-old girl, a friend of my eldest daughter. My husband was also out. He left this morning to go fishing and won't return until about eight o'clock this evening. If I'd had your letter yesterday, he would have stayed, naturally.

I have no big news to report. Everything is going well enough at home. The day before yesterday I received a letter from the Visitation Monastery. I believe Marie is going to become a "Child of Mary" on

---

[284] See footnote in CF 14.
[285] See footnote in CF 12.
[286] Paragraph preserved from the original letter.

July 2. There are only three students in the boarding school who will have achieved this privilege by then.

Pauline writes me that a Jesuit priest is giving a sermon every evening at eight o'clock during the month of the Sacred Heart. She says it's so beautiful, so beautiful, that of course, a sinner she has in mind would convert if he attended it. "It would be impossible otherwise!"

Céline is constantly asking me when you're coming, and I tell her, "During the month of August." She responds, "How many days is that? That's too long! The days won't end so the month of August can arrive."

Thérèse is beginning to say everything. She's becoming cuter and cuter, but that's not a little problem, I assure you, because she's continually at my side, and it's difficult for me to work. So to make up for lost time, I work on my lace until ten o'clock at night and wake up at five o'clock in the morning. I still have to get up once or twice for the little one. Oh well, the more trouble I have the better I am!

Do you remember Madame Leconte, who dined with us during your last visit to Alençon? She died May 3. I'd received her last letter nine days before, which included four closely written pages. I loved this woman almost like a sister, so I felt her loss very much.

She was in Béziers[287] with her son and was quickly carried off by peritonitis.[288] But if you knew how I learned of her death! Imagine I see her son arrive at the house at eight o'clock in the morning. I was surprised and asked him right away for news about his mother. He answered without beating around the bush, "She's at the station, in a coffin." I was dumbfounded. I couldn't speak any more, nor could I believe what he was saying....

I'm giving you a lot of details about someone you don't know, but she's constantly in my thoughts, and I can't help speaking to you about her.

I have to finish my letter because I have an incredible amount of work to do. I'm very calm at the moment. The children went with

---

[287] Béziers is 826 kilometers (513 miles) south of Alençon, located in the southwestern part of France about 10 kilometers (6.2 miles) from the Mediterranean Sea.

[288] An inflammation of the membrane that lines the abdomen.

the maid to pick some strawberries at the Pavilion[289] where we have a lot of them. Isn't it a pity that we're so far away from you! We could supply you with them for the season.

I hug you all with all my heart.

Your loving sister,
Z. Martin

To her daughters Marie and Pauline
June 25, 1874

My dear little girls,

I received your letters, and they made me very happy. I hope Marie will be accepted as a "Child of Mary" on July 2. You have to write and tell me about it as soon as you know.

You'd told me that the pilgrimage to Paray-le-Monial was leaving June 25, and I thought the 25th fell on a Friday. If I'd thought it was a Thursday, I would never have thought of going because it's impossible for me to be away that day unless I'm forced to.[290] This would cause quite a bit of damage to my business. I would leave my workers with nothing to do for a week, and it would delay my orders. That would do me considerable harm.

I have sad news to tell you. Marie S. died last Monday, June 22, at two o'clock in the afternoon. She'd been getting weaker for quite a while. However, she was still going out. She left the boarding school less than three weeks ago. A week ago today she was still up and about, and she gave that up only four days ago. Quite recently she'd run after the maid to ask her for news of Marie.

This poor child didn't realize she was dying, and she didn't suffer very much. Everyone is saddened by her death because she was loved very much. The funeral took place yesterday, Wednesday, at eight o'clock. Léonie, Céline and the maid were there. There were fifty young girls dressed in white wearing a white crown and holding

---

[289] Louis Martin bought this small property with a hexagonal tower on April 24, 1857. It was on the rue des Lavoirs (currently rue du Pavillon Ste. Thérèse), in the Sénatorerie quarter, to the south of the town. After Louis' death, the Pavilion was sold on October 29, 1894 to Henri Rabinel for 2,000 francs.

[290] Thursday was the day Zélie received her workers, who brought their completed work for the week.

a lily. It was very moving and beautiful. Everyone gathered to see this funeral. Unfortunately, upon leaving the church, a heavy shower was falling, and no one was expecting it nor did they have an umbrella. The young girls in white were in a pitiful state. Their dresses and veils were stuck to them to the point that it made it difficult for them to walk. In addition, at the cemetery, they had yellow mud up to their knees. For a while I'd also wanted you to attend this ceremony dressed in white, but I didn't regret it afterwards.

There were many tears shed over this death, and several people let out cries of pain. However, the bitterest tears were those of her poor mother, who had no comfort other than this child. She's not happy with her husband, and her son just enlisted. I pity her with all my heart. Yes, truly, this death saddened me.

The child received the last rites Sunday afternoon. The next morning she didn't recognize anyone anymore. The doctors understood nothing about this illness. I urge you to pray for her a lot because I believe she needs it. This was a good girl, but she was, like the others, by no means perfect, and she didn't have time to prepare for death, which she didn't see coming.

I remember the first time we met her. It was in a field across from the cemetery. Marie was one year old and was there picking daisies with her, who was four months older. I carefully watched to see which one was the prettiest and most advanced of the two, but there was never a big difference. Marie S. was the first in her class. She learned English, German and, in short, a lot of subjects.

Your father just installed a swing. Céline is filled with incomparable joy, but you should see the little one use the swing; it would make you laugh. She holds on like a big girl, and there's no danger of her letting go of the rope. Then, when it's not going high enough, she cries out. We attach her in front with another rope, and in spite of this, I'm uneasy when I see her perched on it.

Something strange happened to me recently with the little one. I'm used to going to the five-thirty Mass.[291] In the beginning I didn't

---

[291] The social classes socialized and functioned mainly within their own class. Mingling of the social classes was not the norm. Thus, attendance at the 5:30 a.m. Mass, which was the worker's Mass, was an extraordinary Christian witness of love and acceptance on the part of Louis and Zélie Martin. They saw the face of Christ in every person.

dare leave her, but seeing that she never woke up, I ended up deciding to leave her alone. I laid her in my bed and moved the crib so close to it that it was impossible for her to fall.

One day, I forgot to move the crib. When I got home I saw the little one was no longer in my bed. At the same moment, I heard a cry. I looked, and I saw her seated on a chair that was close to the head of my bed. Her little head was on the bolster, and there she was sleeping restlessly because she was uncomfortable.

I couldn't understand how she fell seated onto this chair, since she'd been in the bed. I thanked God that nothing happened to her. It's truly providential. She should have rolled onto the floor. Her good angel was watching over her, and the souls in Purgatory protected her. I say a prayer to them every day for this little one. So that's how I explain it... explain it as you'd like!...

Today I learned there will be a pilgrimage from the Diocese of Séez to Paray-le-Monial. It should leave Alençon on Monday, July 13. I've almost made up my mind to go. Léonie doesn't know how to express her joy over the trip because we're going on the train!

Here's the little baby who's coming to stroke my face with her little hand and kiss me. This poor little one doesn't want to leave me, she's continually with me. She loves to go in the garden, but if I'm not there she doesn't want to stay and cries until they bring her back to me....[292] I'm very happy to see that she loves me so much, but sometimes it's troublesome!

I have to finish my letter because today's not Sunday, and I use my time sparingly when I'm working. Give your aunt a big hug for me, and I kiss both of you with all my heart.[293]

---

[292] The passage "Your father just installed... until they bring her back to me" is quoted by Thérèse in *Story of a Soul*, tr. John Clarke, OCD, pp. 17-18.

[293] Following is the version of Sister Marie of the Trinity's copy published in *Vie Thérésienne*, No. 88, 1982, pp. 317-318:

"June 25 – To Marie and Pauline. Have I told you that your father installed a swing in our little garden near the shed? Céline is filled with incomparable joy, but you should see little Thérèse use the swing; it would make you laugh. She holds on like a big girl and there's no danger of her letting go of the rope. Then, when it's not going high enough, she cries out. We attach her in front with another rope to prevent her from falling and in spite of this I'm uneasy when I see her perched on it. Something peculiar happened to me recently with the little one. I'm used to going to the five-thirty Mass every day. At first I didn't dare leave her alone, but seeing that she never woke up, I ended up deciding to leave her. I laid her in my bed and moved the crib so close to it that it was impossible for her to fall. One day, I forgot to move the crib. I arrived home

To her sister-in-law
July 24, 1874

I'm very pleased that you've set the date of your trip to Alençon for August 15. That will give us one more day to spend together. Don't worry about causing me any problems. It's not a problem for me, but a great pleasure. I don't allow myself much recreation, and I can certainly sacrifice a few days a year.

I'm delighted that all our little girls will be reunited. They have to get to know each other. Tell Jeanne we've made her a pretty little garden very near the one she had in the past, which doesn't exist anymore because we put a stone bench in its place.

The children's vacation starts August 3. How eagerly they'll look forward to your visit once they know you're coming! They wrote me two days ago. Pauline tells me she'll probably have only two prizes, and she's very afraid I'll be sad. She advises me not to be because she worked as hard as she could. This is quite true because she's the most studious in her class and among the top students, although she's the youngest.

Marie also tells me she's not counting on having many prizes, and that the teachers are in a very awkward position because there are four or five students equally as learned. Pauline is studying drawing and making remarkable progress. The nuns assured me she had an amazing aptitude, not for one thing but for everything in general.

I'm very satisfied with my two oldest daughters, and, on the other hand, I'm deeply saddened to see Léonie as she is. Sometimes I have hope, but often I lose heart. However, my sister told me that she's convinced Léonie will become a saint.

---

and didn't find little Thérèse anymore. At the same moment, I heard a cry, I looked, and I saw her seated on a chair that was near the bed. Her head was resting on the bolster, and there she was sleeping restlessly because she was uncomfortable. I couldn't understand how she fell seated onto this chair. I thanked God to see that nothing had happened to her. It's truly providential; she should have rolled onto the floor. Her good angel was watching over her, and the souls in Purgatory, to whom I say a prayer every day because of her, protected her. So that's how I explain it... explain it as you'd like!... Here is the little baby who's coming to kiss me and stroke my face with her little hand. I see that she's interested; she needs a "*pécam*," that is, a pin. This poor little one doesn't want to leave me; she's continually with me. She loves to go in the garden, but if I'm not there she doesn't want to stay and cries until they bring her back to me.... I'm very happy to see she has so much affection for me, but sometimes it's troublesome!"

She's going to take lessons in the afternoon at the home of two elderly women (former nuns) who taught in the past and can cope better. I'm happy to have found them, but it's painful to have to go there because she'd be much better off with her sisters.

Soon we'll have the happiness of seeing each other. I hope the political situation doesn't prevent us, neither this year nor the next. I've never had such peace of mind in this respect. I don't concern myself with any events outside of my little Thérèse! I cared about the events too much, and I'm weary to the point that nothing moves me anymore. I've heard too much advice of all kinds, and I finally noticed that nothing turned out the way they thought or said it would.

CF 121   To her brother and sister-in-law
                                                      August 9, 1874

...As we agreed, I'm expecting you Friday evening. Monday I went to pick up my daughters in Le Mans. Marie was nominated eighteen times and received nine beautiful prizes. Pauline was nominated thirteen times and received four first prizes. She's making remarkable progress in drawing. They told me she was an artist and if she was encouraged, she'd go far.

My little Thérèse has been very sick this week. It's true that it was only her teeth, but what a state she was in! Her mouth was a pitiful sight and I was worried about her tongue. It was swollen and so full of big sores that she could no longer take anything, and it was impossible to make her drink. I saw the doctor, who told me to force her to take some milk all the same. It's impossible to tell you the difficulties I had. Day and night, I had to be with her, and she was suffering horribly; this lasted a week. She's much better and is beginning to eat a little baby cereal, but she's very weak and does nothing but sleep. We're very fortunate that this didn't happen during your stay here because we wouldn't have had much pleasure!

During Easter vacation Marie said to me, "Mama, do you think I'll have any more little sisters? That makes me very sad because we're so happy when we have little children."

But this time, she has enough of them! Those poor little girls had a very distressing week; they didn't have a moment's rest. Consequently, Marie is very afraid of having more little sisters and told me that she'll never get married because it's a source of too much trouble!

CF 122 To her sister-in-law
September 13, 1874

...You tell me, my dear sister, that you found your trip to Alençon delightful. I'm very flattered because you didn't find it delightful because of the entertainment I provided, but because of the deep friendship we feel for each other that made us enjoy the time we spent together.

As for me, I was very happy during this too short a time, and I have pleasant memories of it. I was sorry you didn't want to go on the outing I suggested. I would have been delighted to go with you. We went on that outing two weeks ago. We rented a big carriage that could easily hold nine people and went as far as Saint-Léonard-des-Bois, eight leagues[294] from Alençon. To tell you the truth, I hardly enjoyed it, and neither did the children, because of an incident that took place.

The good Sisters who give lessons to Léonie knew about our outing, and they were quick to ask us for a seat. We had to put on a brave face. Marie cried in bitter disappointment, and nothing could cheer her up. It was, in fact, very annoying to have two strangers with us who, after all, we don't like very much.

I must say, I have no luck. Every time I suggest an outing a setback occurs. I notice this often. So I've renounced every kind of recreation, and I don't want to hear another word about it. The most beautiful outing I'd ever been on was to Trouville. How did it end? Just as I was beginning to enjoy myself, I received a telegram that made us disrupt all our plans. I'm sure if I returned there, the sea would swallow me up. So I said good-bye to Trouville, good-bye wholeheartedly, we only see misfortune there!

I would never ask for anything for the small favor you mentioned

---

[294] 19.4 miles or 31 kilometers (one French league equaled 2.422 miles). In actuality, St. Léonard-des-Bois is approximately 20 kilometers (12.4 miles) southwest of Alençon.

regarding Madame Maudelonde's lace. I'd taken it with the intention of mending it myself, but I couldn't find the time and gave it to a worker, and that cost very little.

It's time for me to finish my letter. I'm angry because the entire time I was writing to you I was being interrupted by foreigners wishing to see Alençon lace. It's always like this. Yesterday, a group of English people came who supposedly wanted to buy some. I showed them a piece of lace that I was in the process of assembling, and they asked for one and a half meters. I told them it cost a hundred and fifty francs per meter. Just as I was about to cut it, they presented me with seven francs and fifty centimes because they'd understood five francs per meter! They knew hardly any French. Oh well, I think these inconveniences will end with the holidays.

CF 123

To her sister-in-law
October 11, 1874

Your letter of yesterday, while making me happy, saddened me. I'm constantly thinking of poor little Marguerite Maudelonde.[295] However, according to what you told me, there's no cause for alarm because usually a mucus fever isn't dangerous. And yet I understand your anxiety! She's so perfect, this little one. Children like her are called to heaven sooner than others. But we must hope God will let her perfect herself even more for the happiness of her parents and the edification of everyone. I'd be very pleased to hear more about her.

What you tell me about Jeanne surprises me. I thought she was so reasonable during her stay in Alençon. My sister was talking to me about her last Wednesday when I brought the children back to school. She finds her charming and well brought up. She was amazed to see her remain so well-behaved, as calm as a grown up in her chair. She said to me, "She thinks like an angel." In short, she's delighted with your entire family. "My brother is better than me, his wife is sweet, and his children are jewels." One wouldn't give me such flattering compliments (it's true I hardly deserve them!)

---

[295] Marguerite Maudelonde, seven and a half years old. See footnotes in CF 81 and CF 103. (See the Biographical Guide of Proper Names in the Appendix.)

I have peace of mind today. The maid left yesterday to go to her parents' house. For several days she's had a recurrence of pain and crippling in her limbs, and with that, it's been impossible to find someone to replace her. The person I was expecting got sick, and the home nursing Sister[296] could only come one night. My God, what a sad vacation!

I was so tired it was my turn to get sick. The fever lasted three or four days, and I had a sore throat. However, I had to stay up for part of the nights to take care of the maid. I took on a cleaning woman, but I had even more difficulty. If Louise continues to have such health problems, I've decided to hire another servant. I'll keep her since she wants to stay, but I won't pay her while I'm taking care of her.

Céline is still not going to the boarding school. I'm planning to enroll her in school with the Sisters of the Adoration[297] as a day student around Easter. But I want her to spend this winter at home. It would be too tiring to take her so far twice a day, especially with a maid who can't even walk. And with that, we have to bring Léonie to the good Sisters' house and then go and bring her home. She was in the advanced catechism class today, and she'll probably make her First Communion next June.

CF 124	To her sister-in-law
	November 8, 1874

I'm very happy to learn that little Marguerite is nearly recovered because, in spite of everything, I was very afraid for her. This type of fever is currently all over Alençon. A twelve-year old girl just died of it; she was the sole consolation of her recently widowed mother.

This poor woman lived only for her daughter. She was the most delightful child one could ever see. She was as good as she was beautiful and had converted her mother, who was not practicing her

---

[296] See footnote in CF 92.
[297] The School of the Religious of the Sacred Hearts of Jesus and Mary, also known as the Sisters of Adoration. When Zélie and her sister Élise moved to Alençon, they were enrolled in this school. Prior to that, while living in Saint-Denis-sur-Sarthon, they were enrolled in school in the Church of Saint-Denis-sur-Sarthon, where they were taught Catechism and received Holy Communion.

faith. During her illness she said she was very happy to die and God would not cure her. Finally, she died like a saint. It seems to me that if I had a child like that I would be happy, even though God would take her from me.

And Jeanne? How is she doing in school? Is her teacher cured? Or have you put her in another boarding school? It's very difficult for you to have little ones at home, not having a garden. What a shame to have them so far away from each other; they could come and play with Céline. This one has an excellent character and will be easy to correct, but she's too spoiled by the maid. However, I worked it out, and things are going better.

Since I'm speaking of the maid, I'll tell you she's completely cured, beyond what I was expecting. She feels better than before her illness and is now doing all her work. As in the past, I help her with it. Besides, one person wouldn't be enough to take care of our home, but I prefer to inconvenience myself a little rather than have two servants who would get in my way more than help me.[298]

My little Thérèse is becoming cuter and cuter. She babbles from morning 'til night. She sings us little songs, but you have to be used to hearing her to understand them. She's very intelligent and says her prayers like a little angel; they're perfect!

I'm expecting news from my two oldest girls, and tomorrow will be two weeks since I received any. They were still doing very well, and their aunt was happy with them, although she was far from finding them perfect.

---

[298] In Céline's biographical reflections of her mother, she notes: "There are many witnesses to testify that mother was activity personified. She was constantly busy with her lace-making, house-keeping, working for her children, and her correspondence. Father endeavored as far as he could to relieve her, persuading her to accept helpers. But she never thought of herself – she forgot herself entirely. Her former housemaid, Louise, wrote to the Carmel many long years afterward: 'How many details have come to my mind since her death! For herself, anything was good enough, but for others, it was quite the reverse!' I myself can still remember her distinctly, preparing every morning an excellent breakfast for all in the house; whereas she was satisfied to snatch a little soup for herself which she swallowed hastily, as she was going about." Céline Martin (Sister Geneviève of the Holy Face), *The Mother of the Little Flower,* p. 30.

You ask me what I want as New Year's gifts for my children. I'll tell you on the condition that you do the same for me regarding your children.

For Thérèse, I want a Noah's Ark because this will amuse her better than anything and would do me a great service. She doesn't go to bed before eight o'clock. I don't know what to do with her, she prevents me from working. However, she's very cute, and she doesn't need much to pass the time.

For Céline, I would like a set of dishes made of metal. She has two of them in porcelain and can't play with them because the little one would break them all. They could play together with the ones you send without any danger of breaking them.

As for Léonie, I won't ask you for any toys because she doesn't play with them anymore, she works on her studies. You could give her a rosary for her First Communion, which she'll make on the Feast of the Holy Trinity. She knows her catechism perfectly and answers the questions better than I would have believed. If she didn't become flustered, she would be one of the first in her class. Last Tuesday[299] I took her on a pilgrimage to the Church of the Immaculate Conception in Séez[300] to obtain the grace to make a good First Holy Communion.

---

[299] Tuesday, December 8, 1874.

[300] In 1819, the Diocese of Séez built a Minor Seminary in Sées (formerly known as Séez) dedicated to the Blessed Mother for the young men of the region who were known for the fervor of their faith. A well-known and much frequented Marian pilgrimage site in France, the Basilica of the Immaculate Conception was built as a chapel for this Minor Seminary. This was in response to the Dogma of the Immaculate Conception that had been proclaimed by Pope Pius IX in 1854. As a result, a letter of appeal was sent to all the priests, religious and Catholic teachers of France asking for contributions to finance the construction of this new chapel. This drive was a huge success. To support their decision to build the first church to Our Lady of the Immaculate Conception in France, the Bishop looked to the apparitions that took place in Lourdes between February 11 and July 16, 1858. On March 25, 1858, the apparition revealed her identity saying, "I am the Immaculate Conception." On May 7, 1872, the chapel was consecrated before an immense crowd by Bishop Rousselet. On June 12, 1894, Pope Leo XIII authorized the crowning of the statue of Our Lady that stills stands above the main altar in the chapel. On June 11, 1895, approximately 30,000 people assembled to celebrate the event by offering Our Lady a gold crown with precious stones that was given by the people of the whole region. In 1902, Pope Leo XIII designated the chapel a Minor Basilica. Countless healings and answered prayers have been reported over the years.

For Marie and Pauline, it would upset me if you sent them something. There's nothing to give them, absolutely nothing; they have everything. I beg you, think only of the two little girls. For them, it gives me great pleasure because children their age are so happy that day.

I must finish because it's very late. I had many letters to write, first to the children in Le Mans, then to other people, and, since today is Sunday, I would very much like to go to bed before midnight because I'll be staying up late all week when I'm so harried. However, I give my work of assembling the lace to outside workers as much as I can, but if you only knew how difficult it is to have it done properly. I'm forced to redo part of the work done by the workers, and that's why I'm staying up so late.

CF 126

To her sister-in-law
December 24, 1874

Yesterday I received the box containing all the beautiful and good things you told me about. Truly, you deserve to be scolded. What were you thinking! You sent New Year's gifts for five children and all expensive things. And still, you weren't satisfied with this; you sent me something as well. This isn't sensible.

Oh well, now that I've scolded you, I have to thank you. I'll begin by telling you that you're too good to us, and, despite my being upset, I'm very grateful and love you with all my heart.

At least you made Thérèse and Céline very happy. When their father unpacked the toys, I would especially have liked you to see Thérèse! We said to her, "There are beautiful toys inside there that your aunt in Lisieux sent you." She clapped her hands. I leaned on the box to help my husband undo it. She let out little anxious cries while saying to me, "Mama, you're going to break my beautiful toys!" She pulled me by my dress to make me stop. But when she saw her pretty little house, she remained silent for a moment; she's a child who gets very worked up.

Céline was also delighted. She'll play with her set of building blocks a lot, but she's not happy when her little sister damages her toys, which makes her pick them up. She takes care of her belongings as few children do and prefers not to use them rather than risk having them broken. Léonie is also extremely pleased with her rosary, which is very beautiful.

Since you wanted to give New Year's gifts to Marie and Pauline, you couldn't have chosen better gifts to make them happy. So many times they've told me they would like a travel bag and that all their companions have one except for them. I let them say it, but because I only buy things that are necessary, and, as they could do without them, I didn't consider it appropriate to satisfy them. But now I see their happiness. As for your New Year's gift to me, I thank you a thousand times, although I sincerely regret your having made this expense. It would have been much better to keep this beautiful turkey for yourselves, since there are so many of you.

Forgive me for saying this, but I don't want you to do it again next year. We can find turkeys in Alençon as easily as geese since this is a land of plenty, and there's everything here. For your trouble in having done this, I'm sending you two geese. I'm sorry you won't receive them early enough to put them on the spit for Christmas Day, but when it snows, the trains are late.

I finish by wishing you a good inventory, and I'd very much like to hear comforting news about this.

I kiss you all with love.

Your loving and devoted sister,
Z. Martin[301]

1875

CF•127

To her sister-in-law
January 13, 1875

I've gone such a long time without answering your letter, but you are so good you'll forgive me for it. I should have done it last Sunday, and still I put your letter aside to write to others whom I love much less than you, but who would have been less indulgent.

I begin by thanking you for your New Year's wishes and asking

---

[301] Two lines and the signature are preserved from the original letter.

you to accept mine, which are certainly as sincere. I strongly hope God will make you prosper one day. If the trial lasts a little longer, you mustn't lose heart: "He who trusts in God will never fail."

My big girls were with me for four days and it was a short visit, but we must comply with the regulations. I received news from them yesterday, and they told me that those who delayed their return to school by one day were punished very severely. They were delighted with their travel bags, which they took with them, as you can well imagine! They thank you for them a thousand times.

I'm having so many problems with my poor Léonie. You know that every day she was taking lessons in the home of two elderly retired nuns. I wasn't dissatisfied with the way they were teaching her, and then, all of a sudden, I discovered something about these so-called good Sisters[302] that absolutely prevents me from continuing to entrust Léonie to them.

Imagine that they let languish a poor eight-year-old child[303] they'd adopted, supposedly out of charity. I began to learn of this story two months ago. Before acting, I wanted to be very sure of what I suspected because it would cost me a great deal to denounce them. But last Thursday, an event made up my mind completely.

There's a big uproar here that I won't begin to tell you, but which has already caused me and will still cause me a great deal of concern and a lot of aggravation. I was able to obtain a place at The Refuge for the little girl, and I'm waiting for her mother so she'll take her there. I told the Sisters the whole truth of what I thought of them, these unfortunate hypocrites who pray, or pretend to pray, to God from morning 'til night, and I took Léonie away from them.

CF 128   To her daughters Marie and Pauline
                                                                  January 17, 1875
My dear little girls,

   I received your letters which made me very, very happy.
   I see you enjoyed yourselves a lot, much more than I did, because

---

[302] Two elderly teachers had put on a religious habit to command respect. (See CF 122.)
[303] She is referring to Armandine V. (See CF 128, 129, 145 and 146.)

I can tell you that I just went through the most disturbing two weeks of my life. You're going to ask yourselves, "So what happened that was so distressing?" And perhaps you're going to find that it's nothing when I explain to you that it's about little Armandine V. Since I have nothing new to write you about other than this, I'm going to tell you the whole story.

You know what an unshakable aversion I had to upsetting the good Sisters who are giving lessons to Léonie. It was stronger than I was, I couldn't bring myself to do it. But the Thursday after you left, I learned some things that shook me so much all my scruples vanished.

They had left Armandine without anything to eat from morning until three-thirty in the afternoon. That is to say, at noon they gave her five or six spoonfuls of soup. It's true they would have dined earlier had it not been for a visitor who'd detained them. Finally, at three-thirty they gave her a tiny piece of bread with a little fat from the cold beef stew while they themselves ate mutton. The little one begged them to at least give her a little piece of cheese, and they called her bold. So she had to content herself with her dry bread, and in such small quantity that she pleaded with them for some more, which they brutally refused. Léonie had forgotten to bring her the afternoon snack I usually prepared for this poor child.

In the evening, while going to pick up Léonie, the maid saw Armandine looking haggard and asked her, "Are you sick?" She replied, "I have a stomachache; they don't want to give me anything to eat. They gave me so little that I'm as starved as I was before."

When they told me this, I was so outraged I didn't want to take the time to have dinner. I immediately wrote to the priest in Banner, where the little one is from, to question him about Armandine's mother and if she would consent to come for her daughter and put her in The Refuge.

The next day I sent the little one two slices of bread and jam in a basket she'd forgotten at our house the other day. I had a premonition that everything was going to be exposed that day, so I told Léonie how she had to respond. My predictions came true. Armandine, for fear of being discovered, hid her basket under her apron, even though Léonie had advised her not to do it so she wouldn't look like she was hiding something. That's all it took, and the good Sisters wanted to see what she was hiding.

Finally, an hour later, I received a visit from Sister Saint-Louis.[304] My heart was pounding very strongly, but I'd decided not to show her any consideration, and I was even happy that the situation had presented itself. I told her why I sent bread to this child, and in terms the Sister probably found too strong. However, she wasn't angry; she was even laughing the entire time. She took my hands.... I offered to provide bread for the little one on the condition that they would let her eat as much as she wanted. She answered, laughing the whole time that she wouldn't promise that; and then she left, still laughing!

When the maid went to get Léonie, the scene had changed. Sister Saint-Louis was crying and playing the persecuted saint, saying that this was one more pearl in her crown. She said God had suffered a lot more, and she would return good for evil and take care of my daughter with as much love and concern as in the past....

Louise was confused. As for me, I didn't let myself be taken in because I knew more or less who I was dealing with. My intention was to remove Léonie, but I thought it would be better to send her the next day, which was Saturday, in order to have Armandine come to our house on Sunday. I thought the Sisters wouldn't dare refuse me this, and I wanted to question her in depth.

Saturday morning I went to The Refuge. Faced with such a deed, the Superior welcomed my request right away. She told me they didn't have room, but they would make a place for my protégé.

Finally, on Sunday, I had the little one with me, who had been badly beaten because of all this. Then she said to me, "You know, Madame, since you spoke to them, I eat all that I want." And she told me the foolishness of every kind that Sister Saint-Louis had rattled off against me.

I was committed. That night I wrote a beautiful letter to Sister Saint-Louis, a letter that would have moved the heart of a rock. I assure you, it was nicely phrased! I thanked her for the good care she had given my daughter, but I informed her that, given the present situation, I thought I shouldn't send her to them anymore. In addi-

---

[304] One of the women pretending to be a nun.

tion, I'd thoroughly persuaded the little one to go to The Refuge. She was looking forward to it and had promised to give her mother a warm welcome when she comes to get her.

Tuesday a woman who prepared the child's work – for Armandine worked a little on lace – went to the Sisters' home. The little one begged her to quickly come find me so that I let her mama know right away to come get her because the Sisters made her very unhappy. The next day I sent Louise and Léonie to thank the nuns and pay them. Sister Saint-Louis was just about to leave to pay me a visit. Louise said to her, "Don't go, Sister, it's possible something unpleasant will be said." She answered, "I want to go there."

She did, indeed, arrive, with a courtesy I can't describe. She assured me, while trying to cry, that if I'd thought she was a saint, she wanted to humble herself before me and free me of this notion. She went on like this for a quarter of an hour. I answered, "But, Sister, you use the language of a saint, the saints spoke no better than you do." Her face glowed because she thought she had won me over with her humility and I was going to throw myself at her feet....

I continued, "So, Sister, do you regret what you made the child endure?" Then her face took on a fierce expression, and she declared that none of my accusations were true. I answered her coolly, without getting angry, that everything I accused her of in my letter was the truth, and she left controlling her rage as well as she could.

Then I received a letter from the priest in Banner who had known these unfortunate people. He told me they had never been nuns, they'd worn the habit without any right to do so, and he'd had them thrown out of his parish. He said he wasn't surprised by what had taken place and was going to inform Armandine's mother.

Seeing that she wasn't able to convince me by her humility, Sister Saint-Louis sent Mademoiselle E to see me on Thursday. Mademoiselle E is a good person taken in by beautiful speeches and who, in spite of all that the child had revealed, didn't want to believe me.

I told her nothing would be able to shake my conviction, and I wouldn't have gotten so involved without being sure of the facts. Then she told me the little one had confided in her that she was going to leave for The Refuge and that I had written to her mother. This revelation did not make me happy. I was afraid this young woman would take the initiative and prevent me from carrying out my plan.

Finally, from Thursday to Saturday I heard nothing. I was already anxious, and it seemed to me I would see Armandine's mother at any moment, and then what would happen? I foresaw many difficulties, but I never suspected those that awaited me!

About four o'clock in the afternoon I saw a woman come up to one of our windows that was slightly open, and she asked me if number 36 was nearby. I realized right away that she was the little one's mama. She came in and said to me, "I just left the Sisters' house. I took hold of my child and wanted to take her with me. As I reached the doorway they opened their window and shouted, 'Help! A child abductor!' A crowd gathered, and four sturdy men snatched the little one from my hands while the Sisters were spewing a flood of foolish remarks directed at you, Madame, and at me!"

Faced with this situation, I asked for Mademoiselle X, who knew everything and had offered to act as an intermediary, if necessary. She immediately went to find the Sisters to explain all the trouble they would get into by acting this way. They wanted to hear nothing of it, saying that they would go all the way to the end.

So I saw myself forced to go with your father – I, for the first time in my life – to the Police Station. The Police Chief wasn't there. They told us that they would not remove a child under these conditions, the matter would not be resolved for a while and, finally, perhaps we could see the Police Chief the next day, but it wasn't certain.

The poor mother was devastated. She's a good person who had entrusted her child to the Sisters, persuaded that by doing so, she was ensuring her happiness. The nuns had made her beautiful promises, to the point that Armandine would inherit all that they owned!

"I thought my child was very happy," she continued, "because she just wrote me that she was the happiest little girl in Alençon." Your father, hearing this, was outraged by such a deception and exclaimed, "So the other children are like Blessed Labre, who ate the cabbage cores from the garbage!"[305]

---

[305] St. Benedict Joseph Labre was born March 26, 1748, in Amettes, France and died April 16, 1783, in Rome, Italy. Since early childhood, Benedict Joseph had an intense desire to become a priest. After several unsuccessful attempts to become a Trappist monk, he eventually found his vocation as a pilgrim wandering by foot to the major shrines in France, Spain and Italy living amidst the poor and homeless while he tried

While feeling we had done our duty, he regretted, however, the child's fate that had become known to us. I didn't sleep that night, that is, I had in total two hours of nightmares. I dreamed I saw the little girl, emaciated, begging me to have pity on her, and across from her, the face of Sister Saint-Louis appeared as a diabolical vision and I woke up with a start.

So I got up early the next morning and wrote to the Police Chief to tell him this woman's story, who couldn't remain in Alençon for long because she has a small business. I was insistent that he settle the matter as soon as possible. I even added that she would live on his doorstep until she could see him, quite determined not to leave it in spite of the rain. He didn't wait long. He received her and said many complimentary things about your father.

During this time I was at High Mass. There was a sermon, but I don't know what they preached about. That's how much I was absorbed in my thoughts.

I'm sure you're bored with this long epistle. However, my children, all this is an event for me. I believe God permitted this thing to expose these unfortunate people and snatch their prey from them.

If they had succeeded in keeping the little one for a longer time, they would have taken advantage of it by getting everyone to think badly of me. Out of malice, they would say I'd wanted to rob them of their protégé for my own benefit, but the law decided in their favor. They would have believed it, and I truly had a narrow escape! Finally, thank God, I was relieved of this problem, but Léonie is still there, and what to do about it? I believe the more she goes, the more she finds it difficult to learn. I don't know what's going to become of

---

to keep the integrity of a monk outside the monastery. Humiliated, mocked, and often beaten by those who found him repulsive, he identified with the scorn that Jesus suffered during His lifetime. He slept outdoors in doorways and in fields and at times he was given food by the local monastery. Often he ate the discarded vegetables left in the garbage at the vegetable market and would pick up cabbage cores and eat them as he walked through the market next to the Church of La Madonna dei Monti in Rome. He appeared quite useless and yet the passion for Christ that consumed him was a great inspiration to those who saw him during his continuous prayer, Eucharistic Adoration and charitable works. It was said, "he was a heap of rags out of which emerged the face of Christ" and during his lifetime he was looked upon as a saint. God used his mental illness as part of his ministry to the unwanted and unloved outcasts of society. His life teaches us that God uses even our brokenness to bring us to His love. He was beatified May 20, 1860, and canonized December 8, 1883.

all this. However, if after many trials and tribulations I can succeed as I did with little Armandine, I'd be happier than if she'd always given me satisfaction.

I'd wanted to entertain you with little stories about Thérèse, but this will be for another time. She talks continuously about Marie and Pauline who are in Le Mans. Yesterday, little Thérèse fell against the table leg and cracked her forehead down to the bone. The split was a good centimeter wide, and I think it will leave a life-long scar.[306] I'm devastated over it.

Your father sends you a kiss, and I do, too.

Your loving mother.

CF 129

...Your letter made me sad. I saw my brother was upset, and that upset me, as well. I know his drug business is not doing as well as he would like. I'm very troubled by this, and yet I can't help believing that the day of prosperity will come. But in the meantime, he'll suffer and think he's working in vain. Oh well, this is the cross he must bear, and it's heavy, I understand that. Tell him to take heart. My sister is convinced he'll triumph over all obstacles and, until then, all of us will suffer because I'm carrying a small part of this cross. I would carry more if it would relieve my brother as much, but because of his kind heart, this would probably make his cross heavier.

Since I've written you, my dear sister, I've had many troubles because of these fake Sisters. As I told you, I became aware of the child's sad situation about two months ago. I moaned about it and tried to do everything I could to make it better, but I didn't succeed in calming my anxieties and my scruples. I was constantly haunted by the thought that it was in my power to take her out of that hell, and if I didn't do it, I would be guilty.

My confessor and my sister had advised me to take action, and, in spite of this, I couldn't make up my mind to do so. Finally, a situation so convincing presented itself that I immediately wrote to the

---

[306] Fortunately the scar disappeared completely.

priest at the parish where these elderly women came from.

After many comings and goings on their part to try and calm me down, and seeing that nothing would make me change my opinion, on Wednesday they began to win over the little one by buying her a lot of cake and lavishing a thousand caresses on her. This poor child, who, the day before, made me beg to free her as soon as possible, immediately changed her feelings. As you'll see, I had a hard time with this because this was such a strange story.

On Friday, at four o'clock, the priest from Banner went to the mother's home to tell her what happened. He wasn't able to do it earlier because he had to travel three leagues[307] on a country road to find her. Immediately this woman got ready and left during the night. She had to walk ten leagues[308] to get to the railroad. She traveled all night, and the next day, Saturday, she arrived in Alençon on the two o'clock train. Instead of coming to our house right away, she went to the Sisters', who insulted her in every way and even struck her. There was a great dispute. As if that were not enough, the woman had lost my address. However, having remembered that it was at number 36, she walked from house to house looking for this number because she no longer remembered the name of the street.

Finally, she arrived in front of my house and told me about the scene that had taken place. I wasn't expecting such a thing, and I saw myself in a very awkward position. It was night so I went with her to the home of the Police Chief. They told me we couldn't see him because he was on vacation. What could I do? I was upset. As for the Sisters, they went to the home of the state prosecutor, and they didn't find him.

I couldn't eat or sleep. Finally, after a night of insomnia, without having found a way to fall asleep, I got up and began to pray to Our Lady of Perpetual Help. Immediately, the idea came to me to write to the Police Commissioner. I lit my lamp and set to work.

At eighty-thirty the woman left, and my husband took responsibility for delivering my letter.

Right after reading the letter, the Commissioner approached the little girl's mother, who was waiting for him, and sent a policeman

---

[307] 7.3 miles or 11.7 kilometers (one French league equaled 2.422 miles).
[308] 24.2 miles (38.9 kilometers).

to go get the Sisters. The older one came accompanied by a spinster who lives in the same house, and they both started to slander me, each one more than the other.

The Commissioner told them to go to the Court at one o'clock with the child (and me, of course) because the Prosecutor must be the one to decide the matter. The Public Prosecutor's office was going to meet because of two prisoners who had escaped during the night.

So Louis and I left for the Public Prosecutor's office. I was very upset! Upon arriving there, they told us to go to the Police Station. Then I saw a very distinguished gentleman approaching whom I took to be the Prosecutor. It was simply the Police Commissioner. Unfortunately, I didn't know this until after the session because I would have been less intimidated.

This gentleman began by declaring to us that he'd come out of pure kindness, and he had very little time to give us. Since she's a widow, he told the mother that the Board of Guardians would have to decide if she was in a position to take back her little girl, the matter couldn't be heard as it stands now, she'd given her child voluntarily and couldn't take her back on a whim, and there was indeed a letter from the priest in Banner, but it meant nothing.

The Sisters prevailed. As for me, I was very sad seeing Armandine at their side with a haughty expression she'd never had before. They'd made her drink before bringing her (I found out afterwards) and, what's more, she was upset, and that put color in her cheeks.

One of the commissioners present even began to say, "She doesn't have the expression of a child who doesn't have enough to eat." I saw myself at the point of being accused of fraud. They could have bled all four of my limbs, and I don't think one drop of blood would have come out!

Finally, the famous judge in question had the little one go to another room and interrogated her. When she came out, she didn't dare raise her eyes to mine. I well suspected what she'd said. The old Sister terribly insulted the mother and me. I wasn't determined to defend myself, and I couldn't say a single word.

A few moments later, the so-called Prosecutor came to me and asked me to follow him. I didn't really know if this was to take me to prison, but finally, I followed him. He said some kind words to me that restored my courage and gave me the strength to explain myself. I asked him what the child had said to him. He answered that she felt very well. I asked him to make her speak in front of me, and he took us both with him to a small office.

"Monsieur," said the little one, "I'm very well. I don't want to go with my mama." I asked her, "For how long have you been very well?" "Madame, since you said everything to the Sisters." "And before that, how were you?" Then she admitted everything they had done to make her suffer.

The Commissioner, whom I still mistook for the Prosecutor, said to me, "I see that you're right, but there must be a Board of Guardians because this woman has no certificate, and you don't know her."

Finally, I returned to my seat. He said to a policeman, "Go and see if the Public Prosecutor's Office is meeting again." A moment later, the policeman returned and said yes. "Wait for me," the Commissioner said to us, "I'm going to try and finish this right away."

From that moment on I began to breathe easy, but somebody had to have difficulty breathing, and it was the Sisters' turn! They wanted to leave. Too bad! We were being guarded by three policemen, and there was no way to escape.

It was then that the oldest one began to reel off a string of abuse, and she had a fiendish expression. She who knew how to play the saint so well had thrown off her mask! I didn't answer her, nor did the mother of the little one who had been called a rascal, despicable, etc. She listened to everything with unbelievable humility, and I thought, then, of the scene of the Pharisee and the Publican. The old Sister was so irritated with me that she couldn't control herself anymore, and I don't know what she would have done to me if she had been able to reach me.

Finally, after fifteen minutes of deliberation, the Commissioner returned, saying, "We're returning the child to the appropriate person." Then he said the kindest words to me, as well as to my husband.

The good Sisters took this as an insult to them, and they were angry. He put them in their place with a politeness that reduced them to silence. Then he added in front of those assembled, "Madam, I return this little one under your protection, and since you want very much to take care of her, I will take care of her also. It's so beautiful to do good!" Finally, I can't recall much more of what he said to me, he wanted to pay me some compliments. I didn't know any more if I was dreaming, or if I was awake.

The Sisters were beside themselves and refused to return the child's clothes. The poor mother asked for her umbrella, which she had left at their house during the fight the day before. They turned her down and insulted her. Everyone there was outraged over this. The Police Commissioner exclaimed, "This isn't the first time I've seen women adopt little orphans to gain public esteem, get alms and, under the guise of charity, then make these little ones suffer."

As you see, my dear sister, my affair ended perfectly, and, I may say, in a way I never hoped for. On the contrary, in the usual course of events it would have ended in my shame and embarrassment. I was the sole accuser, and the child was on the side of the two unfortunate women.

Yesterday evening the Superior of The Refuge sent for me to ask what had become of the little one. She'd left with her mother, who seemed truly good. But she's remarried, and the priest in Banner regrets that Armandine didn't enter The Refuge. I received a letter from him today in which he calls the Sisters despicable hypocrites, and he said he's going to speak to the mother again so that her daughter comes to The Refuge. Moreover, this woman promised me that if the child didn't get used to living in her house, she would send her back to me within two weeks. But I'm very afraid she won't keep her word because she needs this little one for her business. She has a shop and is very successful.

All of this worries me a little. Oh well, if God had His hand in this affair, as I believe He did, He'll know how to settle everything for the best. This little girl is very sweet, which is why the wicked women had taken her, by promising her mother they would teach her and, later, leave her all they owned. In the meantime, as soon as Armandine moved in with them, they made a true martyr out of her. She had neither respite nor rest. She did everything; she even made their bed, put on their shoes, and dressed them. Then, like a dog, they would throw her a little piece of black bread with cold fat from the beef stew, and this was her food all week.

They'd made her learn to trace pieces of Alençon lace because she had to earn her living, and, in fact, she was earning it while public charity was giving them clothes for the child, which they never let her wear. They didn't buy her any additional clothes, while I know someone who paid a small sum every year with this purpose in mind. In short, all of this is a disgrace.

They continually beat her over nothing. And to think this innocent creature, after three or four days of good care, wanted to stay with them, and she almost made me appear to be a liar! It seems to me that if it were to happen all over again, I wouldn't have the courage to handle it.

I'm sure, my dear sister, you're bored by all these details and that they're hardly of any interest to you since you don't know these people. But for me, it's a memorable event in my life. I'll never forget it, especially the scene at the Police Station.

It's time that I end this long epistle, I've been writing a good two hours.

CF 130   To her sister-in-law
                                          March 14, 1875

I received your last letter, and you see I'm taking the time to answer it, but I have nothing new to report. I was hoping something would occur and seeing that the delay was getting longer, I decided to break the silence without having anything interesting to tell you.

We're in full-time penance. Fortunately, it will be over soon. I'm suffering so much from the fasting and abstinence! Yet it's not a very severe mortification, but I'm so tired of how my stomach feels, and especially so cowardly, that I wouldn't want to do it at all if I listened to my nature.[309]

For a week we've had two missionaries who give three sermons a day. In my opinion, one doesn't preach any better than the other. We're going to hear them anyway out of a sense of duty, and, for me at least, it's an extra penance.

---

[309] The Martins rigorously observed the fasts prescribed by the Church. They took nothing until noon and allowed themselves a light meal at night.

We're currently celebrating the Jubilee in Alençon.[310] The second procession takes place today, and, fortunately, the weather is good. Last Sunday the weather was awful. Consequently, it put me in a bad mood, and I forgot to recite the stipulated prayers. For my punishment, I had to make a tour of the city five times. I was unaware I would be bound by this practice, and that will teach me for next time. I don't know if it's the same everywhere, but here, those who don't follow the three processions have four churches to visit fifteen times.

Léonie earned her Jubilee indulgence and received absolution. She was afraid of not being prepared well enough and this attitude pleased me. I hope God, in His mercy, answers my prayers for this child, who's one of my biggest concerns.

I'm going to pick up Marie and Pauline in Le Mans on Easter Monday.[311] It's a holiday for them and for me. It's been three weeks since I've had news from them.

Céline isn't going to class anymore. I'm teaching her to read, and she's practically fluent. Also, she's beginning to write. I'm considering having her begin studying with Marie, who's leaving the boarding school this year.[312]

Little Thérèse is always well, and she looks happy and healthy. She's very intelligent and has very amusing conversations with us. She already knows how to pray to God. Every Sunday she goes to part of Vespers, and if, unfortunately, we fail to take her there, she cries inconsolably. A few weeks ago we'd taken her out for a walk on Sunday. She hadn't been to "*mette*,"[313] as she calls it. When we returned home, she let out piercing screams, saying she wanted to go to Mass. She opened the door and, in torrential rain, ran off in the direction of the church. We ran after her to make her come back, and her screams lasted a good hour.

She said to me out loud in church, "Me, I was at Mass here! I really prayed[314] to God." When her father returns home in the evening

---

310 She is referring to the Universal Jubilee Year of the Church in 1875.
311 Monday, March 29.
312 Marie was fifteen and a half years old when she left school.
313 "*Mette*" was Thérèse's childish mispronunciation of the French word "*messe*" (in English, "Mass").
314 She mispronounced the French word "*prié*" ["prayed"] as "*pridé*."

and she doesn't see him say his prayers, she asks him, "Papa, why aren't you saying your prayers? Were you at church with the ladies?" Ever since Lent began, I go to the six o'clock Mass, and she's often awake when I leave. As I'm leaving, she'll say to me, "Mama, I'm going to be very good." In fact, she doesn't move and falls back asleep.

Monsieur M arrived, and my husband went to his meeting. He was unable to have breakfast with us this morning at the house. This annoyed me, but last evening I was rather happy he didn't come because we're fasting. He would have had to eat all alone and would have been embarrassed by this, and we would have been, as well.

CF 131   To her brother and sister-in-law
April 29, 1875

I'm writing to ask you to come to Léonie's First Communion, which will take place on May 23.[315] It would make me happy to have you, but I don't dare hope for such happiness. Oh well, if both of you can't come, at least one of you could. Besides, you would be doing me a great favor.

Not only would I have the joy of seeing you, but I would also be very happy because of Madame X, whom I must absolutely invite. This puts me in an awkward position, knowing that it would be very unpleasant for her to find herself with Monsieur A, whom I'm also forced to invite. They are not on good terms with each other. Monsieur A detests Madame X, and I think it's mutual.... If you were there, that would settle everything. Then I know that she, as well as her husband, would be delighted to come.

I'm also going to ask Monsieur Vital and Mademoiselle Pauline Romet to come. If everything is organized the way I wish, I'll be very happy, but if I see myself only in the company of the A. family and Madame X, that wouldn't be suitable. However, for the reason you know, the latter cannot refuse me without insulting me, and she's too well acquainted with the proprieties to decline my invitation. However, I don't want to insist that you come because you're not obligated to become involved in all this.

---

[315] Léonie received First Communion on May 23, 1875, the Feast of the Holy Trinity, in the parish church of Notre-Dame d'Alençon.

I have my two oldest girls with me, who are on vacation. It's a true pleasure for me, but also a real increase in work because I must take care of everything they'll need for the summer holidays. I'm having all their dresses repaired, so I'm up to my neck in dressmakers. And in addition to this, I have urgent orders due this week; none are completed, and that worries me.

I forgot to give you news about my sister, whom I just saw.[316] My sister is doing well at the moment. I brought little Thérèse with me, who was very happy to go by train. When we arrived in Le Mans, she was tired and she cried. She stayed in the parlor the entire time, well-behaved like a big girl. Her aunt didn't come back, but she usually doesn't. I don't know what was bothering her, but her little heart was heavy. Finally, silent tears came, and she was choking. I don't know if it was the grill that had frightened her, but afterwards, all was well. She answered all the questions as if she were taking an exam!

The Superior came to see her and gave her some little gifts. I said to her, "Ask the good Mother to give you her blessing." She answered, "Mother, do you want to come to our house?" This made everyone laugh.[317]

At the moment I'm alone with her because the maid and the other children went to take Léonie to catechism. I gave her my box of pennies so she would leave me in peace because she was crying very hard when she saw the others leaving without her. But, hearing her father, she said to me, "Mama, Papa's coming. Quick, pick up the pennies!"

I have the feeling we're going to spend this year as peacefully as the previous ones. I continue to remain quite skeptical! I know that at a given time, that only God knows, big disasters will certainly happen that our poor country well deserves, but this may not be for several years.

We had a non-religious burial last week at ten o'clock in the

---

[316] Zélie visited her sister on Easter Monday, March 29, 1875.
[317] Sister Marie-Dosithée mentioned this meeting in a letter to Céline Guérin, her sister-in-law, on April 4: "I had a beautiful little visitor on Easter Monday, whom I wasn't expecting. Zélie brought her little Thérèse; she thought it would make me happy to see her. She's a very cute little girl, with a rare obedience. She did everything we told her to without having to ask her twice, and she was so quiet we could have made her stay like that the whole day, without moving. I was very happy to see her."

morning. The funeral cortege, which left from the rue des Tisons, went through town to go to Notre-Dame Cemetery. It was Monsieur G, a former pharmacist, who had bought himself a beautiful house he was to have moved into on the Feast of St. John the Baptist. He had every possible honor. The mayor held one of the cords of the hearse, all the city councilmen were there, and the representative L'Herminier made a speech at his grave. So, my dear Isidore, this can give you an idea of what has become of our town of Alençon, if you didn't know it well already.

CF 132 To her sister-in-law
May 19, 1875

...I'm only worried about one thing, and that's knowing poor Isidore is so sick.[318] I'm afraid it's dangerous. As for coming to visit, don't even think of it. I find, as you do, my dear sister, that it wouldn't be very wise for you to come, even if he were better, unless he's completely cured, which isn't likely. I was looking forward to seeing both of you very much. I was so happy about it I couldn't sleep last night. This proves that one must never rejoice too much.

I was planning an outing in the country for Monday. I would have invited Madame Y, but all of this has fallen through. My husband just arrived for lunch, and, like me, he was very saddened by your letter. I saw that he very much enjoys having you, too. Oh well, it's a joy we'll all miss.

My little Thérèse is sick. She has a persistent cough with a fever. It doesn't look like a cold to me, and I'm afraid she has the measles. Oh well, everything is turning out so that Léonie's First Communion will be a day of mourning.

I just interrupted my letter to receive a telegram. I was so disturbed I couldn't read it because I thought it had come from you. But no, it's another problem regarding an order of lace that arrived

---

[318] While the nature of this illness is unclear, for several years, Isidore Guérin was subject to a serious liver ailment, complicated by painful arthritis. He also suffered from back pain and gout. It was gout that kept him from attending the funeral of Thérèse. On July 2, 1900, Isidore was also unable to attend Léonie's Solemn Profession due to illness.

for me. Oh well, that's the day so far, and it's still only noon. If this continues, I'll be dead by this evening! You see, at the moment, life seems so heavy for me to bear, and I don't have the courage because everything looks black to me. If I only knew what illness my brother has and whether or not it's serious.

I'm more pleased with Léonie. She does what she can to do well. She gives the correct answers when we question her and knows her catechism perfectly. Every day she tells us that she's going to become a Poor Clare, and I have as much confidence in this as if it were little Thérèse saying it.

I just read my brother's letter to her. I took her aside and I, who never cry, dissolved into tears. She seems very determined to correct her faults.

CF 133

To her sister-in-law
July 4, 1875

Last week I received a letter from my sister in Le Mans telling me that my brother really wants Léonie to go to Lisieux. It wasn't difficult for me to decide because I find, in all fairness, that she should go there, and, without her resistance, she would have gone a long time ago. Finally, I told her my decision, and she came to terms with it willingly.

Now, she's looking forward to it very much and talks of nothing else. She asks me how many weeks until her sisters will arrive, and she says that these weeks aren't getting shorter. She's never seen Lisieux, and she's very happy to go there.

But Céline, who was to go in her place, cried very hard when she learned she wouldn't be going. I had to promise her that she could go, also. I couldn't leave her because she would have been too sad, and I wouldn't enjoy myself knowing that I left a child in such great pain.

So, my dear sister, you'll see five of us descending upon you! It's truly too much, but what can you do? One is put in a very awkward position by our family and friends!

As for Thérèse, when she's five or six years old, we won't be able to leave her home anymore. She'll have to accompany us because I don't think she'll be like Léonie, wanting to give up her place, neither for gold nor silver....

She always has a cold, my little Thérèse, and it comes back every two weeks. The wet nurse had told me that ever since she was born, she doesn't get over one cold without catching another, but the worst thing is that she's very sick. At the moment, she's had a fever for two days and is eating nothing. As for me, I'm not very well. I've had a hoarseness for three months that won't go away, and, with this, I'm coughing a little. But, in the end, I'm not suffering very much and that's why I'm not doing anything to find relief because I firmly believe that all the drugs in the world only keep people waiting to be cured, but cure them, never!

However, I have two packets of St. John's herbs that a good woman gave me a week ago. I smelled them, and I had enough. The woman returned yesterday to see if her herbal tea had done me any good. I told her yes, because I was almost cured. She answered me, "I knew you would be cured because there are no other remedies like that!"

CF 134   To her sister-in-law
July 11, 1875

We were very anxious to receive your letter. I learned about the flood[319] in Lisieux Thursday morning at eight-thirty. I thought it was nothing much, but throughout the day the rumors were more alarming, and I was very worried. The next morning I read about the details in our newspaper, and then I was convinced that you hadn't suffered, since the flood had only reached the low parts of the town. I was going to write you today to ask you for news about all this. I'm very happy to have received news because I'm going to send your letter to Le Mans, not knowing if you've written to my sister.

As you say, my dear sister, all of this is quite dreadful. This is a great curse, but sinful people are hardly benefitting from it. They would need something worse for them to open their eyes. On Wednesday afternoon we had a terrible storm here. It seems it did a

---

[319] A violent downpour in Lisieux seriously flooded the Carmelite Monastery during this disaster.

lot of damage around Sillé;[320] all the hay was lost, and the meadows were flooded.

I'm going to do your errand at Monsieur X's place. He's not there today, he's with Monsieur Vital. He's definitely leaving Le Mans, and he's taking this opportunity to bring together all his friends, twenty of them. He's having a big feast for them in Neuilly-le-Bisson,[321] and my husband is invited.

I'll try to visit you around August 14, the day before the Feast of the Assumption; it's the earliest I can leave. I can't travel the week before because that's the week the children leave school, and I have a lot of things to do for them that wouldn't be ready.

Céline is delighted about what you say about her. She's asked many times what you mean by the word "particularly." We told her that you're inviting her before the others and, if only one person could go to Lisieux, it would be her. You should see how happy she is!

We hear about nothing else but Lisieux from morning 'til night. Even the baby[322] is joining in and also wants to go to Lisieux to see Céline's godmother and little Jeanne, too. Léonie said to her, "I'll bring you all the cake they give me, my little darling. I'm not going to eat one of them." She truly has a heart of gold, my poor Léonie, and she particularly loves her little sister.[323] So, one of the reasons she refused to go to your house was that if she went, Céline wouldn't go.

I must do something for the flood victims in Lisieux.[324] You can always use the money that Madame Y owes me, and if she hasn't already given it to you, ask her for it on my behalf.

---

[320] About 30 to 40 kilometers (19 to 25 miles) south of Alençon.

[321] Approximately 17 kilometers (11 miles) northeast of Alençon.

[322] Thérèse, who was two and a half years old.

[323] From the copy of the letter made by Sister Marie of the Trinity, *Vie Thérésienne*, No. 93, January 1984, p. 73.

[324] In Céline's biographical reflections of her mother, she highlights Zélie's understanding of charity: "She was naturally compassionate, particularly for those who suffer. Public afflictions deeply moved her heart and excited her generosity. Thus, in July, 1875, she sent her offering for the flooded areas of Lisieux. She preferred to exercise charity in the most direct, immediate way; that is, to give daily help to those who seemed to be in need around her, and her faith made her think first of all of souls. Hence she urged us to pray for sinners, for those in the neighborhood who were in danger of death. These she visited, and helped materially, if they needed it; she would tactfully direct their thoughts to God, and call in the priest when there was need of the last sacraments. Her letters contained many instances of this spiritual form of charity." Céline Martin (Sister Geneviève of the Holy Face), *The Mother of the Little Flower*, p. 64.

I just received your letter. I was going to write you today to tell you that we're leaving Saturday morning at ten past eleven and arriving in Lisieux around four-thirty.[325]

For a week we've been talking about leaving Marie and Pauline with you. I can't have one stay without the other because Marie doesn't want to remain without her sister. But as for being separated from them for three weeks, I've decided that's too long, leaving too little time with Pauline before her return to school. You'll have them for about ten days, and then my husband will come get them. He has to leave on the 20th for *l'Abbaye de la Trappe*[326] near Mortagne together with several gentlemen, and they will stay there three days.[327]

I went to Le Mans on the 2nd of this month to bring back my daughters. Marie cried quite a lot while leaving her convent forever. She received six first prizes and Pauline three or four.

I'm very grateful to Madame Maudelonde for delaying her trip in order to see us. I would have felt quite deprived not seeing her and her children, as well.

You said nothing to me of Madame Y. I don't think she'll be at your house at the same time as me. I know she should arrive in Alençon at the end of the week, and perhaps she'll get the idea to come to Lisieux on Monday? That would hardly suit me since I would have to curtsey too many times, and I don't know.

Goodbye, my dear sister, soon we'll have the happiness of seeing you all again.

---

[325] August 14.

[326] The Trappist Monastery of La Grande Trappe in Soligny-la-Trappe, approximately 48 kilometers (30 miles) from Alençon. *L'Abbaye de la Trappe* dates back to the 12th century when it was originally founded. In 1147, it joined the Order of Cistercians, and in 1664, La Trappe became the center of the reform of the Cistercian Order. The reforms were in response to the excesses of the time and the hidden illnesses of the society. The Abbey was closed during the French Revolution, and several monks were martyred and others exiled to other monasteries in Europe. The Abbey was rebuilt in 1815, and is presently an active, working Abbey. The monks live a contemplative life of prayer, work and spiritual readings guided by the rule of Saint Benedict.

[327] Why did Louis go on retreat seeking the quiet and solitude of *L'Abbaye de la Trappe*? One might say that deep within us is an unquestionable thirst for God, and there can be no rest until we find Him. We are all called to awaken and intensify our need for God. However, monastics are called to be open to God's grace and presence

Thérèse at the age of three and a half.

Céline, age twelve, and Thérèse, eight, in 1881.

Isidore Guérin, Zélie's brother, a pharmacist in Lisieux.

Céline Fournet Guérin, Isidore's wife and Zélie and Louis Martin's sister-in-law.

Marie Guérin.

Jeanne Guérin, Isidore and Céline Guérin's first child, born February 24, 1868.

Marie Guérin, Isidore and Céline Guérin's second child, born August 22, 1870.

22 - Marguérite Maudelon

Marguerite Maudelonde.

21 - Céline et Hélène Maudelonde

The Maudelonde children were the cousins of the Guérin children and the playmates of the Martin children.

Céline and Hélène Maudelonde.

Left to right, seated, Isidore and Céline Guérin, Léonie; standing, Marie Guérin and Céline Martin.

A composite photo of the members of the Catholic Circle. Vital Romet is on the left, and Louis Martin is on the upper right.

Pauline Romet (1829-1889).

Vital Romet (1830-1916).

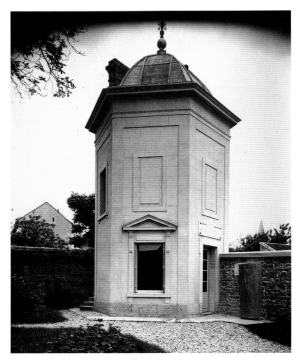

The Pavilion, a small property purchased by Louis Martin in 1857. He often went there to read or pray.

The room on the ground floor of the Pavilion.

The train station in Alençon.

The Visitation Monastery in Le Mans where Zélie Martin's sister, Sister Marie-Dosithée, was a member of the Community. Marie and Pauline (and, sporadically, Léonie) attended the Visitation Monastery boarding school.

PHOT⁺ DE L'ARTISTE

Zélie Martin a few years before her death. An unpublished and undated photo; we are grateful to Madame F. Besnier for allowing its publication.

Louis Martin at the age of sixty-five.

Some of Zélie Guérin Martin's lacemaking tools.

Alençon lace (*point d'Alençon*) made by Zélie Guérin Martin.

Alençon lace (*point d'Alençon*)
made by Zélie Guérin Martin.

Alençon lace (*point d'Alençon*)
made by Zélie Guérin Martin.

36, Rue St. Blaise, 36

A ALENÇON

LOUIS MARTIN

Fabricant

de

POINT D'ALENÇON

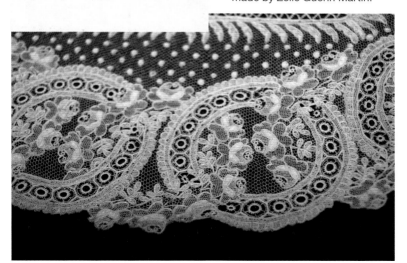

Rose Taillé's house in Semallé, five miles (eight kilometers) from Alençon.

Rose Taillé (1836-1908), the wet nurse
for three of Zélie's children.

Louise Marais (1849-1923) was the
Martins' family servant in Alençon for
ten or twelve years until she left after
Zélie's death in 1877.

The dining room at Les Buissonnets.

Les Buissonnets, the home of Louis Martin and his children in Lisieux.

The Virgin of the Smile.

To her sister-in-law
August 22, 1875

Quite fortunately, we got back Wednesday evening and were lucky enough to be alone the entire journey in a compartment reserved for women. So Céline had a great time! On the other hand, I had a great deal of trouble looking after her, and I didn't have a moment's rest. I had to keep an eye on her the entire time; so much so that when I arrived in Alençon I was so dazed I had difficulty standing.

Thursday my husband left for *l'Abbaye de la Trappe,* and from there he left for Paris. I think he'll be able to be in Lisieux Thursday or Friday.

I saw Madame Y last week. She told me she won't be able to visit you this year since it's impossible for her husband to get away any more. She talked about all her excursions in Brittany, and it was really very interesting. When I'm rich, I intend to go there with my entire family, and I'm fully counting on you being on the trip. It seems that everything is cheap in this region. They sell two chickens for one franc fifty centimes and fillet of beef at sixty centimes per pound. In short, they live cheaply there.

Her sister returned from Eaux-Bonnes.[328] She's still not well, and they're afraid for her chest! However, she's feeling better, although she doesn't have an appetite. They don't know how she's able to live on the little she eats. I'm so afraid she won't live to a ripe old age, and this saddens me because I'm very fond of her.

Now, let's speak of the good visit I just had in Lisieux. You made it so pleasant with your warm welcome and the good friendship you showed me. Those few days did me good. I'm preserving a sweet memory of them, and I'm beginning to regret that they've already passed.

Tell Jeanne that her little fisherman made her little cousin Thérèse very happy. She put it in the big room, and often during the

---

in a special way, and they desire to spend their lives listening to God's call, with the prayers and support of their Community. On retreat, Louis joined the monastic community on their pilgrimage to listen and search for God. It was in deepening his relationship with God on retreat that Louis most probably put before the God he was meeting his hopes and intentions regarding his family.

[328] A resort in the Pyrenees, in the southwest of France, with medicinal springs.

day she goes to admire it, saying that her little cousin sent it to her, and when she comes, she'll give her a big piece of chocolate.[329]

Marie and Pauline must be very happy that you're giving them such a beautiful vacation. When they've returned home, where there will be neither parties nor pleasures, it will be hard for them. As for me, I had trouble getting used to it again, and work seems harder than usual. Though I must take advantage of the few days I'm going to be alone in order to move ahead, because I'm quite behind in my work.

Please, my dear sister, accept my thanks for all the kindness you showed me. Give Jeanne and Marie, who are delightful little girls and whom their aunt loves very much, a big kiss for me.

CF 137   To her sister-in-law
                                                  August 1875

Yesterday my husband ran to the station to see my brother as the train passed through.[330] I would have liked to have gone with him, but, first of all, I wasn't planning on being able to get close to the track, and secondly, I was overburdened that day.

My maid had such a strong pain in her arm she couldn't do anything, not even dress herself. Then, Céline's been sick for a week. She throws up all her food, which only consists of broth and tapioca. I took her to the doctor on Sunday, and he told me she had a stomach irritation and that it would be very difficult to cure.

So I was still very worried. Yesterday, she suffered a lot and didn't know where to settle herself. I put some poultices[331] on her, and that did her so much good she's somewhat recovered. I'm overjoyed because I didn't think she'd pull through. But she played all day and isn't suffering anymore. She tried a little bread today. I'm beginning to think that it was quite simply indigestion, so I'm in better spirits. Yesterday I had a weight on my heart that crushed me, and my sad-

---

[329] From the copy of the letter made by Sister Marie of the Trinity, *Vie Thérésienne*, No. 93, January 1984, p. 73.

[330] Isidore Guérin left on a pilgrimage to Lourdes on August 30, returning September 3. Zélie wrote this letter on August 31.

[331] A soft, heated and sometimes medicated mass spread on cloth and applied as a healing agent to the body.

ness increased more when my husband told me that they had let him approach the train without any difficulty.

I felt very bad that the little girls didn't go with him to greet their uncle. It was their fault. It didn't matter how many times I told them, "Get dressed early." They went about it in a way so as not to be ready on time. They wanted to get dressed when they needed to leave for the station. Louis spoke with my brother for nearly ten minutes. I regretted this disappointment so much that it made me very sad, and Marie was, as well. But I definitely hope to make up for it on Friday, at five thirty in the morning, during my brother's return trip. We'll all be at the station, the father, mother and their five daughters.

I'm sure the time is going to seem very long to you. My dear sister, I also got very bored when my two oldest girls were away. And yet, how calm I was, and how well I worked! I can't do that anymore; I have to cook all day, and it never ends! And when I was alone, I assure you that the cooking was done quickly!

Marie told you about the great adventure that happened to them during their return from Lisieux. Can you see them, the girls and their father, getting off the train in Caen? And me, who'd spent my entire morning preparing dinner for them and was waiting for them to sit down at the table! I was very worried and upset. I had a leg of lamb on the fire that I didn't know what to do with.

Finally, they arrived at five o'clock. No one, of course, was at the station to meet them because by then I didn't expect them until seven-thirty. It's true that the employees should warn passengers in Mézidon that they need to change lines for Alençon.[332] I was surprised by their silence on my last trip, but that didn't prevent me from getting off the train because I like to make inquiries to prevent similar setbacks. I'm very surprised by my husband's absent-mindedness because he's such a perfect traveler.

Marie and Pauline were delighted with their stay in Lisieux. They brought back a good amount of affection for their uncle, but above all for their aunt. Marie says that she has no faults, that she wasn't able to find a single one in her. She's also quite thrilled that her aunt loves her, and now she doesn't doubt it anymore. Before her trip, she'd often ask me, "Do you think, Mama, that my aunt in Lisieux

---

[332] They forgot to get off the train at Mézidon.

loves us?" When she arrived home she said to me, "Now I have no more doubt, I know that my aunt loves me."

I can assure you that her aunt isn't dealing with an ungrateful person, because my oldest daughter is already beginning to pester me to visit you next year.

I'm saying goodbye to you because the children are waking up. Céline took a good nap, and she seems to have made a good recovery.

CF 138	To Sister Marie-Dosithée, a nun at the Visitation Monastery in Le Mans
	August 31, 1875[333]

I was delighted by our trip to Lisieux. I have a sister-in-law who has a kindness and a sweetness that are incomparable. Marie says that she doesn't know her to have any faults, and neither do I. I find that Isidore, in spite of all his problems, is very happy to have such a wife. It would take a long time to tell you her virtues, but that will be for later.

I assure you that I love her as much as a sister, she seems to feel the same way and shows my children an almost maternal affection. She showed them every possible attention and did everything to make our lives pleasant. If I seemed worried, she looked at me with sympathy, this seemed to hurt her. Marie quickly came over to say to me, "Mama, please, look more cheerful. My aunt thinks you're sad, and she's hurt over it." I answered her, "Leave me alone, I can't do better." And I reproach myself for it!

Monday we were in the countryside. I went there reluctantly to accompany the others. Then we settled in a meadow to rest, and during this time my sister-in-law secretly went to prepare a snack for us. When she brought it to us, I was so upset at the trouble she went to that I was far from showing appropriate gratitude. She contented herself with laughing at my apparent coldness.

Oh well, I'm truly not very pleasant. Fortunately, I'm still willing

---

[333] This letter to her sister is the only one that was preserved. It was found among the family papers of Isidore Guérin.

to admit it! But if I don't know how to show signs of affection, I feel the sentiments inside. I believe I wish for my brother's prosperity more than mine. I have a burning desire to see him happy, him and his wife, and I would be ready to make every sacrifice for their happiness.

If I didn't have a home and children, I would live only for them, and I would give them all the money I earn. But since I can't do that, God will provide. Certainly, people like them are bound to succeed, and I have complete confidence in them. Unfortunately, poor Isidore has made hardly any profit from his wholesale drug business, and yet he works hard. This saddens me for him.

CF 139
To her sister-in-law
September 7, 1875

The pilgrimage to Lourdes leaves Séez[334] on Monday, September 27, at nine-thirty in the morning and will pick up the pilgrims from Alençon around ten o'clock. They'll return Friday, around five o'clock.

Our maid is going, and it seems that your chambermaid, Aline, also wants to go? If she decides to go, she should write me immediately, and I'll receive her with pleasure. She doesn't need to bring any provisions because I'll give both of them what they'll need.

As for me, traveling doesn't tempt me. There's only one trip that I would feel a great attraction to, and that would be to visit the Holy Land. And yet, I believe I'll only visit it in the Last Judgment, in the Valley of Jehoshaphat.[335] I'll try hard to see everything while I'm there!

Marie and Pauline were very happy to receive your letter. They're on a pleasure trip. Mademoiselle Romet came to take them on an outing to the countryside with the Benoît girls. There are nine girls, and they're going to have a wonderful time. I don't know what time they're going to return this evening.

---

[334] See footnote in CF 12.

[335] Joel 4:1-2: "For in those days and at that time, when I restore the fortunes of Judah and Jerusalem, I am going to gather all the nations and take them down to the Valley of Jehoshaphat; there I intend to put them on trial for all they have done to Israel, my people and my heritage."

Today Pauline is fourteen years old. She's quite sad to return to the boarding school alone. It's a big heartbreak for her and for me. How happy I would be to keep her here with Marie! If you knew what this child is to me, she's my consolation.

I'm not dissatisfied with my Léonie. If we could manage to triumph over her stubbornness and make her more cooperative, we could make her a good girl, devoted and not afraid of difficulty. She has a will of iron, and when she wants something, she overcomes every obstacle to get what she wants.

But she's not at all devout. She prays to God only when she can't do otherwise. This afternoon I made her come by my side and read some prayers. But soon she'd had enough and said to me, "Mama, tell me the life of Our Lord Jesus Christ." I wasn't sure I wanted to tell the story because it tires me out a lot, and I always have a sore throat. Finally, I made the effort, and I told her the life of Our Lord. When I arrived at the Passion, she was overcome with tears. It made me happy to see her have these feelings.

CF 140   To her sister-in-law
                                        September 29, 1875

It hurts me that my brother is worried. However, I understand because I worry over a lot less. But it's especially the little things that bother me the most. When it's a real misfortune, I'm completely resigned to it and await God's help with confidence.

I certainly share a very large part of all your troubles, and I'm as sensitive to yours as I am to mine. But I have the firm hope that this time of trial won't continue. Why I'm so confident, and nothing can take that away from me, is above all the edifying way in which you keep Sunday holy. All the faithful observers of the Lord's Day, perfect or imperfect, succeed in their businesses, and in the end, one way or another, they become rich.

I'm so convinced of this that I often say to the children, "Your uncle is going to be rich one day." They answer me, "How do you know this, Mama?" I tell them that I know it, and that surprises them a lot. Marie said to me, "So you're a prophet, Mama!" In the end, the future will tell us if I'm mistaken, but I don't believe so.

So my brother went to see the Curé de Malétable?[336] I think he'll return satisfied with his visit. I was reading again, last Sunday, the wonders that took place inside his little church, and it's truly remarkable! They obtain the graces they want, but on the condition that they scrupulously observe the laws of the Church regarding Sunday.

I can't help considering this good priest a saint. I'd wanted to go to him on December 8 to finish a novena I'd been saying for Léonie and to bring the child with me, but I was diverted by two priests to whom my husband had confided my intention. In general, the colleagues of this good priest make fun of him, but weren't all the saints unrecognized? The Curé d'Ars,[337] today almost canonized, was an object of contempt and a laughingstock during his lifetime, even on the part of certain clerics.

As for me, I'm going to be very careful not to buy anything on Sunday anymore. I'm not as strict about this as you and my husband are. For example, when I need a small loaf of bread for my children, I have it bought. But very often I admire Louis' scruples, and I say to myself, "Here's a man who never tried to make a fortune. When he set up his business, his confessor told him to open his jewelry store on Sunday until noon. He didn't want to accept permission to do so, preferring to pass up good sales. And nevertheless, he's rich." I can't attribute the affluence he enjoys to anything other than a special blessing, the fruit of his faithful observance of Sunday.

My dear sister, I've already been in the Association of the League

---

[336] She is referring to Father Jules Clément Migorel (1826-1904), the priest who built a church in Malétable dedicated to Our Lady of La Salette. On September 19, 1846, the Blessed Mother appeared to two poor children tending their cows on the slope of a mountain, high above the village of La Salette in France. In the apparition the Blessed Mother invited the children to be closer to Jesus. She told them, "I am here to tell you great news." She focused on the need to pray daily, and she gave them a strong reminder not to work on Sunday, to keep it as a day of rest and a day to focus on Our Lord. She also encouraged them to deepen their relationship to God, to recommit to God's wishes and to transform their lives. Crowds of people went there on pilgrimage, and this shrine was recognized by Pope Pius IX. Some healings took place after promising to keep Sunday holy. Louis and Zélie Martin were strongly committed to the message of Our Lady of La Salette.

[337] Jean-Marie Vianney, the priest in Ars (1786-1859). He was declared "Venerable" on October 30, 1872, "Blessed" on January 8, 1905, and "Saint" on May 31, 1925 (two weeks after the canonization of St. Thérèse of Lisieux).

of the Heart of Jesus for a long time, but, unfortunately, I'm no better for it because I'm in all the associations, and I don't fulfill the obligations faithfully enough.[338] Every month, a holy young woman comes to preach to me and brings me my little card. I'm glad I received your letter. It's going to motivate me, and I promise you, starting today, I won't neglect any of the requirements.

I never miss, nor does Marie and, naturally, nor does Louis, receiving Communion every First Friday of the month, no matter what difficulties we foresee for that day. We change the time of the Mass we usually go to, and that's all that's needed.

I'm very satisfied with my eldest daughter. She's always working and takes charge of putting the house in order while the maid is away, who left to go home to her parents.

Pauline intends to write to you shortly. I'm bringing her back to Le Mans on Wednesday, October 6.[339]

CF 141   To her daughter Pauline
                                                October 10, 1875

I can't resist the desire to write to you today. This is going to do me good because I think about you all day long. My memory of you isn't fading; it's just the opposite. I've never missed you so much. This is probably because you returned to school alone. Then, you see, my affection for you is growing from day to day. You're my joy and my happiness. Oh well, I must reason with myself and not let my love grow too much because if God was going to take you with Him, what would become of me?

When I left you Wednesday evening I was very sad, and, since

---

[338] "She belonged to several pious associations." Stéphane-Joseph Piat, OFM, *Story of a Family*, p. 148. Among them: *l'Archiconfrérie du Coeur agonisant de Jésus* [The Archconfraternity of the Agonizing Heart of Jesus], *l'Archiconfrérie des Mères Chrétiennes* [The Archconfraternity of Christian Mothers], The Association of Prayers for the Salvation of France, Confraternity of the Sacred Heart of Jesus, The Pious Union of Our Lady of Good Council and the Franciscan Third Order. Thérèse was enrolled in seven associations. (See *Derniers entretiens,* [Last Conversations], Cerf-DDB, 1971, pp. 482-483.)

[339] Zélie made an error. Wednesday was October 7.

you returned to school too early, I deeply regretted the quarter of an hour I would still have been able to spend with you. I waited a full hour at the station. I put myself in a little corner of the waiting room so no one would disturb me, promising myself that I would do my best to enter a compartment with women only.

For three quarters of an hour I was quiet and deep in thought when I saw a brave woman with two little children arrive, one twenty-nine months old and the other two months old. In addition, she had two enormous packages.

Seeing her predicament, I left my thoughts to go help her. She was also going to Alençon and had been traveling for three days like this, even during the night. She was bringing these innocent creatures two hundred and fifty leagues[340] to place them with a wet nurse in her family, not being able to keep them because of a job she has with her husband at the law courts in Valence.

I can't tell you what I suffered to see her abandoning these two poor little ones until the age of ten. And yet she looked like a good mother, but she has a lot more courage than I do, because I would much rather die than leave my children like that. She, on the contrary, didn't seem affected by it.

Finally, I put myself to work helping this woman carry the children and the packages, but it was too much for two people. An employee, seeing our difficulty, took a child in his arms and put it in the compartment for women only. A woman who was already there made a harsh face when she saw the group of children enter the car!

To cheer her up, I wanted to tell her the story of the long journey of this mother and her children, but she didn't answer me. Embarrassed, I said to myself, "I absolutely have to know if she is or isn't a mute." Finally, I was able to make her say a few words. Then I was happy to see that she was neither deaf nor mute, and I left her in peace, that is, not completely, because we were taking care of both of the little babies.

While talking and rocking, we arrived in Alençon. I took the tiny baby, who was well wrapped, and went into the waiting room. Your father was waiting for me there. He noticed the package and

---

[340] 605 miles or 974 kilometers (French league equaled 2.422 miles).

wanted to quickly relieve me of it, and he seemed quite surprised to see me with such a badly wrapped package! As he realized I wasn't letting go, he looked more closely and saw a little hand come out. I told him then that I'd found a little girl, and I'd brought her home. He didn't look too happy....

Finally, the mother arrived. She'd stayed behind to check her parcels. I carried the little girl to the woman's parents' house, and we didn't return home until midnight.

As you see, my dear Pauline, I have the luck of always finding little children along my way.

When we went to Lisieux, it was the same thing. You'll remember for a long time, won't you, the good woman with her two infants who shouted during the entire journey, much louder than her two little ones. Marie felt so awful about it she began to cry. My brother made fun of me as much as he could, and he wasn't wrong because that woman was able to do without me much better than the one on Wednesday.

What else can I tell you because I must write a long letter so my Pauline is happy. I went to visit Monsieur Vital to find out if he's going to Le Mans soon because I have several things to send you. You forgot your scissors, and I bought you a very pretty scapular at the Monastery of the Poor Clares, which I'm enclosing, as well as Marie's book, twenty-five sheets of paper and a box of quills. Buy exercise books and anything else you'll need without worrying about it a bit; I'll pay whatever's necessary. I'm sending you these twenty-five sheets of paper to do with as you'd like.

Thérèse hasn't been well for two days; she has a fever at night and an upset stomach. I hope it's nothing. She's always asking where Pauline is. She says, "I want her to come home, to our house." Then there are some "why not's" that never end.[341] Your father is also sad to be deprived of his Pauline whom he also wants to be with us. I do my best to encourage him to be patient since you have to stay.

If you knew, my Pauline, how pretty I find your drawing. I would never have believed it could have been done so well, and the

<hr />

[341] The passage regarding Thérèse is from a copy of the letter made by Sister Marie of the Trinity, *Vie Thérésienne*, No. 93, January 1984, p. 73.

Ecce Homo[342] is equally beautiful. Continue to draw, I'll frame your drawings with the lovely pieces of wood I put aside; you know the ones I'm talking about. I need six frames for my desk.

Marie misses you a lot and the Visitation Monastery, as well. She even told me she envied your fate when you left because you were going to see your aunt again. I'm very happy she loves her aunt this way, and it's true she owes her tremendous gratitude.

One other thing, you'll make your sister very happy by giving her some details about the students and the new teachers.

I forgot to explain to your aunt that it wasn't your fault if you hadn't done all of your vacation homework, that it was me who prevented you from doing it because there was too much, and you greatly needed to rest because of your frequent migraines. I would even have wanted you to rest completely during those two months. Also tell her that I'm very satisfied with you because you're a good little girl, very affectionate and very sweet. In other words, you're everything that we would want, but still not pious enough.

I hug you with all my heart.

CF 142   To her daughter Pauline
                                              October 14, 1875

Today, my dear Pauline, I'm not going to write you a long letter. You know that on Thursdays I have a lot to do and even more than usual this afternoon because I went out this morning with Marie. I had to do some shopping that I wasn't able to do yesterday because of bad weather.

So I went to the dressmaker's to have your sister's coat mended, and I bought the fur for hers and yours.

Your father isn't here. He left this morning on the five-thirty

---

[342] *Ecce Homo* – In the Latin Vulgate version of the Bible, these words are used by Pontius Pilate when he presented Jesus to the crowd shortly before His crucifixion. Jesus had been scourged, crowned with thorns, and wore a purple robe. Pilate presents Jesus with these words: "*Ecce Homo*" ["Behold the Man" or "Here is your Man"] (John 19:5). For centuries this scene has been widely depicted in Christian art.

train for Mesle-sur-Sarthe[343] in the service of Madame Leconte.[344] I expect him this evening at five o'clock.

Thérèse is still sick, the poor little thing, and we're spoiling her for the moment in order not to make her cry because it's causing her a lot of pain. She always has a fever. I was very worried this morning, but I'm less so now because I noticed she has a big tooth ready to come through. Her gums are very swollen, and it's quite certain that this is what's causing her fever.[345]

It was eleven years ago, yesterday, that little Hélène was born, and I thought about her a lot. I'll be very happy to see her again in the next world.

Madame M[346] is very sick. They believe she's going to die, and no one has yet dared to speak to her about the priest. I'm very afraid she'll die without seeing him. However, the Sisters of Mercy[347] go there every day, and no doubt they'll watch over her.

I'm expecting a letter from you by Monday evening, my Pauline, and I'll be very happy to hear your news. Tell your aunt I very much regret spending so little time with her on my last visit. I forgot to leave her money to have Masses said for the intentions of my father and mother, so I'm enclosing it with this letter.

CF 143   To her daughter Pauline
                                                October 1875[348]

My dear Pauline,

Your letter made me very, very happy. I read it several times, and I would still reread it, but Marie took it as a relic!

I wanted to write to Lisieux today to send the Association bulletins your aunt had sent with your letter. As soon as I received them, I carefully put them back in the envelope and put them in my

---

[343] Currently known as Le-Mêle-sur-Sarthe, it is 25 kilometers (15.5 miles) northeast of Alençon.

[344] Madame Leconte died May 3, 1874. (See CF 118.) She was the wife of the Director of the Hospice Pharmacy in Alençon. (See CF 76.)

[345] The passage regarding Thérèse is from a copy of the letter made by Sister Marie of the Trinity, *Vie Thérésienne*, No. 93, January 1984, p. 73.

[346] Madame Mercier-Pottier, 47 years old, a neighbor of the Martin family.

[347] See footnote in CF 92.

[348] This letter was written Sunday, October 24.

drawer. A moment later, Marie took them out and scattered them on the table without my noticing because I was completely absorbed in my work.

It was nighttime, and Céline and Thérèse were spending the evening with me. Céline, whose only pleasure is cutting everything she can get her hands on, took two St. Joseph bulletins and cut them into pieces. I was not happy, and Louise, seeing this, very quickly took her under her protection and put her to bed. No harm was done to the other bulletins, and one can still read the one for my brother in its entirety. If my sister wants to give me two more, I'll send them to Lisieux right away.

Little Thérèse is much better, and this illness only did her good. Now she's eating better than usual, and with her health, her good humor returned. Céline is learning very well, and I'm delighted about that. In a short time she learns a catechism lesson or a point in Sacred History by heart, and yet without a great deal of effort. She reads fluently. I would see her sometimes, very serious, reading in a low voice, *"Les petites filles modèles."*[349] She thought I couldn't hear her, and she was giving each character the suitable tone of voice.

Marie takes care of them a lot, so she doesn't have time to do much work. She only has her evenings, which aren't as long as mine. I'm not complaining about it, I'm so happy when I see myself freed from all my little children. At least I can work without having to constantly talk. Then, I think about my Pauline, and I build castles in the air and dream about happiness and peace!

But I have too many worries to have total peace of mind, problems with clothes that never end! Yesterday, the entire morning was devoted to buying a complete outfit for Marie, a beautiful dress and a coat very much to her taste. I'll have to do it again for Léonie. I was thinking of giving her your dress, but Marie would be too beautiful in comparison, and everything must be equal.

Oh well, I do nothing but shop every day. Your father says, amusingly, that it's a passion with me! It's no use explaining to him that I have no choice; he finds it hard to believe. But he trusts me; he well knows that I'm not going to ruin him! I'm telling you this to make you laugh!

---

[349] *The Model Little Girls* by the Countess Sophie de Ségur. (See footnote in CF 113.)

Good-bye, my dear Pauline. It makes me sad knowing that your aunt is suffering from a sore foot, but I would be much sadder still if I hadn't seen her so resigned on my last trip to Le Mans. I was very sorry not to have been able to visit with her longer. When I go on New Year's Day, Marie and I will leave at seven o'clock in the morning.

CF 144   To her sister-in-law
October 31, 1875

For two weeks I've had the little bulletins which I've enclosed with this letter. I would have sent them to you sooner, but I was waiting for their number to be complete because something unfortunate happened. Two of them were cut up by the children without my noticing. Last Sunday I wrote to Le Mans asking for replacements, and I still haven't received them.

I would very much like to hear your news, and I do nothing but think of you all. I'm afraid you're upset and having a lot of difficulties. I can't think about my brother's problems without being moved. I assure you, my mind often turns to Lisieux, and it's always longing to see your trials end.

I'm happy with Marie. She usually takes care of Céline, who's learning well. So I won't have to send the little one to boarding school this year. I would have been quite worried over this because she's a very weak child who needs separate food and eats almost nothing. She's always sick, and I'm anxious about it because my little Hélène was like this for months and months before she died.

As for my little Thérèse, although she's not very strong, she has a good disposition and eats perfectly, nothing makes her sick. Last evening, however, Marie made her my patient. She was making her eat by telling her a story. Seeing that the story wasn't ending and the little one was still eating, I said to Marie, "Don't give her any more, I'm afraid it will make her sick." I was busy at my desk and didn't see what took place. Marie ignored my recommendation. So, around midnight, the poor little one was sick, and I held her in my arms for an hour. As for me, I caught a bad cold because I didn't take the precaution of dressing warmly enough. There's a good lesson for Marie.

Pauline is still my *"benjamin."*[350] I love her too much, but I can't help myself, she's so cute. She wrote me that she's on the Honor Roll and that she's so happy to make me happy! My sister tells me she's well liked by the teachers. All of these signs of friendship aren't making her proud; she still has a charming simplicity.

I imagine that Jeanne and Marie are going to the boarding school? Give me their news.

Is your maid, Aline, cured? More or less, I believe, like Louise, who returned from Lourdes with all the infirmities she'd brought with her and, on top of that, bronchitis. But mentally she's not the same anymore. Her enthusiasm knows no bounds, and she's now pious! It's to the point that I, who don't like pilgrimages, am determined to go to Lourdes next year with my three oldest children.

I'm expecting a long letter. Tell me lots of things; you know that everything that concerns you interests me to the highest degree.[351]

CF 145

To her daughter Pauline
November 7, 1875

I can't tell you how happy your last letter made me. I saw how hard you're trying to please everybody in spite of your exuberant nature. I'm infinitely grateful for it. If you knew how I love you, everything about you appeals to me.

It's been several hours since I interrupted my letter for a very sad situation. I was finishing the last few words, completely absorbed in your memory, when I heard the little bell announcing that they were bringing God to our neighbor, Madame M.[352] Louise was supposed to follow with a candle, only they'd told her it would be after Vespers, and it was only two o'clock. Quickly I ran to call her. Fortunately, she was ready, and both of us went to the patient's home.

I attended a ceremony I'll never forget. I saw this poor dying

---

[350] In Emile Littré's *Dictionnaire de la langue française (1872-1877)* [Dictionary of the French Language], *"benjamin"* is defined as the favorite child, so called because of Jacob's preference for Benjamin, his youngest son in Genesis 42:2-5. In current usage, it means youngest child or youngest son/daughter.

[351] This letter had a post-script which was not preserved. The paragraph beginning "Pauline is still my '*benjamin*'" is preserved from the original letter.

[352] Madame Mercier-Pottier. (See CF 142.)

woman, who was nearly my age, leaving so many children who need her so much. They were all there, dissolving into tears, and all one could hear were sobs! She also received Extreme Unction.[353] We're expecting her death any moment, and she's enduring terrible suffering. For the last two weeks she's been spending her nights sitting up and can only take to her bed for a few minutes.

Her two youngest children, Élise and Georges, are at our house, and I'm looking after them this afternoon. They're playing without any worry, and Marie is dumbfounded to see them so carefree. As for me, I'm not surprised; all children are like this. Nevertheless, we should feel sorry for them! Oh well, if it's as I believe, little Élise is going to an orphanage. This will be a good thing for her because, otherwise, she'll probably turn out badly like her sisters.

My God, how sad a house is without religion! How terrible death appears to be there! In the patient's bedroom we didn't see one picture wherever we looked. There were, however, many of them, but all of subjects that had nothing to do with religion! Oh well, I hope God will take pity on this poor woman because she was so badly raised she has many excuses.

I can't get over my emotions. Yesterday I saw the priest from the Church of Montsort[354] and he said to me, "It's been a long time since you've had news of the little girl[355] you freed from slavery? As for me, I've received very bad news. It seems she's developed very serious faults, to the point that the nuns, with whom she's now living, had to expel her from their classes. They asked me to use all my influence with you to pull her back from this precipice."

I was very saddened by this, although I easily guessed whose scheme this was and who would have written this to him. It was prob-

---

[353] Currently called the Sacrament of the Anointing of the Sick.

[354] L'Abbé Crété of the Church of St. Pierre de Montsort, was the successor to l'Abbé Hurel who was both the pastor of this church and Louis' confessor and friend. L'Abbé Hurel married Louis and Zélie on July 13, 1858, in the Church of Our Lady of Alençon. L'Abbé Crété was the one who demolished the medieval church where the Martin children were baptized (except Thérèse, who was baptized in the Church of Our Lady of Alençon) and built the new church which was consecrated in 1884. The original church was demolished because it was too small for the parish. Also of interest, "Montsort was the first of Alençon's suburbs to be developed outside the city walls. It is southeast of the center of Alençon." Pierre-Marie Gautier, *Alençon dans l'Orne*, p. 99.

[355] Armandine V. (See CF 127, 128, 129 and 146.)

ably "the two holy people" from whom I'd rescued this poor little girl, because otherwise people who live thirty leagues[356] from here wouldn't know that the priest in Montsort is my confessor.

However, I'm afraid there may be truth in what they say about the child. The priest in Banner wrote me in his last letter, "I regret that the mother didn't leave her daughter with you. I'll do my best to persuade her."

Oh well, I've almost come to regret not having let her languish in the home of the two elderly women. I knew that her physical life depended on my removing her, but her soul was probably in a good state, and isn't that the main thing?

I immediately wrote to the priest and asked him, should everything they tell me about her be true, to send the little girl back to me if her mother allows it, and I would pay her boarding fees at The Refuge.

As you see, my Pauline, "On earth, all is not roses, Nor happiness nor sweet hope! In the morning, the flower blooms, Often it withers at night."

But to tell you the truth, I'm coming to terms with it! I've already endured so many different things that it's formed calluses around my heart. There are still none around yours, my poor little girl, so you feel the smallest thorn more deeply, but by being pricked you'll end up not feeling the pain as much.

I received a very good, very affectionate letter from Lisieux. They still have their troubles there, but they seem quite resigned to the will of God.

Next time, my dear Pauline, I'll try to write a more cheerful letter because this one is hardly amusing. There are some, however, who are enjoying themselves right next to me. I hear the children giggling, having a party with roasted chestnuts.

Good-bye, my dear Pauline, I kiss you with all my heart.

If you knew how happy your being on the Honor Roll made me! But if you can't be on it again, don't feel bad about it; I won't be sad at all.

Little Thérèse is very good. Today she wore a pretty blue hat for

---

[356] 73 miles or 117 kilometers (French league equaled 2.422 miles).

the first time. Her father spoils her and gives in to her every whim. Two days ago Marie had put her to bed without having her say her prayers, and she put her in the big bed. When I came upstairs to my room I moved her to her bed without warming it because I didn't have a fire. Although she was fast asleep and well wrapped in her nightgown, she noticed this and began to shout, saying she wanted a warm bed. I heard this music the entire time I was saying my prayers. Tired of it, I gave her a little tap, and, finally, she wore herself out.

When I'd gone to bed she told me she hadn't said her prayers. I answered her, "Go to sleep, you'll say them tomorrow." But she didn't let it go. To put an end to it, her father made her say them. But he didn't make her say everything; he had to ask, for the grace of?... He didn't really understand what it was about. Finally, he made a guess, and we had peace until the next morning.

CF 146 To her daughter Pauline
November 1875[357]

My dear Pauline,

Your little letter made me very, very happy. I was delighted to see that you're still on the Honor Roll, and this makes up for all my little troubles. When I think that I have a Pauline in Le Mans, who will come home to me soon, I feel so happy!...

Madame M died last Sunday at a quarter past midnight.[358] I'd been at her house since the morning and seeing her alone, in a room completely dark, made a great impression on me. I was struck by it and began to sob, which is very rare because I can never cry, even when I lose one of my own.

Your father had to go notify the Town Hall and everywhere else because there was no one to take care of it. The burial took place Tuesday morning at eight o'clock.[359] The two oldest daughters of this poor woman were there, and a lot of people went. Marie, Léonie and Céline went with the maid, and I stayed home to look after Thérèse.

---

[357] Letter written Sunday, November 21.
[358] Madame Mercier-Pottier died Saturday, November 13 at 11:45 p.m. (See footnote in CF 142.)
[359] This is an error. It took place Monday, November 15.

When they lowered the coffin into the grave, her daughter Fernande gave out such cries of despair that everyone in attendance became agitated. Her two daughters are much better since their mother's death. If they could only change! I want this with all my heart because I've taken a lot of interest in them. I feel sorry for them. Fernande told me her mother had prayed up until the end. God will have had mercy on her.

I told you in my last letter that I'd written to the priest in little Armandine's parish. Well! My Pauline, I haven't received a response. Thursday Marie said to me, "Mama, so are you writing to the Sisters in Banner?" I didn't want to, being tired of this story, but finally, I decided to do it. I should have received a response today. Nothing! I don't understand such a thing. Of course everyone there is warned against me since the two "holy people" made a visit there. They'd already indoctrinated the child once to make her say everything they wanted, and all it took was one or two caresses. They would have done the same thing in Banner, to make sure I'm thought of as a black crow and that I'm trying to harm the two good Sisters.

The first week I was very sad, but now I'm very calm. No matter what happens, I did whatever was best. On the contrary, my conscience is clear. But one must admit I have no luck, and humanly, it doesn't encourage one to try to do good. If this unfortunate affair only earns me a merciful glance from Heaven, that would be payment enough.

Now what am I going to tell you? I truly don't have any more news, so how can I fill up the rest of the paper? And yet if my Pauline doesn't see my four pages quite full, she's going to be sad!

The little one is by my side, and the others just left to go to Vespers. She's asking me why I'm still writing, and if we're going to leave soon. Sunday I took her to Vespers, and she didn't leave me alone, so we're only going to go to Benediction.

She's asking me to tell Pauline to come home, that she's been in Le Mans quite long enough, and that it's very annoying. Here she is also reproaching me for not taking her to Lisieux. I tell her it's because she's too disruptive. This doesn't flatter her, and she begins to cry. I tell her she's not well-behaved enough in church. Marie loves Céline a lot; she's very gentle and learns very well. It's true Céline will be charming if God lets her live. But I have some doubts, she's always suffering from a stomach ache, and this delicate health is very difficult to maintain.[360]

Every day Marie goes to the six o'clock Mass. I find this too early, and it makes me very unhappy. But I'm no longer the mistress and, so not to upset her, I let her do it. Today she has on a pretty hat that she's wearing for the first time, and she's never had one so beautiful. And yet it's not very luxurious because I take very great care to dress her well while remaining simple. We'll make yours next week, and it will be similar.

I don't know if I'll be able to have you a day earlier for the New Year's vacation this year. I have a lot of things to have you do, and I'm wondering how I'll manage in the few days' leave you'll have. I would have to go pick you up on Tuesday instead of Wednesday, but will they allow me to do so?

Although if they knew what a problem it is to have to dress a child one sees only every three months, I'm sure they wouldn't refuse me. However, I really don't like to ask for preferential treatment and not follow the rules. Let's move on, I'm thinking about this too early, and I still have time to think about it.

I interrupted my letter quite unnecessarily to dress Thérèse, who wanted to go out. When both of us had finished getting ready, it was raining so hard I had to undress her. That resulted in an interruption of three quarters of an hour. Now, Marie has returned from Vespers. She's entertaining the little one, and they get along very well.

Your grandmother[361] just arrived, and I must keep her company. Though I wouldn't mind ending my letter because I have more than a hundred pages of the first volume of the *Life of St. Jane de Chantal*[362]

---

[360] From "I tell her…" to the end of the paragraph are from Sister Marie of the Trinity's copy of the letter, *Vie Thérésienne*, No. 93, January 1984, p. 74.

[361] Fanie Martin, Louis' mother.

[362] St. Jane Frances de Chantal (born January 23, 1572, died December 13, 1641). Zélie identified with Jane de Chantal, the wife of Baron Christophe de Chantal, a landed noble and warrior knight. They had six children, two children died at birth, their daughter Charlotte died at age ten and their daughter Marie-Aimée bore a still-born infant and died a few days later. Jane and her husband's marriage was filled with an extraordinary love and deep spirituality. They both attended daily Mass together and during her marriage, Jane was known as a very holy woman. Jane persuaded her husband to convert several rooms in their castle so that she could nurse the sick,

to read this evening! I have to hurry because I won't have time to read it during the week.

I hear the baby calling, "Mama" while coming down the stairs. At each step she says, "Mama!" and if I don't answer every time, she remains there without moving forward or backward.[363]

You see, I'm having a very difficult time answering your grandmother, the little one, and writing to you! And yet I'm doing everything at once, but I'm not paying as much attention as I did the day I wrote to the priest in Banner. Then it was necessary that no one bother me.

I promised the children we would celebrate the feast of St.

---

feed the poor, assist women in childbirth and care for poor nursing mothers and their children. Jane was an extraordinary businesswoman and managed the family estate and vineyards. During their marriage they were known as excellent business partners who lived the Gospel. They both had made a promise that if one of them died the one left behind would not remarry but would consecrate his/her life to work for God. After nine years of marriage, Jane's husband was accidentally shot in a hunting accident and died soon after. Several years later she met Bishop Francis de Sales, Bishop of Geneva. After years of prayer and spiritual formation under his direction, Jane co-founded with Bishop de Sales (later St. Francis de Sales) the Monastic Order of the Visitation. She founded over 80 monasteries in France before she died on December 13, 1641. She was canonized July 16, 1767. At different periods of her life, Jane lived both the marital and religious vocation. This strongly appealed to Zélie, who never gave up her original wish to become a Daughter of Charity, ministering to the sick and the poor.

[363] On the blank page of her notebook, on the opposite page (that is, on the back of page 41, as Sister Marie of the Trinity only wrote on the front of the pages), she transcribed: "In the same way, she wouldn't go upstairs alone unless she called out to me on each step, 'Mama! Mama!' As many steps as there are 'Mama's'! And if, unfortunately, I forget to answer only once, 'Yes, my little girl!' she remains there without going forward or backward." This is referring to a passage interpolated by Mother Agnès of Jesus in *Histoire d'une Âme*, 1898, p. 8. (See *Histoire d'une Âme*, 1972, p. 327, footnote 6.) It seems that Mother Agnès had reread this episode after Thérèse's death in light of the comparison dear to Thérèse: the episode of the little child at the bottom of the stairs (See *Vie Thérésienne*, January 1979, p. 64) or, better still, that of the elevator: "...I am too small to climb the rough stairway of perfection." *Story of a Soul* tr. John Clarke, OCD, p. 207. This made Mother Agnès reverse the direction, having Thérèse ascending the stairs rather than descending the stairs, which was contrary to the facts. In reality, in Alençon the young Martin children played in a room on the first floor while Madame Martin worked at her lace or wrote letters at the desk on the ground floor, as she was doing this Sunday afternoon, November 21, 1875 (the date is certain). It's by an affectionate whim that the little one calls out to her mother on each step, although the staircase in Alençon is quite steep, and it would be more difficult for a young child to descend the stairs than go up the stairs. One can assume that, at almost three years of age, Thérèse was managing very well on her own. Note that, in 1895, she didn't include this episode in Manuscript A.

Catherine[364] Sunday evening. Marie wants donuts, others want cake, and others chestnuts, but as for me, I would like peace. We're going to invite Mademoiselle Philomène[365] but I would prefer that it were my Pauline!

Monsieur N left a week ago to live in R. He was appointed by the minister and will be entitled to a pension. He'll be the inspector of V's factory where there's a distillery. He asked us to help him get established. His father, who is very well off, didn't want to give him a penny. Well, would you believe he paid a farewell visit to Monsieur L, who had nothing to do with the affair, and didn't come to visit us who, for the last six months, have been taking so many steps to place him. If we didn't work for God, I tell you again, it would be disheartening to do good.

Good-bye, my dear Pauline. As for you, you are my true friend; you give me courage to bear life with patience.

I kiss you with all my love.

---

[364] St. Catherine of Alexandria, the patron saint of lace makers, was born of noble birth and lived in the early fourth century in Alexandria, Egypt. She was a highly educated, intelligent young woman known to be very holy. At the age of eighteen, she publicly challenged the Roman Emperor, Maxentius, with a highly intelligent argument demanding to know, "Why have you abandoned God to worship false gods?" When the Emperor realized that he couldn't argue the case with this intelligent woman, he sent fifty scholars to try to convince her to reject Christ and worship false gods. Instead, the scholars were convinced by St. Catherine's belief in God and were converted and put to death. The Emperor's wife and his soldiers were also converted by Catherine and were beheaded. The Emperor tried to seduce Catherine with worldly riches and also challenged her virginity. When she refused his attempts, he had her tortured and imprisoned. After two weeks, the Emperor summoned Catherine and said, "Today, you shall either offer sacrifices to the gods or lose your head." She said, "Do everything you have in mind to do. I am prepared to bear whatever it is." Maxentius had her beheaded. Catherine was greatly venerated in Europe after the Crusades and especially in France when it was revealed that St. Joan of Arc testified at her trial that St. Catherine was one of three saints who divinely guided her in her war against the English invaders. St. Catherine told Joan of Arc, "Have confidence and abandon yourself to God – that will be your road to heaven." Since St. Catherine was eighteen years old when she was martyred, she was given the title of "Patroness of Adolescent Girls." Her feast day is November 25. St. Catherine stood firm in her Christian faith. She refused to be seduced by the Emperor's promises if she compromised her chaste life. Her strong witness, under extraordinary stress, converted those around her, and Catherine accepted martyrdom rather than betray Christ. Zélie fostered her daughters' awareness and devotion to holy women, and it was these women, strong in their love for Christ, who Zélie held up as models for her daughters.

[365] Philomène Tessier. (See footnote in CF 92.)

CF 147   To her daughter Pauline
                                                December 5, 1875
My dear Pauline,

Your last letter made me even happier than the others and, to complete my happiness, your aunt tells me she's very pleased with you; you're very obedient and quite sweet. So thank you, my Pauline, for being the joy of us all. God will reward you in this world and the next, because we're much happier, even in this life, when we bravely do our duty.

So Wednesday is the Feast of the Immaculate Conception, and it's a great feast day for me! On that day, the Blessed Mother granted me many notable graces. Ask your aunt if she remembers December 8, 1851.[366] As for me, I haven't forgotten it.

Nor have I forgotten December 8, 1860, the day I asked our Heavenly Mother to give me a little Pauline.[367] But I can't think of it without laughing because I was exactly like a child asking her mother for a doll, and I went about it the same way. I wanted to have a Pauline like the one I have, and I dotted the i's and crossed the t's because I was afraid the Blessed Mother wouldn't quite understand what I wanted.[368] First and foremost that she have a beautiful little soul, capable of becoming a saint, but I also wanted her to be very pretty. As for that, she's hardly pretty, but I find her beautiful, very beautiful, and she's as I wanted her to be!

Again, this year, I'll go to find the Blessed Mother at daybreak, and I want to be the first to arrive.[369] I'm going to light my candle to her as usual, but I won't ask her for any more little daughters. I'm only going to ask her that those she's given me all become saints and that I

---

[366] On that day, Zélie, twenty years old, suddenly stopped in the middle of absorbing work and heard an inner voice say, "See to the making of Alençon lace." This inspiration was a determining factor for her future.

[367] Pauline was born September 7, 1861. (See footnote in CF 1.)

[368] Zélie's fear that the Blessed Mother wouldn't understand her needs may have been caused by her mother's inability to gratify her. Zélie, as a child, begged her mother for a doll, and it was never given to her. As Zélie said in letter CF 15, writing to her brother, "My childhood, my youth, was as sad as a shroud because, if my mother spoiled you, as you know, she was too strict with me. She, though so good, didn't know how to treat me, so my heart suffered greatly."

[369] Each year Zélie went to Sées on the Feast of the Immaculate Conception. (See footnote in CF 125.)

may follow them closely, but they must be much better than I am.

At the moment I'm reading the *Life of St. Jane de Chantal*. I told you this two weeks ago, and I was intending to finish the first volume in two hours. But I've found it so beautiful that I've not been so quick to finish it. It's taken me two weeks, and I'm beginning the second volume today.

I'm carried away by admiration. It's all the more interesting to me because I love the Visitation Monastery very much, but now I love it more than ever. How happy I find the people who are called to it! Finally, I don't speak of anything anymore other than St. Jane de Chantal and all that I'm reading.

Louise[370] is angry. When the second volume arrived, she said, "Well! Here's another two weeks of hearing nothing talked about but St. Jane de Chantal and St. Francis!"

My poor Pauline, my hands are so cold I'm finding it difficult to write. Along with this, I can't see, and I can say I'm writing by feeling my way along. I have very bad eyes. It's my Alençon lace that tires me the least, but while writing I see double and often have to close my eyes and cover them with my hand to rest them. It's even worse today than usual.

I'm quite happy with Céline. She's an excellent child who prays to God like an angel, learns well and who's also very docile with Marie. We'll certainly make something good of her with the grace of God.[371]

The baby is an absolute imp.[372] She comes to caress me while wishing me dead, "Oh! How I wish you would die, my poor little Mother!" We scold her and she says, "But it's so you'll go to Heaven, since you say that we have to die to go there." She wishes for the death of her father, as well, when she's in the middle of her outpourings of love for him.[373]

Since your aunt's last letter, Marie is more obedient and doesn't go to the first Mass anymore unless I permit it. I'm very happy to see the influence my sister has over her. First, she venerates her like a

---

370 The servant, Louise Marais. (See footnote in CF 98.)
371 *Carnet manuscrit de soeur Geneviève* [Manuscript Notebooks of Sister Geneviève (Céline Martin)], p. 101. (Not translated.)
372 Thérèse, almost three years old.
373 In 1895, Thérèse quoted these lines in *Story of a Soul*, tr. John Clarke, OCD, p. 17.

saint and loves her a lot, and we have a feeling that she misses her very much. I wouldn't be surprised if she became a nun at the Visitation Monastery. She doesn't have worldly tastes at all. On the contrary, I'm more concerned than she is that she be well-dressed.

One night, quite recently, while saying my prayers after having read Madame de Chantal, I suddenly thought that Marie would be a nun. But I didn't focus on it because I've noticed that the opposite of what I predict always happens.

Don't say anything about this to her because she'll imagine that this is what I want, and, truly, I only want it if it's God's will. As long as she follows the vocation He gives her, I'll be happy.

Here's Céline playing blocks with the little one. They argue from time to time, and Céline gives in to gain a pearl for her crown. I have to correct this poor baby, who goes into a terrible rage when things don't go as she'd like. She rolls around on the floor like a desperate person believing all is lost. There are moments when it's stronger than she is, and she starts choking. She's a very high-strung child. However, she's quite cute, very intelligent, and remembers everything.[374]

Your father often speaks of you and is happy to see you're still on the Honor Roll. He just received a letter from the priest at Montsort who, he said, had an important matter to convey to him. We were quite intrigued. The good priest arrived a moment ago, and it's simply to invite him to have lunch tomorrow at the home of Father de Mieurzé. They're leaving tomorrow at noon, in a carriage.

I'm going to end my letter because I have nothing else new to tell you. I was bombarded by the children who were playing near me, each one talking to me in her turn, so I had to write while talking. Finally, thank God, Louise came looking for them to put them to bed.

Good-bye, my dear Pauline, soon I'll have the happiness of seeing you, and I'm looking forward to it very much.

CF 148

To her sister-in-law
December 28, 1875

I'm sending you the New Year's gifts today. As we agreed, I'm giving a box of paints to Jeanne and a History of France bingo game to

---

[374] Ibid., p. 23.

Marie, then some Christmas cookies in the shape of a little clog with little Jesus cookies and other whimsical objects. They'll find these Christmas morning in their shoes[375] and it will make them happy.

I also made some for my little girls. On Christmas Day they'll receive our presents, and on New Year's Day they'll receive your New Year's gifts.

Céline wrote you a little letter that she composed all by herself. It's not perfect, but it's only been a week since she started to write a little.

Little Thérèse is already beginning to read. She absolutely wants Marie to teach her like Céline, and, since Monday, she's learned almost all her letters.[376] I think she'll learn easily. She often speaks of her uncle and aunt in Lisieux.

Recently I was writing to Pauline, and Thérèse came to ask me if I was writing to her uncle. Then she said to me, "So why, Mama, didn't you take me to visit him so I could see my little cousins and little Céline Maudelonde?"[377] I answered her that she was too little,

---

[375] In France, on Christmas Eve, children place their shoes in front of the fireplace for *Père Noël* (Father Christmas) or *le petit Jésus* (the Child Jesus), who comes during the night to fill their shoes with gifts and sweets. In a letter written to a friend, Marie-Louise Morel, on December 27, 1875, Marie described Thérèse's reaction to a doll she received for Christmas: "What seemed funniest to me was to see a beautiful doll emerging from one of the ankle boots, patiently waiting for the arrival of her mamas. This is what pleased Thérèse the most, too, and when she noticed the famous doll, she cast everything aside to fly to her. Unfortunately, her burst of joy didn't last long, and now that she's acquainted with her charming daughter, she's beginning to neglect her. Today, annoyed to see that she doesn't walk quickly enough, she broke the ends of both feet; one arm is already dislocated, and soon, I believe, that will be the end of this poor doll. But I'm mistaken; when she's absolutely dead, she'll have a funeral for her, and truly, the funeral for a doll is very funny. Thérèse has already experienced this more than once." Stéphane-Joseph Piat, OFM, *Une âme libre: Marie, Soeur Ainée et Marraine de Sainte Thérèse de L'Enfant-Jésus*, p. 39. (Not translated.) [A Free Soul: Marie, Oldest Sister and Godmother of Saint Thérèse of the Child Jesus.]

[376] The same day Marie wrote to her Visitandine aunt, "I think Thérèse is going to become learned because for the last three days she's been constantly hounding me to teach her to read. So the day before yesterday, I got a book on the alphabet and amused myself by showing her the letters, while believing that it was useless. But to my surprise, I saw her arrive with her book the next day, reading to me all the letters I pointed out to her at random without making a single mistake. This little one truly has an incredible facility. I believe that within six months she'll know how to read fluently, because she has an extremely precocious intelligence." *Correspondance familiale de Zélie Martin 1863-1877*, p. 266, footnote 1. [Family Correspondence of Zélie Martin 1863-1877.]

[377] See footnote in CF 103.

and she began to sob, she was a pitiful sight. It was no good promising to take her with me the next time because she said it was too long, it had to be right away![378]

1876

CF 149

To her sister-in-law
January 9, 1876

I'm sure you're not happy with me because I've waited too long to thank you for the beautiful New Year's gifts you sent. They were welcomed with such shouts of joy that I held my head in my hands and put up with it until the evening. And on top of that, some workers were waiting for me. You have no idea of the uproar!

Marie was the only one who didn't make any noise and the only sensible one. She was delighted with her little box, which she put on display in her room with all the jewelry she has.

Pauline made an awful racket over her beautiful stationery and danced for joy enough to wear out the floor. Léonie didn't make a big scene. She enjoyed herself turning her bag over and over again, seeming very happy with her present.

Céline jumped up and down with happiness in front of her "kit."[379] And Thérèse! You had to see her!... Her fortune was made! She wished for nothing more in this world. She's constantly playing with her pretty carriage. In short, I sincerely thank you, and I would like to be able to make you happy as well.

Tell Jeanne that her aunt and her little cousins think of her often, even little Thérèse who definitely wants to call her doll Jeanne Guérin or Jeanne Fournet, that's the latest name she's given her this morning. I don't know where she found that one.[380]

---

[378] From Sister Marie of the Trinity's copy of the letter. *Vie Thérésienne*, No. 93, January 1984, p. 75.

[379] Zélie uses the word "*nécessaire*" which could mean sewing kit (*nécessaire de couture*) or toiletry kit (*nécessaire de toilette*).

[380] From Sister Marie of the Trinity's copy of the letter.

To her daughter Pauline
January 16, 1876

My dear Pauline, it's very cold in Alençon, and I think it's the same in Le Mans. I'm afraid you have chilblains[381] on your feet because you're quite prone to them. I don't know if I'm going to write you a long letter. I don't have any news to tell you, so you see that I'm beginning by....[382]

So I don't dare send Marie to see her aunt, like I'd promised her, although an opportunity presented itself. Mademoiselle Pauline Romet is going there tomorrow. She leaves at seven o'clock and returns on the three-forty train. It's exactly what I needed. But seeing the cold continue, I thought it was better to postpone the trip.

I assured Marie that she would accompany you back to school after the Easter holidays, and then she'll be able to talk freely with her aunt. We'll leave Marie with her aunt in the Monastery, and then the two of us will take a walk. Perhaps I'll bring Céline because the weather should be better at that time.

Here is Marie who dreams of going to live in a beautiful house on the rue de la Demi-Lune across from the Monastery of the Poor Clares. Yesterday she talked about this all evening and you would have thought it was Heaven!

Unfortunately, her desires cannot be fulfilled. We must stay where we are, though not for all of her life. But as for me, I'm only going to leave when I die.

Your sister, though so unworldly, is never happy where she is. She aspires to something better; she would need very large and well-furnished rooms. She couldn't get over her surprise in seeing the wet nurse's little daughter involuntarily letting out a cry of admiration while entering her bedroom on Thursday, and remaining frozen in the doorway, while saying, "Ah! It's beautiful!"

The poor little one believes that there's nothing more beautiful, but Marie knows the opposite from her companions at the board-

---

[381] *Concise Oxford English Dictionary.* New York, NY: Oxford University Press, 2008. A painful, itchy swelling on a hand or foot caused by poor circulation in the skin when exposed to cold.

[382] The unpublished lines that end there were found on the back of a paper stuck in a notebook with a sky blue cover (Archives, Carmelite Monastery, Lisieux).

ing school and dreams of something else. When she has something else, perhaps she'll feel even greater the need for more.[383] As for me, I imagine that if I were in a magnificent chateau, surrounded by everything one could wish for on earth, the emptiness would be bigger than if I were alone, in a little attic room, forgetting the world and being forgotten. So I do nothing but dream of the cloister and solitude. With the ideas I have, I really don't know how this wasn't my vocation or how I didn't remain a spinster, or retreat into a convent. Now I'd like to live to be very old, so I can withdraw in solitude when all my children are grown.

But I feel that all these are only empty ideas, so I hardly pay attention to them. It's better to use the present time well than to think so much about the future.

I'm going to have to find a new dressmaker. I have many reasons to complain about Mademoiselle Irma. However, she's been working for me for such a long time that it's difficult for me to let her go. If your father wasn't encouraging me, I wouldn't be able to make up my mind.

He feels that, if we're paying so much, it's better to hire someone who works reasonably well. Besides, this good young woman believes that everything is owed her, and she doesn't owe anything to anyone else. She doesn't give them the right to reproach her, no matter how gently they go about it, without answering unpleasantly.

Your father is soon going to Paris for the Alençon lace, which isn't going well. I'm very upset over this because the other manufacturers have orders. I'd like to have some also because it makes me so sad to have to dismiss my workers! He's talking of taking Marie with him, saying that it won't prevent him from taking both of you next time. Oh well, he imagines he'd do more business if Marie were with him.

Thérèse is asking if you're going to come home soon. She's always good and an imp.

You can see, my Pauline, that my letter has nothing of interest, but you like long letters, and I'm trying to find something to say.

---

[383] Most of the students at the Visitation Monastery boarding school were from the upper class. It was through the influence of Sister Marie-Dosithée, Zélie's sister, that Louis and Zélie Martin were able to enroll their daughters in this school.

Having no more news, I'll say good-bye to you. In three months we'll see each other again. It will come quite quickly because time passes so fast. I hope you're always a good girl, and you're still on the Honor Roll.

I eagerly await your news and kiss you with all my heart.

CF 151 To her daughter Pauline
January 1876[384]

My dear Pauline,

There's great turmoil on our street today because it's the Senatorial elections.[385] Since this morning, the rue Saint-Blaise has been filled with men. It's seven o'clock in the evening, and we still hear a lot of noise.

It's because of you, my Pauline, that I'm not going to do any pious reading this evening. I'd also like to write to your aunt, and that results in a lot of work for me. What's more, I have a terrible headache like I don't often have.

I had to go out all afternoon; otherwise my letter would be done. But we went to pay a visit to Madame Z, and Marie, as well as the little ones, went with me. We stayed about an hour.

This woman has a little girl who is seven months older than Thérèse, and she's a real little devil! She beats her mother, pinches her, and always disobeys her. She's a wild little child, and yet, her mother adores her! That surprises me because I find her so appalling that I can't look at her.

Poor Marie didn't know whether to laugh or cry. Madame Z wanted her daughter to show Marie her toys, and she never agreed to it, not even to kiss her. If I had a child like this one, no, I could never love her!

Last week she came to the house dressed like a little princess, all in pale blue velvet with gaiters[386] white as snow which she tried very hard to dirty on purpose by rubbing her foot on it. Her mother

---

[384] This letter was written on January 30.
[385] The Prefecture is opposite the Martin house on the rue Saint-Blaise. (See footnote in CF 68.)
[386] A cover of cloth or leather from the instep to the ankle, mid-calf or knee worn over the shoe or boot that closes on the side with buttons or buckles.

wanted to stop her, but she very quickly dirtied the other gaiter. Then she started pinching her mama because she'd given her a little tap!

I took the children to Vespers at the Hospice and from there we went to the square where the booths were set up for the Candlemas Fair. There were a lot of people and a lot of mud. I had my fill and grew tired and bored because there was not much to see, almost nothing, other than frivolous things to entertain young people like you.

Marie kept herself occupied looking at little girls the same age as Céline and Thérèse, envying their outfits and begging me to dress them the same way. You can say again, we're never satisfied! They're both dressed like you'd never been, but that's not enough anymore because they see something better! However, I don't want to escalate this; all of that is a veritable slavery, and one is truly a slave to fashion! Though as you know, when it comes to herself, your sister hates to be concerned about her appearance.

I must tell you how happy your second Ribbon of Honor made me. I'm very satisfied with you, my little Pauline. You give me a lot of joy and great compensation for any troubles I may have. Why, even while writing to you, my headache is almost gone. I'm quite happy to have had this experience, and every time I have a headache, I'll quickly write to you to cure myself. I love you so much, my dear Pauline, that when I talk with you, I forget all my pains.

Good-bye, my dear Pauline, continue to be a good and holy little girl, and if you don't yet have this last quality, try to acquire it.

In the meantime, I kiss you with all my heart.

CF 152 To her sister-in-law

February 6, 1876

Céline is always sick. I'm very happy Marie is here to give her lessons because it would be impossible to send her to boarding school. Sometimes her big sister becomes discouraged, saying, "What good does it do to teach her, if she has to die?" But since we don't know the future, we can't leave her without an education, while making sure we don't tire her too much. They say that children, in their seventh year, change their constitution, and since she'll soon reach that age, I hope she'll do better then.

Oh well, we only live to have torments of every kind. I still have another worry that makes me suffer very much, and that is my poor business, which isn't doing well. I'm sure you're going to laugh and say so much the better because I've worked enough. You're right. I, too, would say the same thing, but there's something else that stops me.

It's not the desire to amass a great fortune that drives me because I have more than I ever wanted. But I think it would be foolish of me to leave this business having five children to provide for. I must go all the way for them, and I see myself in a dilemma. I have workers, and I have no work to give them while other companies are doing very well. That's what distresses me the most! Poor Marie is very unhappy over it. She curses the Alençon lace and declares she would prefer to live in an attic rather than make her fortune at the same price that I've paid. I don't think she's wrong. If I were alone and had to endure all over again what I've suffered these last twenty-four years, I would prefer to die of hunger, because just the thought of it makes me tremble!

I often tell myself that if I'd done half of all this to win Heaven, I could be a canonized saint! I also think of my brother and if he's enduring the same troubles as I am. I feel sorry for him with all my heart, because I know from experience what he's going through!

What a long letter for so few things, but what do you want, it does me good to confide in you. Madame Z is doing better than last year. We thought she had tuberculosis, but, thank God, it was nothing. She's enjoying herself as long as she can, as is Madame X. They offered to look after Marie during their little dances, but it's me who doesn't want it!

While awaiting the joy of reading your letter, I hug you with all my heart.

Your loving sister.

CF 153   To her brother
                                          February 22, 1876

I'm not writing to your wife today because I'm not happy with her. She didn't send me, through Monsieur Maudelonde, a few words in response to my last letter, so I'm not going to write her before she writes to me. Only then will I be completely appeased.

I was quite surprised by Monsieur Maudelonde's arrival. I'm sorry I didn't know in advance because that would have been very helpful. Next time, let us know, even if you don't know the exact day.

However, I was very happy to receive him; he's such a good man. I like him, as well as his whole family. Then he gave me all your news. It seems your wife hasn't been well for some time, and that's probably the reason for her silence. So I don't hold it against her. In fact, I only said it as a joke!

Monsieur Maudelonde went to Le Mans today. He brought Marie with him, who very much wanted to see her aunt and her sister. She had a good day. They asked Pauline to come to the parlor without telling her anything, and, when she saw her sister, she was so shocked she burst into tears. Her aunt promised never to do that again.

Pauline is always charming. My sister is delighted with her, and Pauline gives her a lot of consolation. Recently, she played a role in a play for the Mother Superior's feast day, and it seems she performed perfectly.

Their aunt spoke to Marie about you a lot. She told her that every day she prays that you succeed or you decide to sell the drug business. Meanwhile, you mustn't be discouraged, but have great confidence in God.

CF 154

To her daughter Pauline
February 26, 1876

My dear Pauline,

I must hurry up and write to you; I've just come from Vespers. I won't have enough time after supper because I'm going to have company. I regret it very much because I was looking forward to talking with you this evening while the others are at the theater. Yes, my Pauline, Thérèse and I are the only ones not going to the play! What will you think of us? We've been corrupted very quickly, you say, my Pauline?

And as for me, during this time I'm going to have a visit from

Madame Tessier[387] who asked to come to our house while her husband and daughter were at the theater.

Finally, I mustn't scandalize you any longer. This evening there's a big meeting at the Catholic Circle.[388] The young people are going to put on a very amusing little play, and the parents, along with the Circle Committee, are invited.[389]

I had intended to spend a nice evening with my Pauline and also to read. It disturbs me a little to receive Madame Tessier. I have no need of company because I quite enjoy myself all alone....

Marie was delighted by her trip to Le Mans. She's quite changed since then and does nothing but talk about her aunt. I hope she'll be a good girl, but I would like her to become a saint, as well as you, my Pauline.

I, also, would like to be a saint, but I don't know where to begin. There's so much to do that I limit myself to the desire. I often say during the day, "My God, how I would like to be a saint!" Then, I don't do the work! Though it's high time I started because I could very well do what two people did this week; they died, and their deaths affected me noticeably.

The first is that poor lady V,[390] who was my assembler of Alençon lace for about fifteen years. You know her well; she came

---

[387] See footnote in CF 92.

[388] The Catholic Circle was at the center of the lay Catholic apostolate. It was formed to address the dire conditions of the workers that had resulted from the disruptions caused by the Industrial Revolution: alcoholism; delinquency of every sort; a falling away from the Church; an absence of resources for retirement, health care, maternity and child care; rampant crime; a disconnect from family life and a dissolution of the extended family; child abuse, etc. Catholics in France started local "Circles" to address these issues and to ward off further societal deterioration. They provided a place to gather, connect and socialize with the local people. It offered activities for young workers which fostered a healthy environment in the hope of keeping young workers from delinquency and alcoholism, which were major problems. It provided an environment that encouraged the spiritual lives of the young workers, e.g., spiritual talks, encouragement to attend daily Mass, Nocturnal Adoration and the Conferences of St. Vincent de Paul. In short, it was an attempt to gather young Catholic workers together, to give support to each other – spiritually, emotionally, socially and in the workplace – all under the guidance of the local priest.

[389] In November 1875 Louis Martin participated in the establishment of the Albert de Mun Circle in Alençon. It was named after the man who founded the Catholic Circles in 1871, Albert de Mun (1841-1914). They held concerts and entertaining shows there. They were held at 34, rue de la Gare, under the direction of Father Dupuy. Louis Martin was a shareholder in it.

[390] Madame Vallet died on Monday, February 21, 1876, at the age of 51.

to our house quite often with her little dog. Well, Monday evening, after having served supper, her neighbors heard a heavy fall. They would have paid no attention to it but the little dog was howling so mournfully that they decided to go see what had happened. They found this poor woman lying on the floor, lifeless, the dog licking her hands and face.

Her memory follows me everywhere, and I see her constantly. But what is most painful to me is to think that she never practiced her faith. She only went to Mass two or three times a year, and she was a fanatical Republican.

The other person who died is Madame R, who lives across from Mademoiselle Fany. The whole neighborhood is filled with dismay. She leaves two little children and a very unhappy husband.

All of this is hardly of any interest to you, my Pauline. I'd like to tell you something else to make you happy, but I don't know anything but sorrows. All I know that's cheerful is that your aunt wrote me a delightful letter that I've read and reread in which she gives a lot of compliments to my Pauline, among others that she'll be pious. If you knew how happy that makes me!

Mademoiselle Philomène[391] brought me a biography of Saint Frances of Rome[392] from the parish library. I immediately read about

---

[391] Philomène Tessier. (See footnote in CF 92.)

[392] St. Frances of Rome was born in 1384 to a wealthy, noble family in Rome, Italy, and died at the age of 56 in Rome on March 9, 1440. At the age of eleven she decided to become a nun. However, her father demanded that she marry Lorenzo de Ponziani, a Roman nobleman and commander of the Papal Troops in Rome. Frances' spiritual director persuaded her that this was the will of God. Consequently at the age of twelve, Frances married and had three children. When she was 24 years old, her nine-year-old son Evangelista died, and five years later her daughter Agnes died. They both died of the plague. Frances recognized in her sister-in-law Vannozza a soul with similar yearnings of living a life totally dedicated to God. They became close friends and spiritual companions going to Mass daily, caring for the sick and the poor, visiting those imprisoned, and they set up a secret chapel in their castle to pray together. Frances always realized that her family responsibilities came first and at one time she said, "A married woman must leave God at the altar to find Him in her domestic cares." During the Civil War that broke out in Rome, Frances' husband was critically wounded, her son, Battista was kidnapped and her house was destroyed. However, Frances had total confidence in God. She turned what remained of her house into a hospital and a shelter for the homeless. Frances founded a group of women who lived in the world but vowed to work for God and the poor. They were called Oblates of Mary. Today they are called Benedictine Oblates of St. Frances of Rome and live in Community. After the death of her husband she joined this community and became their superior. It was said that at the age of 52 Frances had the life that she

the apparition of her son. She asked him, "My son, do you think of me, do you still love me?" He told her that in Heaven they are very absorbed in God and can have no pain there.

Finally, I didn't see that he thought about his mother. That hurt me because I have four in Heaven, whom I think about constantly, and to tell me that they could forget me causes me grief, but I don't believe it!

Mademoiselle Philomène, who was there when I read this passage, was very quick to report it to her mother, and, as we returned together from Vespers, her mother spoke of nothing else during the entire journey. Her face became red, and I thought she was going to cry. She eventually said to me that if our dead children didn't think of us, they were "villains." She was so animated and let out this word with such conviction that I burst out laughing, and heartily! It's because she also has two children in Heaven, and she would want them to not forget her. That's why she wants to come over this evening to talk about "villains."

I'll have to leave a page blank to tell you about the play and my evening with Madame Tessier. It's not going to be very entertaining hearing the inhabitants of Heaven discussed all evening because she seems quite determined not to let it go.

There are some very curious things in the life of Saint Frances of Rome. One discovers many mysteries of the other life, and it's very interesting.

So, I spent my evening with Madame Tessier. Your father and the children didn't return until ten o'clock. They rushed to tell me how they enjoyed themselves, and they had a lot of fun. More than 600 people attended, and all the priests of the parishes were there.

As for me, I'd begun by reading about the torments of the damned seen by Saint Frances of Rome; it makes me tremble. I don't like this kind of reading material, but it can be very beneficial.

I talked to your father about it all morning, and he wanted to take the book to his Pavilion. He just left, and I'm finishing my letter,

---

had dreamed of at age eleven. From Zélie's interest in the spiritual biographies of St. Jane Frances de Chantal and St. Frances of Rome, we recognize her identification with these strong women who had been married and later lived the religious life of a nun working with the poor.

which I couldn't finish last night because it was too late. I'm hurrying so it will be mailed before noon.

Good-bye, my Pauline, your father and I kiss you tenderly.

CF 155

To her sister-in-law
March 5, 1876

My dear Sister,

I don't want you to think I'm angry with you any longer, and that's why I'm writing to you. I received your good letter which pleased me very much because I'm always very happy when you send me your news.

I see you're still very satisfied with your two little girls. I'm delighted by this, but it's your little Marie who surprises me. I never would have believed she'd be so well-behaved and have such a developed intelligence.

I can't manage to focus Thérèse's attention, although I believe she would definitely learn if she wanted to. She begged Marie to teach her, and, after 3 or 4 times, she learned all her letters. She would soon learn to read if we gave her a lesson every day.

Monsieur Maudelonde told me your servant, Aline, was still quite sick and coughing continually. I see she wasn't cured in Lourdes. My maid wasn't either, neither in body nor mind, as I had hoped in the beginning, because from here I hear her making such a commotion that it resounds throughout the entire house! I'm getting up to tell her to calm down, but it's useless. She makes me suffer a lot. There's nothing else to do but dismiss her, since I've tried everything. I'd be much happier if I could do my work without needing the service of others.

Céline is doing better. I noticed it was the cider that was making her sick. Since we've stopped giving it to her and make her drink some wine, it's over.

Speaking of wine, ours becomes excellent upon maturing. If you want some of the same kind, let me know this week. If not, there's no need to answer me. We must do as the nuns do, not write during Lent to do penance.

We're going to have a Capuchin friar begin instructions this evening. I'm finishing my letter to go hear him. Whether he preaches well or badly, I'll like him because he's a Capuchin.[393] Just seeing them converts me.

CF 156   To her daughter Pauline
                                                        March 12, 1876
My dear Pauline,

We received your letter last Monday, and I was happy to see that you're still on the Honor Roll. Every day I thank the Blessed Mother for having given me such a good little girl.

You know we're in Lent, my Pauline, so I'm not going to write you a long letter, and, anyway, I have nothing new to tell you. Marie is probably going to tell you about the pretty outfits Mademoiselle G made for your little sisters. I had her in all last week, and she'll come again this week.

I'm still not short of dressmakers. I'm employing three of them at the moment. I took on Mademoiselle Irma again, who ran into me on Wednesday while leaving Monsieur Romet's, where I'd just bought fabric for the little ones' dresses. This poor young lady cried, asked me for forgiveness, and squeezed my hands with so much affection that I couldn't resist. It would have taken a lot less than that to appease me, so we were reconciled immediately.

Mademoiselle G was quite upset, and Marie isn't too happy with it either because the new one has better taste than the former one. But what can I do? I can't resign myself to causing so much grief to a person who's worked for me for almost eighteen years.

Tomorrow a gardener is coming, and the children are delighted because they like this fellow a lot. Marie has become fond of him. He tells curious stories about his good wife who, after her death, came to petrify him, "torment" him, as he says and who asked him to close the door. When little Thérèse sees him, she repeats, in her own way, the fellow's words, "You torment me, my good wife, you torment me." We have to make her be quiet!

Here's Marie bringing me a bed warmer. When I tell her I'm

---

[393] A Capuchin is a Franciscan friar, and Zélie was a member of the Third Order of Franciscans.

not going to write any longer, she begs me to fill four pages because poor Pauline is going to be too sad. "Poor Pauline," she'll have many other sad things in her life!

Mademoiselle X came to give me your news. It seems she saw you on Wednesday, and she told me that you've grown a lot. This made me very happy.

This young lady is a very good person, and it's a shame she has such liberal ideas. I think one day she'll change her opinion, because she's too charitable for God to allow her to always have such a heavy veil over her eyes. Her brother said to us the other day, "God didn't care about us." He'll see if God doesn't care about us, and I believe it will be soon!

It makes me sad that such good friends feel that way. As for me, I know God takes care of me, and I've already noticed it many times in my life. How many memories I have of this that I'll never forget.

My Pauline, my letter isn't very interesting, is it? There are days when we don't have any ideas. I never have a lot, but today is worse than usual. All day was like this. This morning, I slept while I was getting dressed, I almost slept while walking, I slept at the first Mass, while kneeling, standing, sitting, while praying. In short, I was going through the motions all day long. Now I'm quite awake. It's always like this in the evening when I'm never sleepy!

Nevertheless, I have to finish my letter because it's already late, and I get up early, at five-thirty every morning. It's hard for me with the Lenten fast, and I long for Easter. Finally, it will come, and I'll have double joy, even triple. First, because of the beautiful feast of Easter, then my Pauline, whom I'll go and get the next day, and finally, I'll see my sister. There will be so much joy, which I'll look forward to. I only have to wait five weeks, and they'll pass quickly.

Céline is doing quite well now. Little Thérèse is doing perfectly well. She's always very good. This morning she said to me that she wanted to go to Heaven, and, in order to do that, she was going to be as good as a little angel.[394]

Good-bye, my Pauline. All the same, here are my four full pages without my noticing.

I kiss you with all my love. Your mother.

---

[394] From Sister Marie of the Trinity's copy of the letter. *Vie Thérésienne*, No. 93, January 1984, p. 76.

To her daughter Pauline
March 26, 1876

My dear Pauline,

I have to hurry if I want to finish my letter today because we have to attend the Little Office[395] at the Hospice and then go for a ride in the country.

Marie wants to go to the Lorgeaine[396] and we won't return early. Then we'll have to have dinner and go out again for the sermon. If this letter isn't finished, I'll do it when I return. The beautiful days are here, and that makes us want to roam. Even I feel the need for it and often say to myself that if I didn't have the Alençon lace holding me back, I'd go to the countryside every day with my children.

I intend to make sure you have a good Easter vacation. Often we'll go for walks, which will do you good. You'll need a lot of exercise. I was sad to learn that you weren't well, and I do nothing but think about it. We suffer so much from headaches, and at your age, I suffered from them a lot, almost continually. This lasted several years, but now, I rarely have a migraine.

* * *

I was intending to finish my letter before going to Vespers and now it's evening; it's past nine-thirty.

This afternoon, while I thought I was completely at peace, thinking only of you, someone came to disturb me, and I had to stop in order to leave for Vespers and go for a walk. We went to the Count de Curial's château[397] which had burned down. It was much closer than the Lorgeaine, but so much for getting daffodils![398]

---

[395] The Little Office of the Blessed Virgin Mary.

[396] Three kilometers from Alençon, between Saint Germain du Corbeis and Arconnay is the well-known site of the Lorgeaine. In the spring, daffodils grow in the woods of the Lorgeaine and from these woods can be seen the house in Grogny, a nineteenth century family estate of the Monnier family, the home of Madame Tifenne's sister. It is at this estate where Thérèse spent holidays with her family after Zélie's death. Monsieur and Madame Tifenne were close friends of Isidore Guérin and Louis Martin. Madame Léonie Tifenne was Léonie Martin's godmother at Baptism.

[397] The Château du Comte de Curial is known as the "Château de Chauvigny," near St. Germain du Corbeis. After the fire it was rebuilt. In the 17th century, it was a little castle bought by the father of Madeleine de Chauvigny who married Monsieur de la Peltrie. She was one of the builders of the Catholic Church in "Nouvelle France," (Canada) and built the convent for the Ursuline Sisters in Quebec, Canada.

[398] Yellow narcissus with trumpet.

Oh well, God didn't want us to return without having any daffodils. Halfway down the road to the château I saw some little boys who had bundles of them. My intention was to buy them for the little girls. Just as I was thinking of this, I saw one of the boys scatter two big bouquets on the road. Céline gathered them up, and she was very happy, as was Thérèse.[399]

I'm still very happy with Marie and she'll be a very good girl if she continues what she's doing. We see that she takes a lot on. She's made great progress since she visited her aunt, and, with that, she's becoming very pious.

Little Céline will be a good child, very sweet and very pious. Thérèse is a little imp who's the joy of the whole family, and she's extremely intelligent.

Last night she woke us up while calling her father to tell him that she'd hit her head.[400] Her father answered, "Go to sleep, my Thérèse." Then again, "Papa, I hit my head." Finally, he got up to see how she'd hit her head. Actually, her little head was touching the wood of the bed, and every time she moved, she bumped her head. Tonight I rearranged her bed so that she won't hit her head anymore.[401]

She's constantly asking if tomorrow is Easter so she can see "Little Paulin." The day before yesterday, she began shouting in the

---

[399] On a loose sheet, student size, paginated 19-20 and being able to be dated to the years 1920-1930, Sister Geneviève transcribed a part of this letter with variations in form. After the episode of the daffodil bouquets found on the road, one reads this paragraph: "The maid didn't come with us. She had to take Léonie to the Catechism class on perseverance. She answered very well, and the priest complimented her. Louise was so happy over it she didn't regret having missed the outing." *Vie Thérésienne*, No. 48, October 1972, p. 302.

[400] Thérèse uses the phrase *"se toquer"* which in Norman *patois* means to hit one's head against something.

[401] Thérèse quotes this passage in *Story of a Soul*, tr. John Clarke, OCD, p. 24, but speaks of her mother: "You can see, dear Mother, how far I was from being a faultless little child! They weren't even able to say about me: 'She's good when she's asleep' because at night I was more restless than during the day, throwing off the blankets and sending them in all directions and (while still sleeping) banging myself against the wood of my little bed. The pain would awaken me and I'd cry out: 'Mama, I *bumped myself!*' Poor little Mother was obliged to get up and convince herself I really had bruises on my forehead, that I really *bumped myself!* She'd cover me up and then go back to bed, but in a short time I would begin *bumping myself* again, so much so they had *to tie* me in bed. And so every evening, little Céline came to tie me up with a lot of cords that were to prevent the little rascal from *bumping herself* and waking up her Mama; this was so successful a means that I was, from then on, *good* when *sleeping*."

garden, saying to me that it was too long, that she wanted it to be right away.

Céline isn't as sick as her aunt thinks she is. She's very delicate, and she needs great care. But as for the doctors in Le Mans or even those in Paris, not one of them is capable of giving her a strong constitution. There's nothing to do but give her a tonic. I don't need to go find a doctor to tell me this because I know it.[402]

I'm going to tell you about our preacher for Lent. In general, he's not liked. He says things so bluntly that he offends a lot of people, and he has a severe manner.

Last Monday he gave a sermon to the Christian Mothers[403] in the chapel at the Monastery of the Poor Clares. I was almost happy to go hear the terrible compliments he would pay us – a few days before he'd lashed out at doctors. Instead, with us he took a tone of kindness and sweetness which made me think that this wasn't the preacher from Notre-Dame. I was just beginning to think this when he said to us, "I'm sure several of you are going to say, 'This isn't the one who preaches at our parish church?'...."

Marie had wanted to make her confession to him, and I did, too, but he intimidates us. She'll go alone if she wants to.

We've had a little disaster happen to us that I'm going to tell you about. Your father received a letter from Monsieur M, who is building very close to our garden and digging a cesspool. He picked a quarrel, and your father made every concession to make peace. Finally, the neighbor made his hole so close to the wall that it collapsed. The other day, about eight o'clock in the evening, we heard a terrible crash, and it was the wall falling down.

The next morning Monsieur M saw this disaster and got very

---

[402] This paragraph is taken from the *Carnet manuscrit de soeur Geneviève* [Manuscript Notebooks of Sister Geneviève (Céline Martin)], p. 101. (Not translated.)

[403] The Archconfraternity of Christian Mothers was a movement of Catholic women founded by Louise Josson de Bikhem, the wife of a government official, on May 1, 1850, in Lille, France. It was founded in response to fears that the influences of modern society were severely undermining family life and causing husbands and children to lose their faith. Mothers gathered at monthly meetings to pray for one another, their husbands and their children, to discuss their problems, and share ideas regarding the Christian rearing of their children. They were also encouraged to realize the importance of their maternal vocation, to take responsibility for educating and sanctifying the souls of their children by providing a sound Catholic education at home, and by helping the mothers to become a strong spiritual presence within their own family. The Archconfraternity became a worldwide movement that still exists today.

angry, claiming that we had to pay half the costs for rebuilding the wall when the accident was due to his carelessness. He had a summons sent from the Justice of the Peace, and last Friday your father appeared there.

He explained the matter so well that everyone, including the judge, was indignant about our neighbor. But he can make us bear all the costs since the law is on his side because our walls are a few centimeters short of the required thickness.

We asked for an expert who's coming tomorrow at nine o'clock. He already paid us a visit this morning. He confided to us that we weren't in good hands because this Monsieur M knows legal quibbling like no one else and is going to make us eat more than the costs of rebuilding the wall.

That's where we are, and I don't know when it will be over. I'm not too concerned about it. We can only accept disputes with patience, since we must suffer on this earth. If this can spare us a little time in Purgatory, we'll bless Monsieur M in the other world for having made us spend a part of it in this life. But I prefer that he be the one who does us these wrongs rather than if we had to blame ourselves for creating a quarter of them for him. I'll tell you next time how it turns out.

Good-bye, my Pauline, I'll see you soon. We only have to wait twenty-one days, but twenty-one days that go by very slowly, because we must fast! It's very tiring, and last week I thought I was going to give it up. I had such a stomach ache I couldn't bear wearing my dress anymore. I suffered like that all afternoon. I'd made up my mind to give up, but the Capuchin priest gave a sermon that night that restored my courage. Now, it's going better.

I hug you with all my heart.

CF 158   To her sister-in-law
                                                            May 7, 1876

...I just received your letter, which I awaited quite impatiently. I was worried about all of you. I can't tell you that it made me happy. No, on the contrary. I'm sorry to see that my brother is a lot sicker, since they're talking about an operation. I thought he wasn't suffering anymore from his backache. Truly, God is allowing you to have many troubles all at once, but I hope that soon He'll compensate you fully because He doesn't do things by half.

I now have more orders for lace than I would like and an increase in work. Actually, not only must I see to having the various points made, but also assemble them because my assembler[404] just died, and I'll have a difficult time replacing her.

On top of that, summer is here. I have the children's outfits on my mind, which takes up a lot of time. Finally, my thoughts are so muddled in my poor head that sometimes I ask myself where I am.

My dear Marie feels sorry for me and relieves me as much as she can. She avoids asking me for something for fear of adding to my problems. I assure you she's totally devoted, and this gives me complete satisfaction.

Léonie's Second Solemn Communion[405] is set for May 21. Thank God, I won't have the same dilemma as last year with the invitations. That's all I would need!

Céline is still working with Marie. Thérèse is learning very easily, and she's very intelligent. I'm very happy to have her. I believe I love her more than all the others; this is probably because she's the littlest.

I hope we'll have the happiness of seeing you this year in the month of August, on the 15th, as usual. It's still not quite settled that you'll take Marie and Pauline back with you. I think that every other year is enough. Perhaps I'll let myself be won over to make you happy, but my husband doesn't appear to be very willing. Persuade him, if you can. I don't think he'll say absolutely not, but I know it's hard for him to be separated from the children whose vacations he thinks are already too short. Oh well, we'll talk about it again.

In the meantime, I'm going to have a rough day tomorrow, in every way – an order of lace to send out and clothes to choose for my oldest girls. That's what bothers me the most, although I have to dress them beautifully to send them to you!

Good-bye, my dear sister, forgive me for this rambling letter. I'm tired today, and I have a headache, and I see that what I write feels the effects of it!

---

[404] See footnote in CF 154 – Madame Vallet.
[405] See footnote in CF 57.

To her daughter Pauline
May 14, 1876

I'm very afraid that you were quite upset not to have received news from us last week. I'm going to try to make up for it, although I don't have big news to tell you. Life at home is very much unchanged, and what I have to write you is always more or less the same.

I'm beginning my letter a little before the High Mass because this afternoon I intend to go on a walk before Vespers. Afterwards, it wouldn't be easy because I must take Léonie to the Catechism class on perseverance. But this is the last time, because her Second Solemn Communion will take place on Sunday, May 21.

As always, Léonie is looking forward to being all in white. Up until now the material side strikes her more than the spiritual. Yet she hears the other world spoken of so much that she herself speaks of it often, but this only touches her lightly. Oh well, let us hope in God's mercy towards this child.

In some respects, I have many consolations. I'm very happy with Marie, and her ideas please me. This is the opposite of Léonie. Worldly things don't penetrate Marie's mind as much now as the spiritual. However, she still has a long way to go to fully enter the true path of perfection, but the balance tilts strongly in this direction.

My little Céline is completely drawn to virtue. It's the innermost feeling of her being. She has a pure soul and a horror of evil.

As for the little ferret,[406] we don't really know how she'll do. She's so little, so scatterbrained. She has an intelligence superior to Céline's, but much less gentle, and above all an almost invincible stubbornness. When she says no, nothing can make her give up. We could put her in the cellar all day and she would rather sleep there than say yes. However, she has a heart of gold; she's very affectionate and very frank. It's curious to see her run after me to make her confession, "Mama, I pushed Céline once, but I won't do it again." And it's like that for everything she does.

Thursday evening we went for a walk along the side of the station, and she was determined to enter the waiting room to go look for Pauline. She ran ahead of us with a joy that made us happy, but

---

[406] Thérèse, who was three years and four and a half months old when this letter was written.

227

when she saw that she'd have to return without getting on the train to go get Pauline, she cried all the way home.[407]

She's here at the moment, very busy cutting papers, and it's her favorite pastime. She made her choice from all the papers that had fallen around the desk because I'd thrown out some letters. This makes her very happy, but she has the good habit of asking if they can be used. Before touching them, she comes to show me all of them to be very sure that she can cut them. She's quite settled now in her little chair and cuts while singing with all her heart.

Nothing can persuade her to read. This was fine as long as she only had to name the letters, but now she has to spell, and there's no way to persuade her. We promise her everything, nothing works, but she's so little! I'll wait until she's four years old, and I'll be the one who'll make her read.

It's been a long time since my letter was interrupted. Since then, I've been to High Mass, and then we went on a long walk in the fields. We picked beautiful bouquets for the month of Mary, and we were very happy with this outing. On our way back we met a poor old man who had a good face. I sent Thérèse to bring him a few alms. He seemed so touched by this and thanked us so much that I saw he was very unfortunate. I told him to follow us and that I was going to give him some shoes. He came, and we served him a good dinner, he was dying of hunger.[408]

I couldn't tell you how many troubles he was suffering from

---

[407] In *Story of a Soul*, tr. John Clarke, OCD, p. 22, Thérèse quotes the passage beginning, "My little Céline is drawn to the practice of virtue..." to "...she cried all the way home." In Sister Marie of the Trinity's version, "an intelligence superior to Céline's" was replaced with "a remarkable intelligence," probably out of consideration for Sister Geneviève. But Sister Geneviève kept the text copied by Thérèse in the *Carnet manuscrit de soeur Geneviève* [Manuscript Notebooks of Sister Geneviève (Céline Martin)], p. 102. (Not translated.)

[408] As Céline notes in her biographical reflections of her mother, Zélie was very charitable toward the poor: "When she could not go herself, Mamma frequently sent Louise, the maid, to render assistance to needy families. In after years, Louise testified to these acts of charity: 'I alone know how many two franc pieces (of money) as well as the many dishes of stew she sent through me to poor persons around Alençon.' But it was especially her own children whom she taught to be charitable to the suffering poor, and to show them respect. I frequently saw them coming to the house and receiving food and clothing. Mother often shed tears when she heard their tales of distress." Céline Martin (Sister Geneviève of the Holy Face), *The Mother of the Little Flower*, pp. 68-69.

in his old age. This winter he had frostbitten feet, he sleeps in an abandoned hovel and has nothing. He's going to huddle outside the barracks[409] to be given a little soup.

Finally, I told him to come whenever he wants, and I'll give him bread. I would like your father to arrange for him to enter the Hospice; he wants to go there so much. We're going to negotiate the matter.

I'm very sad over this encounter, and I do nothing but think about this fellow who, nevertheless, was delighted by the few pennies I gave him. "With this," he said, "I'll eat soup tomorrow, I'll go to the soup kitchen, then I'll go have some tobacco and get a shave." In a word, he was as cheerful as a child. While he was eating he would pick up his shoes, look at them happily and smile at them. Then he recited a beautiful prayer for us that he always says at Mass.

Another thing, poor Thérèse is very upset. She broke a little vase, as big as my thumb, that I'd given her this morning. As usual, when the accident happened, she came right away to show me. I appeared a little displeased, and her little heart swelled, and she was choked with emotion. A moment later, she ran to find me, saying, "Don't be sad, my little Mother. When I earn a lot of money, I promise you, I'll buy you another one." As you see, I'm not about to get one.

I was intending to go to the Marian devotions, but I forgot the time. Now I would get there too late. In fact, I don't like this ceremony very much. One hears intolerable singing there; it's incomprehensible cooing. You would think you were at a café with live music, and that annoys me! Before, it was much more pious. Oh well, it seems that's progress!

Tomorrow and all week I'll be very busy. I'll be at the dressmaker's every day. I'm having made for you, as well as Marie, a beautiful dress that will be made as you wish, with an abundance of pleats, but your aunt is going to grumble! She'll have good reason, because nowadays people don't think of anything anymore except their appearance. I would prefer things not be like this. However, we have to make some concessions to fashion, when it's not objectionable.

---

[409] The military had a dominant presence in Alençon in the 19th and early 20th centuries. There were three army barracks in Alençon housing more than 2,000 soldiers. Pierre-Marie Gautier, *Alençon dans l'Orne*, p. 94.

I'm also having two black dresses made for you. Marie needs one to attend the retreat with you at the boarding school.

Madame Maudelonde had a little girl last Monday, and Jeanne is going to be the godmother.[410]

I see that my paper is full, although I must tell you something else. You know that your aunt, during my last trip to Le Mans, had mysteriously given me a letter that I couldn't show you. You now know what it contained....

As soon as I arrived at the station, I quickly went up to a gas streetlight to read this mysterious letter. I was very happy to see that you were going to receive many decorations and the Cross of Excellence. I want to congratulate you with all my heart.

You'll tell me in your next letters if the China aster seeds I gave your aunt have come up, and if the verbena is sprouting, although the weather isn't favorable.

I commend to your prayers and, above all, to those of your aunt and good Sister Marie-Gertrude, whom I like, a poor man who's going to die. It's been forty years since he's been to confession. Your father is doing all he can to persuade him to convert, but the man thinks he's a saint. Like Saint Paul, he thinks that nothing more remains for him than to receive the crown of justice!

It's true that he's a brave man, but he's more difficult to convert than a bad one. Only a miracle of grace could make fall the thick veil in front of his eyes.

I'm thinking whether or not I have anything else to tell you, and I don't find anything. So I'm going to kiss you with all my heart, as I love you, and I love you a lot, a lot.

CF 160

To her daughter Pauline
May 21, 1876

My dear Pauline,

I'm very tired this evening. We left at half past noon to go to the cemetery, and it was oppressively hot. Little Thérèse couldn't walk anymore and I had to carry her home. I put her to bed, and she

---

[410] Jeanne Guérin was the godmother of Hélène Maudelonde (May 9, 1876-June 6, 1944).

had a good two-hour nap, as did Céline. During this time I went to Vespers while your father watched them.

Léonie will be confirmed tomorrow morning.[411] She prayed very piously during Mass for her Renewal.[412]

It's almost nine o'clock. We're returning from a long walk, for which we left at six-thirty, and the weather was much better than this afternoon.

Tomorrow afternoon the children are going on another walk with their father. But I'm not going with them because I have an order of lace to make by Tuesday, and I don't have time to lose.

Marie is in the process of writing to you. I always tell her to take care of her letters on Saturday, but she doesn't listen to me, so it's going to force her to stay up quite late. On Sundays during the summer we have little spare time. The entire day is spent in church or out walking. If I had free time during the week, I wouldn't keep my letter writing for that day.

Your sister didn't want to go out this evening so that she could write, but I didn't want her to stay home all alone. She's strange, because all week she moans about never having any fun, and that she must always be confined, but when Sunday arrives, she dreads it. We're all a little like that, wanting what we can't have, and then, when we get it, showing ourselves to be blasé.

I was quite saddened by the deaths you told me about, especially that of the good Mother Superior, whom I loved a lot. I have a picture from her that I keep like a precious memento. She gave it to me seven years ago, and it's signed in her hand.

Friday I received a box of candy from Lisieux, from the baptism of little Hélène Maudelonde. Thérèse was the one who was happy. It was funny to see her jumping up and down and clapping her hands. Last evening we were talking about a rich proprietor, and Louise, who always envies the rich, said, "If only that were mine!" But the little one quite quickly said that she liked the box of chocolates much more than all of that. They're so happy at that age! It's a shame to leave it!

Marie loves her little sister very much, and she finds her very

---

[411] Léonie received the Sacrament of Confirmation on May 22, 1876.

[412] Léonie received her Second Solemn Communion on May 21, 1876, the date of this letter. (See footnote in CF 57.)

good. She could be quite difficult because this poor little one has a great fear of upsetting her.

Yesterday I wanted to give her a rose, knowing this would make her happy, but she begged me not to cut it because Marie had forbidden it. She was red with emotion. In spite of this I picked two of them, but she didn't dare go into the house anymore. It was no good telling her that the roses were mine. "But no," she said, "They're Marie's." She's a child who gets emotional very easily.

As soon as she makes the slightest mistake, everyone has to know. Yesterday, having accidentally ripped a little corner of the wallpaper, she put herself in a pitiful state. Then she had to very quickly tell her father. When he returned four hours later, everyone had forgotten about it. But she ran up to Marie, saying to her, "Quick, tell Papa that I ripped the paper." She behaved like a criminal awaiting her sentence, but she has it in her little head that we'll forgive her more easily if she takes the blame.

I was delighted by your letters, my dear Pauline, they are full of heart. I'm quite consoled to see you with such fine sentiments, and you make me happy.

I don't know if I'll be the one to bring Marie to the retreat, but I will certainly go get her, and I hope to take you out for a walk. I'm happy that your sister is going to make this retreat and that she'll have the happiness of spending a few days with her good aunt because this will do her a lot of good. She loves her dear Visitation Monastery so much and finds no other boarding school comparable.

Good-bye, my Pauline, write soon. You'll tell me if there's another Superior. Give your aunt a big hug for me.

CF 161 To her sister-in-law
June 4, 1876

I'm very late responding to your good letter and thanking you for the box of candy you sent me, which made Thérèse's happiness complete!

I was happy to hear of the birth of Madame Maudelonde's little girl, and I hope you'll send me news of them. Jeanne must be very happy to be the godmother?

I worry a lot about my brother's health. What did the doctor in Paris tell him? Also, how is his business going? My God! How I would like to see him succeed with his drug business![413] There will come a time when, with God's help, your hopes may be exceeded, but, in the meantime, we worry in spite of ourselves. We'd have to be saints to do otherwise.

Marie is always a good girl, but a little unsociable and too shy. She has unusual ideas. One day when she was wearing a new outfit for the first time, could you believe she went into the garden and cried, saying that we dressed her like a young girl whom we wanted to marry off at all costs, and that it would certainly be because of us that she would be asked! Just the thought of this makes her beside herself because, at the moment, she'd prefer to have her throat cut!

Recently Louise was telling me that a maid in the neighborhood had told her that her mistress knew a young man for whom Mademoiselle Martin would do quite well. Marie heard this and burst into tears, and we couldn't console her. Consider for a moment if there's anyone like her! I don't think she'll ever get married, although she doesn't seem to have a religious vocation. However, she's not the type of person to remain alone.

Every day she talks about you and your trip to Alençon. If I listened to her, I would spend a lot of money to entertain you. She asks for too much all at once, and I can't satisfy her.

I would have to wallpaper, polish, buy new curtains for all the beds, and put trellises all over the garden. Some of this has been done. There's also a swing for the little cousins from Lisieux to play on and a little garden for Jeanne. "Finally," like Marie says, "When my uncle and aunt come, everything must be in order." But I have a lot to do for that to happen, too much, because everything must be accomplished the same year, and then I have so many things on my mind!

But I've chatted enough, not saying anything of great importance. It's time I finished my letter because it's time for Vespers. Good, Grandmother Martin's arriving. Fortunately I've finished because, soon, I'm going to have a lot to do in order to see to everything!

Good-bye, my dear friends. I hope my letter finds you all happy and in good health, that's my dearest wish.

---

[413] Zélie's brother, Isidore Guérin, had opened the drug business in May 1870.

CF 162

My dear Pauline,

I've been very worried since I received your letter because your aunt tells me you always have migraines and aren't eating. I think you're going to need rest, and I'd like you to give up your prizes for this year. I'll buy you beautiful books that you'll have well earned because you've worked too much. So you'll leave your compositions and not worry anymore about your drawing.

I don't know if they'd want to allow this change to your routine, but if they can't, I've decided to come get you as soon as Monday. I'm waiting for an answer from your aunt about this. If you want to return to the Visitation Monastery next year, you'll need rest, otherwise it will be impossible. I prefer you to be less learned than to see you die, and if we wait too long it will turn into an illness that will not be easy to cure.

I'm not going to write you a long letter today since I'm going to see you in a couple of weeks anyway. If they permit it, I'm going to take you out all day on the 26th until eight o'clock in the evening. I don't know if Marie will go into the Visitation Monastery right away to make her retreat. We're leaving here at seven o'clock in the morning, and perhaps I'll bring Céline.

Your sister told you that last week there was a rabid dog that did a lot of harm in town. It bit four people, two very seriously: Monsieur Boulant, a locksmith, and a little boy of the regiment.[414] They were taken to the Hospice not so much because of the injuries caused by the dog, but for the cauterizations. They went across his leg with a branding iron. Recently, they were saying that he was going to die because they're convinced he has rabies. Monsieur Boulant is very sick, although he's beginning to get up, but he needs crutches to walk because he was horribly burned.

Your father and your two little sisters were nearly bitten; they passed quite close to the dog. They'd left to go for a walk, and the

---

[414] In the 19th century, the French army supported and educated the sons of soldiers; they served as uniformed members of the French army and were known as *"enfants de troupe"* ["children of the regiment"]. Louis Martin, the son of an officer, was an *enfant de troupe* in Strasbourg from the age of three and a half to seven (1827-1830).

dog was following them. The police ran after the animal and shot it with a rifle, but it was only wounded. It was quickly coming back down our street when a man who was working a few meters from the house broke his shovel on its head. The beast gave out a big howl, but it was his last. Everyone went to see the poor dog, which they carried away like a trophy on the end of a stick.

Good-bye, my dear Pauline. Above all, don't be sad over not having any prizes. As for me, this doesn't make me sad at all, I assure you. Rest your head in order to be able to work a little next year.

See you soon, my Pauline. What good times we'll have together!

To celebrate your arrival, Léonie absolutely wants me to keep two ducks that we bought on Thursday because she claims we mustn't eat them without you. We had to promise her we'll buy another two as soon as you arrive!

CF 163 To her sister-in-law
July 9, 1876

I received your nice letter, which I eagerly awaited! I was anxious, thinking that perhaps you were sick. I wasn't mistaken since you tell me you've suffered a lot with your teeth. I'm acquainted with this awful pain; we suffer horribly from it. Now, I hope you're all in good health and that soon we'll all have the pleasure of seeing you.

Pauline is suffering a lot. She's prone to headaches, but in the last few months they've gotten noticeably worse. She returned home four weeks ago. Her aunt sent her home to me because she was incapable of following her classes in the state she was in. However, since Marie had to go on retreat the 26th of June, I also wanted to bring Pauline, who wanted to go very much. Her teachers and her aunt saw fit then to keep her until the vacation, which begins August 1. Really, I wasn't annoyed; I regretted her not finishing the year and losing her prizes.

Last Monday I returned to pick up Marie, together with Céline. I made Pauline go out all day long, and she had a violent headache. I really wanted to bring her home with me, and, if the vacation hadn't been so close, I wouldn't have been able to resign myself to leaving her so tired. Her diligence has hurt her a lot. My sister advises me not to send her back next year because she thinks Pauline knows enough. That's probably what I'll do because she may not be completely recovered. This has lasted far too long, and she must have a lot of rest. I'm very upset about it. Her teachers are so pleased with her. She's considered the best student and will be very much missed.

I found my sister in very poor health. She couldn't make the slightest effort without spitting up blood. I'm afraid we won't keep her with us; she seems ready for Heaven. To dispel my fears, she tells me that the doctor assures her she can live like this another twenty years, but I doubt it very much. If I weren't so used to often seeing her sick, I could well believe her to be close to death.

I couldn't pull Marie away from the Visitation Monastery, and she spent the whole day in tears! She only left in the evening to take the train. She was telling me she's so sad because she's sure she'll never see her aunt again. I can't imagine things are at that point because I've already seen her this tired many times. But to tell you the truth, never as thin as this, and this is what worries me the most. It will be a great loss for me, but for her, a great happiness. She spoke to me about you a lot, and we didn't talk of anything else. This interested us both. She consoled me a great deal about you. I would have liked you to have heard her because it seems to me that you would have been as happy as I was. I returned so relieved of all my concerns!

Marie is completely changed since her retreat. It seems the Jesuit priest who gave it is a saint.[415] There were mysterious things said between them. I asked her aunt for some information, but there was no way of finding out anything... What I learned was from Pauline. Moreover, it was very little information. I told her aunt about it, who begged me not to publicize it, since Marie prefers to hide everything from me. I wouldn't want you to mention what I'm telling you for anything in the world, neither in letters (she reads them) nor in any other way.

In short, I think she's going to be a nun, although she does everything possible to convince me otherwise. Pauline, with her usual honesty, told me that she herself was taking spiritual direction from

---

[415] The retreat was held June 28 to July 2, 1876, and was preached by Father Cartier. Guy Gaucher, *Sainte Thérèse de Lisieux (1873-1897)*, Paris, France: Les Éditions du Cerf, 2010.

this priest and that he'd said to her, "My child, I think your vocation is to be a nun."

To throw me off the track about herself, Marie told me that he'd advised a few girls to get married as soon as possible. But as for her, she doesn't whisper a word about her affairs, and I don't try to find out her secret. All of that doesn't keep me from worrying a little. In spite of my great desire to give them to God, if He asked me, right now, for these two sacrifices, while I would do my best, it wouldn't be easy.

Please, my dear sister, not a word in your letters about this. We'll talk about it again when we're together.

Today I offered Marie the opportunity to go hear music, but, no, she doesn't need the crowd or getting all dressed up. We had to get angry this afternoon to make her dress. She doesn't like any of her hats, one no more than the other. She has a very pretty toque, and she can't look at it. She has a hat that she puts on carelessly, and that's even worse! In short, she only wants to go out wearing her everyday hat because it has a large brim that hides her more.

Pauline isn't that way. She wants everything that we want and is always quite agreeable to anything. I like that much better than being in an endless discussion about hats.

The next letter I want to receive from you must tell me the date of your arrival. I'll be very happy to see all of you, and I'm delighted you're coming. But I won't have time to do everything I would like to do to welcome you. I'm very overworked because I lost my assembler, and I have to work far too much. I'm truly unhappy over it, and I'd very much like to have a little rest before I die.

CF 164 To her daughter Pauline

July 16, 1876

My dear Pauline,

Yesterday I sent you Céline's photograph as well as the one of Thérèse.[416] I knew you wanted them very much, which is why I in-

---

[416] The photograph of Thérèse at three and a half years of age was taken in the middle of June 1876 by a professional photographer in Alençon. This photograph was preserved.

sisted that you not have to wait until your vacation to see them.

I just received a letter from Lisieux, and my sister-in-law tells me she'll arrive August 5. She definitely intends to take you home with her, you and Marie. This upsets me, I admit, and I'm only giving in reluctantly, just to make them happy. I would much prefer to keep you with me.

I think of you often, my Pauline. It seems to me you always have a migraine, and I'm extremely distressed by this. But I console myself by thinking that I only have to wait two more weeks for your return.

As usual, I'm delighted to go to Le Mans, and nothing delights me more. It's my greatest pleasure, and, to think that if you don't return next year to the boarding school, I won't have any more opportunities to make the trip! Oh well, everything comes to an end in this world, pleasure as well as pain, and the only thing to do then is to resign oneself, although I find it quite difficult to do so, especially today. I feel an oppressive sadness, like the heat. What's more, I believe there's a reason for it.

This morning at Mass I couldn't pray, and I said to myself, if I were a nun at the Visitation Monastery I would nevertheless have to pray. Then this thought helped me to respond. It seems to me that one is not sad like this when one is a nun. First of all, nuns have fewer problems, and I have them over my head.

Marie is no longer keeping secret what the Jesuit priest said to her during the retreat. She ended up confiding in me more than you had told me. I'm very pleased with her.

Monsieur de C, our neighbor, was buried yesterday, and this had a great effect on Louise. She can't understand how one could die "when one is so happy on earth!" I think she would gladly sacrifice her share of Heaven to be eternally here below, as happy as the rich people whom she imagines in perfect happiness. It's no use telling her that they're no happier than anyone else because she doesn't want to believe any of it.

I'm sorry I entrusted the two photographs to Monsieur Vital because I'm afraid he'll make you wait for them. Céline's isn't good, one eye is half-closed. She had to do it over again three times, as did Thérèse, who, for all that, was no more successful. The poor little one was afraid of the photographer. She, who's always smiling, was pouting as she does when she's about to cry. We had to reassure her.[417]

Every day the little one asks if Pauline is going to return soon. Yes, she's going to return soon, but to go to Lisieux, which doesn't make me happy! I think if your uncle and aunt knew how upset I am over this, they wouldn't ask us for these separations, and we would see each other every year as was agreed.

Marie is delighted to have you home soon. It's true she has hardly any entertainment. Besides, she misses everything and doesn't like society. I suggested going to hear music at the Promenades, but she didn't want to go; she preferred to write to Pauline.

I'm ending my letter because your grandmother just arrived. We're going to sit down at the table in a moment, then take a little walk to I don't know where.

I'm coming to get you Tuesday, August 1. Meanwhile, I kiss you with love.

CF 165

To her sister-in-law
July 23, 1876

I received your letter Sunday, and I'm counting on you for August 5. I think you'll arrive on the seven-thirty train, and we'll be expecting you for dinner.

I hope you'll stay with us a good week, and we'll try to make it as pleasant for you as possible. If you want, we'll go on an outing in a carriage to Saint-Denis[418] and from there to Saint Anne[419] which is very close, in the middle of the woods.

I think this trip will appeal to my brother. It's such a long time since he's seen his hometown. He was two years old when he left it and doesn't remember anything, but it's not the same for me. This town is full of memories. However, I think this little party will please

---

[417] *Ibid.*

[418] Saint-Denis-sur-Sarthon is 11 kilometers (7 miles) from Alençon and is where Isidore Guérin was born.

[419] Chapelle Sainte-Anne in Champfrémont, where there is a spring that is known to have cured childhood diseases, particularly those affecting the eyes. Jean-Marie Foubert, *Sainte Thérèse, Zélie et Louis Martin, Alençon.* Cully, France: Orep Editions, 2009, p. 11. (Not translated.)

all of you, especially the children, and then the pilgrimage to Saint Anne is charming. Unfortunately, her feast day will have passed.[420] They say, "Once the feast day is passed, good-bye to the saint!" We won't say good-bye to her!

Marie and I were invited to go there Wednesday the 26th. We must leave Tuesday night for Saint-Denis and the next day, the feast day, get up at four o'clock to make the pilgrimage. But I decided it's better for us to go there all together. Like at Lourdes, there's a miraculous spring there where many miracles have taken place.

I see you worked wonders for the Feast of Corpus Christi. May God reward you a hundred times over!

So you're intending to take Marie and Pauline. However, I assure you that's not how I understood the arrangements. When you come to Alençon, it's agreed that we don't go to Lisieux. I will have to go pick them up and that would be a great inconvenience to me. You might say to me, "Monsieur Martin can very well go there." Yes, that's true, but the absence of his daughters is very hard for him, he wouldn't like it,[421] and, even if he did like it, I would regret not going there myself to see you one more time!

Finally, last night, I asked him for his opinion. He said that if he saw you were insisting too much, he wouldn't want to upset you. So, you'll do as you think best.

You don't need to write me again to confirm your arrival. I'll forget neither the day nor the hour because here we talk about it enough so that I'll remember it myself!

CF 166

To her sister-in-law
August 20, 1876

I was happy to learn that you all got back to Lisieux in good health. I was only afraid that you might be annoyed with me for not letting Marie and Pauline go with you. It hurts me that I've upset you, but I would have been sorry to see Pauline leave, she's here for such a short time. I have a lot to do for her at the moment. I must replace her wardrobe for next year.

---

[420] The feast day of Saint Anne, the mother of the Blessed Virgin Mary, is July 26.
[421] See footnote in CF 65.

240

She's very sad today because we received a letter from her aunt in Le Mans who tells us very few things, but these few say a lot. She admits she's getting weaker and weaker, although she believes she'll be able to go on for a few more months. They're not giving her any more medicine. However, the Community surrounds her with the most loving care. She asks that Marie go on the retreat next year because she'll then have the consolation of praying at her grave!

As you can imagine, all of this doesn't fill our hearts with joy, so we've been sad all day long. I wouldn't have written to you this evening because it's late, but I was afraid the Malaga wine[422] you'd promised to send my sister had been mislaid. She seems very touched by the affectionate way in which you offered it to her and appears to want it.

You asked for news of my mother-in-law? She's completely recovered, and it was only a minor illness.

Good-bye, my dear sister, forgive me for having hurt you. I'll try to make up for it next year, but if you hold a grudge against me until then, I'll be upset! A thousand kisses to the little ones. Jeanne's letter is charming.

CF 167

To her brother
The beginning of October 1876

It's been two weeks since I received a letter from my sister, as well as the Superior of the Visitation Monastery. They asked me not to send Pauline back to school because of the prospect of her aunt's imminent death, and since Pauline is very sensitive, they wanted to spare her this pain.

Pauline wrote a letter to her aunt that brought tears to my eyes. Finally, she went back to school. As for me, I'd replied to the Superior that if she thought my sister was going to suffer more by Pauline's presence, I'd keep her home.

I saw my sister Wednesday, and she's very sick, very changed. She can only walk with the help of a cane and the infirmarian, who supports her. However, she spent two hours with us on two separate

---

422 Wine from Malaga, Spain.

occasions, and even her voice was very strong, much better than I'd thought it would be.

She told us that she's "the happiest patient in the world." Her face radiates joy, and she's awaiting the hour of her deliverance with a heavenly peace. I've never seen anything so edifying.

She spoke to us a lot about you, and I think I saw that she's had a few illusions about your success. I didn't want to take away her peace of mind, although not entirely sharing her way of thinking.

After you left Alençon, your wife wrote me that you'd forgotten to send the Malaga wine to Le Mans because of the large number of orders you found upon your return. My sister learned of this, and she immediately deduced from it that the novena for your business was answered in such a miraculous way that she had to publish this grace in the *Annales de Notre-Dame du Sacré-Coeur*![423]

I said to her, "You need to wait longer in case it hasn't continued." But she didn't have a shadow of a doubt that the matter was certain. So, I left her in her conviction, although I, myself, not being sure that she wasn't prophesying, promised myself to speak to you to find out whether or not it was so. Regrettably, I see from your letter that it's the complete opposite. That made me come down to earth because my holy sister had almost persuaded me!

I saw the Superior of the Visitation Monastery alone. She told me that the doctor believed our dear patient wouldn't last until the end of the year, but that she'd walk up until the end. She gets up at five o'clock in the morning after a night spent coughing in her bed. Her feet are always swollen, but she still goes downstairs to take her meals with the Community. She has a raging fever every day from two o'clock in the afternoon.

Pauline should write me on the 15th. I'll let you know as soon as I receive her letter and will do so each time I receive news. I think you can still wait until All Saints' Day to go to Le Mans, but later, our dear sister would be too sick and perhaps dead. All the Sisters I saw think she doesn't have much longer to live, and almost all of them came to see Marie.

She's thought of as a true saint within the Community, and the nuns told me that their Superior cites her as an example.

---

[423] *The Annals of Our Lady of the Sacred Heart.*

If you're going to see her, write me before Thursday. If I were you, I wouldn't delay long.

CF 168

To her sister-in-law
October 20, 1876

I'm sending you Pauline's letter. The best that it says doesn't make me very happy. It's like St. Martin's Summer[424] announcing the ice of winter. They are, in my opinion, the last rays of sunlight. Oh well, those who leave are happier than those who stay, as you and I well know. I was sad today, above all because of you. You have so many struggles, my God! When will it end? When will we be happy?

As for being unduly distressed over my bothersome gland,[425] I'm not convinced it's necessary. If God allows that I die from it, I'll try to accept it as best I can and resign myself to my fate to lessen my time in Purgatory. But I hope all will be well. I'll make your remedies exactly to put my mind at rest because I don't have great confidence in all that. Oh well, it will be like the blessing about which the Bishop of Séez's servant said, "If that doesn't do you any good, it won't do you any harm." Do you know the story?...

I was looking forward to your letter. I wanted to know if you were keeping the student,[426] but I see that was completely impossible. What are you going to do? I'm going to ask God to send you a suitable one. I'm beginning a novena with Marie, and our prayers will be answered. God knows well that you need it, and He always gives us what we need. Let us all have courage.

Please, don't worry about me. In no way am I suffering from the gland, and the little shooting pains I thought I felt are completely gone. I think it will be nothing, or, if it's serious, it will only be much later, when it will be time to die.

Marie read your letters with great interest and wants to faithfully follow all your advice for the treatment to be applied to me. I told her I didn't need to be looked after by her, but the maid replied that if

---

[424] Currently known as Indian Summer, in Europe it was formerly called St. Martin's Summer. The feast of St. Martin of Tours is November 11.
[425] During the Guérins' vacation in Alençon, Zélie confided her suffering to them.
[426] Pharmacy student.

they didn't prepare for me what was needed, nothing would be done. She said I needed to be hounded and that they are quite determined to do both! Oh well, I'll let them. Actually, it will be easier for me to see it all prepared.

CF 169

To her daughter Pauline
October 22, 1876[427]

My dear Pauline,

It gave me great joy to read the few lines from your aunt. She tells me that her strength is returning and may this continue! Céline has a special affection for her aunt. When we received your letter, she said to us, "I knew God would answer me; I do so many practices for her."[428] Actually, she does several of them every day. Today she only did one, which isn't surprising since she played all day long, and she didn't think of it anymore. I believe Céline will give me many consolations; she has an angelic nature. She's already seriously thinking about what she'll have to do to make her First Communion.

God is very good to grant me compensations which diminish the bitterness my poor Léonie causes me. I can't get through to her anymore; she only does what she wants and as she wants.

She just noticed that I was writing and said to me, "Mama, don't say anything to my aunt about me, I'll never do it again." I didn't answer her, but she started again so as to prevent me from writing. To have peace, I said, "No." I'm not lying because it's not to her aunt I'm saying it, but to you.

Oh well, here is everyday life, which isn't cheerful, I assure you.

---

[427] The date is deduced from the content of the letter. The second paragraph is taken from the *Carnet manuscrit de soeur Geneviève* [Manuscript Notebooks of Sister Geneviève (Céline Martin)], pp. 104-105. The paragraph about Léonie is original (*Vie Thérésienne*, No. 49, January 1973, p. 67). The paragraph about Thérèse comes from Sister Marie of the Trinity's copy of the letter (*Vie Thérésienne*, No. 93, January 1984, p. 77).

[428] Thérèse was taught by her mother to do everything to please God. From an early age, she learned the practice of self-sacrifice and was given a chaplet of movable beads that indicated the many daily sacrifices she made. They were called "practices." As an adult, she did away with the method of counting, and Thérèse came to understand that suffering was a gift and that all the sacrifices she continually made she transformed into acts of love and offered them to God. Hence, the many daily trials became fuel in her steady outpouring of love to God.

But often, to console myself, I think of my dear Pauline, who makes my consolation. It's a balm on my wound, and I find myself happy. Marie also makes me happy. Certainly, I have nothing to complain about. On the contrary, she does everything she can to make me happy. She's very pious and doesn't go a single day without saying her rosary.

Thérèse is still the same little imp. She often speaks of Pauline and says she's very annoyed not to see her returning from Le Mans. This evening she thought that we were going to wait for you at the station because your father went out to take Marie to Mademoiselle Pauline's house. She put up a struggle "to go get Pauline, too."

Yesterday morning, Céline was pestering your father to take her and Thérèse to the Pavilion, as he'd done the day before. He said to her, "Are you joking, do you think I'll take you every day?" The little one was there playing with a stick and didn't seem to be listening to the discussion, she was too absorbed. While playing her little game, she said to her sister, "We mustn't have the nerve to think that Papa will bring us every day." Her father laughed with all his heart.

The day your uncle was in Le Mans, at ten o'clock I received a letter from his wife, who was in very big trouble. The student they'd had for four days to take care of the pharmacy was intoxicated to the point that they had to put him to bed. Your aunt was alone, not knowing what would happen. She asked me to tell my brother, who was due to return to Alençon on the five-thirty train.

After dinner he left on the eight-o'clock train, which arrived in Lisieux at midnight. We hardly enjoyed ourselves, he was too worried.

I received a letter from them on Thursday. My brother didn't see the student again because Monsieur Fournet had given him his notice. Now, the most difficult thing is to find another one. Marie and I are going to say a novena to the Sacred Heart that your uncle finds what he needs. We'll begin on Wednesday so that we'll finish on the first Friday of the month. If you want, you can say this novena with us.

I'm certain our prayers will be answered because our Heavenly Father always gives us what we need.

I'm eagerly awaiting your letter, and you know you have to

write me every week. You did well, my Pauline, in wanting to return to be with your aunt, and how sad I would have been if it had been otherwise! I didn't want to tell you in order not to influence you, but I wanted it very much.

Please tell me how many times per week you see your aunt and for how long. Above all, during these moments, that are so short, try hard to show her your gratitude and affection for all she's done for you.

What a lovely evening I'm having writing to you, my dear Pauline! Also, I'm not bored while waiting for Marie, who's not going to arrive home before ten o'clock in the evening.

Here's Léonie coming downstairs to bring me my rosary, and who's saying to me, "Do you love me, Mama? I won't disobey you anymore." Sometimes she has good moments and good resolutions, but they don't last. Tell your aunt not to worry about me regarding the little illness I have and which isn't really an illness, since I'm not suffering from it at all. I'm making some remedies my brother sent me, and he assures me that they're infallible. In any case, there's nothing to worry about.

Good-bye, my dear Pauline. Give your aunt a big hug for me and tell her that I love her like those I love the most after God.

CF 170   To her daughter Pauline
October 29, 1876

My dear Pauline,

I'm sure you're not expecting to receive a letter today. I'm sending it to you secretly, without your aunt knowing. I'll send you another one Sunday, that is, when you will have written me the letter that she has to see, but I'd like another one from you, between now and then, to have reliable news of her health.

Sister Marie-Louise de Gonzague[429] will be kind enough to put a few words at the end of your letter to give me some accurate information about your aunt's health. Then, if there's cause for rejoicing, it will be without reservation, but in any case, I prefer to know the truth.

---

[429] A nun at the Visitation Monastery in Le Mans and the director of the school.

So, my little Pauline, as soon as you have a moment, write me a few lines. In next Sunday's letter, act as if you hadn't already written me, and I will do the same in my response.

Take heart, my dear Pauline, whatever God sends us, we must submit to it. If I lose my dear sister, I won't cry for her but for myself, because she'll be happy, and we'll be sad! This pain, however, will be soothed by the certainty of her happiness.

Marie isn't writing you a letter this time, it will be for Sunday. Above all, don't send her a letter in this secret mail; I don't want to see it.

I have nothing new to tell you. Céline is always doing her "practices,"[430] and she did 27 of them today. It's easy for her with her little sister.

That one is truly funny sometimes. The other day she asked me if she would go to Heaven. "Yes, if you're very good," I answered. "Ah! Mama," she continued, "If I'm not good, then I'll go to hell? But no, I know what I'll do. I would fly off to be with you who'd be in Heaven. Then you would hold me very tightly in your arms. How would God be able to take me?" I saw in her expression that she was convinced God could do nothing to her if she was in the arms of her mother.[431]

The day of your return to the Visitation Monastery, poor Céline cried all day to the point of getting sick over it. Everyone abandoned her at the same time, her dear Pauline and also her little friend Élise, whom she loved very much and who was leaving Alençon for good. She still found a little consolation in the hope of seeing Marie and me again when we returned, but our train was an hour late, and instead of returning at eight o'clock, we arrived at nine o'clock.

I assure you I was very worried knowing that your father was waiting for us at the station. I said to Marie when we left Le Mans

---

[430] See footnote in CF 169.

[431] Thérèse quotes this letter in *Story of a Soul,* with some variations: "Little Thérèse asked me the other day if she would go to Heaven. I told her 'Yes' if she were good. She answered: 'Yes, but if I'm not good, I'll go to hell. But I know what I will do. I will fly to you in Heaven, and what will God be able to do to take me away? You will be holding me so tightly in your arms!' I could see in her eyes that she was really convinced that God could do nothing to her if she were in her mother's arms." *Story of a Soul*, tr. John Clarke, OCD, p. 18.

at a quarter to eight, "Your father is already at the station at this moment" and I wasn't wrong. He waited for us an hour, he who doesn't like to wait. Imagine how he was enjoying himself!

I'll think of you a lot on Thursday, my little Pauline, and I'll be very sad all day long, knowing that you'll be deprived of going out. If I could be there, I would, but you know I can't be away on Thursdays. Oh well, it will be All Souls' Day, and that will be good. We'll offer all our hardships for the poor souls in Purgatory, who are much more deprived than we are, and, above all, for the souls of our relatives.

Good-bye, my Pauline. I must end my letter, although I'm having difficulty making up my mind to do so because it makes me so happy to write to you. I love you so much. If you knew how you're always on my mind, I don't think there's a moment during the day when I'm not thinking about you. I'm always seeing your beloved face, and I don't need your picture to remember it.[432]

Good-bye once again, my little girl who's loved very much. I kiss you with all my heart.

Your mother,
Z. Martin

CF 171   *To her sister-in-law*
November 2, 1876

I received very good news from Le Mans a week ago. My sister tells me that she's doing much better. She's sleeping well and doesn't use a cane anymore. But her throat is hurting her a lot to the point that she's not able to speak, and I shouldn't count on having any news for 9 days.

Last Sunday I wrote secretly to Pauline, without her aunt knowing, and I asked the head mistress to put a few words in the little girl's letter to find out if she really has improved. I'm enclosing Pauline's response and that of the nun.

I should have written you yesterday, but I wasn't able to because the services were very long. Today I think I'm going to miss the cutoff for the post. I'm always being disturbed, so I don't know where I am

---

[432] From "Good-bye, my Pauline..." to the end of the letter, the text from the original letter is preserved.

anymore. However, I had many little things to tell you, but I'm going to have to leave it there.

I'm properly making the remedies you sent me, only when I put the fresh ointment on the area to be treated, it hurts. I feel nothing only when it's dry. It probably must be that way for it to work well?

I kiss you with all my heart.

Your very loving sister, Z. Martin[433]

CF 172

To her daughter Pauline
November 3, 1876

My dear Pauline,

Since you want me to write to you today, my letter will not be as long as usual because I have hardly any time, being very harried by work and busy in every way. Also, I long for rest. I don't even have the courage to continue the fight. I feel the need for a little quiet reflection to think about my salvation, which the troubles of this world make me neglect.

And yet I should remember these words from the *Imitation*: "Why do you seek rest, whereas you are born to labor?"[434] But when you are too engrossed in your work and no longer have youthful energy, you can't help wishing to be relieved of it, at least in part. Oh well, I live in this hope. It seems to me, for many reasons, my business is winding down.

If I were free, my dear Pauline, I would go to Le Mans tomorrow with Marie. That would please me as much as you, and I would have the happiness of seeing my dear sister one more time. I think she's better, and if God wants to keep her with us a few more years, we'd all be very happy.

Little Céline is very cute and makes many sacrifices for her aunt. Sometimes, however, she's not consistent, like last night. She didn't want to give something to her little sister. I can't remember what it was, even though everyone was asking her to do it. Marie and Louise

---

[433] These last two lines are preserved from the original letter, as well as a few lines at the beginning of the letter.

[434] Thomas à Kempis. *The Imitation of Christ*. New York, NY: Alba House, 1995. (Book II, Chapter X, line 1-2, p. 127.)

made silly remarks to her, saying, among other things, that she only made sacrifices that pleased her and she'd be better off not making any at all. I told Marie she was wrong to discourage her that way, that it was impossible for such a young child to suddenly become a saint and that she had to overlook little things.

Even Thérèse wants to join in doing the practices.[435] This little one is a delightful child, perceptive and very lively, but she has a sensitive heart. She and Céline love each other very much, and they only need each other to entertain themselves.

The wet nurse gave Thérèse a small rooster and hen, and the baby quickly gave the rooster to her sister. Every day, after dinner, Céline goes to get her little rooster. She catches it with one swoop of her hand, as well as the hen which, nevertheless, isn't easy to grab, but she's so quick she swoops it up on the first try. Then both of them come with their animals to sit by the fire and play like this for a very long time.[436]

Sunday Thérèse took it upon herself to leave her little bed to go sleep with Céline. The maid was looking for her to dress her. She finally found her, and the little one said to her, while hugging her sister tightly, "Leave us alone, my poor Louise, you can see that we're both like the little white hens; we can't be separated!"

This evening Léonie and Céline went with their father to the Catholic Circle and left poor Thérèse home, who well understood that she was too little to go. She said, "If only they wanted me to sleep in Céline's bed." But no, they didn't want it. She said nothing and remained alone with her little lamp. She was sound asleep a quarter of an hour later.[437]

---

[435] See footnote in CF 169.

[436] This entire passage comes from the *Carnet manuscrit de soeur Geneviève* [Manuscript Notebooks of Sister Geneviève (Céline Martin)], pp. 102-103.

[437] Thérèse quotes this letter in *Story of a Soul*, with some variations: "Even Thérèse wants to do little acts of penance at times. She's a charming child, very alert, very lively, but she is very sensitive. Céline and she are very fond of each other, and are sufficient unto themselves for passing the time. Every day as soon as they've eaten dinner Céline takes her little rooster; she catches Thérèse's little hen with one swoop of her hand, something I can never do, but she's so lively she gets it in one bound. Then they come with their little pets and sit before the fireplace and amuse themselves for long hours at a time. (*It was little Rose who gave me the hen and the rooster, and I gave the rooster to Céline.*) The other day Céline slept with me and Thérèse had slept on the second floor in Céline's bed; she had begged Louise to take her downstairs to dress her. Louise went up to get her but found the bed empty.

As for me, I stayed home to look after her. I read until eleven o'clock because I had to wait up for Marie, who spent the evening at Madam X's house.

That poor lady! Despite all her millions, I know she's not happy, and yet she has the most beautiful house on the rue de Bretagne, with beautiful drawing rooms that are very vast and very elaborate, but for what? No one goes there except the people she wouldn't want to see because she finds them beneath her. Her daughter's isolation was so great that she recognized the need to make her associate with some young ladies her own age. Her sister-in-law told me this, not as clearly as I'm telling you, but I'd guessed as much a long time ago!

In short, my Pauline, one cannot be happy in this world.

When one has a fortune, one wishes for honors. I see this in all the people who become rich.

For Madame X, it's stronger than she is. I predicted to Marie that her invitations wouldn't last, I know this lady too well, and as for me, that would make me happy deep down.

I know Marie has nothing to fear in this gathering of young ladies, but I don't like seeing her with such rich people because it arouses unhealthy envy. I have no desire to associate with these people. I would be rather humiliated by them. I think that it's from pride on my part, but what can you do, I would have to spend too much to please them, and I would risk wasting my time and my money.

I must have nothing to tell you to speak to you of such little things, but it's so you'll be happy in seeing four very full pages. If I could only think of some news that would be of great interest to you! I don't know of anything, everything is very calm at home.

Marie will have told you that she no longer goes to Mass alone; that's over. She was never able to get used to it, and I myself insist that she never do it again because she's too shy. Then, she's too dressed up,

---

Thérèse had heard Céline and had come down to be with her. Louise said, 'You don't want to get dressed?' Thérèse answered, 'Oh no! Louise, we are like the two hens, we're inseparable!' Saying this they embraced each other and both held each other tightly. Then in the evening Louise, Céline, and Léonie left for the meeting of the Catholic Circle and left little Thérèse all alone. She understood she was too little to go to the meeting and she said, 'If they would only let me sleep in Céline's bed!' But no, they didn't want it, so she said nothing and stayed alone with her little lamp and fifteen minutes later fell into a sound sleep." *Story of a Soul*, tr. John Clarke, OCD, p. 25.

and it's not appropriate. When you're home, my Pauline, this will be more difficult because you like to sleep in the morning and go to bed late, and then chat with Marie until eleven o'clock in the evening. This concerns me because this has already troubled me many times. So I'll see what I can do to find a way of having you both go at different times. If, then, I'm not making Alençon lace any more, it will be very simple, but if not, I'll still be in a quandary. Oh well, we'll work it out for the best.

Every time I receive a letter from you, I send Lisieux news of your aunt. How I look forward to Tuesdays! How would I have done this if you hadn't returned to the Visitation Monastery? Is it not, my Pauline, that we were both inspired to want you to go back? It was God who guided us.

Good-bye, my dear Pauline. Tell your aunt that I pray for her every day. However, I find it quite peculiar to pray for a saint, I who am covered in weakness. What can God do with my prayers, as long as I'm not transforming myself? But it seems to me I'll be much better when I'm no longer making Alençon lace because at least I'll have the time to work on my perfection! Ah! What a beautiful day it will be for me when I'm freed from it!

I kiss you with all my heart.

CF 173 To her sister-in-law
November 12, 1876

I'm happy to see that you've finally found a good student in the pharmacy. If he could only stay with you a long time! That would make me very happy.

Tuesday I received news from Le Mans. I'm not at all reassured about my sister's health. I think it's still declining and soon it will be over. This gives me sad thoughts, and it seems to me I'll find myself abandoned. I need her and her advice. Oh well, I have to resign myself. I'm sending you the few words that she wrote me. Please put aside all her letters to return them to me because I want to save them. You see how happy she is, it's truly amazing. Usually suffering makes one so sad, and she's always filled with joy!

My brother wants me to give him some news about my health.

It's very good, and, apart from my mood, I'm not suffering at all. I'm certainly not filled with joy. I'm extremely worried, right or wrong. Ah! If only I were freed from my business, I would be happy. But no, my poor Léonie would be there preventing me from being completely happy because I fear for her future. What will become of her when we're no longer here?

I'm doing my remedies properly. Supposedly, they're necessary to take away this lump, but they take absolutely nothing away. Oh well, I feel guilty when I miss it, which, from now on, I don't want to do anymore, I promise you.

You haven't told me anything about your little girls; they're probably doing very well. Marie and I were talking about you this evening, and she's delighted to see that you love her; this seems to surprise her. She said to me, "Next time, you have to let us go to Lisieux, you can't do otherwise." I said, "Yes, and for at least three weeks."

But above all, she wants her sister and herself to be very beautiful to honor you. So you see this will be an expense. However, she's not particular about her appearance. I wanted to buy her a fashionable coat for the winter, but she doesn't want it, preferring to wait until next year so that she and Pauline will be the same. But for her little sisters, she doesn't give me a moment's peace. There must always be new things, and she doesn't like to see others dressed better than they are.

And as for me, if you knew how she hounds me so that I'll be more fashionable. It's truly painful for her not to see me well dressed. I'm forced to do more than I'd like in order not to always be hearing complaints. However, it's completely against my will because I detest dressing up myself.

A moment ago I received a letter from Le Mans. Really, our sister is better, and I don't understand anything anymore. What happiness if God wants to keep her for us!

But I'm surprised by some of her comments. Where did she get the idea that I think you don't write me often enough? It's probably because I recently said to Pauline that I was impatiently waiting to hear from you.

And also, she thinks I desire great suffering because I told her, if I had the choice, that I would prefer to die from a slow illness.

But great suffering, no. I don't have enough virtue to desire that; I dread it!

Then, her aunt didn't like Marie telling Pauline that she was going to Madame X's house every two weeks. Although there's no harm in this; there are a dozen young ladies there, all well brought up, who have a good time among themselves. So do I have to shut her up in a cloister? We can't live like wolves in the world! I would take all "the holy girl"[438] tells us with a grain of salt. First, I'm not sorry that Marie finds a little entertainment, it makes her less unsociable, and she's already too much so.

It's Mademoiselle S who organized these little get-togethers for her "beautiful niece" who is pining away from boredom. Madame X had never been able to make up her mind to associate with the "little" people. She was hoping that by having her mansion on an aristocratic street, she would end up softening the hearts of high society. But no, it's harder than she thought, and there's a deathly silence in her beautiful drawing room.

She told me that this year she'd finally been able to get permission to take her niece on outings with her cousins and other young ladies of her acquaintance, but her sister-in-law will never get over it. Her millions torment her.

It's quite true that one is never happy in this world. I know many others who ended up with a great fortune and are unhappy because of that very thing.

To be frank, I would rather that Marie not go there. Madame X believes she's bestowing on me a great honor, and, on the contrary, she's not at all.

I'm very worried about my little Thérèse. She's felt a heaviness in her chest for several months, and it's not normal. As soon as she walks a little quickly, we hear a sound like a strange whistling in her chest. I consulted a doctor, and he told me to give her something to make her vomit. I gave it to her, and she's even worse. I think a vesicant would do her good, but it's frightening to think about it.

My God, if I were to lose this child, how sad I would be! And my husband, who adores her!... You wouldn't believe all the sacrifices he makes for her, day and night. I'm going to see the doctor again, but

---

438 Sister Marie-Dosithée.

Louis doesn't want him to apply a vesicant, and yet it seems to me that would be the best thing because she's very sick at the moment.

Good-bye, my dear friends. Don't write back to me right away. You see in the letter from my sister in Le Mans that she's telling me to do penance.

I hug you with all my heart.

CF 174   To her daughter Pauline
                                                    November 19, 1876[439]
My dear Pauline,

Your last letter amused me very much with your story about the ink. Incidentally, let me say that you're a little careless. You made the good nuns go to a lot of trouble to clean all this, and then you weren't scolded!

Marie was telling me that one time, when she was six years old and a day student in Alençon,[440] she'd knocked over an inkwell, and what was her punishment? First they made her dip her hands in the ink and then smear it on her face. She was so angry telling me this. There's quite a difference between this approach and that of the Visitation Monastery!

Marie can thank God for having a Visitandine aunt. Being meticulous, she needed a lot of gentleness, and it was the only way of making her more accommodating. Also, her memories of her aunt and the convent are still vivid for her. She speaks of them with nothing but great affection and gratitude.

Let's come back to events that aren't very interesting. Céline was sick Thursday, and she spent the entire day in bed. She had a very high fever, and we thought she was going to be sick, but now she's much better, although not strong. She had three bad nights. I had her sleep with me last night, and she slept well. This morning at five-thirty, when I got out of bed, she woke up. I asked her if she

---

[439] The three extracts quoted here that differ from CF 174 in the 1958 edition of *Correspondance familiale 1863-1877*, pp. 323-324, come from a fragment of the original from the *Carnet manuscrit de soeur Geneviève* [Manuscript Notebooks of Sister Geneviève (Céline Martin)], pp. 103-104. (See *Vie Thérésienne*, No. 49, January 1973, pp. 72-73.)

[440] See footnote in CF 6.

wanted a little piece of chocolate. She didn't answer me because she was very attentive in offering her heart to God. She's a good little girl who gives me great hope, if, however, God lets her live because I have some doubts. She has an angelic nature, in spite of the little faults that result from the fact that Louise spoiled her and still spoils her. No matter what I do, I can't stop her, but with reason, all this will pass. She's very good with Marie. She's obedient beyond compare and does everything she can to please her.

This morning, while laughing, I called her my holy angel, and I said to her, "Who used to call you that?" "It was my nurse," she said. I said to her, "Do you think about praying for her since she died?"[441] She answered, "Ah! I haven't even missed once. Every day I say an Our Father and a Hail Mary for her, and, when you're dead, I'll say them for you, too."

Céline said to me this morning, seeing that I was showing great affection towards Thérèse, "Tell me, Mama, if you love me better." I answered that I loved both of them a lot. Finally, to please her, I told her I loved her a little bit more. This didn't satisfy her completely, and she answered, "Love me like you love Pauline. You know you love her more than a little bit better than Marie." I said to her, "For heaven's sake, don't say that to Marie!" "Oh, no!" she said, "There's no danger of that."

She asked me to hug her tightly, and Thérèse, who heard her, quickly answered, "And me, too, and tell her that I love her with all my heart." So the messages were delivered.

Tomorrow morning your father is going to Héloup[442] to buy apples. He's going to make cider again this year, and it's a savings by half. The children are overjoyed, even Marie, because they want to see the fellow who amuses them so much, with his good wife who returns at night to tell him to close his door![443]

We don't have any news about Mademoiselle Philomène.[444]

---

[441] Céline's third wet nurse was Madame Georges, known as "*La maîtresse Georges*." The Georges family lived in Samallé, not far from the Taillé family. (Rose Taillé was the wet nurse for three of the Martin children.) In a note written March 20, 1952, Sister Geneviève wrote, "I was perhaps six-years-old when she died," which would have been in 1875. (See footnote in CF 48.)

[442] See footnote in CF 61.

[443] See CF 156.

[444] Philomène Tessier. (See footnote in CF 92.)

They don't mention her anymore, and I don't know what's become of her. Her mother always appears very cheerful, and I think this is a little affected. She can't be as happy as she seems since she didn't want to give Philomène consent to enter the convent.

Thursday, Louise went to the market to buy a goose. I don't like to send her by herself, she always does stupid things. A few weeks ago she'd bought two of them, one to send to Lisieux and one for us. Ours was very small; however, she'd paid as much for it as the other one, believing she'd heard that it weighed the same. Thursday she gave eighty cents too little to the woman who sold vegetables and who didn't know how to count any better than she did. I wanted to send her back to run after her, but where to find her? This poor Louise has a mind like a sieve. She takes ten steps when she would only need to take one and quarrels while wanting to be right.

The other day, we were really annoyed by a cat. The poor animal was lost, and it came to us looking for shelter with such pleading eyes that I felt very sorry for it. She didn't want to hear about it and was looking at it in a menacing way, promising it some good blows with a stick as soon as I wasn't there to protect it. This really made me angry. I want to be free to help a cat if it makes me happy!

Come on, my Pauline, that's enough. I can't think of any more anecdotes to tell you, so I must say good-bye. This is a little hard for me to do. I'd still like to talk with you, but it's difficult to always be talking and talk well, so all that I tell you might not be very good....

Thank Sister Louise de Gonzague very much for me. She had the goodness to give me news of your aunt. Give her my regards.

I hug you with all my heart.

CF 175

To her daughter Pauline
December 3, 1876

My dear Pauline,

The first of the year is fast approaching. Soon I'm going to come and get you, and I'll have the happiness of seeing your aunt. You only have to write me twice between now and then. We're all going to be very happy to have you with us a few days. Marie is very much rejoicing over it, and little Thérèse made her little preparations for "when Pauline will be here." To listen to her, we'll be in a holiday mood the whole time. Perhaps we'll have the night to rest, but I don't think she'll want us to go to bed!

Two weeks ago Thérèse, finding Céline so happy to be sick and wanting so much to be in her place, came down as she did with a high fever and all the symptoms of measles. Thank God, at the end of four days she was cured.

At the moment, all children are sick and many are dying. Little Moisy was taken ill like your sisters. On Sunday she was better, since she wanted them to bring her downstairs to the table, and Tuesday morning she died. She was Thérèse's age.

We asked Thérèse if she was happy to be sick like Céline, but no, her wish had passed. She said, "I wanted to be sick as big as the head of a pin, but not like this." And she said this to us while crying.[445]

To amuse you, I had several of her funny remarks to tell you, but I can't remember any more. I should make a note of them right away. Next time, I'll fill my four pages with them, and I'll have to, because sometimes I'm quite at a loss and can think of nothing more, like today.

Oh well, I remember that Sunday we celebrated the feast of Saint Catherine[446] with donuts. The children and even Marie were intending to have a good time, but I said, "We won't have fun; Pauline isn't here." Marie exclaimed, "So we have to do without everything because Pauline isn't here! It's already more than enough that she's not here."

I wasn't mistaken, we didn't enjoy it, and almost all the donuts remained. We'd eaten too much at dinner, and there was no more room. The celebration was ruined.

At that moment, I heard the sermon bell sound, it was seven o'clock. I didn't have to go there because of the celebration for Saint Catherine, but as we looked at the donuts without being able to eat them, I said, "I'm going." Marie answered me, "Do I have to go, too?" "No, stay and eat your donuts, if you can!"

---

[445] Paragraph taken from the copy of the letter made by Sister Marie of the Trinity, *Vie Thérésienne*, No. 93, January 1984, p. 78.

[446] See footnote in CF 146.

Then I went up to my room to get dressed. Here's Marie, feeling a twinge of conscience, also going upstairs, and we left to celebrate Saint Catherine with a sermon!

I have to tell you about two events that happened this week. I already spoke to you about a poor man whom we've known since spring. He was in the most extreme poverty, since he didn't have any shelter and slept in a barn with an openwork door, which caused him to get frostbite on his fingers and feet. No one took care of him, and he asked for nothing and only went to the door of the barracks to have a little soup. He was starving. Your father had noticed him in the doorway of the Hôtel de France in such a miserable state and with such a gentle expression that he took an interest in him.

As for me, I wanted to know more about him, and while on a walk, I approached the fellow. I brought him home and questioned him. I then discovered that he was childlike and languishing without any help. I asked him to come here every time he needed something, but he never came.

Finally, in the beginning of winter, your father met him one Sunday. It was very cold, and he had bare feet and was shivering. Overcome with pity for this unfortunate man, he began to take all kinds of steps to have him enter the Hospice. How many steps he took, and how many letters he wrote to get a copy of his Baptismal certificate! And the petitions! But all of this was a waste of time because we discovered the fellow was only sixty-seven years old, three years less than the required age.

However, your father did not admit defeat. He took this cause to heart and prepared for the assault once again to have him enter the Home for the Incurables. The poor man has a hernia, but usually they won't take someone in for such a little thing, and I had no hope. Finally, he entered there last Wednesday, against all expectations. Your father went to track him down in his barn Tuesday evening, and the next morning he admitted him. He saw the old man again today, who cried tears of joy to find himself so perfectly happy. In spite of his weakened mind, he tried hard to thank him and prove his gratitude.

The other story is sadder. Last Monday, after the six-o'clock Mass, your father, Marie, and I came out of the church and were passing through the market when we heard awful cries. We headed in that direction, full of dread, and through an open window we saw a lady who appeared panic-stricken. Her husband had just fallen dead on the floor.

They went to look for a priest and a doctor, but it was too late. The day before he had gone to bed in good health, and I'd spoken to him Saturday morning.

Monsieur X, a haberdasher, was your father's age. He was a strong and handsome man, who thought more of himself than God. He had all kinds of civil honors, such as city councilman, president of the court dealing with trade disputes, etc. It's all ended. It's very sad to die that way, especially when one doesn't practice his religion.

Every week there are sudden deaths here, and we risk nothing being ready.

I don't think these stories entertain you very much, but, you know, I must fill my four pages. I can't talk to you about politics because that would interest you even less![447]

Now, I'm going to get ready for bed, but before I do, I still have a lot to do. Good-bye, my Pauline, give your aunt a big hug for me.

CF 176   To her sister-in-law
                                            December 7, 1876

I received your good letter and Pauline's the same day, which I'm sending you. She's not very reassuring, and I see that there's no hope. But I had no great illusions. I never believed our poor sister would pull through unless there was a miracle, which I wasn't counting on.

You're already speaking to me of New Year's gifts! That comes as such a shock.... How quickly the years pass, and how often this month comes! It's a true nightmare. Oh well, since you want to, send New Year's gifts to everybody. And what to give? I don't know.

For Marie, perhaps a sewing box and also one for Pauline. She'd told her sister what she wanted, but Marie can't remember it anymore!

As for Léonie, she's constantly saying that she wants a knife that closes. I told her that's not something she should ask for, but it's no use. She wants one and a drinking glass.

---

[447] Pauline is not yet fifteen years old.

Céline wants a little copper foot warmer. For Thérèse, you can give her whatever you'd like. As for toys, she has carriages and dolls.

For me, a jar of ointment because the one I have is almost finished. Although, it seems to me that the ointment is hurting me because now it's red. To tell you the truth, I'm a little worried about it, but I say nothing about it at home. If it's dangerous, they'll know it soon enough.

But let's talk about New Year's gifts again, and tell me honestly what would please Jeanne. She's already a big girl, and it's harder to know what to get her. As for Marie, I'd like to buy her a little set of dishes that I saw. They're very pretty and not breakable because they're made of strong papier-mâché decorated like china, and there are many pieces. Let me know as quickly as possible, so I'll be able to send you all this the Thursday before Christmas, as usual.

I hear Thérèse crying very hard while saying, "I'm so unhappy!" And it's because Céline is telling her that her dolls are badly brought up and she gives in to their every whim... Pauline writes Marie that her aunt wants me to bring Léonie to Le Mans when I go to pick her up for the New Year's holidays. I'll do it to make her happy, but to what purpose? None, unless my sister has the power to perform miracles. Marie will return to accompany Pauline to see her aunt one last time, if she's still in this world. All this is very sad, but we'll still have the consolation of knowing she's in Heaven, and for me, that's the main thing.

We often see sudden deaths in Alençon. Last week it was Monsieur X, who had very progressive ideas. Monsieur V thinks the town is losing a lot, but as for me, I think they're losing nothing there.

Good-bye, my dear sister, I don't think I'll write you again for another two weeks. I'll give you reliable news from Le Mans, where I'm going to pick up Pauline the Wednesday before New Year's Day.

I hug you with all my heart, as well as your children and my brother.

Your devoted sister,

Z. Martin[448]

---

[448] The passage from "before New Year's Day" to the signature is preserved from the original letter.

My dear sister,

My heart is pounding thinking of how much I'm going to hurt you. I hesitated a moment whether or not to tell you the entire truth, but I feel I must, I need your advice.

I'd made up my mind, last Sunday, to go find a doctor. I was more worried than I wanted to make known, seeing my disease getting worse. If I delayed so long, it was because I was doing my brother's remedy, and he didn't advise me to see a doctor.

I also knew there was nothing to do except have an operation, and the thought of that makes me tremble. Not because of the suffering, but because I was convinced that from that moment on, I would go to bed and never get up again.

Finally, upon receiving your letter, I would have gone to find Dr. X if I hadn't had a shipment of lace to do. So I waited until Friday. My husband, reading your letter, began to become more worried. He went to find Monsieur Vital Romet because I was saying I didn't want to see a doctor. Monsieur Vital came and insisted on an operation, naming several ladies whom I knew and who'd pulled through.

In the end, I went to see Dr. X, who, after having examined me thoroughly through touch, said to me after a moment of silence, "Do you know that what you have there is of a very serious nature? It's a fibrous tumor. Would you shrink from an operation?" I answered, "No, although I'm certain that instead of saving my life, this operation would shorten my days." I added proof to support this, so much so that he continued immediately, "You know as much as I do, all this is the truth. Also, I can't advise you because it's quite uncertain." I asked him if there was a one in a hundred chance, and he answered evasively.

I'm very grateful to him for his frankness because I'm going to hurry to put my affairs in order so as not to leave my family in an awkward position.

He offered me a prescription. I said to him, "What will it do?" He looked at me and replied, "Nothing, it's to make the patients happy."

I couldn't help myself from telling my family everything. I

regret it now because there was a grief-filled scene... everyone was crying, poor Léonie was sobbing. But I named so many people who'd lived ten or fifteen years like this, and I didn't seem very upset, doing my work as cheerfully as always, perhaps more so, that I calmed everyone down.

And yet, I'm quite far from deluding myself, and I have trouble falling asleep at night when I think about the future. However, I'm resigning myself as best I can, but I was far from expecting such a test. My sister is very happy to die. She'll know nothing of these sad affairs because I don't want to poison her last days. I won't say anything more to Pauline. If she knew, she wouldn't be able to return to boarding school. Knowing her as I do, that would hurt her more than seeing me.

If you have any advice to give me about the operation, please write me this week because Pauline arrives Wednesday, and I don't want her to see your letter.

My husband is inconsolable. He's given up the pleasure of fishing and put his lines up in the attic, he doesn't want to go to the Vital Circle anymore. It's as if he's shattered. That same night he went to find Monsieur Vital to give him an account of the consultation, and Monsieur Vital still says the operation is very necessary. Please, give me your advice.

I'm not suffering a lot. There's a numbness along the whole side to just under the arm and a dull pain on the right side of the lump. I can't lie down on that side anymore.

I would like that this not worry you too much and that you resign yourself to the will of God. If He found me useful on earth, certainly He wouldn't permit me to have this illness because I've prayed so much that He not take me from this world as long as I'm necessary to my children.

Marie is now grown-up. She has a very, very serious nature and no youthful illusions. I'm sure that when I'm no longer here she'll make a good mistress of the house and do everything possible to raise her little sisters well and set a good example for them.

Pauline is also charming, but Marie has more experience and, moreover, she has a lot of influence over her little sisters. Céline shows the best tendencies, and this one will be a very pious child. It's quite rare at her age to show such an inclination towards piety. Thérèse is a true little angel. As for Léonie, only God can change her, and I'm convinced He will.

I hope to go and see you one more time, and if I notice that the illness is progressing too much, I'll go before the vacation. If Pauline were here, I would have taken her and Marie to stay with you, and I would have left them with you several weeks, in fear that it may not be possible this summer.

They'll be very happy to have you when I'm no longer here. You'll help them by your good advice, and, if they have the misfortune of losing their father, you'll take them into your home, won't you?

It consoles me a lot to think that I have such good family and that they'll be good replacements for us in case of misfortune. There are poor mothers much more unfortunate than I who don't know what will become of their children and who leave them in need without any help. As for me, I have nothing to fear in that respect. In short, I don't look at the dark side of things. It is a great grace that God is giving me.

Since I wrote you the above lines, quite a lot of time has passed. I was waiting to send my letter until I received the one that arrived today from Le Mans, and which I'm enclosing in mine.

Don't worry about me at all. I'm hardly sick at the moment. It's a little thing, and if I didn't see the lump, I would think it's nothing. I have a corn on my foot that hurts me much more, and I don't have to see it to feel it. Be that as it may, let's make the most of the time that's left to us and not worry. Besides, it will still only be what God wants. If the illness gets worse, I'll go on some pilgrimages. If I'd listened to Louis, I think we would have been to Lourdes already, but it's not urgent.

I would wish, for a moment, to go spend a day with you, and you'd see that I look well, my appetite is good, and I'm very cheerful. It's true that I'm not sad.

While waiting to hear from you, I hug you with all my heart.

CF 178

To her brother
December 1876

My dear brother,

You put death in my heart with your operations. I know enough about it to be sure that my days would be shortened by it. Please, let me live and don't try to find a doctor who says the same as you. We like Doctor X, and you trust him since you'd asked me to consult him. I told you the whole truth. He is far from advising me to have an operation. If you don't rely on my word, write to him or come speak with him.

Finally, to make you happy, I'll go to Lisieux on Saturday.[449] I'll leave at eleven-ten in the morning.

I'll spend Christmas with you. I don't want to go to Paris to consult with a doctor right away. I trust Doctor X and Doctor Notta completely.[450]

Good-bye, until Saturday. Don't worry, you'll see that I'm not dying, I'm absolutely fine except for this little booboo with which I can live many years, if they leave me alone.

You know that it's a period of fasting, and I'm fasting because I'm not sick enough to exempt myself. So don't get anything ready for me, please.

Marie is not coming this time.

CF 179

To Louis Martin
December 24, 1876

My dear Louis,

I arrived in Lisieux yesterday afternoon at four thirty. My brother was waiting for me with a carriage, where I found a good foot warmer. Upon arriving at his house, I saw Madame Fournet and Monsieur and Madame Maudelonde, who gave me a very warm welcome.

---

[449] December 23.

[450] Doctor Alphonse Henri Notta (1824-1914), a famous surgeon in Lisieux. In 1883 he took care of Thérèse and, in 1889, signed the voluntary placement of Louis Martin to the Hospital of Bon-Sauveur in Caen. He published *Médecins et clients* [Doctors and Patients], second edition in 1877.

After dinner I did everything possible to cheer up my brother and give him a little courage. He spoke to me a lot of Monsieur Vital, who'd written to him the same day, telling him about the consultation with Doctor X and begging him to act forcefully and take me to Paris. I would have wanted to see this letter, but they refused to let me see it.

Finally, I slept perfectly last night, against my expectations, but I was tired from the trip. The doctor arrived this morning at eight-thirty. He examined the area of the illness well and gave exactly the same advice as Doctor X, that an operation wasn't necessary and that it would be a big mistake to try. He prescribed some pills, and I don't know what else. Now my brother is quite certain and no longer wants to take me to Paris.

Doctor Notta finds it very regrettable that, from the very beginning, they didn't do the operation, but now it's too late.

However, he seemed to think that I can go on a very long time like this. So, let's put it into the hands of God because He knows much better than we do what we need. "It is He who causes the wound, and He who binds it."[451] I'll go to Lourdes on the first pilgrimage, and I hope the Blessed Mother will cure me, if it's necessary. In the meantime, let's stop worrying.

I'm rejoicing very much at the thought of seeing you all again. How long the time seems! How I would like to come home today! I'm only happy when I'm with you, my dear Louis.

I have to end my letter because it's time for supper, and Monsieur and Madame Fournet are going to join us. I've just spent the best moment of my day with you because I'm a little bored of going to pay visits and receiving them, but this isn't going to last long.

I'm going to Midnight Mass with my brother. Madame Maudelonde is also coming, for the first time in her life.

Nevertheless, I have to finish, but I very much regret the blank paper that remains. I would tell you much more.

I'm leaving Tuesday morning[452] at nine-thirty, arriving in Alençon at one-forty. I kiss all of you. Good-bye.

---

[451] Inspired by Job 5:18.
[452] December 26.

So here is another year passed.... As for me, I'm not sorry. I impatiently await the end of next year. Yet I hardly have cause to rejoice in seeing the time pass, but I'm like the children who don't worry about the future, I always hope for happiness.

I've thought of you many times since I left you, and I still see you surrounding me with every possible care. Truly, if I stayed with you a long time you would spoil me completely. Do you know, afterwards it seems hard going back to work and having all kinds of troubles? I'd very quickly get used to the gentle life you gave me for those three days.

I think I'm cured, or on the road to being cured, because I haven't felt the slightest pain since Thursday. In any case, I'd be able to go a very long time like this. It won't be the same for my sister. We don't expect anything anymore except very sad news. It's sad for us but not for her because I find her very happy having prepared for such a holy death.

As for me, I'm trying to convert myself, but I may not get through it. It's quite true that we die as we lived. We can't go against the current when we want. I assure you, I realize it well, and sometimes I become discouraged by it. And yet they say it only takes a moment to make a reprobate a saint, but I think that's only a very little saint! Oh well, there must be all kinds. In spite of my wanting to hide my illness from Pauline, she's already heard too much about it. This morning she asked me what it all meant. I told her I could live fifteen to twenty years like this, and she was very reassured. It seemed like an eternity to her. That's how it is when we're young; we don't worry about something so far away.

So on Wednesday I'm going to take her back to the Visitation Monastery. I'm very afraid that something tragic will happen to my sister between now and then. If it does, I don't know if I'd have the courage to return to Le Mans.

I have to finish my letter because it's time for the post. I wish you much happiness in the New Year. If God grants my wishes, you'll be as happy as Adam and Eve in the Garden of Eden. They would have done well to stay there and not to have cast us into misery as they did. I'm not grateful to them for it.

I kiss all of you with all the affection I'm capable of and thank you a thousand, thousand times for all your kindness towards me.

1877

CF 181

Your letter announcing your favorable balance sheet for the year gave me the greatest pleasure. I told you you'd succeed. It's a small beginning, but later it will be quite different, you'll soon see. Oh well, this good news cheered us all up, even my husband, who's been so sad because of my health.

You're going to see, in the enclosed letter, that Pauline is going to leave alone on Monday. I'm very upset about this because I'm convinced I'm not going to see my sister anymore. A moment ago I just received a telegram, and immediately I said, "My sister has died!" Pauline began to sob. I opened the telegram... it was an order for lace. Sadly, though, I think we'll soon receive the announcement of her death.

I wrote to the Superior last Tuesday, and I sent the famous sweet cider that she wanted. Mademoiselle Pauline Romet went to the Visitation Monastery the next day to learn news of our dear patient. They told her that her condition had not changed.

The extern Sisters entered the enclosure on New Year's Day, and they gave her their messages for Heaven. A good priest wrote to her asking that she obtain a favor for him, promising her nine Masses if it was granted.

Monsieur, Madame and Mademoiselle X, who have different ideas about the afterlife, laughed in the face of the good Sister who gave them these very details. They told me all this, saying that she must have taken them for heathens.

I forgot to tell you that I received the medicine. You're going to a lot of trouble, my dear sister, and I'm truly very grateful to you for all your kindness. I'll use it to make you happy. However, I don't believe anything will be effective.

Please thank the ladies from the P family[453] for me, who commended me to Lourdes. In fact, I don't count on anything anymore except the help of the good Mother! If she wants, she can cure me, she's cured much sicker people.

However, I'm not convinced that she'll cure me. After all, this very well may not be the will of God. Then we must resign ourselves, and, I assure you, that is what I'm doing.

I don't understand my brother still wanting to take me to Paris. And why do it? I wouldn't rely on what the doctors there would tell me; I only trust Doctor Notta. The day he considers an operation necessary, it will be decided at once. So let's go on as we are and as cheerfully as possible. Now they're less worried at home, and I'm trying harder than ever to keep it that way.

So I would really like us not to talk about all this anymore! What's the point! We did everything we had to do, and let's leave the rest in the hands of Providence. I'm going to have a good protector in Heaven in the person of my sister, and if I'm not cured, it's because God will be firmly resolved to have me....

CF 182

To her sister-in-law
January 8, 1877

I've just come from Le Mans, and I'm hurrying to give you the news about our dear sister. I found her better than I did two weeks ago, and she spoke to us for two hours without seeming too tired. I was quite surprised by this because I was expecting to see her in a sadder state.

However, towards the end of our parlor visit she had a bad attack, and I thought she was going to die. Quickly she asked for a glass of cold water, which was quite slow to arrive. As soon as she took a drink, she felt better.

She talked about you a lot, how she loves you with such deep affection. I had to read my brother's letter, and afterwards this letter

---

[453] The Pigeon family.

was passed around the convent. As for me, when I read it out loud, I had a lot of trouble holding back my tears, but in the end, I didn't cry.

Here are the messages that I gave my sister for Heaven. I told her, "The moment you're in Heaven, go and find the Blessed Mother and tell her, 'My good Mother, you played a joke on my sister by giving her poor Léonie. She's not a child like the one she asked you for, and you must fix this.'

"Then, go and find Blessed Margaret Mary and tell her, 'Why did you miraculously cure her? It would have been much better to let her die, and you are bound by conscience to repair this misfortune.'"

She scolded me for talking like this, but I didn't have any bad intentions, and God knows this very well. It doesn't matter, perhaps I did something wrong, and for my punishment, I'm afraid of not having my request granted.

The Superior's Assistant[454] came to see me in place of the Superior, who was sick. I'd received a letter from her Saturday morning responding to a question I'd asked, telling me what would make my sister happy. Can you imagine, it was to eat goose, but a goose cooked at our house... It seems the Mother Superior had a good laugh about the patient's wish.

I said to my sister, "Thursday I'll send you two geese, and I want you to treat all the sisters to a delicious meal. These good nuns never eat any, and they're forbidden to buy any poultry. They only have some when it's given to them. So I'm very happy to offer them this treat at the same time as you." They'll only have to have them roasted because if I send them already cooked, they would hardly be presentable.

That's enough about geese. In that way, our meeting was almost cheerful.

However, I don't have a cheerful heart. My little Thérèse is sick, and I'm worried about her because she has continual colds that cause a heaviness in her chest. This usually lasts a couple of days. She's a child who can neither walk fast nor play like the others without be-

---

[454] The nun who takes on the duties of the Superior when she is unable to attend to them.

ing out of breath. I have to consult the doctor, but he's going to tell me to put vesicants on her, and that terrifies me. This evening I find her almost cured.[455]

This morning I received a letter from a merciless merchant who now no longer wants some orders that he placed with me. This is the third piece of lace he's refused. I've been sad about it all day long.

We're in the process of selling our business, and perhaps this will be concluded tomorrow. We'll benefit from the existing orders. Naturally, the person who buys the business will take all the merchandise. I don't have a lot at the moment, except for the three pieces that were refused. But he wants our house and to sign a nine-year lease. It annoys me to have to move because I was used to living here. Finally, tomorrow we'll know what the terms are.

CF 183   To her daughter Pauline
                                                January 1877

My dear Pauline,

I want to put your mind at ease about your little sister, who was so sick when you left. When I arrived Monday night she came with the maid to meet us, but not as far as the station. She ate with us and was very cheerful. In other words, the illness had disappeared. I don't understand this illness which she gets quite often and never lasts more than a day or two. Afterwards, it's completely gone.

I have nothing new to tell you. I'm taking advantage of an opportunity to write to you; otherwise you wouldn't have had any news today. You know I'm very busy on Thursdays.

Marie is sending you all of her pictures. Try and make do with them, and if you don't have enough, buy some from the Visitation Monastery.

The deal for the sale of the Alençon lace business hasn't been completed, and I don't think it's going to take place. I don't want it for several reasons. Besides, I prayed to the Sacred Heart that it won't go through if it's a bad business venture for the people who want to buy it.

---

[455] The paragraph about Thérèse comes from Sister Marie of the Trinity's copy of the letter, *Vie Thérésienne*, No. 93, January 1984, p. 79.

If we'd wanted, the sale would have been concluded, but I thought I should open the eyes of the potential buyers about certain difficulties because they saw everything in a positive light, and I didn't like that. For me, who sees everything as black, there's a big difference!

Oh well, I'll continue until further notice, and we'll see what we'll do, but I'm very weary of business. I don't have the necessary energy anymore. I feel I need rest, but I'll hardly have any before the eternal rest....

My dear Pauline, continue to be a good girl, very gentle and good towards everybody. You will be rewarded, even here below: "Blessed are the meek, for they will inherit the earth."[456]

I'll write you a long letter a week from Sunday and a very interesting one, if possible, because I'll need to have something new to tell you, and that's not always the case.

When your aunt has no more oranges, give money to Sister Félicité[457] so she can buy some.

I kiss you with all my heart.

CF 184   To her sister-in-law
                                                  January 18, 1877

Monday I received a letter from Le Mans in which my sister wrote a few lines in pencil. She tells me her condition is still the same and the progress of her illness is hardly noticeable. She adds that the Community received the geese and that I can't imagine the pleasure it gave them. They talk about it at recreation.

She adds, "As for me, I desire nothing more than eternal life.... I will pass along all the messages for Heaven.... Hello to the dear family in Lisieux. Already I'm unable to write these lines anymore." Pauline tells me that the Superior and the head mistress agreed to let her see her aunt every morning around seven-thirty. Pauline's school report is excellent, and she's going to become a Child of Mary on February 2. Her aunt confided in Marie that if her sister continued,

---

[456] Quotation from Matthew 5:5.
[457] The extern Sister at the Visitation Monastery in Le Mans.

she would receive the "white crown" when the prizes are given out. This is a crown of white roses – the highest award there is, and it's almost never given. Marie only saw it awarded once in nine years.

Now, I must respond to your good letter. I see that you're very worried about me. My condition hasn't changed since I saw you. I'm hardly suffering at all, only the glands in my neck are swollen.

We haven't sold our business. We found out some things about the buyers, and it's worse than you can imagine. This gentleman has already lost thirty thousand francs borrowed in small sums from unfortunate workers who had trusted him, and we found out several other facts of this kind.

I'm happy the sale wasn't concluded. These people would have caused us great inconvenience. Anyway, I prefer to give it up very gradually. Besides, I'm going to be forced to because I don't have any more orders.

Léonie had begun a letter to you, but that was the end of it. Nevertheless, she has to write you. Marie is giving her lessons with Céline, and she's pleased with her. Yesterday she said to Marie, "I'm going to write to my aunt in Le Mans before she dies and give her my messages for Heaven. I want her to ask God to give me a religious vocation."

Marie pretended to make fun of her to see what she would say, but she persisted and said, "Everybody can make fun of me, I don't care, but I want to tell her this before she dies." Finally, today she wrote her letter all by herself, without anyone saying a word to her to give her any ideas. This is what she wrote:

"My dear aunt, I still treasure the picture you gave me. I look at it every day to become obedient, like you told me to. Marie framed it for me.

"My dear aunt, when you're in Heaven, please ask God to give me the grace of converting me and also to give me the vocation of becoming a true religious because I think of it every day. I beg you, don't forget my little message because I'm sure that God will answer your prayer.

"Good-bye, my dear aunt, I kiss you with all my heart. Your very loving niece...."

What do you think of this? As for me, I'm very surprised. But where did she get these ideas? It certainly wasn't me who put these ideas in her head. I'm even quite convinced that, without a miracle, Léonie would never enter community life.

It's her future that worries me the most. I say to myself, "What will become of her if I'm no longer here?" I don't dare think about it. But I assure you that this little letter renews my courage, and I find myself hoping that perhaps God has merciful plans for this child. If it only took the sacrifice of my life for her to become a saint, I would give it willingly.

We had a beautiful ceremony Monday for the transfer of soldiers killed in the fighting in Alençon on January 15, 1871. The entire town was standing, and it lasted five hours.

Our mayor returned home so tired that he went to bed and wasn't able to go to the Prefecture for the official dinner. His wife thought he was sleeping well, but she noticed that his sleep was un-natural. She sent for the doctor who was unable to wake him up, and he's been sleeping since Monday. He'll probably remain asleep until the end of his life, at least that's what the doctors are saying because he's paralyzed and had a stroke. It seems there's no hope for him.

It's very sad to die in one's sleep. As for me, I'd prefer to be fully awake and see death come. It's time I finished my letter. I've been writing this letter quite a long time. I've had to come back to it many times because I was often interrupted.

While I was writing you I saw Madame Z, who is going to the grand ball being given at the Prefecture tomorrow. She told me all kinds of things about her ball!

Good-bye, I kiss you with love.

CF 185   To her daughter Pauline
                                                January 21, 1877

My dear Pauline,

I don't know if I'm going to have time to write you a long letter today because it's already a quarter to one. At one-thirty I have to go pay a visit to Madame M, later to Vespers, and then to the closing of the retreat at St. Léonard's at seven-thirty.

However, I have to find enough time to write a long letter to my Pauline to make her happy. I also have to write to your aunt and then to a nasty merchant who wants to make me lose a lot of money, quite unjustly. I'm more appalled by his injustice than by the loss I'm going to bear.

Oh well, I see it's quite a busy day, and yet my letter must be sent this evening, or tomorrow morning if I finish it too late.

I think you're going to write me today. I'm almost going to regret it because I would have liked a few words from your aunt for Léonie. There's quite a story behind this.

Last Wednesday, while Marie was giving the class, Léonie said in a very serious tone of voice, "I want to write to my aunt before she dies and give her my messages for Heaven."

Marie, very surprised, asked her what it was about. She told her that she wanted to be a religious, and her aunt would have to obtain this grace for her. Marie made fun of her, but she persisted, and Thursday morning she wrote her note, which I think is rather good for her.

I said to Marie that evening, "There's one thing that surprises me; it's that she wrote 'a true religious.'" Marie, also surprised, said, "I really wanted her to erase the word 'true.' I pointed out to her that it didn't mean anything, but she stood firm saying, 'Please, let me put it in, I want it to be that way.'"

The next day Marie asked her, "What does that mean, 'a true religious'?" Léonie answered, "It means that I want to be a completely good religious and in the end become a saint." I don't know what I should think of all this because the poor child is covered in faults like a blanket. We don't know how to handle her, but God is so merciful that I've always had hope, and I still hope.

Yesterday she had an awful day. At noon I told her to make some sacrifices to conquer her bad mood, and that, for each victory, she should put a hazelnut in a drawer I pointed out to her, and we would count them that evening. She was very happy about this, but there were no more hazelnuts. I made her bring me a cork that I cut into seven little slices.

That evening I asked her how many "practices"[458] there were.

None! She'd done the worst she could. I wasn't happy and

---

[458] See footnote in CF 169.

scolded her bitterly, telling her that she certainly shouldn't ask to be a religious under these conditions.

Then she started to cry because she was sincerely repentant, and she flooded my face with her tears. Today there are already little slices of cork in the drawer.

Now, my Pauline, I'm leaving you. I have to get dressed to go where I told you, and this annoys me very much. Until this evening....

It is now, in fact, this evening, and it's ten o'clock. We're just coming from the closing of the retreat. It was magnificent, a beautiful sermon on virginity and a spiritual enlightenment without equal.

Yet it was very hard for me to go, I was thinking about my letters. Marie would have liked to see me stay home. I told her I wasn't asking her to go with me, that I would go alone. But it was like the Feast of Saint Catherine, and she was seized by remorse and followed me.[459] Now she's very happy to have gone, and the two of us just made a wonderful late-night snack.

We had a very enjoyable day. I was at the home of the beautiful lady who wasn't there. That is to say, she was there, but there was a carriage at her door, and she was about to pay her last visits of the day. Marie was very frustrated by this. She was anxious to see her to ask her for information about certain things that interest Marie.

Afterwards we attended Vespers at the Hospice, and we all went for a walk in the country. The weather was so beautiful this afternoon, and it had been such a long time since we'd gone out! So this did us a lot of good.

Now I must tell you about an adventure that happened to us last night.

The maid was in the process of drying the dishes. It was already dark, and she was getting ready to cut the bread for the soup when she was interrupted. Léonie, always quick to help her, took hold of the bread and sliced it.

Finally, here is the soup ready to serve, with the soup poured over the bread. It was purée of pea soup, which Marie likes a lot. She

---

[459] Zélie is referring to an incident that took place when she and the children were celebrating the Feast of St. Catherine of Alexandria. (See CF 175.)

said, "Papa's at a grand dinner at Monsieur Vital's house, but he won't have soup as good as this!"

We all sat down at the table. I began to serve the soup, but I couldn't push the spoon in, I felt a tremendous resistance. I said to Louise, "What have you put in here? I can't find any bread; are there only vegetables on the bottom of the soup tureen?"

Finally, I tried to pull out whatever was blocking the spoon, and after many tries I pulled up... the dishtowel. Léonie had cut the bread over it without noticing!

The soup wasn't eaten, but on the other hand, we had a good laugh! Your father said it was like the little shoe of the man from Auvergne! "It's not that it's dirty, it's that it takes up space!" You know the song.

Marie didn't want me to tell you this. Last night I heard her say, "I'm sure Mama is going to tell Pauline, and the teachers will know. I'm ashamed of it." I answered, "I'll tell her all the same, they can laugh about it if they want."

Now, what else can I tell you? I don't know anything else very interesting.

Last Monday, in Alençon, there was a beautiful and sad ceremony for the transfer of the remains of the soldiers killed in the fighting in Alençon in '71. There was a huge crowd, and the bishop, the prefect and the mayor gave speeches.

The mayor, upon returning home, got dressed to go to a grand official dinner at the prefect's house. He felt very tired, and his wife advised him not to go and to rest. He gave in and went to bed, soon lost consciousness, and, the next morning, he was paralyzed on one side with a stroke. The doctors expect that his faculties will remain greatly diminished if he comes out of it.

It's a great tragedy for his wife and daughter because his affairs are in a very bad state, and he's going to leave them without any resources. His wife wanted too much to be socially prominent, and that's what ruined them. Nevertheless, when Marie spoke of the mayor's daughter, she'd tell us everything. Now she no longer envies her fate, if she ever envied it.

I received your letter and your school report which pleased me very much. The few lines that your aunt wrote me made me very happy. Your father said, "We must save this letter," and he put it away carefully. But I went and got it to learn by heart what your aunt had written.

Good-bye, my Pauline. If your letter hasn't been sent, all the better because I would very much like a few words for Léonie. This poor child went to the instructions at the retreat every morning at six o'clock; she was very afraid of failing. I didn't want to wake her up so early, but she woke up on her own. Once she didn't have time to put on her shoes and, without anyone noticing, she went wearing some kind of worn out slippers. Fortunately it was dark out, but she was strongly scolded, and I told her she wouldn't do that again.

I kiss you with all my heart.

CF 186 To her sister-in-law
January 28, 1877

I received your letter as well as the telegram, and truly, you go to far too much trouble for me. I'm quite overcome; I don't deserve anyone taking care of me so much. My life is not so precious, and, if I die, there won't be any more unhappiness over me than for someone else. There are so many people who are dying and would like to live, who consider themselves useful and whom God sees fit to take because, after their death, everything will only go better.

This doesn't keep me from praying that the Blessed Mother will cure me. I'm impatiently waiting for a pilgrimage to Lourdes, and certainly, if my family needs me, I'll be cured, because it's not faith that I'm lacking. Nor do I lack the will to live, the future has appealed to me for some time. My illness may have thrown a little water on the fire, but it's still not completely extinguished.

Tuesday I received news from Le Mans and my sister is still the same. The headmistress, who wrote to thank me for the geese, told me that they understand nothing more about her illness. However, the swelling is still getting worse, but very slowly.

The teacher sang the most flattering praises of Pauline; in short, she's perfection.

My dear sister, you ask me for something that is very hard for me to do, to go to the doctor without having need of him. Didn't he tell me there was nothing he could do and the medications were prescribed to make patients happy? I've had enough! You want him to determine if the illness has progressed? For that, I can inform you better than he can because I know it much better.

He'll ask me my opinion on it, as he did when I went to see him with my brother, because there's not enough progress for him to be able to remember one consultation from the other. When I'll have informed him of any progress, what do you want him to tell me? He won't talk about an operation. Quite certainly, that's less necessary than ever.

Oh well, if you insist that I consult him, I don't want to upset you, you who are so good to me. And yet he's a rude character, whom I don't really like. There needs to be a very good reason for me to speak to this man.

Look, if you don't mind, let's not talk about my illness anymore; it's beginning to become boring. Let's put it aside and talk about more cheerful things.

I see you mistook our mayor for a dead man. I didn't tell you he'd died, but that he was still sleeping. That was true and that lasted until Saturday, after which he recognized the doctor. He's paralyzed and can barely speak. Yesterday they were saying he's much worse.

In the end he didn't die. Unfortunately for him and his family, he owes a lot of money. His wife is ruining him with her luxury. Without his job paying fifteen thousand francs, he would have nothing, but now the job is lost! If he dies, his widow will have fifty thousand francs from a life insurance policy that he took out. I thought they were very rich but "all that glitters is not gold!"

I'm not waiting for any news from Le Mans to send you in this letter because I already took too long to answer you. You're going to think I'm quite indifferent.

I kiss you with all my heart, my dear sister, and I thank you a thousand times. To please you, I'll still go to the doctor.

My very kindest regards to everyone.

I'm sending you a letter from my sister that I received a week ago.[460] I'm also enclosing a letter from Pauline, who quite entertained us with her story of Father La Colombière.[461] Last week she wrote us that the Community was saying a novena to him and that if it were answered it would be used for his beatification.

She added that her aunt was hardly happy with this and that she preferred the miracle be for someone else other than her. So if the good Father wanted to do it for me, he could, because I'm not in such a hurry to leave, nor am I prepared well enough.

I'm still the same, yet the illness is slowly getting worse. They're saying a novena to the Blessed Mother for my intentions. I put on Lourdes water and drink some of it, but I have to use it sparingly because I'm not at the source!

If I were in the Blessed Mother's place, I would very quickly give in to so many prayers to free myself of people. The Poor Clares are also going to start a novena, but I don't like asking for prayers for myself because it would be better for me if it was for the intentions of others.

Tell Jeanne and Marie that if they were in Alençon at the moment, in the Place du Palais de Justice, they would think they were in Lisieux, because all the booths that I'd seen there during my trip to visit you have returned to our city. It's an "open air dancehall" that could drive you crazy.

Sunday I took the children there to make them happy, and I recognized everything that had been at the Lisieux fair, even up to the carousel horses, the weightlifters, and everything else.

---

[460] This was the last letter from Sister Marie-Dosithée to her family.

[461] St. Claude La Colombière (1641-1692). In June 1674, the newly appointed Jesuit superior of Paray-le-Monial was asked to be the confessor of Sister Margaret Mary, later known as Saint Margaret Alacoque at the Visitation Monastery in Paray-le-Monial. In time, she revealed, only to him, that Jesus had appeared to her and that He had revealed the secrets of His Sacred Heart. Father La Colombière requested that she write what was being revealed to her. With her permission, he revealed it to the world and devoted himself to the institution of the feast in honor of the Sacred Heart and spreading devotion to the Sacred Heart of Jesus. Father Claude La Colombière was beatified by Pope Pius XI on June 17, 1929, and canonized by Pope John Paul II on May 31, 1992.

There's nothing new to tell you. Everyone here is well. My husband is here by my side, saying to me, "Give them my best regards."

CF 188

To her daughter Pauline
February 13, 1877[462]

My dear Pauline,

I received your letter this morning. I saw you thought I was going to send it to Lisieux because of all the compliments you paid your aunt and uncle. Don't go to so much trouble the next time because I'm not going to send them anymore, although your aunt in Lisieux told me that they amused her very much. So then, write to me openly, as you have in the past, and that will make me happier.

I'm sad to see that your aunt is still doing very badly, and I'm sorry that she's languishing such a long time. However, God does what's best for us, and it's to purify her completely so she'll no longer have the slightest imperfection to atone for.

This afternoon, when I was with Marie making my hour of adoration, I saw Mademoiselle Pouplain, who lives in Le Mans very near the Visitation Monastery. Then I had this idea. My sister had wanted to eat goose cooked in Alençon, and I still have a little left. Should I ask this good young lady to take on this errand?

So that's what I did. I took advantage of the occasion to also send her gumdrops and some spice bread.[463] I don't know if she'll like it. If I only knew what would make her happy!

What more can I still tell you, my dear Pauline? I truly don't have very much to tell you. I can't think of anything. We hear a terrible racket on the street, it's the torchlight procession. Now it's a group of people wearing masks who are letting out piercing whistles. I truly believe they're devils personified!

They can throw themselves into such entertainment because the next day they'll cover their heads with ashes and do forty days of penance, but I suppose these people are hardly thinking of that.

---

[462] Mardi Gras, the Tuesday before Ash Wednesday.

[463] *Pain d'épices* [spice bread] was a type of bread made with rye flour, honey and spices.

However, our carnival wasn't very cheerful. We did little out of the ordinary. This evening Louise made some donuts, and, after eating the donuts, we went to hear the sermon.

Even little Thérèse came, who gets rather bored. She said, "It's more beautiful than usual, but it's still boring, all the same." We heard a superb sermon. It's too bad she didn't understand anything. It may as well have been in Hebrew for this poor baby, and she heaved sighs over it! She's truly too little to keep her in church a long time, but it's quite annoying to stay home on a day like today because of her. Oh well, she was compensated for it with the torchlight procession.

It's nine o'clock, and the little ones went upstairs to bed. This is good for me because they were making a lot of noise.... Even your father had joined in. There were only Léonie and me who were as quiet as a picture.

In spite of her calm, this child is a great worry to me. When my eyes rest on her, I feel intense pain. She always does what I wouldn't want her to do, and the older she gets the more that makes me suffer.

Sometimes Marie would say to me, "When Pauline is here, everything is more cheerful." Then she would smile at the thought of seeing you soon.

She wants a letter from you very much. Write to her on Sunday, but I don't want you to write to me. I forbid it; you have too little free time. The letter to Marie will be enough for me.

Thank Sister Marie-Louise de Gonzague[464] very much for me for her kindness in sending me news of your aunt and the very affectionate words she wrote me which touched me tremendously.

I'm going to have to end my letter, my dear Pauline, because I still have to write to your aunt, and I can't think of anything else of great interest to tell you. I don't know anything amusing to tell you about Thérèse, except this little detail which comes back to me.

The other day I wanted to kiss Thérèse before going downstairs. She seemed to be in a deep sleep, and I didn't dare wake her up when Marie said to me, "Mama, she's pretending to be asleep, I'm sure of it." Then, I bent down over her forehead to kiss her, but she immediately hid herself under the blanket, saying to me, sounding like a spoiled

---

[464] See footnote in CF 170.

child, "I don't want anyone to look at me." I was less than pleased, and I let her know it.

Two minutes later I heard her crying, and the next thing I knew, to my great surprise, I saw her at my side! She'd left her little bed all by herself and came down the stairs barefoot, encumbered by her nightgown which was longer than she was. Her little face was covered in tears. "Mama," she said, while throwing herself at my knees, "I was naughty, forgive me!" Forgiveness was quickly given. I took my little angel in my arms, pressing her to my heart and covering her with kisses.[465]

When she saw herself so well received, she said to me, "Oh! Mama, if only you wanted to wrap me in a blanket like when I was little! I'd eat my chocolate here at the table." I took the trouble to go look for her blanket and then I wrapped her in it like I did when she was little. I looked like I was playing with a doll![466]

Good-bye, my Pauline. I'll write you a week from Sunday to make up for such a short letter, and I'll try to make it longer next time. Meanwhile, I hug you with all my heart.

Your mother who loves you tenderly.

CF 189

To her sister-in-law
February 20, 1877

I'm enclosing a letter I just received a moment ago which doesn't leave us any more hope, as you can see.[467] Last week I sent some

---

[465] A passage from this letter was included in *Histoire d'une Âme* [*Story of a Soul*] 1898, p. 10, as follows: "One morning I wanted to kiss little Thérèse before going downstairs; she seemed to be in a deep sleep; so I didn't dare wake her up, when Marie says to me, 'Mama, she's pretending to be asleep, I'm sure of it.' Then, I bent down over her forehead to kiss her; but she immediately hid herself under the blanket while saying to me, sounding like a spoiled child: '*I don't want anyone to look at me.*' I was less than pleased, and I let her know it. Two minutes later I heard her crying, and the next thing I knew, to my great surprise, I saw her at my side! She'd left her little bed all by herself and had come down the stairs barefoot, encumbered by her nightgown which was longer than she was. Her little face was covered in tears: 'Mama,' she said, while throwing herself at my knees, '*Mama! I was naughty, forgive me!*' Forgiveness was quite quickly given. I took my little angel in my arms, pressing her to my heart and covering her with kisses." (Thérèse did not include this passage in the original Manuscript A of *Story of a Soul*.)

[466] Sister Marie of the Trinity's copy of the letter was used for this passage. *Vie Thérésienne*, No. 93, I, January 1984, p. 79.

[467] It's about the health of her sister, Sister Marie-Dosithée.

roasted goose to my sister since she'd wanted to eat some cooked in our house. I also sent her a pound of gumdrops and a dozen cakes, but Pauline wrote Marie that she gave almost all of them to her.

Finally, I think her death is imminent, and it makes me very sad. But on the other hand, I want my poor sister to be freed as soon as possible.

Thursday I received your letter. I was thinking about you, and I would say to myself, "They're angry because I didn't want to go to the doctor." I saw my brother telling you all kinds of things against me!

At the same time, I heard the bell ring violently, but it was only the postman, who rang it again, just as violently.

It was, in fact, your letter. I can't tell you how happy it made me. I was consoled by it all day long.

I'm not any sicker, and I'm still suffering very little. The most sensitive spot to touch is where the second gland is near my neck. However, it's nothing compared to the lump.

Finally, God is granting me the grace of not being afraid. I'm very calm, and I find myself almost happy. I wouldn't change my lot for anything.

If God wants to cure me, I'll be very happy because, deep down, I want to live. It's hard for me to leave my husband and children, but, on the other hand, I say to myself, "If I'm not cured, perhaps it's because it will be more helpful for them if I go away...."

Meanwhile, I'm doing everything possible to obtain a miracle. I'm counting on the pilgrimage to Lourdes, but if I'm not cured, I'll try to sing on the return trip all the same.

This time, our mayor is really dead. He wasn't conscious enough to go to confession. His wife is even more unfortunate than I am because she has nothing but debts. Six months ago her husband sold the fifty thousand franc insurance policy that she should have received after his death; he sold it for fifteen thousand francs, which he was unable to borrow.

I see you had a lot of fun on Mardi Gras,[468] especially Jeanne and Marie. I would have liked to have seen them in their little peasant costumes; the children here talked about it enough!

---

[468] Tuesday, February 13.

I return to my sad thoughts. I believe this is the last letter I'll write you to give you news of my sister. If the tragedy hasn't happened, I'll send you a note next week, because I receive news every Tuesday.

I kiss you all with love.

CF 190

...I have no more information than you do, my dear Isidore, about the death of our holy sister. Here are the contents of the letter from Mother Superior, written Saturday night:

"It was this morning[469] at seven o'clock that our very dear Sister Marie-Dosithée finished her so edifying life by a death worthy of envy.

"For two days a significant weakening told us that the end was approaching. Difficulty breathing and a sort of perpetual anxiety made our patient suffer more, our patient who never lost her sense of peace, her perfect resignation and who felt more and more the desire to go see Our Lord.

"Yesterday she again had the consolation of receiving Holy Viaticum,[470] then several indulgences. Her presence of mind, her serenity, were admirable up until the end. We can say, dear Madame, that you and we have one more holy protector in Heaven (...), because it would be difficult to end a more virtuous life in a more saintly way.

"I had the consolation of assisting our beloved Sister until her last moment. She had all the help, all the overabundant graces one could possibly want, and her heart, full of faith, expressed to us, even this night, all her gratitude towards the good God who was so generous to her.

"Her death was very gentle, and we can say that our dear Sister truly didn't suffer a lot. Tomorrow at twelve-thirty we will take her to her final resting place, surrounded by the regrets of our Community, who were deeply attached to her.

---

[469] Saturday, February 24, 1877.
[470] The Holy Eucharist given to a person in danger of death.

"This morning we gave your good little Pauline the sad news. The poor child is very sensitive, but her faith and her piety gave her courage.

"P.S. That same night our beloved Sister, at our request, blessed you all from the bottom of her heart.[471] Oh! How she's going to pray for her two dear families, whom she loved so tenderly."

When I received this letter I never found the courage to open it because I knew too well what it contained. Finally, Louis took it from me and read it, and I ended up reading it, also, a long time after he did. Now, I don't want to part with it. When you write me, return Pauline's last letter to me. It includes a few lines in my sister's hand, and these are the last she wrote. I'd like to see them again.

Yesterday I wrote back to the Superior and sent her some money to have Masses said.

As for the information you asked for regarding dates, my sister was born May 31, 1829, and she entered the convent April 7, 1858. All of us were born in Saint-Denis.[472] It's there that we were baptized, and yet, although my sister and I were born in the market town, we lived in the village of Gandelain.[473]

I'll write to you next week. Pauline will give me the details. I asked her for them, but I don't think she knows very much because she hardly saw her aunt this last week.

CF 191
To her sister-in-law
March 4, 1877

Tonight I received, through Mademoiselle Pauline Romet, a small package containing the objects mentioned in the Superior's letter. I'm sending you this letter, as well as Pauline's, which is touching. I'm happy she was at the Visitation Monastery at the time. It's true that it was very sad for her, but I would very much have wanted to experience that sadness.

Here, I found myself with so much commotion that I suffered

---

[471] The passage "the regret... bottom of her heart" is preserved from the original letter.

[472] Saint-Denis-sur-Sarthon (Orne), 11 kilometers (7 miles) from Alençon.

[473] The passage "As for the information... the village of Gandelain" is preserved from the original letter. Gandelain is 5 kilometers (3 miles) from St. Denis-sur-Sarthon.

from it from the bottom of my heart. I was overworked preparing the mourning clothes and by visits from people I'd told about our dear sister's death. What a busy week!

We'll divide up my sister's relics. I'd very much like to keep the rosary so I can use it when I'm really sick. You can take what you want from the other mementos, although I'd like to keep all of them until my death so I can have the cross that received her last kiss. You'll lend me the *Ecce Homo*[474] that was in her cell, won't you? In the meantime, I'll send it to you the next opportunity I have.

As for her hair, I'll keep very little of it and give you the rest, as well as the pictures.

I've been suffering a little more these last few days, but it's still not acute. I'd very much like to see Doctor Notta again because I don't have nearly as much confidence in Monsieur X.

I'm sending you a little article from the newspaper that Madame Deverny sent me because I had to tell her about my situation so she would leave me alone about her orders.

That didn't prevent her from giving me an order of fifteen meters of lace to make in four months, so I'll have to work up until the end!

As for the remedies she told me about, I don't trust advertisements in newspapers, and I wouldn't dare put myself in the hands of that sorcerer!

I checked to see if there would be a pilgrimage to Lourdes in the diocese, but there won't be. As soon as you become aware of one, tell me, and I'll join it no matter where it is. I don't want to go there except on a pilgrimage, or at least I would wait until I'm close to death.

CF 192

To her daughter Pauline
March 4, 1877

My dear Pauline,

This evening, after Vespers, I went with Marie to see a poor worker and her husband who have both been sick for almost four months.

Upon returning, I found the package containing the objects

---

[474] See footnote in CF 141.

of devotion that your dear aunt kept up to the end: her rosary and the cross she kissed before her last sigh, as well as her *Ecce Homo* and also her hair.

Marie and I hurried to read the letters. Marie cried a lot while reading yours, which touched me deeply, but consoled me at the same time. If you knew how much good this letter did me, you would be happy.

Yes, my dear Pauline, you will be a saint[475] like your aunt; I have hope of it. Nevertheless, she was much better than you at your age.

I loved her so much, my poor dear sister! I couldn't do without her.

One day, shortly before she left for the convent, I was working in the garden, but she wasn't with me. I couldn't remain without her, and I left to look for her. She said to me, "What are you going to do when I'm no longer here?" I answered that I would leave, too. In fact, I left three months later, but not by the same road.

I went to see her for the first time at the monastery on my wedding day.[476] I can say that on that day I cried all my tears, more than I'd ever cried in my life, and more then I would ever cry again. My poor sister didn't know how to console me.

And yet it didn't make me sad to see her there. No, on the contrary, I would have liked to be there, too. I compared my life to hers, and I cried even harder. In short, for a very long time, my mind and my heart were only at the Visitation Monastery. I often went to see my sister, and there I breathed a calm and a peace I can't express. When I went back, I felt so sad to be in the middle of the world. I would have liked to hide my life with hers.

You who love your father so much, my Pauline, are you going to think that I was hurting him and that I'd ruined our wedding day for him? No, he understood me and consoled me as best he could because his inclinations were similar to mine. I even think our mutual affection grew from it. Our feelings were always in accord, and he was always a comfort and a support to me.[477]

---

[475] This is a fragment preserved from the original letter.
[476] Zélie and Louis Martin were married on July 13, 1858, by l'Abbé Frédéric Hurel at midnight in the Church of Notre-Dame d'Alençon.
[477] This paragraph is considered an interpolation by Mother Agnès of Jesus (Pauline); the date is unknown.

But when we had our children, our ideas changed somewhat. We lived only for them. They were all our happiness, and we never found any except in them. In short, nothing was too difficult, and the world was no longer a burden to us. For me, our children were a great compensation, so I wanted to have a lot of them in order to raise them for Heaven.

Four of them are already in a better place. The others, yes, the others will go there as well, to the heavenly kingdom, laden with more merits since they will have fought much longer.

It's only Léonie who's still a very heavy cross to bear. May her dear aunt obtain for me a change in my poor child, I'm always hoping for it. This evening she came to ask me if she could see her aunt's mementos. Céline and Thérèse looked at them at the same time and kissed them.

You didn't say, my Pauline, if you received the cinchona bark wine[478] I sent Wednesday; don't forget to tell me in your next letter. Write me on Sunday so I'll know if you're still in the infirmary because that worries me.

When you see Mother Superior, thank her for her kindness in having sent me the objects used by your aunt and also for her lovely letter, which made me extremely happy.

I'm very happy that she's permitting Sister Félicité to bring you home on Easter Monday. This good Sister is going to be happy to see the Poor Clares again, who like her so much! I'm going to tell them about her arrival, and they'll be equally delighted. I hope she'll receive permission to have dinner with us again.

On Easter Monday there's going to be a big celebration that will gather together the entire population. They're organizing a colossal cavalcade like the one seven years ago. Although it's hardly the time for cavalcades! And everyone must give money for it. The gentlemen on the Town Council are going to collect from all the houses, saying that it's for the poor. Yes, "for the poor," who won't get any richer from it!

Don't forget to tell me the time you're arriving. I'm the one who's going to bring you back! It's going to be very hard for me not see your

---
[478] Cinchona wine is made with a medicinally active tree bark and has been given for a number of medical reasons.

aunt again. She was a part of my happiness in this world.

I had an enormous amount of work this week, my dear Pauline. I had to see to the mourning clothes, and that took all my time. Then I had a lot of visitors because all the people I'd told about your aunt's death came, except for Madame X.

And to think that we've only been good to these people, as much as it was possible for us. I think that's why they don't like us and especially because our convictions are so far from theirs! It's a mountain that separates us.

So if I could tell you something that interests you, it would probably have to be about your little sister, would it not?

Thérèse is always very sweet and as intelligent as can be. She likes to know what day it is, so this morning she barely had her eyes open, and she asked me, "What day is it?" Again this morning she was saying to me, "Today is Sunday, tomorrow is Monday, then after that Tuesday," and so on. She knows all the days of the week and doesn't make any more mistakes.

The most curious thing is her chaplet of practices[479] which doesn't leave her for one minute. She even marks them a little too much, because the other day, getting it in her little head that Céline deserved a reprimand, she said, "I said a naughty thing to Céline. I have to mark a practice." But she saw right away that she made a mistake. We pointed out to her that, on the contrary, she had to quickly remove one. She answered, "Oh! Well, I can't find my chaplet."

The day before yesterday she was at the grocer's with Céline and the maid. She was talking about her practices and discussing them loudly with Céline. The woman asked Louise, "What is she talking about?" When she plays in the garden we hear her talking about nothing but practices. Madame Gaucherin[480] sticks her head out to try to understand what this debate about "practices" means.

This dear little one makes our happiness. She'll be good, and we can already see the seed. She speaks of nothing but God and wouldn't miss saying her prayers for anything. I wish you could see her recite her little stories. I've never seen anything so cute. All by herself she

---

[479] See footnote in CF 169.
[480] A neighbor on the rue Saint-Blaise.

finds the right expression and tone that's appropriate, but especially when she says:

> "Little child with blond hair
> Where do you think the good God is?
> He's everywhere all over the world
> He's up above in the blue Heaven."

When she comes to the words, "He's up above in the blue Heaven," she looks up with an angelic expression. We don't grow tired of having her say it, it's so beautiful. There's something so heavenly in her expression that we're delighted by it.

She and Céline are inseparable, and you couldn't find two children who love each other more. When Marie comes to get Céline for her lessons, Thérèse is in a flood of tears. Oh no! What is she going to do? Her little friend is going away.... Marie feels sorry for her, so she takes her as well, and this poor baby sits in a chair for two or three hours.

We give her beads to string and a little piece of cloth to sew. She doesn't dare move and often heaves big sighs, especially when her needle becomes unthreaded, because she can't manage to rethread it and doesn't dare disturb Marie. Then we see two big tears running down her cheeks. Marie consoles her very quickly, rethreads the needle, and then the poor little angel smiles through her tears.[481]

The time didn't seem long, my dear Pauline, and here it is chiming ten-thirty, and I thought it was only nine o'clock. I've been writing since six-thirty and this is my fourth letter. I wrote to Lisieux, to the uncle in Paris, to Alphonsine[482] and, then, to you.

Good-bye, I kiss you with all my love.

CF 193

To her sister-in-law
March 12, 1877

...I think my sister has obtained a great grace for me. You know that I wasn't able to have any influence over Léonie; she ran away

---

[481] Thérèse quotes some of the passages in this letter in *Story of a Soul*, with some variations. *Story of a Soul*, tr. John Clarke, OCD, pp. 26, 28-29.
[482] See footnote in CF 114.

from me.... I'd tried everything, nothing worked! She was fascinated by the maid[483] who, nevertheless, made her very unhappy without my realizing it.[484] Marie is the one who discovered everything and told me about it.

I've suffered a lot, I assure you, not understanding this child's very strange behavior. Consequently, I didn't think there was any need for me to live, not being able to be helpful to her at all. But since Saturday, everything has changed, and in such a way I never hoped for, and I can't get over it.

I don't have time to give you a lot of details, but all I can tell you is that she doesn't want to leave me. I'm taking care of her exclusively, as is Marie. The other one has lost her influence forever. I can do as I please with Léonie. Before, I couldn't persuade her to get dressed to go out, but yesterday and today she put on an outfit to come with me and wants to follow me everywhere. She was sorry this morning because she didn't have enough time with me and is asking me when this letter is going to be finished so she can talk to me and sit by my side.

I received your good letter which I was awaiting impatiently. So I see that there's no hope for me as far as the doctor goes, but yet, I want to live, especially now, to begin to raise my Léonie.

Yes, I have hope that the Blessed Mother will cure me, but I still want to go on a pilgrimage. I'll go by myself only as a last resort. Don't think that it's to save money, it's not, but I have more confidence that way. I don't want to go there with Louis either. Out of kindness, he would want to take me from town to town to make the trip more pleasant, and I wouldn't be cured!

I'll look for a pilgrimage in the direction of Le Mans. I'll bring

---

[483] Louise Marais. (See footnote in CF 98.)

[484] On three different occasions, people employed to help in the care of the Martin children were found to be extremely abusive, leading to severe consequences. Céline wrote that, in 1869, she, as an infant of a few weeks, was the victim of severe neglect by her wet nurse. It was her father who saved her from death. (See footnote in CF 48.) Again, in 1870, Marie-Mélanie-Thérèse was starved to death by another wet nurse. (See CF 61.) And again, as per this letter, Zélie became aware that Léonie had been physically and emotionally abused by Louise Marais, the family servant. This resulted in Léonie enduring extreme pain in her childhood and ensuing difficulties in her adulthood. It was Marie, the oldest daughter, who was extremely perceptive and intuitive, who realized the wrongdoings in both cases and quickly reported her observations to her mother.

my three oldest girls, and the Blessed Mother will cure me because they'll pray so much for me that our good Mother will never be able to refuse us.

If I receive nothing this time, I'll return in six months; the sicker I am the more hope I'll have.

I don't accept your understanding regarding my sister's mementos. First, because I would keep them too long and you would be deprived of them because I'm not going to die for a long time. And as for you taking them back right after my death, the children wouldn't want that, they would treasure them too much.

I'll send you the cross, the *Ecce Homo*, half her hair and the pictures. I'll keep the rosary.

Last Sunday I received the newspaper. I thought it was the announcement of a pilgrimage that you wanted to bring to my attention. I'd looked for it a lot but I could find nothing of interest. Finally I said to myself, "They didn't send me this newspaper without a reason. Let's look more carefully." And I found it.[485]

We were very touched reading what you wrote to us about Jeanne. What a good heart she has, and how she already understands and feels things! This is extraordinary in a nine-year-old child.

Send me a letter soon. Though I don't like going to you so often for help, but you know that I only have you now.

CF 194   To her daughter Pauline
                                                  March 12, 1877
My dear Pauline,

Your letter to Marie surprised us beyond anything I can say to you and, at the same time, filled us with joy. Is it possible that you had the happiness of seeing your aunt in a dream and talking to her? Oh, my Pauline, that is a gift that's priceless. Yes, it's certain that God gave you a special grace.

Today my mind no longer inhabits the earth. It's travelling among higher spheres, and I'm not going to be able to speak to you about things here below. But, sadly, since it's too limited to speak of

---

[485] The response to what she found appears in CF 196, dated March 25, 1877.

the wonders of Heaven, I don't know what to say.

I believe I've obtained a great grace through the prayers of your aunt. I've commended my poor Léonie to her so many times since her entrance into Heaven, and I believe I'm feeling the effects of it.

You know what your sister was like: a spirit of insubordination, never wanting to obey me except by force, acting defiantly, doing the complete opposite of what I wanted, even when she would have wanted to do it, and, finally, obeying only the maid.

I'd tried everything in my power to draw her to me. It had all failed until today, and that was the greatest sorrow I'd ever had in my life.

Since your aunt died I've begged her to return this poor child's heart to me, and Sunday morning my prayer was answered. Now I have her heart as completely as possible: she doesn't want to leave me for a moment, she hugs me to the point of suffocating me, does everything I tell her without arguing, and works by my side all day long.

The maid completely lost her authority, and it's certain that she'll never again have any influence over Léonie by the way in which things happened. She found it a severe blow, and she cried and moaned when I told her to leave immediately and that I wanted her out of my sight.

I'm going to wait some time before I make her leave because she begged me so much to stay, but she's forbidden to direct a word to Léonie. Now, I treat this child with so much gentleness that I hope to succeed, little by little, in correcting her faults.

Yesterday she came with me to go for a walk, and we went to the Monastery of the Poor Clares. She whispered to me, "Mama, ask the cloistered sisters to pray for me so that I become a nun."[486] Finally, all is well, and let's hope that this continues.

---

[486] After Zélie died on August 28, 1877, the Martin family moved to Lisieux. Six years later, from August 20-September 3, 1883, Louis Martin, Marie, Léonie, Céline and Thérèse returned to Alençon to pray at the grave of Zélie and visit family friends. They visited Alençon again in October 1886. It was during this visit on October 7, that Léonie abruptly asked to be accepted into the Monastery of the Poor Clares and was promptly admitted that same day. Pauline had already entered the Lisieux Carmel on October 2, 1882, and Marie was to enter the Lisieux Carmel on October 15, 1886, eight days after their return from Alençon. In trying to understand the abrupt nature of Léonie's entrance into the Monastery of the Poor Clares on October 7, it is possible that Léonie, in a panic and feeling abandoned by the four maternal figures she lost

My dear Pauline, since you're so favored by your aunt, pray to her so that she cures me of my illness, which you know about. I want now, more than ever, to stay with you. It's more necessary for Léonie than for the little ones. Oh well, if it's as helpful as I believe it is, the Blessed Mother will certainly cure me. I'll definitely go to Lourdes this year. I would very much like to join a pilgrimage, but there won't be one in our diocese. If you could find out if there will be one in Le Mans, we'll all go, that is, Marie, you, and Léonie, and I'm sure I'll return cured. You'll pray so well for me that your prayers will be answered.

I also commend myself very much to Saint Joseph. I have great confidence in him. Join your prayers to ours during this month dedicated to honoring him. He'll intercede with the Blessed Mother, who will give you back your mother.

Don't be distressed by what I'm saying to you, my dear Pauline. If I knew you would be hurt by this, I wouldn't say anything to you, and God wouldn't be happy with you; it would be a lack of trust. Let's abandon ourselves to His goodness and His mercy, and He'll arrange everything for the best.

Never worry about the suffering you may assume I feel. I'm suffering very little, since I sleep without waking up, but that doesn't prevent the illness from being there, threatening. I wouldn't tell you this if you hadn't had the vision of your dear aunt, which was so comforting, and I feel the need to have you pray for me with love and confidence.

Your good aunt in Lisieux is having prayers said everywhere to obtain my recovery.[487] If you knew how good she is; she's truly a dear sister to me.

---

in the previous nine years (her mother; her aunt, Sister Marie-Dosithée, who was a positive maternal figure in her life; her sister Pauline; and now, her eldest sister Marie, who took Zélie's place as the mother of this family) thought she would find the motherly love and support that were now absent in her life. Because of this profound loss and a desperate need to connect to a maternal substitute that she needed for nurturance, protection and a sense of well being, she might have felt that through connecting to the Poor Clares, she would stay connected to her mother, since Zélie's heart and commitment to Christ were with this Franciscan community in Alençon. On December 1, 1886, three months after her entrance into the Monastery of the Poor Clares, Léonie had to leave because of poor health.

[487] Céline Guérin asked Mother Marie de Gonzague, Prioress of the Carmelite Monastery in Lisieux, to have a novena said for the cure of her sister-in-law.

Write to her as soon as possible. This would make her, as well as your uncle, very happy. Tell them about your aunt because they also loved her very much. They're begging me to tell them all the smallest details that you can give them.

I had no choice but to send them the letter you wrote to Marie last week, and I asked them to return it to me immediately, but they replied that they wanted to copy it and I would have it next time. Jeanne cried as though her heart would break; anyone would have done as much. My Pauline, I don't regret having sent your letters. Besides, it's done now, there's nothing more to talk about.

Write me one more time before Easter because you have to tell me what time you're arriving, whether it's seven-thirty in the morning or two-thirty in the afternoon. I inquired about it, and there's no train in between. Bring everything you have to be mended. I can't wait to see you. You'll have so many things to tell us and we, also, to tell you.

Good-bye, my dear Pauline. I kiss you with all my love.

CF 195 To her daughter Pauline
March 22, 1877

You tell me that my letter surprised you very much, and yours was no less surprising, so, we're even.

I can't tell you that your famous dream didn't affect me deeply. If it was, in fact, as you told it to us, it's a little out of the ordinary. It seemed like a dream to me. Oh well, let's say it is a dream. That doesn't prevent it from being very consoling. As for me, it gave me great joy.

How I loved seeing my sister "incomparably beautiful and holding out her arms to you." Yes, I'm going to believe that it's true, and it makes me feel happy. At the risk of being seen as my having an overexcited mind, it consoles me. I like to think about the supernatural, it raises my soul towards Heaven.

Marie was also very touched by it, and we talked about it for a week! Your letter yesterday disenchanted her a little, but not entirely. She's very much looking forward to seeing you, and I am, too, I assure you.

Don't worry, my Pauline, I don't think you're a saint. It takes a lifetime to reach perfection, and you still only have good intentions. That makes me hope you'll be a saint someday, if you persevere.

That's really what I think of you. Sadly, I also think that when you're no longer at the Visitation Monastery you may not be as good, and, because of this, I'm not happy to see the time come when you return home for good.

Secondly, I think the death of your aunt made some very good impressions on you and a shower of graces fell on you. Also, I'm grateful to have overcome all the obstacles that stood in the way of your return to the Visitation Monastery. Everything that happened is what I wanted for you and for me.

Now, may your holy aunt obtain for you the grace to persevere in your good resolutions so that your life may be similar to hers in the vocation that God will be pleased to give you.

I didn't have the courage to give the maid all the messages that were in your letter. I don't at all profess to be as sympathetic to her as you are, especially recently. I know she's devoted and attached to us in her own way, but I'm not happy with her violent nature.[488]

I won't be sorry to see her go, especially since I discovered what she'd put Léonie through. That, you see, I'll never forget. I would never have believed that one could have done, for so long and so coldly, the things she did to a poor creature who didn't dare complain "for fear of it getting twice as bad," as she now admits.

---

[488] In the memoirs of Sister Marie of the Sacred Heart (Marie), written in 1909 at the request of Mother Agnès of Jesus (Pauline), she wrote: "...later we had a maid who had the unhappy talent of freezing with just a glance my three little sisters Pauline, Léonie and Hélène; I was the only one she didn't catch in her net. I saw that poor little Hélène was very sad when she happened to get a spot on her stockings or her apron; she didn't dare to play for fear of having that happen and then being scolded by Louise. But I did it on purpose to show her I wasn't afraid of her and when she reproached me I answered her back immediately, 'I'm free, I am.' She nicknamed me 'I'm free, I am' and it was she who was afraid of me. Since I'm on the chapter about Louise, I will say that that poor girl made my two little sisters Léonie and Hélène very unhappy. She did love very much little Hélène who was ravishing and had the sweetness of an angel, but as Louise was lacking in judgment, she didn't see that she was terrorizing that poor child and really hurting her. Mama saw this one day and said to her, 'But it seems to me that you are making these children unhappy. I forbid you to scold them for nothings, like you do.' Then seeing that the two little ones were always around her and seemed to love her, this poor little mama trusted Louise." *Thérèse de Lisieux.* "Marie, L'Intrépide" [Marie the Intrepid], February 2010, p. 2.

And would you believe this girl claims that she was being a great help to me, thinking she was very clever to have been able to control your sister, who, in her opinion, no one else was able to tame? But brutality never converted anyone, it only makes slaves of people, and that's what happened to this poor child.

I'm still convinced that it's your aunt who's responsible for this being discovered. Now Léonie doesn't leave me for a minute. She goes everywhere with me, showing a happy face and, little by little, giving up her bad habits.

She no longer puts up any resistance to me. On the contrary, she anticipates everything that would please me and doesn't wait for my instructions.

I didn't know why she never wanted to take a minute of play-time. When a meal was finished, she would clear the table, put the room in order, and in short, do the servant's work. I was tired of saying to her, "Go outside and play in the garden. I don't want to see you here while everyone else is enjoying themselves."

She would say to me grudgingly, "I want to stay here." I've since learned that the maid had said to her, "If your mother tells you to go play, go, but you know that afterwards you're going to pay." You see, all of that outrages me to a point I can't express.

I went to the Monastery of the Poor Clares to consult an elderly Sister who has the face of a saint. She was accompanied by a younger Sister who, despite her great qualities of devotion, wanted me to dismiss her immediately. The older one said to me, "Wait. Don't rush into anything." That's where things stand now.

Now Léonie plays with the joy of a four-year-old child. She makes a little too much noise and isn't quiet enough, and I have to calm her down, but she tries very hard. Let's hope that, little by little, she'll change completely with God's help.

That's why now I have a desire to live that I never knew until today. My child needs me very much. After I die, she'll be too miserable, and no one will be able to make her obey except the one who made her suffer so much. But no, this won't be because when I'm dead she'll have to leave right away. I don't think they'll refuse to carry out my last wishes.

But I trust in God, I'm asking Him now for the grace to let

me live. I know very well that He won't take away my illness and my dying, but I ask that He grant me enough time so that Léonie won't need me anymore.

I'm not worried about the two little ones; both of them are very gifted. They have exceptional natures, and they'll certainly be good. You and Marie will be able to raise them perfectly. Last night around ten o'clock, while I was going to go to bed, I went to Louise's room. I thought she was in bed since it had been two hours since she'd gone upstairs. I found her reading library books. I scolded her very loudly, which woke up Céline. After the storm had passed, Louise went to bed, and the little one said to her, "Please, my little Louise, most of all, don't forget to give your heart to God." That's good for such a young child, so I thank God with all my heart. Céline would never commit the smallest fault deliberately.[489] As for Thérèse, she wouldn't tell a lie for all the gold in the world. She has a spirit like I've never seen in any of you.[490]

Finally, my dear little Pauline, I do have hope of being cured and that you'll be praying for me. For a week I haven't been suffering at all. I trust that God is going to stop the progress of the disease, which was frightening, and that He's going to do for me what He did for your aunt, because twenty-four years ago she was condemned to death. The doctor told my mother she could barely live more than three months.[491] She prayed and made a novena to Our Lady of La Salette[492] to obtain the grace of dying a religious. The illness never disappeared, but she lived another twenty-four years.

I'm not asking for as many as that, but I hope to obtain enough years to raise my children. Commend me to the prayers of your good teachers, whom you love so much.

So it's been decided that you'll arrive in Alençon at two-thirty on Easter Monday. That will be just the time the cavalcade is leaving the fairground. That's why I would have preferred that you arrive on the seven-thirty train, if that had been possible. The street will be so

---

[489] *Carnet manuscrit de soeur Geneviève* [Manuscript Notebooks of Sister Geneviève (Céline Martin)], p. 105. (Not translated.)

[490] Thérèse quotes this passage in *Story of a Soul*, tr. John Clarke, OCD, p. 28.

[491] See footnote in CF 47.

[492] See footnote in CF 140.

congested, and we'll have to pass through all those crowds, so not all of us will be going to meet you.

If Sister Félicité took the first train with you, she would still have the possibility of hearing several Masses, and she'd even be able to attend the eight-o'clock Mass at the Monastery of the Poor Clares. But you would have to get up at four-thirty, which would be very early, so perhaps it's better to take the second train.

Pray well to Saint Joseph for the maid's father, who's gravely ill. I would regret it very much if this good man died without confession.

CF 196 To her sister-in-law
March 25, 1877

Wednesday we received a letter from Pauline, who strongly advises us not to think of her as a saint and not to consider the dream she had as a vision.

She tells me that the Superior strongly advised her about it. She seems delighted with her direction. In short, from what I can see, she's thinking about becoming a nun, her letter implies it enough. The Superior told her she has time to think about it, and she's quite right.

As I've already told you, Léonie is considerably changed. She's no longer the same person. She left all her "deception" without a word. Until then, I'd been unable to keep her from helping the maid. Supposedly that was the only work that pleased her, but she's given it up so well that now she has to force herself to help around the house.

I assure you she's never far from my side. She's always working with me, and I can't go out without her. It's her greatest happiness. Before, it was impossible for me to take her anywhere without causing a scene. She never played with her sisters, which surprised me very much. How blind I was! I didn't notice that she was spellbound by the maid, and I could have no influence over her.

Finally, it's absolutely over. Léonie only wants one thing now, to see that girl leave because she's uncomfortable in her presence and doesn't dare kiss me. I can't tell you how many times a day she comes secretly to shower me with kisses. She does exactly everything I tell her to do joyfully and promptly. Now she's like a normal child.

I think her desire to see the servant leave will soon be fulfilled. The girl's father is dying, and her mother is clamoring for her. The poor girl, who at the same time is deeply attached to us, finds herself totally perplexed at the moment. On the one hand, she'd like to stay, but on the other hand, her mother is pulling her. I don't know, should I be rejoicing over it?

As for me, I was quite surprised to see I was mistaken about Monsieur David. I would never have been able to think it was for Monsieur Chesnelong, whom I think about so little, when you sent me the newspaper![493] However, I would have liked to see this speech again because it had to be worth it, but it disappeared. I think my husband took it.

I'm anxiously awaiting Easter Monday to see my Pauline and to find out if it was a simple dream she had or a dream with an important message. I'll see it in the answer that was given to her, and I'll find out what she had asked her aunt. I find all of this very intriguing.

She's not arriving until two-thirty. It's a little late because a beautiful cavalcade representing Charles VII and Joan of Arc with the entire court should pass in front of our house at two o'clock. I'm not going to invite you to come; I know you wouldn't want to. However, if it tempts you a little, you know I'd be delighted to have you.

The mayor's wife obtained a post office. It's a little hard when one lived in such luxury. But we hardly feel sorry for her. We feel sorrier for the one whom she made lose eighty thousand francs.

CF 197   To her sister-in-law
                                                        April 12, 1877

I received your letter telling me to expect a visit from Monsieur Maudelonde on Friday, so what a surprise it was to see him arrive the day before at three o'clock. To make matters worse, I was alone because everyone had gone for a walk. I had to go shopping and prepare the food. I closed the door and left to make my purchases.

Finally, around four o'clock, the maid returned. She'd left the children with a woman who'd insisted on keeping them. She had to

---

[493] See footnote in CF 193.

return to the other side of town to get them in the evening.

They were back at five o'clock, and at six o'clock my dinner was ready. I was pleased with myself, I'd done a good job, and they found my cooking excellent. I'd made, in fact, a nice dinner, and the whole time I was making it, I was saying to myself, "What would they do if I weren't here?"

It seems impossible to me that I can go away. So then, I believe I have to stay and that I will stay. I'm like all the people I knew, not seeing their own condition. Only other people see it clearly, and they remain dumbfounded that they promise themselves unlimited time when their days are numbered. It's truly curious, but that's how it is, and I'm like everyone else!

So Pauline arrived Easter Monday[494] with a headache that still hasn't gone away. I keep her until Tuesday, and I'd like to keep her indefinitely because it's hard for me to send her back while she's suffering. However, she wants to return very much. She loves the Visitation Monastery almost as much as God!

She would like to go there again next year. I'd promised her that I would persuade her father, who doesn't believe she should go, but I've changed my mind. She's had enough school, and she needs to rest until she returns there permanently as a nun. I have good reason to believe that this is what she wants. Oh! If she knew that I'm telling you this, all would be lost.

If I learned anything about it, it's very much against her will; the famous dream betrayed everything. If you knew how much she regrets having told us about it. She tries every possible means to avoid anyone alluding to it.

You understand what I want to say because I'd sent you her letter, where she told Marie that she'd written to her aunt in Heaven and that her aunt had answered her in a dream. She saw her with such a beautiful face that she's never been able to pray for her since then, that's how much she looked like a blessed soul.

Marie was foolish enough to answer her in a completely flattering way. As for me, I said what I thought about it. The Superior read it and, afraid that Pauline may see herself as a privileged person, she diminished its importance completely while admitting, all the same,

---

[494] April 2, 1877.

that it was a grace, but not a vision.

The extern Sister who brought Pauline spoke to me a lot about my sister. She was generally thought of as a saint, not only in the convent, but in town. Everyone was saying, "The saint died!" And the day when she was laid out by the choir grill, a number of people brought religious objects to touch them to her. When they carried her to the cemetery, nothing gave an impression of sadness, rather it seemed like it was a triumph. The nuns said they'd never felt that before.

Since Pauline's been in Alençon, we've hardly had any good weather. Finally, Monday we went to the country. It was a beautiful day from noon until six o'clock, but then a terrible storm broke. We were in an open carriage, and, in spite of our umbrellas, we were drenched. The children were soaked to the skin when they got home.

Pauline wore a pretty, brand-new hat that was completely ruined. You see, we don't have any luck.

We had a very beautiful cavalcade that made a lot of noise. It only lacked one thing, a little more distinguished king. The one we had rather looked like a stableman. He greeted no one, not even the Prefect, who had come to wait for him on the doorstep of the Prefecture.

There was a magnificent ball for all the shopkeepers, but the highest ranking refrained from going. So there's anarchy in town at the moment.

You're going to think that I don't have much news to tell you, and you're going to be right, but I would very much like to fill up the entire page; I regret the little bit that remains. What could I say to you now? I can't think of anything else.

I just told you that I didn't have any luck on my outing on Monday with my ruined hat, but listen, there are poor people who have to lament other misfortunes!

Monsieur Hommey, a banker, went on an outing with his brother-in-law. And while they were on their way home, the horse knocked over the carriage. Monsieur Hommey has a bad gash on his head, and his brother-in-law broke his leg so badly they had to cut it off that evening. Don't speak to me of fun when it costs you so dearly!

I had something else to tell you that I can't remember; it will be for next time. Meanwhile, I kiss you with all my heart.

CF 198 To her daughter Pauline

April 29, 1877

Dear Pauline,

I regret not having written you on Sunday because, again, I see I must wait a whole week to hear from you. And yet I'm anxious to know how your poor head is doing. Every day I tell myself that it's hurting you, and that makes me sad.

I wish the three long months that separate us from your vacation were over, so you could rest. Above all, don't push yourself too hard in doing your homework. If you don't receive any prizes I won't be sad at all, I know very well that you're doing your best.

At the moment, my Pauline, I have no idea what I'm doing because your grandmother is talking to me while I'm writing to you, the maid is arriving with the little ones, and they're making quite a lot of noise.

I think I'm going to have to abandon my letter until this evening, when they've all gone to bed, since one can't have a moment's rest here. I'm sure that all the boarding school students at the Visitation Monastery combined couldn't make as much noise. It's a good thing I have the ears for it!

The maid spent a week at her house, and she returned on Friday night. Her father is failing quickly and doesn't want to hear about confession. However, he hasn't professed irreverence for God.

I strongly advised his daughter to inform the priest in time for him to come and prepare him gradually, but she didn't want that. She's like her mother, who says, "We have plenty of time; he's not that sick." I'm absolutely appalled by this and get angry with her.

Finally, I'm free for a moment. Léonie, who saw me forced to hold a conversation with her grandmother while writing, took pity on me. She said to her, "Grandma, so you're not thinking anymore about going to visit Madame Tessier?"[495] And your grandmother left

---

[495] See footnote in CF 92.

right away, very happy to have been reminded of her oversight.

Good! Here I am, once again, pestered by the little ones. This time I'm leaving my letter because I have a headache. My God! How unhappy I am that it's raining; if it wasn't, they'd all go for a walk!

I see that while waiting for good weather, I'm not saying anything of value to you, not even for you to write back about or think about. I hear Vespers sounding, and I have to leave you. Perhaps after this evening, I'll know something new....

It's evening now, and I know nothing new, except that we couldn't go out all day because of the rain. Your father offered to take Marie to the Catholic Circle where there's a little performance this evening, but she declined. There already was one last Sunday, and she didn't go to that one either.

What brought about this evening's performance is a peculiar incident. Since there were a very large number of people there on Sunday because Monsieur de Cissay was to speak, two hundred letters of invitation were sent to the "beautiful ladies" and postcards to the "less beautiful," and care was taken to put a barrier between the two categories.

And then a woman whose son was one of the principal actors and who only had a card, said, "If they don't want to let me sit with those who have letters, I'm going to go and get my son and he won't perform."

However, she didn't sit with those who had letters and didn't dare take her son away, but it resulted in a general discontent among those with cards.

To prevent an insurrection, today they gave a little party where there was no more distinction. These gentlemen are truly at a loss to please everybody. It's certain that the great ladies wouldn't come if the best seats weren't reserved for them, and, on the other hand, it would cause bitter disappointment among the mothers whose children took part in the performance to be relegated to the last row. But it's no use. Only in Heaven will the poor be able to have the best, on earth one mustn't think of it.

I see I didn't have to squeeze my lines so closely together, I have nothing more to tell you. I must absolutely finish my letter here.

I anxiously await hearing from you. Above all, tell me if you still have a headache. This worries me. And, please, force yourself to eat. If you don't, you won't get better. On the contrary, the illness gets even worse when you're weak.

Do you know how I amused myself yesterday in the garden? Counting all the white flowers and wishing that they were on your aunt's grave. They bother me in the garden and I'd like not to see them there anymore.

Good-bye, my Pauline, it seems like it's been a hundred years since I've seen you. I'd find it very difficult not to go and spend a day with you when the weather is good, but the idea that I won't see your aunt anymore casts a shadow on the pleasure I would have on this trip.

I kiss you with all my heart.

CF 199   To her daughter Pauline
                                         Alençon, May 1, 1877[496]

My dear Pauline,

I was very upset to learn that you're still suffering, I've been thinking about you constantly since you left. Now I'm worrying a little less since you're hardly doing any work anymore and you follow a good regimen.

This is what I recommend, that you neither worry about your prizes nor the white crown. I only ask for one thing, that your teachers be satisfied with you, and I see with great happiness that this is so, because Sister Marie-Louise de Gonzague[497] wrote me today.

I don't mind if you're not taking any courses as long as you're not bored, because if you get bored, your headache will get worse. So you must give up your studies for the moment, if necessary, but while distracting yourself by drawing or doing whatever activity your teachers tell you to do.

To come back to your report, I think it's very good, and I could hardly wish for better. I don't know what you have to worry about. As for me, I'm very satisfied.

I'm still thinking about the pilgrimage from Laval, if, however,

---

[496] A fragment of the original letter preserved, "Alençon, May 1, 1877."
[497] See footnote in CF 170.

it's true that there is one. My intention is to take you with me. We'll pray to the Blessed Mother so that she takes away your migraines.

As soon as you have information about this pilgrimage, write to me so I can make arrangements for tickets. If your father's not opposed to it, we'll also take Marie and Léonie with us.

Am I right in thinking that you received my letter when I received yours this morning?

I have nothing new to tell you. We're all well, I'm almost not suffering at all, and I very much hope that the Blessed Mother will cure me.

I kiss you with all my heart.

CF 200   To her sister-in-law
                                           May 10, 1877

...I'm very worried about Pauline. During her two-week vacation she had a headache constantly, and, if I hadn't been afraid of upsetting her, she wouldn't have returned to school.

I gave her a letter for the headmistress in which I made my concerns known. This poor child didn't dare complain for fear of displeasing the nuns and was certainly doing work that was too much for her.

The headmistress answered me a week ago. She told me that the headache hasn't let up and they made her see a doctor, who prescribed some tonics and, above all, almost complete rest.

So Pauline follows a separate regimen and is almost like a boarding student without a schedule. I would prefer to see her here, but I know the Sisters would be very upset, and I'll wait until the vacation. Since then, a letter from Pauline confirmed that she's not doing any better, and I'm very sad over this. Marie has to go on the retreat for former students, which begins June 11. I'm waiting anxiously for the moment I see my Pauline again. All of these concerns make me forget my illness. I hardly have time to think about it, and I'm always imagining that my death is remote and in the distant future. However, sometimes I have a flash of reality, and I care about pilgrimages more than you can believe. I'm always in search of information to find out if there's one on the horizon.

I'm about the same. I'm not suffering a lot, and yet now I feel, almost continuously, the inner work that the illness is doing, but the suffering is quite bearable.

I hope the Blessed Mother will cure me, if not completely, at least so I'll have the time to raise my children. At first, I always asked her for it. If it's necessary, I'm certain I won't be refused, and I believe this grace is more necessary now than ever because of Léonie.

Yes, I see a shining ray of hope for her that foretells to me a complete change to come. Up until now, every effort I've made to become attached to her has been fruitless, but it's no longer the same today. She loves me as much as it's possible to love, and, with this love, little by little the love of God penetrates her heart. She has unlimited trust in me and goes as far as revealing to me her slightest faults. She truly wants to change her life and makes many efforts that no one else can appreciate like I do.

I can't get the idea out of my head that this transformation is due to the prayers of my holy sister because everything changed two or three weeks after her death. She's also the one who obtained the grace for me to know how to manage to attach her heart to mine. I hope God will let me complete my task, which is far from being finished. It takes time to conquer such a nature, and I see that this mission was entrusted to me. No one else could carry it out, not even the nuns at the Visitation Monastery; they would send her away, as they've done before.

So I'm really giving up my Alençon lace and beginning to live off of my investments. Anyway, I think it's time. My biggest fear is not enjoying my retirement for very long. It would be a shame. I really earned it, and I can say that it cost me dearly.

I may be mistaken, but I believe the other manufacturers will be right behind me because the events that are developing won't help this kind of industry. Ladies make do with flowers, even the "middle class ladies," who are wearing veritable flower beds on their heads this year. It's strange, but not beautiful!

It's time that I finished my letter. It took me several attempts to write this long letter. I hope Madame Maudelonde is recovered now and that you've finally found a student. I always say it, and I'll never stop saying it: God will give you what you need at the right time. You are Christians who are too good for Him to do otherwise.

To her daughter Pauline
May 10, 1877

My dear Pauline,

I was very anxious to receive your last letter. I'm still concerned about your health, and then I wanted to know if you would tell me about the much desired pilgrimage which, unfortunately, isn't taking place. I'm beginning to fear that I won't find one. However, it's very rare that there isn't one sometime around the month of September.

It's still quite settled that you'll go with Marie and Léonie. Your father, seeing that I want them to come, gave his consent right away.

As for Marie's retreat at the Visitation Monastery, you know how little your father likes to be separated from you,[498] and at first he'd categorically said she couldn't go. I saw that he was so determined I didn't try to plead her case. On the contrary, I agreed, quite resolved in fact to try again.

Last night, Marie was moaning about this. I said to her, "Let me take care of it. I always manage to get what I want without fighting. It's still a month away, that's enough time to persuade your father ten times."

I wasn't mistaken because when he returned barely an hour later he began to talk in a very friendly way to your sister, who was working energetically. "Good," I said to myself, "Now's the time!..." And I brought up the matter. "So you really want to make this retreat?" your father said to Marie. "Yes, Papa." "Oh well, you can go."

And he, who likes neither absences nor expenditures, declared to me again yesterday, "I don't want her to go, and she certainly won't go; the trips to Le Mans and Lisieux are never-ending."

I said all the same things, but with an ulterior motive. I learned the tricks of the trade a long time ago! So, when I say to someone, "My husband doesn't want it," it's that I don't want the thing any more than he does because when I have a good reason, I know how to persuade him of it. And I found that I had good reason to want Marie to go on the retreat.

It's true that's it an expense, but money is nothing when it's

---

[498] See footnote in CF 65.

about the sanctification and perfection of a soul, and last year Marie returned to me completely transformed. The fruits still last, yet it's time for her to renew her reserve. Besides, deep down, your father feels the same way, and that's why he gave in so kindheartedly.

I'll try to find an opportunity to send her to you on Sunday or Monday morning, although I don't like anyone travelling on Sunday unless it's absolutely necessary. Then I'll go get her and have you come home at the same time.

Now, let's talk about Léonie a little bit, my poor child who caused me so much fear! How many times I trembled at the thought of the unhappy future that awaited her, yet I always had hope, and I believe I see the dawn of better days.

Grace has been working in her since your aunt's death, when she began to show an affection for me that's constantly growing. She can't leave me anymore; she even goes as far as confiding in me her most secret thoughts. Fear and love of God are penetrating her heart little by little.

But if you knew how gently I treat her! I'm surprised at myself. I'm quite sure your aunt also obtained for me the grace to know how to handle her. She wants to receive Communion at the end of May, and that means constant preparation every day. Oh well, may God be blessed!

That's why I feel needed, if not indispensable, so, I very much hope the Blessed Mother will cure me. So pray hard, my Pauline, during this beautiful month, so that our good Heavenly Mother comes to our aid.

Our dear little Céline and Thérèse are always angels of benediction, with little angelic natures. Thérèse makes Marie's happiness and glory; it's incredible how proud she is of her. It's true she has answers quite rare for her age. Céline said to her the other day, "How is it that God can be in a tiny host?" Thérèse answered, "It's not surprising since God is all powerful!" "And what does all-powerful mean?" "It means He can do whatever He wants!"[499]

---

499 Thérèse quotes this passage in *Story of a Soul*: "Our two little dears, Céline and Thérèse, are angels of benediction, little cherubs. Thérèse is the joy and happiness of Marie and even her glory; it's incredible how proud she is of her. It's true she has very rare answers for one her age; she surpasses Céline in this who is twice her age. Céline said the other day, 'How is it that God can be present in a small host?' The

I have many other things to tell you, but I don't have time. They'll be for next time. Good-bye, my Pauline, I look forward to hearing from you. I kiss you with all my heart.

CF 202   To her daughter Pauline
May 13, 1877

You should have received the letter I mailed to you on Thursday. By the date, you see that I didn't wait very long to answer your letter, which reached me last Friday.

I was very happy to hear your news, but it hurt me to hear that you're still suffering. If I didn't have to go to Le Mans soon to take Marie, I would have been to see you right away. I'm worried in spite of myself. Your father reassures me by saying it's not dangerous, that all you need is rest. I'm afraid you're still tiring yourself by studying. In your next letter tell me if you have more of an appetite, if you're sleeping well, in short, give me the details.

I see you're very worried about me. As I told you, I hope to be cured by the Blessed Mother. When you write me that the good teachers are praying for me, it gives me even more confidence.

The other day, Mademoiselle X was preaching to Marie so she would be resigned to seeing me die. Your sister told her she hoped for a miracle. Yes, but… this young lady, who's no more pious than that, looked at us like we were very simple and said, "Oh, yes! If your mother were cured, that would be the greatest miracle for me. I can't imagine anything greater than that."

Marie was saying to me this morning, "Oh, Mama, how surprised she'll be! This time, she'll believe in the miracles at Lourdes, she who criticizes pilgrimages so much." In short, your sister is rejoicing in advance over showing Mademoiselle X she's wrong and reducing her to silence.

I intend to bring Marie to the retreat on Sunday, June 10. We'll go to the five-thirty Mass and leave on the seven o'clock train, arriv-

---

little one said, 'That is not surprising, God is all powerful.' 'What does all powerful mean?' 'It means He can do what He wants!'" *Story of a Soul*, tr. John Clarke, OCD, p. 27. Sister Marie of the Trinity's text includes some variations. *Vie Thérésienne*, No. 93, January 1984, p. 80.

ing at the Visitation Monastery at nine o'clock, just in time for High Mass, after which I'll take you out.

We'll go to the processions at the cathedral because it will be the Sunday of the Sacred Heart. In Alençon there are processions like those on the Feast of Corpus Christi. I think it's the same in Le Mans. Then, in the evening, I'll leave Marie at the Visitation Monastery. I'd like you to ask if they'll allow you to go out that day. If not, I won't go.

The last time I wrote to you, Marie asked me to tell you some stories about our roofer. I didn't want to because I didn't think you'd find it very interesting, but today, since I have nothing to tell you, I'll talk about this roofer who was working for us all last week. He's a good man who has, no more and no less, the manner of a saint who performs miracles. He stays in church a very long time, kneeling on the ground, with an angelic manner. If anyone talks to him, he answers with admirable simplicity and gentleness. He works without wasting a minute, praying continually while working, and fasts every day.

He told me that on Wednesday of Holy Week, while on top of a roof, he saw a big bright cross in the sky. The sun was below the four arms of the cross.

I found this hard to believe, although he told the story with such sincerity that I really didn't know what to think. But the recounting of his visions didn't stop there. He spoke of so many kinds of visions that I saw he was crazy....

First of all, he knows what God's angels don't know – the week when the world is going to end… (it's the first week of January 1880!) Then, his mission is to go find all the bishops in the world to announce this to them, and he's already put his house up for sale to make his journey. I'll spare you the rest because I'd fill my letter with nothing but this nonsense!

This story amused Marie a lot. It was said so seriously and with so much humility that if one didn't understand the absurdity of it, one wouldn't know what to make of it.

We must recognize that it's a peculiar madness, because this poor man, in some respects, seems very well. But the strangest thing is that his wife believes in this as much as she does in the Gospel! She's also going to leave and take him to Saint-Denis, near Paris. There's a woman there whom she knew in the past. She was sick, and the roofer promised to pray that she'd be cured. They've had no news about her since, but he claims to know, by revelation, that she's cured. As you see, this fellow's madness....

My dear Pauline, I went no further than this last word. Sunday evening at seven o'clock your father came to ask me to go out with him, and, as I'm very obedient, I didn't finish my sentence! So I don't remember anymore what I wanted to say about the fellow's madness.

At the moment, I'm concerned about something much more serious that preoccupies me completely. I've learned that there's a pilgrimage to Lourdes leaving Angers[500] on June 10, and I'm going to write to Sister Marie-Paula[501] to get the necessary information.

My illness is still progressing, although I'm not suffering a lot. But before you returned to school, sometimes I would go a week without feeling anything, and now I'm suffering continuously.

However, I'm confident I'll be cured. It was ten or fifteen days after your aunt's death that, rightly or wrongly, I began to feel this confidence that I can't understand and also a great desire to live a few more years to raise my children.

Before, I thought I wasn't very useful and that perhaps everything would go better after my death, but now Léonie worries me. She truly needs me, and I need time to finish the work that God has put in my hands. So, I'm sure He'll give it to me, although I know it's a lot to ask Him to disregard the laws of nature to prolong one wretched life.

Oh well, what's certain is that He does it often through pure goodness and mercy, and, if He does it for me, I'll try to make Him not regret it.

I don't need to ask for your prayers. Thank the good teachers who want to take an interest in me. I commend myself especially to the prayers of Sister Marie-Gertrude. Don't forget to give her my message.

---

[500] Angers is approximately 140 kilometers (87 miles) southwest of Alençon.
[501] Sister Marie-Paula was a former headmistress at the Visitation Monastery of Le Mans boarding school who had been living in Angers for several years.

I'll expect your letter for Sunday.

Meanwhile, I kiss you with all my heart.

Z. Martin.

I just learned how many leagues it is from here to Angers, it's 38.[502] Perhaps I'll bring you. We'll decide that soon.[503]

CF 203 To her sister-in-law

May 29, 1877

I should have written to you a week ago, but I didn't find the time. However, I have to decide to do it today because I have good news to tell you.

I saw in *La Semaine religieuse*[504] from Séez[505] that a pilgrimage to Lourdes will leave from Angers on June 10. I wrote to a nun at the Visitation Monastery in Angers who had been my oldest daughter's headmistress for seven years in Le Mans and asked if she would be kind enough to provide me with information about it.

She replied that the pilgrimage will depart June 18 and not the 10th, and that she was responsible for the tickets. I asked her for four of them since Marie, Pauline and Léonie will come with me.

It's quite a lot of trouble and expense, but if I obtain the grace we wish for so much, it will not be too much to pay dearly for it. And it seems to me that the more sacrifices we make, the more the Blessed Mother will be inclined to answer our prayers.

Only yesterday I received a letter from the good nun giving me some new information. The pilgrimage leaves Angers on Monday, June 18, at seven-fifty in the morning and arrives in Lourdes on Tuesday, the 19th, at eight o'clock in the morning. We stay until eight o'clock Thursday evening and return to Angers on Friday around eight o'clock at night. This way we'll spend three days in Lourdes, which isn't too much for me. In addition, this dear Sister tells me not to

---

[502] 92 miles (148 kilometers) from Alençon to Angers (French league equaled 2.422 miles).

[503] From "Meanwhile" to "soon," original text preserved.

[504] *La Semaine religieuse* [Religious Week], the religious newspaper of the Diocese of Séez.

[505] See footnote in CF 12.

worry about looking for a hotel in Angers, that an extern Sister will meet us at the station and provide suitable accommodations. "And who knows," she adds, "if Providence won't have a pleasant surprise in store for you?"

I don't know what this pleasant surprise can be. Marie thinks she may want to give us a room in the extern Sisters' residence. Sister Marie-Paula also tells me that the entire Community is praying for me. In short, all of this makes me happy and gives me courage. Yes, I truly hope the Blessed Mother will cure me.

The disease is progressing and spreading more and more. I expect the tumor will burst[506] before the month of August. I'm still suffering very little, but the mild suffering is almost continual and, at times, quite violent. For about a month I've also had pain in my arm.

I don't need to ask you for your prayers, I'm quite sure there's no shortage of them, nor those of your good family who show me so much sympathy.

The decisive moment is approaching. I'd like all of us to make a novena that would end Wednesday or Thursday, June 21, the day I leave Lourdes.

I'd intended to go see Doctor X before leaving so that if I'm cured, he'll be able to certify that it was a miracle. My husband doesn't agree with this idea. Tell me, what do you think?

My Pauline still gets headaches. I'm hoping she'll find some relief in Lourdes.

Léonie continues to become a good child, but it's difficult land to cultivate. It definitely needs the dew of Heaven, which, I'm sure, won't fail us. I'm doing everything possible to cultivate it well, and God will make the flowers and the fruits grow. This little one has a heart of gold. You only have to know how to handle her, with a great deal of gentleness.

---

[506] "The bursting which she anticipated was the dreadful symptom of advanced cancer, when the tumor broke the flesh and opened an ulcerated and suppurating wound.... Throughout her whole correspondence, no mention was made of the stench, which is one of the distressing effects of an advanced tumor. By June 1877, the breast cancer had followed a familiar pattern of generalization and had spread into the bones of her upper spine. She complained of pains in the neck as the chief symptom of her illness." Therese Taylor, "'Purgatory on Earth': An Account of Breast Cancer from Nineteenth-Century France," *Social History of Medicine*, Vol. 11, No. 3, 1998, p. 394.

I'm so gentle with her that they criticize me for it, but I know what I'm doing and don't listen to these criticisms. She was brought to this point by an extreme harshness that I didn't suspect and under the influence of the maid who went about it very badly, although she's a nice girl deep down.

Oh well, who knows? I believe God allowed this bad treatment, which I was unaware of, to first subdue this strange nature and make it more accommodating so that the task may be easier in the future. Otherwise, she would never have known the value of gentleness and friendship, but it was important that it ended as quickly as possible, or else she would have been lost.

If my wishes aren't granted and I'm not cured, the maid will leave as soon as I return from Lourdes. I don't want this child to fall under her control ever again. I hope God will help me find the kind of person I want to raise her, but rather let's hope that I'm the one He's chosen for this task.

However, the servant is very devoted. If I'm not cured she wants to take care of me up until the end, but I can't accept her devotion for fear that she'll stay on after I'm gone.

I'm leaving June 10 to take Marie to the retreat at the Visitation Monastery. I'll pick her up on the 17th along with Pauline, and we'll leave for Angers.

CF 204
To her daughter Pauline
May 1877

My dear Pauline,

I just received your letter and, at the same time, I received Sister Marie-Paula's, as well. The pilgrimage leaves June 18 at seven-fifty in the morning, so we'll have to leave Le Mans on Sunday. As you know, I don't like travelling on Sunday, but God knows that this time we have no choice. We'll take an afternoon train in order to be able to attend all the morning services.

So I'm taking you, my dear Pauline, as well as Marie and Léonie. We'll arrive just in time for the end of the retreat, which should end Friday. I'm asking the director of the boarding school, Sister Marie-

Louise de Gonzague, if she would be kind enough to keep Marie until Sunday.

Before leaving, I'll attend the first Mass here and arrive in Le Mans at nine o'clock. I'll still have time to go to High Mass, after which I'll go and get you.

The pilgrimage won't return until Friday. I think we'll remain in Angers until Saturday because I'd very much like to see Sister Marie-Paula again. She was so good to you that we can't pass through Angers, so close to her, without visiting her. It's quite probable we won't be able to if we continue on that night because we'll arrive too late. This good Sister offered to find me at the station, and this will be a great help to me.

In the beginning, your father didn't approve of my taking all three of you, but now he wants me to, saying that no sacrifice is too great to obtain such a great miracle. And even if I don't obtain it, I'll never regret having taken you there. We must be open to generously accepting God's will, whatever it may be, because it will always be what's best for us.

In any case, my Pauline, we must prepare ourselves well for this pilgrimage. I'm counting more on you than on the others for this. I don't know why I have this idea because Marie is praying for me so much, also with all her heart.

Your little letter made me very happy. Don't write me anymore now until my arrival. We'll spend a lovely day together. I'm delighted by it already, my beloved Pauline, but if you have a headache, I'll be sad.

As for the dress you asked me for, I can't have one made for you without a model. Instead, on the 10th, I'll bring home the one that's torn, have it repaired, and bring it back when we go on the pilgrimage. It's not worth buying you a black dress for the two months you have left at the Visitation Monastery. I'll try and make sure that the ones you have last.

I'll see you soon, my dear Pauline, pray hard for me since I'm especially counting on you.

Your mother who loves you dearly.

To her brother and sister-in-law
June 7, 1877

My dear brother and sister,

I received your letters which I was anxiously awaiting. I'll do my best to follow the good advice you've given me. So I intend to go to see Doctor X next Wednesday, fearing I won't find him available the last few days before I leave for the pilgrimage.

Soon I'll really need you if the Blessed Mother doesn't cure me because my illness is getting worse and worse. Last night especially I suffered a lot for two hours. It's no longer possible to touch the sore spot, it's too sensitive.[507] I wouldn't be at all surprised if it burst[508] before I left.

As long as hemorrhaging doesn't occur, because it seems that this happens when the illness is far along. Oh well, it's in God's hands! I'll have to be very sick not to go.

Yet I'm still hoping to be cured, perhaps too much. If I'm not, I'll be much more disappointed. I tell you again, it was from the moment I saw what was happening to Léonie that I became attached to life. Now I know how much she needs me. That servant, whom I trusted, tricked me....

However, I have nothing to reproach myself for, God sees well that I did the best I could.... I did the work of four people, who still wouldn't have had time to waste. I led a difficult life that would be very hard to do all over again. I don't think I'd have the courage.

And just when I would finally be able to breathe, I see the signal to leave, as if they're saying to me, "You've done enough, come rest." But no, I haven't done enough; these children aren't grown up yet. Ah! Except for that, I wouldn't be afraid of death.

Look, I see I'm wasting my time saying nothing. So I'll finish by leaving you free to do whatever you'd like regarding a Mass in Lourdes. I believe the Blessed Mother will cure me without it, since

---

[507] "I was only eight years old when my mother, at my request, showed me the sore; I have always kept an unforgettable memory of it. All of the upper part of the right side of her breast as far as the shoulder and the base of the neck was bright red with inflammation, while darker red streaks ran through it, up and down." Céline Martin (Sister Geneviève of the Holy Face), *The Mother of the Little Flower*, p. 103.
[508] See footnote in CF 203.

it's so difficult to arrange for it. My little girls will pray so hard for me that it's impossible the Blessed Mother won't let herself be touched.

If you only saw Pauline's letter, she gives me confidence. No, never has Heaven seen, nor will it ever see, such fervent prayers or a more lively faith. And then I have my sister in Heaven who will take an interest in me. I also have my four little angels who will pray for me. They'll all be in Lourdes with us.

If I'm cured, I'll send you a telegram. We're arriving home Saturday, and I won't be able to write you until the next day.

On Sunday[509] I'll begin a novena to the Sacred Heart. I'll also say one to the Blessed Mother and one to Saint Joseph that will end Wednesday. Perhaps I'll only be cured on Thursday; it's the last day.

I'm hurrying because the bell for Benediction is sounding, and I want to attend. I had something else to say, but I don't have time. Nevertheless, I must bring up my brother's idea that God will only cure me for His glory. I say that everything is for the glory of God, but that He doesn't think absolutely only of Himself. He would perform a miracle for me even if no one in the world knew about it.

I'll pray with all my heart for all of you.

I'll try to get a seat in the corner of the railroad car, as my brother recommends, but this won't be for me. I don't want the corner; any place will do. This will be for my Pauline, who always has a headache, and also for Léonie, who will want to see everything and believes she's going to Paradise.

CF 206   To her brother
                                              June 11, 1877

I'm quickly writing to reassure you. I had the impression I should write you while I was having a bad feeling that has since gone away. My illness is not as intense as it was and doesn't prevent me from sleeping anymore. I've even suffered little since then.

I'm hoping that my trip will go without a hitch. I'm expecting this favor from the Blessed Mother, and I'm very sure she won't refuse me.

---

[509] June 10, 1877.

Yesterday I went to Le Mans to take Marie to the retreat. I'll pick her up Sunday morning with Pauline, who's determined to force me to say that I'll be cured because, they assure her, it's a sure sign of healing when patients have a lot of hope. But I can't satisfy her this time because my hope doesn't go as far as certainty.

If I'm not cured instantly, I don't know what poor Pauline will do; she takes everything too much to heart. It will be a severe blow.

I saw the Superior at the Visitation Monastery who promised that the Community will receive general Communion[510] for me. In short, I have high hopes. But sometimes I say to myself, "Why would there be a miracle for me rather than for other people I knew, who died leaving a big family and were better than I am?"

It's true that they hadn't gone to Lourdes, and yet there was a young lady in Alençon with an illness in her chest who wanted to go and died there two days later. She was only twenty years old and left two little children.

It doesn't matter. I have a lot of hope, but I'm quite resigned to accept whatever God wants. This way, in case it's not successful, the disappointment will be less.

There's not a single ticket left for the pilgrimage. If Louis came, as you'd like him to, he would have to take poor Léonie's ticket, whom I want to bring. If the Blessed Mother doesn't heal me, at least I'll ask her to cure my child, to open up her intelligence and make her a saint. So, let's leave all the arrangements as they are. They seem very good to me. Then let's put ourselves in God's hands.

Sunday morning I leave for Le Mans after the first Mass. I almost have scruples about traveling this way on a Sunday, but I don't believe I'm doing anything wrong since it's impossible for me to do otherwise. Besides, it's not to entertain myself but, in fact, to do true penance.... I'm especially talking about myself because I dislike travelling so much.

Good-bye, I won't write you anymore except by telegram to announce my cure.

I'll pray very hard for you and above all for my little Jeanne so that the Blessed Mother heals her completely and that she's a good little girl.

---

[510] General Communion is an offering of a common intention upon receiving the Eucharist.

Even if Louis were to come, I assure you that the two youngest girls could very well stay home with the maid. She loves them very much, of this I'm sure. It was only towards Léonie that she was so mean. As for the others, she spoils them more than I do and makes sacrifices for them.

I kiss all of you with love.

Z. Martin[511]

CF 207

To her sister-in-law
June 14, 1877

…So yesterday I went to see Doctor X. I told him I came back to consult him to find out if there was anything else that could be done now.

He didn't seem to know what I was asking of him. Finally, he wrote me a prescription.

Seeing that he'd decided to say very little, I tried to pull a few words out of him. I asked him if he thought the tumor would soon burst,[512] and I got no answer.

I asked him again if he thought they could perform the operation, and he answered, "You well know that idea was abandoned."[513] Then, finally, he said to me, "It's so much better if it does burst, the illness will run its course that way." I answered, "Yes, when I'll die." "Yes, that's possible," he admitted, "but it's not impossible that you'll be cured. We don't know how it will turn out."

All of this was said in an indifferent, bored tone with a forced grin that made a profound impression on me.

It will be very hard to go back to this man if I'm cured. Either he'll not pay attention to what I'm telling him or he'll reel off a lot of

---

[511] The last line and the signature are from the original letter.

[512] See footnote in CF 203.

[513] "Zélie Martin realized, when her doctor declined to describe surgery as a cure, that he judged her case to be hopeless. One specialist warned the doctors on the subject of recommendation for surgery: 'There is a moral aspect involved in this line of conduct, because these poor women, in general, know only too well that the refusal to operate is the equivalent of a death sentence.'" Therese Taylor, "'Purgatory on Earth': An Account of Breast Cancer from Nineteenth-Century France." *Social History of Medicine*, p. 391.

foolishness to me because he believes nothing. All the same, I'll go, but it will be the last time.

If I'm not cured, I'll never go back, and he'll never treat me again because just the sight of him would make me sick. Nevertheless, he once did me a favor, it was the day he told me the truth. That consultation was priceless for me.

I could see he regretted it, and as he doesn't know how to say a good word or even how to be kind, he contents himself with showing complete indifference. He seemed to be saying to me, "What are you doing here? Didn't I tell you, for the first and last time, that there was nothing to be done, that the medicines I prescribed were just to make the patients happy?" This poor man! He doesn't know how much I do remember it and how few times I've used his remedies and his prescriptions.

The last one I threw into the fire when I got home without even reading it. You're going to say I'm in a very bad mood, but what do you want? It's beyond my will. I feel so deeply repulsed by the harshness of this man that I can't express it.

It's a good thing I find more sympathetic souls along the way. Without them I'd be running after death and not after life, like I'm going to do.

Good-bye, my dear sister, thank you for all that you do for me, I'm touched to the bottom of my soul. I'll ask Our Lady of Lourdes to give it back to you a hundredfold, in this world and the next.

I kiss you with all my love.

P.S. Do you know that I'm still making Alençon lace? I received some orders, very few, it's true. Well, I'm fulfilling them, and we'll go on like that up to the end.

CF 208

To Louis Martin
Angers, June 1877

My dear Louis,

Léonie and I have arrived in Le Mans[514] and we attended Mass before going to the Visitation Monastery. At nine-thirty I asked for Marie and Pauline, who were already worried about us!

---

[514] June 17.

The Superior had arranged for a good lunch to be prepared for us with coffee and all kinds of desserts. She came to see us and promised me prayers and a general Communion[515] offered up by the Community. For my intention, on Tuesday evening, all the nuns and the students will make a pilgrimage through the gardens where there is a statue of Our Lady of Lourdes. They're taking as much interest in me as they possibly can.

After lunch we left for Angers, and we arrived at three o'clock. An extern Sister was waiting for us at the station and took us to the Hotel de France, right across from the station. I brought my luggage since it was so close. We have a room with two beds. The good Sister came to help us get settled and then brought us to the Visitation Monastery. We're not going to leave there until around eight-thirty.

Sister Marie-Paula doesn't want to leave the children. She cried when she saw them again and Marie did, too. The Mother Superior stayed with us for an hour. She's going to have the entire Community pray for me. The Chaplain, who has the face of a saint, also came to visit us for three quarters of an hour. Never have I seen such a good and pleasant priest. On the way back from Lourdes I was planning to take the train that left Angers at six o'clock in the morning in order to arrive in Le Mans early and be home by five o'clock in the afternoon. But this excellent priest told me that if I were cured, he himself wants to say a Mass of thanksgiving on Saturday and have a beautiful ceremony, which he explained to me. I don't remember it anymore, but he always wants there to be a lot of people!

In short, if I'm cured, I don't think I'll be able to arrive in Alençon before eight o'clock at night, and if I'm not, it will be at five-thirty.

We saw the Bishop of Evreux[516] at the Visitation Monastery in Angers, who spoke to us with kindness and had us kiss his ring.

I'm writing to you while Sister Marie-Paula is talking to the two oldest girls, and she's having a hard time leaving them. Pauline is enjoying herself immensely at the Visitation Monastery in Angers. On the other hand, Léonie is here at my side and very bored!

---

[515] See footnote in CF 206.

[516] Bishop François Grolleau, Bishop of Evreux from 1870 to 1890. Evreux is approximately 130 kilometers (81 miles) northeast of Alençon.

The surprise that the good Sister had mentioned to me is that the extern Sister is going on the pilgrimage with us.

We leave tomorrow morning at seven-thirty. I'm finishing my letter because it's getting dark. Give my little girls a big hug for me.

I send you all my love.

CF 209 To her brother and sister-in-law
Alençon, June 24, 1877

I think you must be worried about how my trip went. I wish I could have sent you a joyful telegram, but unfortunately, I'm not cured. On the contrary, the trip made my illness worse.

However, I'm not at all hopeless. I believe I'll be cured, and this idea came to me at my last good-bye at the Grotto, so I was very happy on the return trip. I sang as well on the return trip as I did while going, but the children didn't do the same, they're desolate.

I had quite a hard time calming them down. Pauline didn't want to eat anymore. I had to say to her an hour after we left, "I truly believe I'm getting better." A sudden joy lit up her face, and she told me that she was overcome with hunger. She ate well and fell asleep.

I'll remember this trip for a long time because of the misery and fatigue I endured. I wanted to bring three children, believing it better to do so and more easily obtain the grace we wished for so much, but it cost me a lot of trouble and turmoil of every kind.

First, in Le Mans, an extern Sister had to lend me a "very handy" container to put some water in. We already had one, but it was full of good wine, and we needed water. She filled it, and there we were on our way when we noticed it was leaking. We had to bring it back to her.

After arriving in Angers we went to the Visitation Monastery; it was three o'clock. There we waited a long time for Vespers to finish, and around four o'clock we saw the Superior and the Sister who used to be headmistress of the boarding school in Le Mans.

At six o'clock, I wanted to leave so my daughters could have dinner. The Sister wanted to keep them until eight o'clock. I didn't want that, we were dying of hunger. She told me to take them to the hotel and afterwards bring them back right away, but it was too far.

To go and come back would be a league[517] and I couldn't agree to this arrangement.

Finally, the good extern Sister took it upon herself to give them a piece of bread with a little chocolate. I wasn't very happy, but Sister Marie-Paula wanted so much to keep them with her and the girls wanted so much to stay, that I didn't dare hurt any of them. Pauline was as happy as a queen with her piece of bread!

They gave us another container. We brought it with us to the hotel, and the next day, upon leaving, we filled it with water. This one, too, leaked like a watering can. The manager gave us a bottle, and off we went.

But this was only the beginning of my trials and tribulations. In spite of the loving protests of my daughters to let them take care of me, it was I, in fact, who took care of them. Sometimes one of them was thirsty, sometimes another one was hungry. What's more, Marie was afflicted by a big speck of dust in her eye and moaned about it for four hours. Finally, Léonie's feet were swollen, and she cried because her shoes were hurting her.

At the end of the journey I was so worn out by fatigue, I was afraid I would faint. Finally, towards the end of the night, I slept for two hours, during which Léonie, while dreaming, got up, came to throw herself on top of me and from there against the door which, fortunately, was closed.

I let out such a cry of surprise and terror, not knowing where this had come from, that I woke up all the other travelers, who laughed heartily. Finally, I made Léonie sit near the door so that the same thing wouldn't happen again.

We arrived in Lourdes at five o'clock in the morning. At that early hour I couldn't bother Father Martignon, whom I'd first asked to find me a place to stay. Then later, having indicated to him another address that had been recommended to me, I didn't know if he'd received this second letter. Finally, I nevertheless decided to go to this second address.

We were beginning to get settled when this good priest arrived and said to me, "I saw you pass by my window and, based on the information you'd given me, I thought I wasn't mistaken. You

---

[517] See footnote in CF 64.

mustn't stay here. I reserved a room for you with the Sisters from the orphanage in Nevers." And he said to the proprietor of the hotel, "Madame, yesterday I came to see you twice but in vain, so I looked for other accommodations for Madame Martin whom, first of all, we must take care of."

I was only half pleased by all of this. Finally, haphazardly, we had to pick up our luggage again and follow Father Martignon, who got us settled with the Sisters while asking them to treat us well.

This was all well and good, but I said to myself, "I wouldn't normally put up with this arrangement for a long time. Oh well, I'll live with it for the moment." The children were hungry so I ordered a good tapioca. As for me, I took nothing because I wanted to go first to the Grotto and then to the spring, although I was completely worn out.

When I arrived at the Grotto, my heart was so tight I couldn't even pray. During Mass I was very close to the altar, but I was so exhausted I didn't understand a thing.

I left in a state of total collapse, and from there I went to the spring. I looked with terror at the freezing water and the deathly cold marble. But I had to do it, and I courageously threw myself into the water. Yes, but... I almost couldn't breathe, and I had to get out almost immediately. I should have gone in more gently.

Then I went into the first restaurant I could find to have a cup of chocolate, and at eleven o'clock we had lunch at the Sisters'. There was a magnificent table with many rich pilgrims, but the menu was quite meager.

I said to myself, "Here's one meal, but there won't be two of them because I'm uncomfortable with all these people, and I prefer to stay in my room with my daughters." So I told the Sisters that I'd brought enough provisions, and I would tell them when I needed anything.

I did the right thing because I wouldn't have had enough money. Nevertheless, I'd brought a sufficient amount, and I returned with five francs!

Father Martignon was to see us again at noon in order to let us know the time of the Mass. I wanted to go to his house to spare him the trouble of going out, but he was entering the Sisters' house as I was leaving.

He celebrated Mass for me on Wednesday[518] at six o'clock at the altar of the Sacred Heart in the Basilica in Lourdes. Léonie became sick during the journey and was unable to receive Communion.

This good priest is truly a saint. I wanted to see him again, and I went to his house four times. On my first visit, he was at the Bishop's house, so I went there, that's how much I wanted to speak with him. They told me he'd left and handed me a letter from him. While leaving Lourdes I tried one last visit, but again he wasn't home. I was very sorry about that. Oh well, I'll write him soon, and I fully intend to be able to tell him that I'm cured because I still have hope.

I'm going to continue the novenas with the Lourdes water that I'll apply every day. I brought back three liters, but what trouble I had with the containers! Again, one of the containers I bought was leaking, and I had to return it to the shopkeeper. Only countless misfortunes and miseries happened to me.

I lost my sister's rosary that I'd brought with me, hoping it would bring me happiness. However, I was so afraid of losing it that I never put it down for one minute, and I constantly had it intertwined between my fingers.

I said I didn't put it down for one minute, but unfortunately, while I was buying some groceries, I gave it to Marie to keep. When we returned there was no more rosary. This hurt me very much; it was the only relic I had of my sister and the one I wanted the most.

Pauline also lost her rosary to which two of her aunt's medals were attached. She cried over her poor rosary. As for me, I didn't cry over mine, but it left me with a pain deep within my heart. Oh well, God allowed it, an ordeal for which He'll compensate me.

I had many other distressing adventures, but they were of little importance, and it would take too long to tell you about them. Finally, we arrived in the Angers train station at eight-fifteen on Friday night.[519] The good Sisters at the Visitation Monastery had asked me to have breakfast with them Saturday morning.

The Mother Superior wanted me to go to Notre-Dame de Sous-Terre[520] in Angers, where miracles occur, but I declined and

---

[518] June 20.
[519] June 22.
[520] A shrine to "Our Lady of the Underground."

thanked them for all their offers because I wanted to take the first train to Le Mans.

When I arrived at the hotel I told the manager that I was going to return to the station to inquire about the exact time of the train. He declared that there was no need, that he had all the fares and that the schedules had changed the day before, and consequently, there was only the seven o'clock train.

So I relied on that and didn't go to the station. Besides, I'd just torn my dress in such a way that I couldn't walk anymore because my two feet got caught in the tear. I even almost got crushed by a carriage that I clearly saw coming towards me, but I couldn't get out of the way. Finally, I had dinner and then repaired my dress.

The next morning at a quarter to seven I was at the station. The employee who was selling tickets said to me, "The train left an hour ago. The new schedule doesn't start until the 25th."

I knew that Louis would be waiting for me in Alençon at five-thirty, and I had to bring Pauline to the Visitation Monastery in Le Mans. What could I do with only my half-hour stop in Le Mans? When we arrived there, I decided to put Pauline alone on the omnibus. She was crying and was very unhappy. I wasn't happy, either.... I was worried the whole rest of the journey and still am. I'm afraid the conductor took her I don't know where. I'm going to write to her today to find out if she got back safely.

Not having been able to leave Angers until noon, I forgot to tell you that I went back to the Visitation Monastery and, at the plea of the Superior, went to Notre-Dame de Sous-Terre. I was still hoping to obtain my cure there, but I wasn't cured. That will be for another time. Let's wait patiently for God's time, who wants to test us for a while.

The good nuns wanted to see me cured as much as I did. They said endless prayers and novenas, those in Angers, as well. The Sister in this town, who taught my oldest children, cried part of the day on Thursday because she didn't receive the telegram I'd promised her.

At eight o'clock in the evening they heard a little bell in the cloister sound only once. It did no good to try and find out who rang it, nobody had touched it. They believed it was a miracle and that it was Our Lady of Lourdes letting them know that a miracle had taken place… or rather, that it hadn't!

I lit a beautiful candle for you in the Grotto of Lourdes and three others for Monsieur Fournet, the Maudelonde family and the ladies of the P family.[521] I plunged into the spring four times. The last time was two hours before we left. I was in the icy water just above my shoulders, but it wasn't as cold as the morning. I stayed there more than a quarter of an hour, still hoping that the Blessed Mother was going to cure me.

While I was in there I didn't feel any pain anymore, but as soon as I got out, the sharp pains began as usual.

The Blessed Mother left more people than me with a trial to bear. I saw many sick people, among them a young thirteen-and-a-half-year-old girl whose poor mother carried her around on her shoulders during the processions and throughout the day. She was in a pitiful state with paralyzed legs and a hideous sore covering her entire back which I only had the courage to look at from a distance.

She left Lourdes without being cured, as well as two poor sick people who came there for the second time. I saw the funeral of a seventy-two year old man who had died almost unexpectedly on Tuesday because the day before he drank too much water from the Grotto while being in a sweat.

Last Wednesday, while taking down a vase full of water, I missed two steps and strained my neck so badly[522] on the side that isn't sick, that it's impossible for me to make any movement in bed. This morning I needed a lot of help to be able to get up. However, today I'm feeling better than yesterday.

Tell me if one could have a more unfortunate trip? Of course, there are great graces hidden at the bottom of all this that will compensate me for these miseries. With faith, I put the miraculous water on my Léonie's forehead.

I'm finishing my letter; I think you know enough about my trip. I thank you, as well as the good ladies of the P family, for all

---

[521] The Pigeon family.

[522] "In Lourdes, she slipped on some stairs and jarred her neck. She must have damaged the weakened bones in her upper spine, and from this moment forward she continuously suffered neck pain which is characteristic of advanced breast cancer." Therese Taylor, "'Purgatory on Earth': An Account of Breast Cancer from Nineteenth-Century France." *Social History of Medicine*, p. 398. (See footnote in CF 203.)

you've done for me. I would have been twice as happy to be cured because of you. Unfortunately, the Blessed Mother says to us, as she did to Bernadette, "I will make you happy not in this world but in the next."[523]

I don't regret having gone to Lourdes, although the fatigue has made me sicker. At least I won't blame myself for anything if I'm not cured. Meanwhile, let us hope.

Many people here know that I'm returning from Lourdes, although I hid it as much as I could. But one person would tell another, so now almost everybody knows.

I don't like it because I see some smiles of disbelief on the part of even those who advised me to go on the pilgrimage. These people were thinking that I wouldn't be cured because they don't believe in the miracles of Lourdes. So they have a triumphant air, not that they wish me ill, of course. Finally, to tell you the truth, I'm very unhappy over it and don't know where to hide myself.

Good-bye, I look forward to hearing from you. Today I'm starting another novena, and I won't stop saying it unless I'm cured or I die. Meanwhile, I kiss you with all my heart.

My husband asks me to give you his best wishes. He had a hard week, always hoping to receive the "miraculous" telegram which never came!

CF 210   To her daughter Pauline
                                               June 25, 1877

My dear Pauline,

I couldn't help having a painful feeling when I saw you disappear on the omnibus. This feeling stayed with me, and yet I believe there was no reason to worry like this. You must have gotten back to your dear convent very quickly, where you found friendly hearts which consoled you and also the calm you needed after that trip.

We didn't arrive in Alençon until six-thirty;[524] the train was almost a half hour late. Your father was waiting for us for an hour

---

[523] The words said by the Blessed Mother to Bernadette Soubirous on February 18, 1858, in the third apparition.
[524] Saturday, June 23.

with the two little ones. He was happy to see us, although quite sad. He'd had some difficult moments since Thursday expecting the famous telegram at any moment, and each time the bell rang, he would jump.

He was very surprised to see me return as cheerfully as if I'd received the much desired grace. This renewed his courage and put everyone in a good mood again.

I still have a very strong hope of being cured which only increases. I see a look of disbelief on the face of certain people who come to ask about the results of my pilgrimage, but that doesn't trouble me.

First of all, I can't help having the feeling of confidence that invigorates me. I'm saying my novenas again, and every night I put Lourdes water on my wound, and after that, I live in hope and peace, expecting that God's time has come.

Yesterday I saw Mademoiselle X, who admitted to me what I already knew – that she doesn't believe in miracles. However, I told her that I was hoping for one all the same. She agreed with my words, but I could tell what she really thought. Oh well! As for me, I'm still expecting a miracle from the goodness and omnipotence of God through the intercession of his Holy Mother. Not that I'm asking Him to take away my illness completely, but only to let me live a few years to have time to raise my children and, especially, poor Léonie, who needs me so much and who I feel so sorry for.

She has fewer natural gifts than you, but in spite of this, she has a heart that asks to love and be loved. Only a mother would be able to continually show her the attention she's hungering for and follow her progress closely enough to do her good.

My dear child treats me with infinite tenderness. She anticipates my wishes and nothing is too much. She looks into my eyes to try and guess what would make me happy. She's almost doing too much.

But as soon as anyone else asks her for something, her face clouds over and her expression changes instantly.

Little by little I'm managing to make her get over this, although she still often forgets. However, with time, I'm sure I'll be able to manage to make her love God a lot and be pleasant to everyone.[525]

---

[525] "[Léonie] accepted generously, in silence, the stinging words of some of her companions – as she pardoned Louise Marais, the maid who had once tyrannized her in

I forgot to return your badminton racquet. Mademoiselle Pauline R[526] has taken responsibility for bringing it to you, as well as the ribbons you asked for. You'll probably receive them this week. I'm going to give her everything today or tomorrow, so don't expect a new letter to accompany what I'm sending you.

Write me on Sunday because I want to know what state of mind you're in and if you're still angry with the Blessed Mother for not wanting to make you jump for joy. As I just wrote in a letter to Lisieux, she says to everyone as she did to Bernadette, "I will make you happy not in this world but in the next."[527]

So don't hope for a lot of joy in this world; you'll have too many disappointments. As for me, I know from experience how much to count on the joys of this world, and if I wasn't hoping for those of Heaven, I would be very unhappy.

I don't have time to write anymore. I'll do so after I receive the letter you'll write to me. Above all, courage and confidence! Pray faithfully to our merciful Mother, who'll come to our aid with the kindness and gentleness of the most loving mother.

I kiss you with love.

Your mother,
Z. Martin[528]

CF 211

To her daughter Pauline
June 29, 1877

My dear Pauline,

I had told you I wouldn't write you a letter when I sent you your little package, but I'm only sending it today, and I don't know when you'll receive it.

The Mass you wanted will be said tomorrow.

Alençon. Louise – who had become Madame Legendre, a wife and mother – died in December 1923." Léonie forgave Louise Marais. She said, "I forgive my tormentor with all my heart and I am grateful to her for looking after my mother so well during her last illness." Marie Baudouin-Croix, *Léonie Martin: A Difficult Life*. Dublin: Ireland. Veritas Publications, 1993, p. 86.

[526] Pauline Romet.

[527] See footnote in CF 209.

[528] From the paragraph that begins "Write to me on Sunday" to the signature are three passages preserved from the original letter.

Don't worry about me. I'm not worrying at all, and I'm putting everything in God's hands. I'm longing to hear from you. Are you fully recovered from your fatigue?

I'm hoping and waiting for a good letter. I don't have time to write any more, they're taking mine this moment.

I kiss you with love.

Your mother.

CF 212 To her sister-in-law
July 8, 1877

I think you're expecting news from me which is why I decided, with regret, to write you today because I have nothing satisfying to tell you. Not only is the illness still progressing and continuing to ooze since it burst[529] two weeks ago, but the strain in my neck that happened when I tripped in Lourdes makes me suffer immensely, especially since last night. If this continues, it will be terrifying; I would have to remain completely immobile.

It still doesn't hurt during the day, but at night, when I have to lie down or get up, it's awful. It gives me a terrible jolt, and I'm ready to faint.

Up until now it's been bearable, and last night I was even happy to notice that I could turn over a lot more easily. So I fell asleep almost right away and began to dream again of my processions in Lourdes, because every night I dream about Lourdes and miracles.

Around a quarter to twelve I woke up and wanted to turn over. It was then that I felt the most violent pain one could possibly have. Finally, after incredible effort, I succeeded in sitting up, but I felt as if my head was going to fall off. Then I got up and took a handkerchief which I soaked in Lourdes water and applied it to my neck. But how could I lie down again? I asked the Blessed Mother to help me lie down in the direction I wanted, and I managed to do it because the slightest movement in the opposite direction caused me acute pain. Then I was able to fall back asleep until four-thirty.

I had to get dressed at five o'clock to go to the first Mass. I was

---

[529] See footnote in CF 203.

alone because Louis was at Nocturnal Adoration. I got up to look at the time, and fortunately, the Blessed Mother helped me because I don't know what I would have done. It was still too early.

I sat down on my bed. I didn't dare lie down so as not to have to sit up a half hour later. Finally, at five o'clock I called Marie to help me get dressed. I had a great deal of difficulty sitting down and kneeling in church. I had to stop myself from crying out, so I'm not going to go to High Mass anymore.

However, it's better at the moment, and, if I'm very careful, I'm able to move a little. If I could manage not to strain it any more, I would be cured of this, but unfortunately, that's hardly possible.

On top of that, this week I felt a general malaise that took away all my strength. I'm feeling better today, and I feel like I have more energy. If I didn't have this pain in my neck, it would seem as if I were freed from all my other illnesses.

Let's continue our prayers and applying the Lourdes water. I still have hope. However, I'm not sure I'm going to be cured, and sometimes this thought makes me sad. What will become of my poor Léonie?

Soon the maid must leave for good, and I still don't have anyone in mind to replace her. Oh! If God gave me the grace of curing me, I wouldn't want any more servants. Marie knows a lot about running the house. She's the one who takes care of the bedrooms and takes care of her little sisters. Pauline and Léonie would also help, and we'd be happy like I've never been before.

Do I have to see my entire life's dream vanish just as it's going to become a reality? We're so at peace when we have no strangers in the house. During the ten days the maid was away, everything was in the most perfect order because my children gave me great satisfaction. However, I still have one hope that consoles me in case God doesn't consider it advisable to perform a miracle in my favor. I have a worker who's about forty years old and who lives alone in Ancinnes.[530]

You see few or none like her. In the twenty years she's worked for me, I've come to appreciate her. She's an angel of gentleness and devotion joined to a very sound mind and good judgment. As soon

---

[530] Ancinnes is approximately 10 kilometers (6.2 miles) southeast of Alençon.

as she heard that I was sick, without knowing exactly what I had, she came specially to see me. That was nearly two months ago.

I told her everything, and she burst into tears and showed me as much sympathy as if she were my own sister. She anxiously awaited the outcome of the pilgrimage. I'd told her that I'd thought of her to look after my children if God called me home. She answered, "I would make many sacrifices for you."

This answer said everything to me. I'm sure she would come. Such a person would be a true treasure and a gift from Heaven. Marie saw her and said, "If we had a girl like that in our home, we would be happy."

I hope to be well enough to go to Lisieux next month; we'll leave August 18. I want to spend the Feast of the Assumption in Alençon because perhaps the Blessed Mother will begin to cure me that day, and I wouldn't be able to prepare myself for such a grace while on a trip.

It's quite settled that I'll only bring Marie and Pauline with me, and they'll stay with you for some time. But, I beg you, don't talk to me about bringing the others. That would upset me and my husband, as well.

The little ones know quite well that the two big girls must leave, but if one of the other three girls came, there would be tears and lamentations that would lead to my bringing all five!

The little one[531] will be the most eager. She'll remember for the rest of her life that we left her in Alençon two years ago, and when she talks about it she starts crying at once. My Thérèse is a charming little creature. I assure you that this one will turn out well.

My husband saw Monsieur Vital, who told him that he paid you a visit and that you have two sweet little girls who are so well brought up.

My brother tells me nothing new about Monsieur X. I knew him a long time ago, and I heard him say that God doesn't worry about us and all kinds of nonsense. I'm sure he thinks I'm crazy because I declared to him that, in spite of my failure in Lourdes, I knew without a doubt that He works brilliant miracles there and I hoped to be cured sooner or later.

---

[531] Thérèse, four-and-a-half years old.

He shook his head and winked while laughing, he believed absolutely none of it. If I told him this, it's because he wanted to convince me that it was impossible that a cure takes place suddenly. I was determined not to appear to share his opinion. In short, he thinks he possesses the truth in its fullness and that everyone else is more or less an "idiot."

Regarding my trip to Lourdes, we had an adventure on the train that I forgot to tell you about. There were two women in our compartment who seemed to be very good and very charitable. On the other hand, they took the best care of themselves day and night. They went down to all the buffets, but that wasn't enough, they'd brought a spirit stove[532] and a coffee pot with them, and they set about making coffee in the train car.

As soon as I saw this paraphernalia and the flame flickering back and forth, I was afraid of a fire, and I was anxious. A moment later they let out a cry of fright, and everybody moved away. The children rushed over to me, I was literally crushed, and I still didn't know what had happened.

It was the little table holding the cups that had just fallen over. Fortunately, they held on to the stove in time, but the flood of coffee (at least eight cups) happened on our side, and all our provisions were soaked. The linen I'd brought had to be wrung out, our bread was nothing but coffee....

Oh well, I was dreading a worse misfortune. Fortunately, the children were wearing black dresses because otherwise I don't know what we would have done!

I'd wanted to get angry but these good women were so pleasant and so upset by the event that I stopped myself, especially since they were heating the coffee for us, as well.

What a commotion! When I wrote to you about my adventures two weeks ago, I thought my brother was going to say, "It's not surprising. What happens to her never happens to other people." I was pleasantly surprised by your good letter which in no way seemed to laugh at me.

I'll return to my illness since the details interest you. The very violent pains I feel in my neck make my husband and Marie believe

---

[532] A small portable stove fueled by alcohol.

that the Blessed Mother wants to cure me, otherwise she wouldn't permit so much pain at once, and pain that stems from my pilgrimage.

I think you're right. If the Blessed Mother prolongs my existence, it's not so that I earn money. So, last month I was sad to see a new order arrive, not knowing if I should accept it or let it go because of the hope I still have of being cured. I have enough business, although now that I have big girls it would be less painful than it was before when, because of it, my family was too much at the mercy of silly or malicious servants.

I think that's enough for today. I'll write you again in two weeks, and let's hope the news will be better.

I kiss you all with love.

CF 213   To her sister-in-law
                                                      July 15, 1877
My dear Sister,

Your letter is truly touching, as well my brother's. It brought tears to my husband's eyes. He admires your devotion, and, I assure you, it consoles me greatly when I contemplate my leaving this world, to think of the help you'll be for my dear children.

As for going to live in Lisieux, my husband says neither yes nor no; we must let time take care of it.[533]

If he had a person helping him with the children like the one I have in mind, perhaps it would be very difficult for him to decide. But if, on the contrary, it's someone who resembles ordinary mortals, it would be a different matter.

But you know, "Man proposes, but God disposes."[534] It's not easy to say what one will do in the near future. It's like me who, with good reason, was counting on the person in Ancinnes. Oh well! On Thursday I received a letter from her. For three months this holy girl has had a problem with her foot that appears dangerous. She told me

---

[533] Response to a suggestion from the Guérins that Louis Martin come live in Lisieux, near them, in the event his wife dies.

[534] Thomas à Kempis, *The Imitation of Christ.* New York: Alba House, 1995. (Book I, Chapter XIX, p. 67.)

about her sufferings and that she's offering all of them to the Heart of Jesus for my cure, adding that she would gladly sacrifice her life to save mine. She thinks she's good for nothing in this world and says it would be a compensation if her life could buy back another that she believes useful. I wasn't mistaken, this is an exceptional soul. I'm going to send her Lourdes water and say a novena for her. God absolutely has to cure one of us. I'd be almost as happy if it were her rather than me, although I don't have her selflessness, and I don't feel determined to sacrifice my life for hers.

As I told you, the maid must leave next month, but, seeing that I'm no longer capable of anything, she wants to stay until my death. I can't refuse her this under the present circumstances.[535] She's very devoted and does the best she can. It's a shame I have to reproach her for such serious things. She claims that no one will care for me like she will, and I think so, too.

Again, you ask me to speak to you about my illness. Sadly, what can I tell you about it? Except that the illness is getting worse every day. I can neither get dressed nor undressed by myself anymore, and my arm on the side where I'm sick refuses to do anything, but my hand still wants to hold a needle!

What's more, I feel a general malaise, some intestinal pain, and I've had a fever for about two weeks. Finally, I can't remain standing and have to sit down.

As for my neck, it's not cured, but I haven't endured as much pain as I felt the Sunday I wrote to you. I have almost no attacks during the day, it's only at night when my nerves tense up, and then I have to take unbelievable precautions to change my position. However, I've learned by experience, and I'm beginning to know how to go about raising myself up so that it keeps me from having an attack.

I've been sleeping well enough for the last three nights. The previous nights were very bad because I was too restless. Not being

---

[535] From Céline's biographical reflections of her mother: "With her own personal experience of daily work, the servants were the object of great concern to her; as a result, they remained long in her service. The servants for us were part of the family. It was on that account when it was decided to dismiss the maid who had so wrongly treated Léonie, the poor girl wept so much that she was allowed to stay, to take care of Mamma, whose illness was making frightful progress." Céline Martin (Sister Geneviève of the Holy Face), *The Mother of the Little Flower*, p. 35.

able to move myself overexcited me more, so I decided to go out every night into the garden and tire myself out a little bit. This experience did me good.

You tell me not to lose confidence, and I'm certainly not losing confidence. I know very well that the Blessed Mother can cure me, but I can't help fearing that she doesn't want to, and I'll tell you honestly that a miracle seems very doubtful to me now. I've taken that stand and am trying to act as if I have to die. It's absolutely necessary that I not lose the little time I have left to live, these are days of salvation that will never come again, and so I must make the most of them.

I'll have double the benefits. I'll suffer less by resigning myself, and I'll do part of my Purgatory on earth. So please, ask for resignation and patience for me, I need it very much. You know that I have hardly any patience.

This week I wasn't expecting to be able to go to Lisieux anymore, but I truly feel better. The fever disappeared, and I believe I'll still be able to make this trip one more time. In any case, I absolutely insist that we bring Marie and Pauline to you. I can't tell you how long they'll stay, that will depend on circumstances.

I see that your little Jeanne is still not well; it's been a very long time. I was like that from the age of seven until eleven or twelve. Afterwards, I had a serious illness, and I was completely cured. But I think she'll be cured much earlier than I was because I was a lot less strong and also not cared for as well.

Here is Léonie who wants to die in my place, and she prays for this every day. However, she's beginning to lose heart because she's not getting sick!

I shouldn't be writing to you today. I'm doing so because I saw that it would make you happy. I also have to write to Pauline for the last time because we're going to pick her up August 1. She'll shed a lot of tears because she loves the Visitation Monastery very much.

I dread her arrival home. She'll hardly be happy. I would like her to return again next year, but her father and, especially, Marie, don't share this opinion. She has to take on her share of the crosses.

You don't need to answer all my letters because I write you too often. You can answer the next one, which you won't have to wait long for. I hope to tell you Sunday that the improvement continues.

I kiss you with all my love.

Your very loving sister,
Z. Martin

As for going to the doctor, I'm undecided about it. He would make me worse, he makes too much of an impression on me. If he could still do something, I would overcome my repugnance, but I know he can do nothing, neither for my neck nor anywhere else, if this continues.[536]

CF 214	To her daughter Pauline
	July 15, 1877

My dear Pauline,

Yesterday I wasn't expecting to have the pleasure of receiving a letter from you; I was only counting on it for Tuesday. When it arrived I was out with Léonie. We had gone to Mass and shopping. Your father had left at six o'clock to take Marie to confession, and then they had to go to the Pavilion to gather strawberries and red currants.

Since Léonie and I weren't very far away from the garden, she begged me so much to take her there, that I went. I found Marie quite busy filling her little basket. It had rained, and she was rather wet. Your father had left her alone to do her gathering and had returned to the house to get his newspaper.

When he arrived back at the Pavilion, he told me that he'd received a letter from Pauline and also from the Mother Superior. He regretted very much not bringing them to me, but he wasn't expecting to find me there.[537]

I urged Marie to leave. I was longing to see your letter. Finally, I had the time to read and reread it, I don't know how many times, throughout the day.

I have good news to tell you today. My neck has felt better since yesterday, even a lot better, and I don't feel anything anymore except a slight numbness.

---

536 The passages "you tell me..." through "hardly any patience" and "I dread..." through "can do nothing" are preserved from the original letter. The unfinished postscript is also original (*Vie Thérésienne*, No. 55, July 1974, p. 232). This postscript, on the back of the letter, was stuck and deciphered with difficulty.

537 The passage: "When he arrived back at the Pavilion..." through "a letter from Pauline" is preserved from the original letter.

You tell me that you would like to suffer for me. I would be quite annoyed by this. So, you don't want me to gain Heaven; you would like it all for yourself.... Go right ahead, my Pauline! And for my part, I would have maybe a hundred years in Purgatory to do! Do you want to do that for me, too? If you're taking it on, you might as well take it all!

It's like Léonie, who read in *Le Semaine Catholique*[538] that a saintly soul had offered her life for the Pope and her prayer had been granted. She hasn't forgotten it, and here she is beginning some novenas to die in my place. Thursday morning she went to find Marie and said to her, "I'm going to die, God has answered me; I feel sick."

Marie just laughed, but this mortified Léonie, who was speaking seriously, and she started to cry. A quarter of an hour later her tears were dry, and, with her unpredictable spirit, she had something else in mind; she needed tapestry slippers.

I said to her, "But since you want to die, it would be a waste of money." She remained silent, probably hoping to still have time to wear out her slippers. Perhaps she would have put this in the terms of her sacrifice and would have made them last a good long time, only wearing them on the great feast days.

So the first of August is the day of departure, that's to say the endless vacation![539] This is a sweet word, and yet you'll find it painful to leave the good teachers. They'd like to keep you longer. If you want to continue your studies at the boarding school, you'll return there. I really think so, and I could well persuade your father. You know that when I want something, little by little I come to get what I want.

Oh well, let's think about it while you're on vacation. Meanwhile, let's all rejoice knowing that you're coming home to be with us. We're intending to go on several outings to the country, among others, to the forest.

We'll leave August 18 for Lisieux. They're eagerly looking forward to your visit and intend to show you the best time possible.

While awaiting the happiness of seeing you, my dear Pauline, I kiss you with all my heart.

Your mother.

---

[538] *Catholic Week.*
[539] This sentence is preserved from the original letter.

CF 214-a   To Sister Marie-Louise de Gonzague Vétillart[540]
                                      Alençon, July 15, 1877[541]
My dear Sister,

I'm just responding to the little note you sent me in Pauline's letter. I find, my dear Sister, that you're right in deciding that she leave on the first train, and I thank you for your concern. But I'm in a very awkward position to refuse her this little pleasure because, when I saw her last, she asked me many times to let her spend as full a day as possible on her last day at the Visitation Monastery, and I don't dare refuse her. Perhaps it's weakness on my part, but I'm also afraid that the abrupt departure which she's not expecting will upset her too much. So, my dear Sister, if you don't find any harm in it, I will comply with her wish and have her leave at 5 o'clock. She'll cry but perhaps this will make her feel better. At least she won't regret the moments she could have spent with you and your dear teachers since she'll stay until the last moment.

I'm taking advantage of this occasion, my dear Sister, to renew my feelings of profound gratitude for the truly maternal concern you've shown for Pauline and for me. I could never repay my debt of gratitude to you for all the prayers you've said to obtain my cure.

I dare to recommend myself again to your charity to obtain from the Heart of Jesus, if not my cure, at least perfect resignation to the will of God.

Please accept, my dear Sister, my feelings of deep affection and gratitude.

Sincerely yours in Our Lord Jesus Christ,

                                                          Z. Martin

CF 215   To her brother and sister-in-law
                                                July 24, 1877

I'd promised to write you on Sunday, but I couldn't, and here's the reason:

I'd had a pretty good week. While the pain in my neck hadn't

---

[540] See footnote in CF 170.
[541] This letter, published for the first time in *Vie Thérésienne*, No. 55, July 1974, pp. 232-233, is the only complete original letter preserved (21 x 13.3 cm. or 8.3 x 5.2 in).

disappeared, it had lessened quite a bit. So Sunday morning,[542] after a night that wasn't too bad, I got up at five o'clock to go to the first Mass.

While Marie was combing my hair, all of a sudden I let out a piercing scream; I had twisted my neck again. I thought the pain was going to pass. All the same, I wanted to go to Mass, but I couldn't take one step without extreme caution. When I had to step down from the sidewalk, it was quite an affair. Fortunately there were hardly any people on the street. I promised myself I would never go to Mass again in this condition.

The following night was one of the worst because I had a terrible toothache. My cheeks have been swollen before because of my teeth, but never like this. I was afraid of erysipelas.[543]

Last evening I was afraid of the night, judging by what the day had been like. I asked the Blessed Mother for the grace to be able to stay in bed, and my prayer was answered. I was even able to rest from ten o'clock in the evening to one o'clock in the morning.

I saw Monsieur Vital on Sunday. He insisted that I didn't have a fever, but I felt that it was wearing me down! He told me the pain in my neck was from the little strain I'd given it, but that there was an imbalance in the organs. This I believe because the pain comes and goes, and just when I'm feeling better, it comes back.

Today we received a letter from Pauline who tells us about all her little parties there and that she's "very happy that Mama is so well now!" She arrives August 1[544] and is begging me to bring her home on the last train. She believes that I'm coming and going like I did when I was in Lourdes, but things have changed since then, and I won't be in any condition to go to Le Mans. Her father will go and bring her back on the six o'clock train.

I hope, though, to visit you one more time unless the pains in my neck come back with intensity.

Poor Marie is very sad because of me, and she's as good to me as she can possibly be. Every day she says it's going to be very difficult for her to go to Lisieux and be out and about while I'm sick. But during

---

[542] July 22.
[543] See footnote in CF 21.
[544] Wednesday.

their stay with you, I'll do what I did for Pauline at the Visitation Monastery. I'll write and tell them that I'm doing well so they won't worry. If I don't, you'll never be able to make them stay.

My brother isn't right to scold me so much about the Alençon lace. I had some orders long before I saw the doctor for the first time. These orders are still not completely finished, and yet the four last ones should have been sent out this week if I hadn't been sick. It's true I took on a new order for eleven meters, which will also soon be finished.

Last month I turned down eighteen meters of flounce, and now I refuse everything that comes in. I had twenty-four meters begun on my behalf, or for Madame Deverny, which are still far from being finished. I very much regret having them, but they're too far along to not finish them.

I kiss you with all my heart. Your devoted sister,

Z. Martin[545]

I got up four hours ago, and I'm not at all tired. I think I'm going to have a good night.

CF 216   To her brother
                                          July 27, 1877

My dear brother,

Yesterday I called out for you in a loud voice, believing that you alone could relieve my pain. For twenty-four hours I suffered more than I'd ever suffered in my entire life, so those hours were spent moaning and crying out. I begged all the saints in Heaven, one after the other, but no one answered me!

Finally, not being able to obtain anything else, I asked to be able to spend the night in my bed. I hadn't been able to stay there in the afternoon. I was in a dreadful position, it was impossible to rest my head anywhere. We'd tried everything, but my poor head could touch nothing, nor could I make the slightest movement, even to

---

[545] From "I kiss you…" to the signature is preserved from the original letter.

swallow some liquid. My neck was stiff on all sides, and the gentlest move put me in atrocious pain.[546]

Finally, I was able to stay in bed as long as I was sitting up. When I began to fall asleep, the imperceptible movement I made no doubt woke up all my sufferings. I had to moan all night. Louis, Marie and the maid stayed by my side. From time to time poor Louis would hold me in his arms like a child.

The doctor came this morning at eleven o'clock and prescribed a sedative, but I haven't taken it yet since the big crisis has passed, although I continue to suffer all over.[547] [548]

You're right to get ready to come, I would be happy to see all of you. However, it would be better to wait until the week of the 19th because the house is too messy at the moment, and we have to get it in order. I'm going to begin to bring people in to do quite a few things. The Sisters of Mercy[549] are going to take care of me starting today, and they won't stop until I die.

I can no longer write to you. I can't see anymore, and I'm incomprehensibly weak.

A nursing sister just came. She can't stay tonight. She tells me that she's cared for several people suffering from the same illness as

---

[546] "Zélie Martin's body was exhumed and reburied at the Lisieux Basilica in 1958. The doctors who witnessed the appearance of her skeleton noted that the three vertebrae at the base of her neck, as well as her left shoulder-bone, were corroded with profound lesions." Stéphane-Joseph Piat, OFM, *Une âme libre. Marie: Soeur Ainée et Marraine de Sainte Thérèse de l'Enfant-Jésus*. [A Free Soul. Marie: Older Sister and Godmother of Saint Thérèse of the Child Jesus], p. 53. (Not translated.)

[547] "When Marie Martin recalled her mother's sufferings from the perspective of the early twentieth century, she commented: 'In those days there were no pain killers as there are now.'" *Ibid.*

[548] "There were no morphine injections, but only orally administered extracts of opium, especially Laudanum. That Zélie Martin did not even begin using sedatives until she had reached her very deathbed, was not necessarily due to the heartlessness of her doctor, but to a shared unwillingness, by both doctor and patient, to have recourse to addictive drugs. Astonishingly, even at the last stage of her illness, when she had received the sedative tonic following an attack of pain, Zélie Martin hesitated, 'I have not yet taken it, for the great crisis is passed, although I continue to feel pain everywhere.' She did not elaborate on the reasons for her indecision, but the harmful condition of Laudanum addiction was well known by the 1860's. It was also known that if invalids began taking opiates too soon, they would develop a resistance to their effectiveness." Therese Taylor, "'Purgatory on Earth': An Account of Breast Cancer from Nineteenth-Century France." *Social History of Medicine*, p. 393.

[549] See footnote in CF 92.

me and that they also had pain in their neck, but not the terrible pain I'm going through.

The Blessed Mother didn't cure me in Lourdes. What can you do, my time is at an end, and God wants me to rest elsewhere other than on earth.

I kiss you all with love.

Z. Martin[550]

CF 217 To her brother
Thursday, August 16, 1877

...I saw the doctor the day I received your last letter. I showed him the packets, and he told me they were good but as... [sic] I'd asked for it for my stomach and intestinal pains. I was expecting a treatment that would have relieved me, but he only prescribed a bottle of mineral water! Yet it seems to me that they could do something to relieve my pain because I can no longer stand up. I hardly ever go downstairs. I go from my bed to the armchair and from the armchair to my bed. I just spent two very cruel nights.

Two days ago I washed myself with Lourdes water, and I've suffered a lot from that moment on, especially under my arms. Really, the Blessed Mother doesn't want to cure me.

I can't write any longer, my strength is at an end. You were right to come to Alençon when I could still stay with you.

What can you do? If the Blessed Mother doesn't cure me it's because my time is at an end, and God wants me to rest elsewhere other than on earth....

---

[550] From the passage "The Blessed Mother" to the signature is preserved from the original letter. *Vie Thérésienne*, No. 55, July 1974, p. 233.

ZÉLIE MARTIN: HER FINAL DAYS

Marie, the Martins' oldest child, wrote four letters to her aunt and uncle, Céline and Isidore Guérin, during the last few weeks of her mother's life. These letters provide objective insights and details that give the reader a fuller picture of Zélie's final days. Transcripts of these letters can be found in Appendix One.

July 30, 1877	Céline and Isidore Guérin came to visit Zélie.
August 26, 1877	Zélie received the Last Rites surrounded by her family.
August 27, 1877	Isidore and Céline Guérin came from Lisieux to be with Zélie as she dies.
August 28, 1877	Zélie died on Tuesday at 12:30 a.m. surrounded by Louis, Isidore, Marie and the nursing sister.
August 29, 1877	Zélie's funeral occurred on Wednesday, August 29, 1877, at 9 a.m. in the Church of Notre Dame d'Alençon. Her family and friends were present.
August 29, 1877	Zélie's burial took place in the Cemetery of Notre Dame, in Alençon.
October 1894	After Louis' death, Isidore Guérin arranged for the bodies of Zélie, Louis and Zélie's four children who had died, Zélie's father, Louis' mother and other family members to be exhumed in Alençon and moved to the family vault in Lisieux with Louis.

PART TWO

The Letters of Louis Martin

CF 218   Louis Martin to his five daughters in Lisieux
                              Alençon, November 25, 1877

My dear daughters,

I'm hurrying to send you a few words today, Sunday, the day when I'm least busy.

I can't wait to be with you again,[551] and I'm urging the workers to finish the Alençon lace that I still have with several assemblers. So, I hope that on Thursday we'll have the happiness of being all together again, not to be parted from each other for a long time.

My dear Marie, tell "Little Paulin" that her gold shells[552] will not arrive until next Tuesday and I asked for three of them instead of

---

[551] The five Martin girls had moved into Les Buissonnets on November 16, 1877. As Céline wrote in her biographical reflections of her father: "The devoted tenderness of his [my father] became still more evident when we moved to Lisieux. After the death of our mother, a very important question arose for him with regard to his five daughters, the eldest of whom was seventeen and the youngest only four-and-a-half. Many friends, even his Spiritual Director, advised him to place us all as boarding pupils. Again he had influential relatives and friends among the upper classes of Alençon, and all urged him not to leave the town. Besides, was he not too advanced in years to change all his ways, to uproot himself, so to speak, and begin a wholly new life? With his outspoken ways, my uncle, Monsieur Guérin, rather frightened my father, who was by nature so simple and reserved. It would be introducing the 'Patriarch' into quite a wholly different environment. But the love of his children had first place in his heart. He sought their welfare, their greatest welfare, without taking his own into consideration. It was on that account, after having consulted his older girls, that he made the decision to go to Lisieux in order to be nearer the influence of Madame Guérin, an angel of peace and of sweetness. 'I ask your advice, children,' he said, 'for it is solely on your account I am making this sacrifice, and I do not wish to impose a sacrifice on you.'" Céline Martin (Sister Geneviève of the Holy Face), *The Father of the Little Flower*, p. 42.
[552] To be used to make miniatures on parchment, this was the big form of leisure for Pauline.

two. As for your pins, I think we'll find these more easily in Lisieux. The moss you mentioned isn't available during this season, but we'll try to get some later.

My children, pay attention to all the recommendations of your uncle and your good aunt. You know the great sacrifices I had to make to obtain for you the help of their good advice, so don't let a single opportunity to benefit from it pass you by.

You, my Marie, my big girl, my first, you know how much I love you. Well, continue to devote yourself more and more to your sisters. Try and make sure that in seeing you, they'll have in front of them a good example to follow.

Tell Léonie that if she continues to be a perfectly good girl, I'll definitely give her something on New Year's Day that will make her happy.

Good-bye, my dear children. I press you all lovingly to my heart, and I entrust you to your holy mother.

CF 219   Louis Martin to his daughters in Lisieux
Alençon, November 29, 1877

My dear children,

I'll do my best to arrive tomorrow, Friday, around seven-thirty in the evening. Fortunately, I've finished all my business, and I can't wait to be with you again. So, I'll see you soon.

The two little notes I received – from you, my Marie, and from my Pauline, made me very happy, and the errands you asked me to do will be, I hope, carried out well.

A thousand best wishes for Monsieur and Madame Guérin and a big kiss for the five of you.[553]

CF 220   To Monsieur Nogrix, an old friend of
Louis Martin's from Brittany
Lisieux, 1883

My very dear friend,

You see that I'm hurrying to answer your good letter.

---

[553] Louis rejoined his daughters on Friday, November 30, as planned, after having settled various matters in Alençon.

It's because I feel the need to congratulate you, or rather to thank the Lord with you, and with all my poor heart, for the great favor He was kind enough to grant you last December, a time we'll always remember!... As for this favor,[554] we won't know the true value of it until much later....

If "God blessed the house of Aaron,"[555] He also blessed the house of Nogrix, because your family "is sailing along at a good speed." Let's hope the wind doesn't change and all return safe and sound.

Your letter made me even happier because I'm living on almost nothing but my memories. The memories of my whole life are so pleasant that in spite of the ordeals I've been through, there are moments when my heart overflows with joy....

I'll tell you that Thérèse, my little Queen (which is what I call her because she's a beautiful girl) is completely cured, I assure you.[556] The many prayers finally took Heaven by storm, and God, who is so good, in His kindness gave in.

I told you before about my five daughters, but I forgot to tell you that I have another four children who are with their saintly mother

---

[554] Louis' friend had returned to God and religious practice.

[555] An allusion to Monsieur Nogrix's letter and a paraphrase of Psalm 115:12.

[556] On May 13, 1883, Thérèse, ten years old, was cured when she saw the statue of the Blessed Mother smiling at her. The Statue of the Virgin of the Smile is a copy of Bouchardon's Madonna that stands in the Church of Saint-Sulpice in Paris. It was given to Louis by Mlle. Boudouin, the woman who helped Louis set up his clock and watch making business. She was also the president of the Society of Eucharistic Adoration in Alençon. The statue was placed in the garden of the Pavilion. After the marriage of Louis and Zélie, this statue was placed in their house, and after Zélie died, it was moved to the home of Louis and the children in Lisieux. After Pauline, Marie and Thérèse entered Carmel, it was given to the monastery and placed in the care of Sister Thérèse. Presently, it rests above the reliquary of St. Thérèse in the Chapel of the Carmelite Monastery in Lisieux. Per Céline's biographical reflections of her mother: "It was at the foot of this statue that she made us say our prayers, and we used to kiss it so often that its fingers were all broken, and it was necessary to keep in reserve more than one pair of hands! During May we used to assist at the May devotions in the church. Besides that, mother wanted to keep a special month of Mary at home. The shrine had to be so beautiful that my sister used to joke about it, good-naturedly, and say 'that it rivaled the decorations of the parish church,' Notre Dame, Alençon. It is true that it was gorgeous, for besides lace hangings over a blue background, Mamma used to hire a poor woman to bring whole armfuls of flowers and blossoms from the country, and branches of white thorn. These were placed in vases and reached up to the ceiling, to the great delight of little Thérèse who would clap her hands with glee." Céline Martin (Sister Geneviève of the Holy Face), *The Mother of the Little Flower*, pp. 50-51.

in Heaven, where we hope to rejoin them some day!… So, I won't say anymore, "Oh! Who will give me back my Hélène?"[557] – With Hélène there are also two little Josephs[558] and a pretty little Thérèse.[559]

Last Easter I was in Paris with two of my oldest children, and we spent five whole days that were very pleasant. On March 25,[560]in Notre Dame, I took part in a magnificent agape.[561] There were at least eight thousand communicants, all men. Bishop Guibert[562] gave out Communion, and Father Monsabré[563] spoke to us. We stayed at the Hotel for the Catholic Missions on the rue Chomel.

So you had the chance to see our friend Aimé Mathey?[564] This reminds me of a little act of madness of my own, which I have to tell you about.

Once, about twenty-five years ago, like you, I had rushed through my little business matters in Paris when I got an idea, "Oh, wouldn't it be fun if I went to surprise Mathey?"

It didn't take very long for me to go from the idea to carrying out my plan. So I headed toward the station and took the train to Strasbourg. When I arrived, as I did once at your shop, I pretended to have my eye on a winder in the display window of his watchmaker's shop. After I'd played my trick on them, they received me with open arms, and I gave his little girl, who is now Madame Antonin, then sleeping in her cradle, a silver rattle.

---

[557] An allusion to a verse in François Chateaubriand's poem *"Combien j'ai douce souvenance"* ["What Sweet Memories I Have"]. Louis and Zélie's daughter Hélène died February 22, 1870. (See footnote in CF 52.)

[558] See footnotes in CF 21 and CF 36.

[559] See footnote in CF 60.

[560] On March 25, 1883, Louis, Marie and Léonie were in Paris for Holy Week when Thérèse became ill on Easter night. They were notified and returned home immediately.

[561] "Agape is a Greek word used in reference to the Eucharistic celebration of coming together at Mass to celebrate the life, death and resurrection of Jesus as we anticipate the 'heavenly banquet' that awaits us. At the heart of the liturgy is the offering of the body and blood of Jesus Christ, truly present in the Sacrament of consecrated bread and wine." Richard P. McBrien, *Catholicism*. New York, NY: HarperCollins, p. 1068.

[562] Cardinal Joseph Hippolyte Guibert, Archbishop of Paris from 1871 to 1886.

[563] Father Louis Monsabré, a famous Dominican preacher (1827-1907). He preached at Notre Dame in Paris and throughout France.

[564] A member of the Mathey family of Strasbourg, where Louis had perfected his work as a watchmaker.

How long ago that was, and how much I would like to see these good people return to the Church's embrace! For one who has faith, it's so sad to see a good young man like Mathey, and so many others, go peacefully along without worrying about what awaits them.

And Lange, the gullible one, you have nothing to tell me about him? And yet enough times he ran up our stairs four at a time.... You must admit we had good times together!

Have I babbled on enough? It's been a long time since that's happened to me. Could I, by chance, be getting younger?

All my best to you, my old friend, I love you like a brother.

Please pass along my good wishes to Madame Nogrix and your children.

CF 221   Departure for a long journey[565]

Paris, August 2, 1885

My very dear daughters,

You're very kind to have let me take this little break, and I will be very grateful to you all my life. Besides, if distance separates us a little, my heart is always close to you. So don't worry and don't be sad, my children.

If, however, you are too sad, write me honestly, my Marie, and send your letter to Munich (Bavaria), General Delivery, and I'll leave Father Marie high and dry.[566]

I'm sending you a dozen gold shells. Give two to Céline and two to my little Queen[567] while giving them a big kiss on both cheeks. And you, my big girl, take comfort, and once again, I assure you you'll never regret having let me leave. I send you, also, as well as my Léonie, a very big kiss, very big.

---

[565] The letters CF 221 to CF 229 were written by Louis Martin while on a pilgrimage. Paris, Munich, Vienna, Budapest, Bucharest, Varna, Constantinople, Athens, Naples, Rome, and Milan are some of the stops on this trip which lasted almost two months. Louis Martin had hoped to reach the Holy Land, but lack of possible transportation made him abandon the idea.

[566] Father Charles Marie, the curate of the Church of St. Jacques in Lisieux with whom he was traveling. In 1910, he participated in the Ecclesiastical Proceedings for the Beatification of St. Thérèse. He died at the age of 63 in 1912.

[567] Thérèse.

Don't forget to give the eight gold shells to "my fine Pearl" of Carmel.[568]

All yours in Our Lord.

P.S. Many kind regards to your uncle, your aunt and your cousins. I'm hurrying because I have to be at the station at nine o'clock, and I don't have much time.

A thousand kisses to everyone in my family.

(Your father who loves you.)

CF 222   *Munich, Thursday, August 27, 1885*

My Marie, my big girl,

I don't want to leave Munich without having given you a sign of life.

We've already visited several beautiful cities. Yesterday we climbed the "Bavaria" statue,[569] and this was quite interesting. Imagine a bronze statue that is very high and of such size that one could easily sit on its nose. We've also seen the museums, which are very beautiful.

I devoured your letter, which I have in front of me, and I thank God for having given me such good children. You did well not to show your letter to your uncle because I think the good Father Marie is happy I'm with him. We get along well, he's very pleasant and I like him very much.

You see by the postcard I'm sending you that we didn't choose

---

[568] Pauline had entered the Carmelite Monastery in Lisieux on October 2, 1882, and was given the name Soeur Agnès de Jesus (Sister Agnès of Jesus).

[569] A bronze-cast statue of a female figure representing Bavaria's power and strength, erected in 1850. A guidebook published in 1914 describes the statue as follows: "On a block of granite-like marble, 29 ft. high, stands a statue cast in bronze, the imposing colossal figure of this majestic Teutonic woman, as the patroness of her country. The figure is 53 ft. high; to the tip of the wreath, 62 ft. ...The head is accessible; at the back of the pedestal a bronze door leads into the interior. 60 stone steps lead from the socle [base] up to the knee and then a cast-iron winding-staircase of 60 steps through the hair into the head, where there are two seats of bronze for 6 persons. Through the holes in the locks of the hair one can enjoy from here a fine view of the alps." A. Bruckmann, *Guide to Munich and Its Environs.* Munich, Germany: A. Bruckmann, 1914, p. 63.

the smallest hotel, so I think it's going to be more expensive this time. Oh well, war is war!

Thank Madame Marie de Gonzague[570] well for me and tell my "Little Paulin" that I think of her often. Also give the same message to Léonie, Céline and Thérèse.

Now I must finish my letter to rejoin my companion. I assure you that I would like to have all five of you with me. Without you, I'm missing the greatest part of my happiness. Meanwhile, continue to pray for us.

Your father who loves his big girl even more since he's far away and who kisses her many times, as well as his other four of the same brood.

Above all, don't worry.

CF 223   *Vienna, August 30, 1885*

Dear Marie,

You must have received a letter from Munich telling you that all was going well and that I was very happy with all of you. But I'm very surprised that you haven't received the shells and my keys. You will do well to inquire at the post office in Lisieux because Monsieur Marlier, 211 rue Saint-Martin in Paris, must have sent the package.

Now, what will I tell you? That it's "like the late Monsieur Nicolet, stronger and stronger." Father Marie always seems radiant, and he's almost tireless. Sometimes it's hard to keep up with him.

Yesterday we visited the Monastery of the Religious of Saint Norbert[571] where we could not have been better received. Father

---

[570] The Prioress of the Carmelite Monastery in Lisieux.

[571] In the town of Schlägl, 239 kilometers (149 miles) from Vienna. The Order of the Religious of St. Norbert is an international community of men and women religious known as the Canons Regular of Prémontré. They are also known as the Order of Premonstratensians (named after their ancient mother abbey in Prémontré, France), Norbertines, or White Canons (in the British Isles). They were founded by St. Norbert on Christmas Day in 1121. Living a communal life in priories and abbeys, they follow the Rule of St. Augustine, rich in liturgy, with a special emphasis on the sung Divine Office.

"Their goal is to be living examples of the 'community of God' spreading the Good News of God's love for humanity. They do this by expressing God's love in living a simple communal life as close to Christian perfection as possible while remaining

Marie presented them with a letter from R.P. Godefroy[572] whom we saw at Saint Jacques.[573]

The city is exquisite and with bridges like I've never seen before, even in Paris. There are also some Carmelites, but who don't keep as good a table as we had at the good Premonstratensians because imagine that each of us were served an entire pigeon or partridge and enormous pieces of hare. These excellent religious have the reputation of being very charitable, and we could see that.

All the delightful letters that arrived for me in Vienna made me very, very happy. Thank Léonie, Céline, Thérèse and my "fine pearl" of Carmel for me for their feast day wishes.

It seemed like I was seeing you all around me in the belvedere and my little Queen,[574] in her pleasant, gentle voice, almost singing her little compliment to me. That moved me so much that I would have liked to be back in Lisieux to hug you all with love.

Why don't you want to accept your aunt's invitation to go see them in Trouville? It seems to me that you're making a mistake. Oh well, do as you wish.

---

very involved in the life of the Body of Christ outside their communities. Their vocation strives to balance a life of action and contemplation. Their charism is to use Christian love as a tool to promote faith in Christ and unity of purpose and action. Over the 888 years of their existence, they have achieved a consistent balance between the contemplative religious community and the intense caring involvement with fellow Christians. Today their involvement in Christian faith and action involves spreading the word of God by: preaching the word of God in parishes, educational institutions and on the Internet, promoting Christian unity, outreach to those less fortunate, parish support and assistance to diocesan clergy, participating in appropriate reform efforts and transition throughout the church, missions to remote communities in need of hearing the Good News, teaching in, and operating educational institutions, Third Order and Associate participation in the Norbertine communities, and lastly, opening Norbertine houses to the laity and inviting their witnessing of and participating in the religious community." It was this aspect of their apostolate that Louis Martin witnessed and experienced. (Information obtained from the Norbertine international website, www.premontre.org.)

572 It is of importance to note that on October 29, 1897, Mother Marie de Gonzague wrote to Father Godefroy Madelaine (1842-1932), a Norbertine father, and a great friend of the Carmel of Lisieux, requesting that he read and correct the manuscript Thérèse had written in the last year of her life. He was the Prior of Mondaye Abbey and later was the influential Abbot of Frigolet. It was his idea to entitle Thérèse's obituary letter "Story of a Soul." Céline reported that later he was called the "Godfather of Story of a Soul." He also worked to obtain Bishop Flavien Hugonin's Imprimatur. Two months after he had given his Imprimatur, the Bishop died unexpectedly. Céline Martin (Sister Geneviève of the Holy Face), *The Father of the Little Flower*, p. 62.

573 In Lisieux.

574 Thérèse.

Take care of Félicité[575] and don't forget to pay her quarterly wages.

If you receive any letters for me, open them if you want and put them aside for me.

Finally, my Marie, my big girl, my first, continue to lead your little battalion the best you can and be more sensible than your old father, who's already had enough of all the beauty that surrounds him and dreams of Heaven and infinity. "Vanity of vanities, and all is vanity except loving God and serving Him alone!"[576]

The one who loves you all and carries you in his heart.

CF 224   On board ship on the Black Sea
                                                    September 7, 1885
Dear Marie,

You should have received my news from Monsieur Retout. I'm still in good health, as well as Monsieur l'Abbé.[577] We still have three days before we arrive in Constantinople.

The country is magnificent, but up until this point, I don't find what I would call, as Father Baudry[578] claims it to be, "a corner of Heaven forgotten on earth." Unquestionably, it's very beautiful, but I don't quite share my good companion's[579] enthusiasm.

Above all, don't be sad because of me. If you could write me a few lines and send them to Naples, General Delivery, that would make me very happy because I often think of you all and say to myself, "Oh! If I could only have them with me, then all would be well!" But, seeing that there's no way, this casts a shadow. Oh well, before long we'll see each other again and not leave each other anymore.

Last evening we met the priest from Varna.[580] He's a very young priest who knows eight languages, and he gave us such a warm wel-

---

[575] Marie-Françoise-Félicité (October 27, 1860-August 25, 1930), a servant in the Martin home.

[576] Thomas à Kempis. *The Imitation of Christ.* New York: Alba House, 1995. (Book I, Chapter I, paragraph 3, p. 20.) See also Ecclesiastes 1:2.

[577] Father Charles Marie.

[578] A religious and friend of Father Charles Marie who had made the same trip three years before.

[579] Father Charles Marie.

[580] Varna, Bulgaria, on the coast of the Black Sea.

come that all my life I'll preserve the memory of the pleasant moments spent with him. I'll tell you about it later on, and the things I'll have to tell you! But you'll have to wait.

We didn't feel seasick. The sea remained calm and majestic, although they had depicted it as very rough.

In your next letter, tell me if you received the package sent from Paris containing my keys.

Give a big hug from me to my little "pearl," as well as Léonie, Céline, "my courageous one," and the Queen[581] of my heart and give my best wishes to the entire Guérin family.

Tell my "Little Paulin" that her memory is very present to me and that I'd like to be able to send her all the big fish I see from our deck jumping about in the Black Sea. How many there would be heading toward the Carmelite Monastery in Lisieux!

Soon we're going to sit down at the table to eat because I see they're setting it near me while I'm finishing my scribbling.

Good-bye, my beloved. Say a Hail Mary for us.

CF 225   *Constantinople,[582] September 11, 1885*

My poor big girl,

I see that you're worrying far too much about me, so I'll tell you, as I did in my other letters, that I couldn't be better.

Your delightful and much wished for letter was handed to me by a Vincentian Father when we were still on the small boat before we went ashore. I often think about all of you, and recently I had a very beautiful dream in which I saw all of you so clearly that it almost seemed real. If I could only make you feel everything I feel while admiring the great and beautiful things unfolding before me! My God, how admirable are Your works!

Constantinople is wonderful and well worth the effort to visit, but it's so far! We just climbed the Galata Tower from which one discovers the entire city, a unique sight in this world. We've already seen the Sultan and his three sons, the oldest of which appears to be eighteen years old, and the whirling dervishes, poor people to be

---

581 Thérèse.
582 Today known as Istanbul.

pitied with their diabolical movements and ways.

We're like family, staying at the home of Madame Matich, who remembers very well having received Father Baudrey three years ago.

You tell me that the good Mother Marie de Gonzague and all the Carmelites are riddling me with prayers. In return, I want you to bombard them for me with big boxes of tuna. Please represent me to them as best you can.

A thousand loving wishes to my dear little pearl, who so well smoothed over all the obstacles to my trip. Tell her I love her even more, if that's possible.

Tell my good Léonie, who did what she could to calm you and persuade you to let me leave, that I would like to know what kind of souvenir from Rome would make her happy.

Again, tell my Céline, "the courageous one," and my "Queen of France and Navarre"[583] that they can also let me know what would make them most happy.

In my last letter, I told you that I would be very pleased to receive your letters in Naples. As I'm remaining a few days in Constantinople, I hope you'll have time to write me immediately so that I can receive them here.

Reassure your uncle about the safe. There's nothing to fear, no one knows where it is. So just lock the door of the cupboard, take the key, and, God willing, all will be well.

You didn't tell me, did you receive the little souvenir I sent you from Vienna?

Once again, I see so many beautiful things that I could easily exclaim, "It's too much, Lord! You're too good to me!"

In a few weeks it will no longer be a dream, and we'll be together again for as long as God, in His goodness, wants us to be.

I kiss you, my dear Marie, Pauline, Léonie, Céline and Thérèse.

You see that I wanted to make you happy because we arrived this morning and I'm already answering your letter. So, give me the sweetest pleasure possible by writing to me, as well.

Your father who loves his oldest child so much.

---

[583] Thérèse.

Constantinople, September 16, 1885

Dear Marie,

I have a moment, and I'm taking advantage of it to send you a few lines while Father Marie is on a walk in Scutari.[584] We're feeling very well and find ourselves wonderfully situated in this lovely private home which the Vincentian Fathers recommended to us. We would have left for Smyrna[585] today, but the boat service is

---

[584] Scutari, today known as Uskudar, is on the Asian side of the Bosphorus, opposite Constantinople (today known as Istanbul). It is 3 miles (5 kilometers) from Istanbul. The Bosphorus is the strait that links the Black Sea with the Sea of Marmara that separates Europe from Asia. It resembles a river with a beautiful stretch of scenery on each shore. From the shores of the Bosphorus, Louis could see imperial palaces, seaside mansions, foreign embassies, fortresses, mosques, ruins, gardens and beaches.

[585] Smyrna, today known as Izmir, incorporates the ancient city of Ephesus on the Aegean Coast. Ephesus is 33 miles (54 kilometers) from Smyrna and 204 miles (328 kilometers) from Constantinople, today known as Istanbul. Of the three apostles, John, Barnabas and Peter, who traveled to Asia Minor (now modern day Turkey), it was St. John who was the first to preach in Ephesus. St. John the Apostle, the Evangelist and author of the 4th Gospel, founded the Church in Ephesus and was its first bishop. He was martyred and buried in Ephesus. Later, St. Paul evangelized in Ephesus between 52 and 54 AD and established flourishing communities in the three years that he lived there. It is thought that these communities expanded to several cities, including Smyrna, through his exhaustive missionary evangelization. In the 2nd century, Smyrna was also important under its bishop, St. Polycarp, who was the successor of St. John. St. Polycarp also suffered martyrdom. The Church in Asia Minor also produced great saints and Fathers of the Church, including St. Basil the Great, St. Gregory Nazianzen, and St. John Chrysostom, who was the Patriarch of Constantinople. Also important to note, the first seven Ecumenical Councils of the Church were held in Asia Minor, which defined the fundamental truths of the faith. The House of the Virgin Mary, known as the Sanctuary of Meryem Ana Evi, is located in Ephesus. It is believed that it is here the Blessed Mother came to live with St. John the Apostle sometime after the crucifixion of Jesus. It is also believed that she died and was assumed into heaven from Ephesus. Pope Paul VI "unofficially" confirmed its authenticity when he visited this Sanctuary on July 26, 1967. Pope John Paul II visited it on November 30, 1979, and Pope Benedict XVI on November 29, 2006. Also located in Ephesus is the 6th century Basilica of St. John the Apostle. This basilica was built over the tomb of St. John the Apostle by Emperor Justinian. Since Louis was on a religious pilgrimage and traveled by boat from Constantinople to the ancient seaport of Smyrna, one might think that he would have visited the city of Ephesus, 33 miles (54 kilometers) from Smyrna, since the city was in close proximity. The pilgrimage to Ephesus would have been to recall the missionary work of the apostles and the flourishing Christian life that existed there, in what has been called "The Cradle of Christianity." A pilgrimage to this city would usually include a visit to the tomb of St. John the Apostle and the House of the Virgin Mary. [*Inside the Vatican*, New Hope, Kentucky: Urbi et Orbi Communications, November, 2006, pp. 8-14 and December, 2006, pp. 14-21.]

disorganized, and we'll have to wait until Thursday or Friday.

Now what can I tell you about this beautiful city of Constantinople? I've been all over the city, and the more I see, the more I admire it. There are some magnificent things, and we've visited several mosques, of which the most beautiful is certainly Santa Sophia in Stamboul.[586] It was built by Constantine the Great in 325.

That basilica was completely destroyed by fire in 532. Emperor Justinian I rebuilt it, and it is to him that this building owes its current form. Justinian wanted this monument to be the most enduring and the most magnificent of all time. The entire Empire was stripped in order to decorate it.

The Grand Bazaar in Constantinople is a curious thing. This complex labyrinth forms a city within a city with its streets, alleyways, passageways and intersections.

Each street is assigned a specialty. The Grand Bazaar closes every evening before sundown and doesn't open until around nine o'clock in the morning.

On Friday the Turkish shops are closed, on Saturday it's the Jews' turn, and on Sunday, it's the same thing for the Christians.

We visited the Cistern of Asparis. It rests on 64 columns and was built under Leo the Great.[587]

Now, my first, my big girl, my diamond, let's talk a bit about our little affairs. In rereading your last letter, I see that what you're doing couldn't be better while I'm not there. So continue, and you'll

---

[586] Santa Sophia is more popularly known as Hagia Sophia. In Greek, "Hagia" means "holy" and "Sophia" means "wisdom," thus, the Church of Holy Wisdom. Following the destruction of the original Hagia Sophia built by Constantine the Great in the 4th century, the second church was built by his son, Constantius and the Emperor Theodosius the Great. During the riots of Nika in 532, the church was destroyed by fire, though fragments remain and have been preserved. A third church was constructed on the original site by Emperor Justinian I and has been preserved and exists today. For nine hundred years it was the seat of the Orthodox Patriarch of Constantinople and a principal setting for Church councils and imperial ceremonies. In 1453, after the conquest of Constantinople by Sultan Mehmet the Conqueror, he converted the church to a mosque. Hagia Sophia served as the principal mosque for almost 500 years. After World War I and the fall of the Ottoman Empire, Turkey became a secular state and the mosque was turned into a museum and remains a museum today with no religious ceremonies. It is one of the greatest examples of Byzantine art and architecture, rich with marble and world famous mosaics. When Louis visited the Hagia Sophia, it was one of the most important mosques in that part of the world.
[587] Leo I, Byzantine Emperor from 457 to 474.

make me happy. My poor big girl, how I would like to have you with me during my entire beautiful journey!...

Tell my dear "Little Paulin" that I think of her often, too, and I thank God for having given her such a lofty vocation. Thank her well for me for her lovely letter, and also don't forget to pay my humble respects to Madame Marie de Gonzague.

We expect to be in Athens on Sunday, and from there we're going to Naples. Only then am I intending to go look for news from all of you at the Post Office General Delivery.

Give a big, big hug for me to my Léonie, Céline and my Queen.[588] As for my beautiful little Pearl, sadly, it's impossible to pass through the grill! Finally, say many kind things to your uncle and aunt, as well as Jeanne and Marie. A little pat on Tom's head, the brave, faithful dog.[589] Is he still crying for me?

Your father who loves you.

P.S. You did well to give some pears. Give, give always and make some people happy.

CF 227   *Naples, September 25, 1885*

My dear big girl,

I just spent a very nice morning. I visited several magnificent churches, and all were filled with superb mosaics, they're very beautiful and very elaborate.

Naples is an enchanting city, but one is tormented by all sorts of beggars. Even the flies get into the act, and it's like a small persecution, but we're in good health, and I see with gratitude that God continues to lavish his goodness upon us.

Yesterday we visited Pompeii. It was very interesting, and I'll give you the details later.

...I'm sorry, I have to accompany Father Marie, and I'm hurrying to write these few lines. They're only to make you happy and

---

[588] Thérèse.
[589] Louis Martin had given this spaniel to Thérèse on June 26, 1884. He was with him at the Château La Musse until Louis' death on July 29, 1894.

give you a sign of life; you must realize that. Soon, in Rome, I'll write you a longer letter.

Come, my dear daughters, always be my joy and consolation on earth and continue to serve the Lord well. He is so great and admirable in His works!

So good-bye, dear children, I thank you a thousand times for the kind prayers you say for the travelers.

Father Marie is here behind me, and I'm forced to finish my letter.

I kiss you with all my heart.

CF 228   *Rome, Sunday, September 27, 1885*

Dear Marie,

We finally arrived in Rome at six thirty in the morning. For me, Saint Peter's is really the most beautiful thing in the world. I prayed for you, whom I love so much. It's so pleasant to pray there!

But how sad that the Holy Father[590] is in captivity. This casts a shadow, and this shadow makes one melancholy in spite of everything.

Father Marie was touched by the little note from Carmel mentioned in my "fine Pearl's" letter. How I'm consoled when I see that she's so completely happy and that Jesus, even here below, really wants to visit her as only He knows how to do! Let us truly thank God, my big girl, and pray to Him with all our hearts that He'll also shower our poor, dear Léonie with His graces.

Tell Céline and my little Queen[591] that I think of them a lot and that if you're happy with them, I'll reward them.

I went to the post office with Father Marie, and we found nothing. He was a little disappointed because he was expecting at least a letter from his pastor. As we hope to be in Milan Tuesday of next

---

[590] Leo XIII, pope from 1878 to 1903, was in conflict with the Italian government. (See footnote in CF 69.) Also, Louis Martin, with Céline and Thérèse, had an audience with Pope Leo XIII on Sunday, November 20, 1887. It was on that occasion that Thérèse asked the pope for permission to enter the Carmelite Monastery.
[591] Thérèse.

week, send me your news if you can. Also, I'll be very happy to know if you received my two letters from Constantinople.

I'm hurrying because my good Father Marie is coming soon to take me again to visit all the beauties of Rome. It's certainly here that I feel the happiest. Tell my "fine Pearl" that I'm too happy and that I'm "bracing myself" because this can't last. I'm delighted that I'll see her soon.

As for you, my dear big girl, I fully intend to kiss you on both cheeks with all my love, that is, with a resounding noise. I also kiss my Léonie, Céline, and my little Queen.

Your father who loves you a lot, a lot.

P.S. After lunch we're planning to visit the Catacombs of Saint Agnes.

I place you all in the grace of God and pray for you every day in Saint Peter's. The thought of your mother also follows me constantly.

I'll see you soon… soon… soon!

CF 229   *Milan, October 6, 1885*

My dear big girl and my first,

I'm writing to you in haste because we're about to leave, and Father Marie is hurrying me.

I received your lovely letter, as well as my Pearl's, and they made me very happy. I needed them because while leaving Rome I was "like a black one-eyed cat, purring at the corner of a post on a rainy day."

You ask when I'll arrive. I hope it will be Saturday night at nine-thirty.[592] But plan on my returning from Alençon because I have to go there next Tuesday.

I thought of you in all the sanctuaries that we visited, but there was no way of seeing the Holy Father. I'll tell you all about that.

---

[592] Louis Martin was writing on Tuesday, October 6. "Next Tuesday" can only be the 13th, so he would have returned to Lisieux on Saturday, October 17, 1885.

Everything I see is splendid, but it's always an earthly beauty, and our heart is satisfied with nothing as long as we're not seeing the infinite beauty that is God.

Soon we'll have the intimate happiness of the family, and it's this beauty that brings us closer to Him.

I kiss all five of you with all my heart.

Your father who loves you.

CF 230   To the Nogrix family
                                          April 10, 1888

...Thérèse, my little Queen, entered Carmel yesterday! God alone could demand such a sacrifice, but He's helping me so powerfully that through my tears, my heart abounds with joy.

One who loves you,

Louis Martin.

CF 231   To his Carmelite daughters
                                                        1888

I want to tell you, my dear children, that I have the urgent desire to thank God and to make you thank God because I feel that our family, though very humble, has the honor of being among the privileged of our adorable Creator.

Original Undated Notes

These are copies of rare fragments of original manuscripts preserved in the archives of the Carmelite Monastery in Lisieux.

My very dear daughter, Sister Marie of the Sacred Heart. If you love me, you will pray to God for your godmother and my brother.[593]

The one who loves you,

Louis Martin.

On his calling card: "Louis Martin – Lisieux."

Respect and friendship to Madame Marie de Gonzague. Happy little feast day to my beloved diamond, without forgetting my dear little fine pearl.[594]

On an envelope, this address:

To my dear little daughters, all possible happiness.

For my diamond and my fine pearl!

On the back of the note, this text copied in his hand:

†The Imitation of Christ, Book I, chapter XX

What can you see elsewhere which you see not here? Behold the heavens and the earth, and all the elements; for out of these are all things made. What can you see anywhere which can last long under the sun? You think perhaps to be satisfied, but you cannot have this. If you could see all things at once before you, what would it be but a vain sight?...[595]

On the back of a picture of Saint Alphonsus Liguori:

Love has only one word: still it never repeats itself.

Father Lacordaire[596]

At the bottom of this picture:

Thérèse, my little Queen, entered Carmel on April 9, 1888. Pauline, my fine pearl, entered Carmel October 2, 1882. My diamond, October 15, 1886.

---

[593] Marie's godmother was her paternal grandmother, Marie-Anne-Fanie Boureau Martin. Louis Martin's brother Pierre, born July 27, 1819, died at sea.

[594] Diamond – Marie (Sister Marie of the Sacred Heart). Pearl – Pauline (Sister Agnès of Jesus).

[595] Thomas à Kempis. *The Imitation of Christ.* New York: Alba House, 1995. (Book I, Chapter XX, paragraphs 7-8, p. 71.)

[596] Henri Dominique Lacordaire, OP (1802-1861).

Letters from Marie Martin to Céline and Isidore Guérin

Letter 1

July 28, 1877

Letter from Marie to her Aunt Céline Guérin

"Since the beginning of the week, Mamma has been much worse. On Sunday she still wanted to go to the first Mass; but she needed super human courage and had to make incredible efforts to get as far as the church. Every step she took seemed to react on the pains in her neck. Sometimes she was obliged to stop in order to regain a little strength.

"When I saw that she was so exhausted, I begged her to return home, but she wanted to go on to the end, believing that the suffering was but a passing attack. It was by no means that; on the contrary she had much trouble on the return journey, so she will not again be so imprudent.

"Besides, it would be impossible for her at present, for, since last Monday, she has been unable to leave the house. She no longer goes to her office; Louise and I attend to the lace-workers. Mamma is continually in her room, either lying on the bed, or seated in an armchair. She feels very uncomfortable in bed, on account of her neck, which causes her frightful suffering.

"We have put four pillows behind her shoulders, in order that she may be in practically a sitting position in bed; she has to keep her neck absolutely straight, without moving it at all. When she is tired from having her head in that one position, we raise her very gently with the pillows until she is sitting erect. But every change of position means incredible suffering, for the least movement makes her utter piercing cries.

"And yet, with what patience and resignation she is bearing this dreadful illness! Her rosary beads never leave her fingers; she is praying constantly in spite of her sufferings. We all have great admiration for her; she has such courage and surpassing energy.

"Until two weeks ago she used to recite the five decades of her beads on her knees, before the Blessed Virgin, in my room, which she loves so much. Seeing her so ill, I wanted to have her sit down, but it was useless to ask her.

"Mamma quite approves of your idea of coming to Alençon, for we cannot go to Lisieux this year. She would like to have you arrange your trip for the week after the feast of the Assumption, because if the Blessed Virgin were to cure her that day, we should all go to Lisieux, as already planned. Let us hope that the dear Mother will have pity on us, and that she will be touched by our prayers and our tears.

"P.S. I forgot to mention that Dr. X came to see mother today. He ordered a sedative for the pains in her neck which, he explained, are the effect of her illness. I thought so myself, for a simple strain would not last so long.

"He was very polite and very kindly. I think he does not frighten her so much now."

Sister Geneviève of the Holy Face (Céline Martin), *The Mother of the Little Flower*, pp. 101-103.

Letter 2 *August 9, 1877*

Letter from Marie to her Aunt Céline Guérin

M. and Mme. Guérin came to Alençon on July 30. After their return to Lisieux, Marie wrote regularly to give news of the dear invalid:

"Since you left, Mamma continues to suffer more and more, and there are new trials every day. For the past two or three days she has constantly complained of heart seizures. She passes very bad nights, and it is absolutely heart-rending to listen to her moaning.

"Yesterday evening, she was suffering so much that she kept saying out loud: 'Ah! my God, You see that I have no longer any strength left to suffer. Have pity on me! Since I must remain here on this bed of pain, without anyone being able to give me relief, I beg You not to abandon me.'

"Sometimes she weeps, and keeps looking at us one after the other. Then she says: 'Ah! my poor children. I can no longer take you for a walk, although I have been so anxious to make you happy! And I had so desired to give all the pleasure I could to Pauline during her holidays; now I must leave her to herself, or let her go out without me! O dear little ones, if I could only go with you, how happy we should be.'

"In a word, our poor dear mother forgets herself to such a point that she is happy only when she sees us going off for a walk. In order to please and humor her, Papa took my sisters for a boat excursion. But what pleasure can we find, when we know our mother is so ill.

"Mamma wrote last Sunday to Abbé Martignon of Our Lady of Victories, in Paris, and to the Sisters at Lourdes. We began on Monday the novena that is to close on the feast of the Assumption. I am making it with the greatest confidence. I trust that the Blessed Mother will not abandon us. If she does not cure Mamma she will at least bring her relief, and diminish her suffering, which seems to be growing in intensity.

"Whom would the Blessed Virgin protect if she would not protect Mamma who is so good and so courageous? Last Sunday morning she again wanted to rise in order to go to the first Mass, because she thought that her neck was not so sore, and that she could move it more easily. If you only knew, dear Aunt, all the difficulty I had to keep her from rising. If she could have dressed herself alone, she certainly would have done it.

"Last Friday morning she went to the 7 o'clock Mass, because it was the First Friday of the month. Papa helped her along, for, without him she could not have gone at all. On arriving at the church, she admitted that if someone were not with her, she would never have been able to push open the door of the church!"

Ibid., pp. 103-105.

Letter 3   *August 25, 1877*
Letter from Marie to her Aunt Céline Guérin

"I have sad news to tell you. Mamma is very much worse. Her illness is making frightful progress from day to day. The nights are terrible for her. She is obliged to rise every quarter of an hour, as her suffering prevents her from remaining in bed.

"The least little noise brings on terrible crises. Even a whisper, or walking barefoot, wakes her up. Her sleep is so light that the slightest sound awakens her.

"For the past two days she appears to be less nervous, and her pains do not seem to be so violent or acute as at the beginning of the week. On Monday and Tuesday we did not know what to do. Her sufferings were atrocious. We could not relieve her in any way, and no remedy seems to quiet her.

"These incredible tortures have given way to an extreme weakness. She is no longer able to utter a moan – she has not enough strength – and one can scarcely hear her when she speaks. It is only by the movement of her lips we can understand what she wishes to say. Yesterday she was weak, but today she is still weaker.

"Last night she had a hemorrhage, which has increased her weakness. Papa spent the whole night beside her; he was so distressed. Fortunately, the hemorrhage did not last long. It seems that it is very dangerous.

"I hope that Mamma will regain a little strength and that she will not remain as weak as she is today. It is true that she seems to suffer less, but the weakness frightens me. When she is asleep, one would say that she were no longer living; that is the impression it gives.

"Do you believe, auntie, that this weakness will last long? I think that she would overcome it if she would take some nourishment, but nothing seems to agree with her. Her whole nourishment consists of two or three cups of bouillon, and even that much she cannot always retain."

Ibid., pp. 107-109.

Letter 4   *August 26, 1877*

Letter from Marie to her Uncle Isidore Guérin

"Yesterday, I forgot to tell auntie that Mamma's legs have become swollen, and papa wishes me to write to you about it immediately. I would have written about it, anyway, for I am very disturbed myself.

"The swelling began about a week ago. I realized it only this morning; until then I did not pay much attention to it. Her arm is quite swollen, and she can scarcely move it at all.

"Besides that, she is in a state of complete exhaustion. Today, even more than yesterday, she can speak only by signs. If she were left alone in her room, she would die rather than call for help.

"She also has just had another hemorrhage. All this has changed her very much, making her emaciated! Papa is so anxious that he has just told me to beg you to come as soon as possible, in order that you may at least find her fully conscious."

Céline goes on to say: "It was the evening of August 26th, or the following morning, before the arrival of M. and Mme. Guérin, that she received the Last Sacraments. Thérèse alone mentions it: 'The ceremony of Extreme Unction,' she writes, 'made a deep impression on me.'"

Céline again reflects:

"It also left a lasting impression on my soul. We were all kneeling beside her bed, in order of age, with Thérèse beside me. Our poor dear father could not restrain his grief.

"As for our mother, she remained calm and self-possessed. She was to die thus in a truly saintly way, giving us, to the very end, the example of complete self-forgetfulness and most lively faith.

"In the moments of anguish during her malady, her sorrowful plea would rise to Heaven: 'Oh! Thou Who hast created me, have mercy on me!' And God had pity on her by hastening the progress of her disease; for, at that time, there were not, as now, sedatives to relieve the pains of poor sufferers.

"It was on Tuesday, August 28, 1877, half an hour after midnight, that our admirable mother was taken from us. She was only forty-five years and eight months old."

Ibid., pp. 109-110.

* * *

In her turn, Marie has left us the expression of her own recollections:

"During the course of the day I often went close to the body of my dear mother. I never tired of looking at her. She seemed to be but twenty years old. I thought that she was beautiful. I felt a supernatural impression as I stood beside her. It struck me, which was quite true, that she was not dead, but more alive than ever."

Ibid., p. 111.

APPENDIX TWO

Textual Commentary

Letters of Zélie Guérin-Martin

The two hundred and eighteen letters published here are only a part of the correspondence spanning from 1863 to 1877. According to the correspondents, many were lost or destroyed.

Sister Marie-Dosithée, a religious at the Visitation Monastery of Le Mans and Zélie's older sister, preserved none of her sister's letters and, what's more, none of her other correspondents' letters, either, according to the custom of Visitandine religious life at the time.

Only one of Zélie's letters to her sister was found among the papers of Isidore Guérin. This is letter CF 138 dated August 31, 1875.

Marie, the Martin's eldest daughter, kept all her mother's letters for a long time, but the servant, Louise Marais (1849-1923), used all these letters to light a fire.

Isidore Guérin, archivist and conservator of the family papers, kept everything carefully. But in 1905, when he was asked to give his papers in view of the process of Thérèse's beatification, he destroyed everything that seemed too intimate to him.[597]

The three Martin sisters, Mother Agnès of Jesus (Pauline), Sister Marie of the Sacred Heart (Marie), and Sister Geneviève of the Holy Face (Céline), collected their archives and those of their uncle.

They also erased or deleted what seemed too intimate to them and that which concerned third parties. They cut everything that could appear unfavorable to "poor Léonie" expressed in her mother's concerns for this difficult child.

---

[597] Sister Geneviève of the Holy Face testified to this in a letter to Father Stéphane-Joseph Piat, OFM, dated January 2, 1958. (The Archives of the Carmelite Monastery in Lisieux.)

Everything concerning Thérèse was reviewed and corrected from the perspective of the period to eliminate everything that seemed too childish in view of the beatification process.[598]

Various Copies of the Original Documents

"At least two handwritten copies were made: one by Sister Marie of the Sacred Heart, finished January 11, 1911, and the other, probably less complete, by Sister Geneviève of the Holy Face in 1922-1924."[599]

In addition, Sister Geneviève copied some extracts concerning herself in a personal notebook[600] which she entitled "*Passages des lettres de Maman adressées à Pauline et qui parlent de la petite Céline*" ["Passages from Mama's letters addressed to Pauline that speak of little Céline".]

In March 1926, Mother Agnès of Jesus gave her mother's letters to Sister Marie of the Trinity (1874-1944), Thérèse's former novice. Not the original letters, but in all likelihood the abovementioned copy made by Sister Geneviève.[601]

Thus Sister Marie of the Trinity, in two school notebooks, on 50 and 28 pages written only on the front, recopied extracts from Madame Martin's letters that only concerned little Thérèse, "*Sainte Thérèse de l'Enfant-Jésus*" (1872-1877). (Therefore, the copy was made after the canonization in 1925.) On March 10, 1926, she wrote to Mother Agnès of Jesus, "I'm captivated by the letters of your holy mamma; they make me laugh and cry at the same time."[602]

As for the original letters, they were destroyed by the Martin sisters, probably before 1941. A note in *Vie Thérésienne* (No. 49,

---

[598] One finds the same problem regarding Thérèse's letters. See *Correspondance générale de sainte Thérèse de Lisieux, Tome I, 1877-1890*. Paris, France: Éditions du Cerf-Desclée de Brouwer, 1972, pp. 29, 30, 31, 32, 59, 60. [Saint Thérèse of Lisieux, *General Correspondence*, Volume I, 1877-1890. Tr. John Clarke, OCD, Washington, DC: ICS Publications, 1982, pp. 29, 30, 31, 32, 59, 60]. Moreover, this was done with the encouragement of the Vice Postulator, Mgr. Roger de Teil (see pp. 29-30).

[599] See *Correspondance générale, tome II, Sainte Thérèse de l'Enfant-Jésus et de la Sainte-Face* [General Correspondence, Volume II, Saint Thérèse of the Child Jesus and the Holy Face] (*Nouvelle Édition du Centenaire*, Paris, France: Éditions du Cerf, 1992, p. 1240).

[600] *Carnet manuscrit de soeur Geneviève* [Manuscript Notebooks of Sister Geneviève (Céline Martin)], pp. 97-105. (Not translated.)

[601] *Vie Thérésienne*, Nos. 88, 89, 93.

[602] *Vie Thérésienne*, No. 89, January 1983, p. 66, note 7.

January 1973) indicates that, according to oral tradition, "The main objective of the destruction of the originals would have been to spare Léonie Martin any pain should she have wanted to reread the maternal correspondence" (p. 57, note *b*). Léonie, who became Sister Françoise-Thérèse at the Visitation Monastery in Le Mans, died June 16, 1941.

Consequently, all that remains at the Carmelite Monastery in Lisieux are about 130 rare fragments of the original manuscripts, a few words to a few lines, of which a third are glued either on four loose sheets or in a 25.5 x 18 cm. notebook with a blue cover, consisting of 10 sheets.[603]

History of Publications

Between May 1941 and November 1954, the Martin sisters published fragments of their mother's correspondence in the *Annales de sainte Thérèse de Lisieux*. In issue number 3-4, March-April 1941 (pp. 35-37), Bishop François-Marie Picaud, the Bishop of Bayeux and Lisieux, addressed a letter to Mgr. Octave Germain, rector of the Pilgrimage Office and Director of the *Annales,* about the publication of the *Lettres familiale de Mme. Martin* [Family Letters of Madame Martin], to strongly encourage him in this undertaking. In issue number 5-6, May-June 1941, publication began (the letters were published over a period of thirteen years) preceded by an historical foreword (pp. 66-71) which gave some information on the fragmentary publication. It was emphasized – we know – that this correspondence is far from being complete, since the letters sent by Zélie Martin to her daughter Marie were destroyed inadvertently by the servant, Louise Marais, in Alençon. Moreover, the letters sent to Sister Marie-Dosithée, the

---

[603] See *Correspondance générale, tome I* [General Correspondence, Volume 1], p. 1240. In the Archives of the Lisieux Carmel one finds, in a white colored file, 52 fragments of original documents glued on 4 pages (21x13.5 cm.), plus one fragment on a loose sheet. In a sky blue notebook, there are 37 fragments (of which 29 are signatures) glued in the notebook with 20 pages (25.5x18 cm.), 2 sheets serving as an envelope (address and stamp), and 37 fragments in some envelopes. In total, there are 127 fragments. Some glued fragments have text on the back, and at times it is possible to decipher some words. Only one complete original letter remains, CF 214-a, dated July 15, 1877, addressed to Sister Marie-Louise de Gonzague Vétillart, the director of the boarding school at the Visitation Monastery in Le Mans. The letter is written on a folded double sheet (21 x 13.3 cm), with the second page blank.

Visitandine in Le Mans, were not preserved by her.

The foreword adds, "Following the advice of the Bishop of Bayeux, we respect as much as possible the integrity of the original text of this correspondence, even if it means allowing for some repetition…" (p. 70). We shall return to this assertion.

In 1958, when the Carmelite Monastery in Lisieux undertook the publication of this family correspondence in one volume, Father Stéphane-Joseph Piat (1899-1968), a Franciscan and author of *Histoire d'une famille* [The Story of a Family], 1946, wrote the Foreword for it, pp. 5-11.[604]

He emphasized some variants between the publication in the *Annales* and the 1958 edition: "Needless to say, the original language was restored in the present edition" (p. 10, note 1).

But we know that this "original language" was taken from nothing but copies of destroyed original documents.

The few comparisons possible when original fragments remain – or initial copies, like those of Sister Geneviève and Sister Marie of the Trinity – point to the following modifications:

1. Alterations of style - According to the custom of the Martin sisters and as was done at the time, when one didn't pay a lot of attention to an exact copy of a text. The punctuation was rationalized and misspellings corrected.

2. Omissions - Omissions were made for various reasons. We mentioned the concern to spare Léonie, but the copies were also cut or "rearranged" to avoid hurting members of the family or out of concern for edification, which remained the primary objective of the publication.

3. Interpolations - For example, a sentence Zélie wrote on July 24, 1877, was transposed to August 16, 1877 (CF 217).

4. Combining of text - One can infer that texts were combined without being able to prove it definitively, due to the lack of original documents.

5. Changing the order of paragraphs.

6. Passages concerning Thérèse - Thanks to Sister Marie of the

---

[604] Zélie Martin, the mother of Saint Thérèse of the Child Jesus, *Correspondance familiale (fragments) 1863-1877.* The Carmelite Monastery of Lisieux, copyright by Office Central de Lisieux, 1958, 462 pages with illustrations.

Trinity's copy, we realize that everything that showed the little girl to be very spirited, even unruly, was toned down, if not erased. Without any doubt, this version is much closer to the original documents.

The current concept of sanctity, which takes root in a very concrete humanity, prefers this reality to an idealization, a characteristic attitude of the time.

Precise comparisons made between the texts of the *Annales*, the 1958 book and the various copies[605] show that all the liberties taken by the Martin sisters posed no problem to them, their primary objective being the edification of the readers, while the modern historical method cares, above all, about scrupulously restoring the original texts.

Finally, let's not forget that in her first manuscript, written in 1895 (Manuscript A), Sister Thérèse quoted from her mother's letters twelve times.[606] There is every reason to believe that she used the original documents preserved by her sisters. According to the customs of her time, Thérèse herself probably copied them without scrupulous concern about reproducing them exactly as the original. And yet, we notice that these quotes are identical to the texts in *Correspondance familiale* [Family Correspondence]. Be that as it may, these publications always indicated that they were only "fragments."

Our Edition

It was necessary to publish a new edition that could benefit from those versions closest to the original documents, fully knowing that a critical edition is impossible due to the lack of original documents (except some rare fragments).

Therefore we reproduced the text of the 1958 edition, but, whenever possible, we used the versions in Sister Geneviève's notebook and Sister Marie of the Trinity's notebooks, which are probably closer to the originals. The letter found dated July 15, 1877, was put in its chronological place. The footnotes were expanded and updated to include the knowledge gained over the last forty years. It's absolutely

---

[605] These works exist but would weigh down this edition considerably.

[606] Manuscript A, 4 v° (CF 147); 5 r° (CF 119); 5 v° (CF 170 and CF 160); 6 v° (CF 104); 7 r° (CF 159); 8 r° (CF 147); 8 v° (CF 172); 9 r° (CF 192); 10 r° (CF 201); 11 r° (CF 195 and CF 192).

essential to consult the *Archives de famille* [Family Archives] published in the journal *Vie Thérésienne* from October 1969, number 36, to January 1994, number 133. One finds an inexhaustible source of information there on the Martin and Guérin families and their environment (1,340 published letters).[607]

In regard to the present edition, we summarized the issues of *Vie Thérésienne* (VT) that we consulted; they are indicated in the footnotes throughout the text:

- VT number 44, October 1971, p. 239: Madame Martin to Pauline, July 16, 1873.
- VT number 47, July 1972, p. 229: Madame Martin to Madame Guérin, October 31, 1875.
- VT number 48, October 1972, p. 302: Madame Martin to Pauline, March 26, 1876.
- VT number 49, January 1973, p. 67: Madame Martin to Pauline, October 22, 1876.
- VT number 49, January 1973, p. 72: Madame Martin to Pauline, November 19, 1876.
- VT number 55, July 1974, p. 232: Madame Martin to Madam Guérin, July 15, 1877.
- VT number 55, July 1974, p. 232: Madame Martin to Sister Marie-Louise de Gonzague, July 15, 1877.
- VT number 55, July 1974, p. 233: Madam Martin to Monsieur and Madam Guérin, July 15, 1877.

The 218 letters of Zélie Martin, from January 1, 1863, to August 16, 1877, are distributed as follows: 4 to Louis Martin; one to her sister (Sister Marie-Dosithée); 56 to Isidore Guérin, her brother; 93 to Céline Guérin, her sister-in-law; 13 to the couple together; 42 to Pauline; and one to Sister Marie-Louise de Gonzague Vétillart, headmistress at the boarding school in Le Mans.

The Dates

Zélie Martin dated her letters, but when she didn't, sometimes the date could be deduced from the context. She usually wrote on

---

[607] This work spanned twenty-five years. Usually signed DCL (*Documentation Carmel de Lisieux*) [Material from the Carmelite Monastery in Lisieux], it was the work of Sister Cécile de l'Immaculée, OCD. It was carried out with the same critical meticulousness as the *Édition du Centenaire* [Centenary Edition], (Cerf-DDB), 1992. See *Vie Thérésienne*, No. 133, pp. 67-68.

Sunday. By comparing with other letters that specify "last Sunday," "the day before yesterday," "next Wednesday," etc., we managed to date certain letters. Sometimes it was a political or local event that allowed us to specify the date. In total, 13 letters were able to be dated in this way.[608]

When all is said and done, it's absolutely clear that the destruction of Zélie's original letters is an irreparable loss. With our current criteria for publication of the texts, we deplore it.

It remains that the general meaning of this correspondence was preserved and continues to be an important source of knowledge regarding Thérèse's mother and her family.

After a very rigorous and very precise job of comparing the texts, the authors of the *Positio* could conclude: "We can point out once again that, if we have to lament the loss of the original documents, at least we can think that the modifications carried out successively did not substantially alter the text and the thought of the Servant of God."[609]

It's interesting to note the opinion of a great Theresian scholar, the Carmelite priest François de Sainte-Marie († 1962), editor of the *Manuscrits autobiographiques* [Autobiographical Manuscripts] of Saint Thérèse of the Child Jesus and of the Holy Face, who said in 1956 regarding this correspondence: "After having questioned those responsible or the witnesses of these alterations, I believe I can affirm that these modifications, however regrettable they may be, have hardly affected the form of the letters."[610]

Letters of Louis Martin

The sixteen letters of Louis Martin were published in the book written by Céline Martin (Sister Geneviève of the Holy Face), *Le Père de sainte Thérèse de l'Enfant-Jésus. Témoignages et documents.* Carmel de Lisieux, 1955, 136 pages, in an Appendix (pp. 109-129). The English translation of this book was originally published in 1955 under the title *The Father of the Little Flower* (Fr. Michael Collins, SMA, transla-

---

[608] All of this work was done in *Vie Thérésienne* when the Family Archives were published; one can refer to it. See the work of the *Positio*, volume II, pp. 354-366.
[609] *Positio*, Volume II, pp. 365-366.
[610] *Ibid.*, p. 436.

tor). The current edition is published by TAN Books and Publishers, Inc., Charlotte, North Carolina, 2005, with an Appendix containing the sixteen letters of Louis Martin, pp. 126-150.

They date from October 8, 1863, to April 10, 1888. One was addressed to his wife; thirteen to his daughters; and two to his friends, the Nogrix family.

Here again, the original letters were destroyed. Sister Geneviève explained this in a note dated July 16, 1956:[611]

"[The letters] were published in full, such as we owned them, except for two words: one, an error by the copyist and the other, the correction of an error of place.

"If they were burned, it was, I must admit, due to a groundless fear motivated by some indiscretions which took place in Portugal after the death of Father de Santanna, S.J.

"This religious had translated *Story of a Soul* into Portuguese. Naturally, he corresponded with us to do research. We were very grateful to him for having dedicated his work to our pious parents and our letters had a certain tone of intimacy.

"And yet, after his death, this correspondence appeared in the Portuguese press, and we had to have the Patriarch of Lisbon intervene in order to stop this indiscreet publication.

"Since then, the original documents in general inspired terror in us, and, panic stricken, we burned our father's letters, keeping only the signatures.

"It was then, also, that it was asked of all our correspondents, under threat of not writing to them anymore, that they destroy our letters after reading them.

"Having made this sincere statement, I can take an oath on the text printed in the pamphlet, '*The Father of Saint Thérèse of the Child Jesus*,' and that I testify to the Process."

The Archives of the Carmelite Monastery in Lisieux do not possess the original letters of Louis Martin except for some fragments, sometimes reduced to a few words or a signature.

In our edition, we have inserted Louis' letters in their chronological place, among those of his wife.

---

[611] A typed sheet of paper with her handwritten signature and date. (The Archives of the Carmelite Monastery in Lisieux.)

Genealogy of the Martin and Guérin Families

The Paternal Family of Thérèse

Paternal Grandparents

Pierre-François Martin (April 16, 1777-June 26, 1865).
Marie-Anne-Fanie Boureau (January 12, 1800-April 8, 1883).
They married in Lyon on April 4, 1818.
They had five children – three daughters and two sons.
 Pierre born July 29, 1819.
     He died in a shipwreck when still very young.
 Marie-Anne (September 18, 1820-February 19, 1846).
Louis-Joseph-Aloys-Stanislaus (August 22, 1823-July 29, 1894),
    father of St. Thérèse.
Anne-Françoise-Fanny (March 10, 1826-October 9, 1853).
  Anne-Sophie (November 7, 1833-September 23, 1842).

The Maternal Family of Thérèse

Maternal Grandparents

Isidore Guérin, Sr. (July 6, 1789-September 3, 1868).
Louise-Jeanne Macé (July 11, 1805-September 9, 1859).
 They married in Pré-en-Pail on September 5, 1828.
 They had three children – two daughters and one son.
  Marie-Louise (May 31, 1829-February 24, 1877).
      She became Sister Marie-Dosithée
      Visitation Monastery, Le Mans.
  Marie-Azélie (December 23, 1831-August 28, 1877),
      known as Zélie
      the mother of St. Thérèse.
Marie-Victor-Isidore (January 2, 1841-September 28, 1909),
      known as Isidore
      the uncle of Thérèse. He became
      a pharmacist in Lisieux.

In Lisieux, on September 11, 1866, he married
Élisa-Céline Fournet (March 15, 1847-February 13, 1900).
They had three children:
Jeanne (February 24, 1868-April 25, 1938), cousin of Thérèse.
On October 1, 1890, she married Dr. Francis La Néele
(October 18, 1858-March 19, 1916).
Marie (August 22, 1870-April 14, 1905), a cousin of Thérèse.
She became Sister Marie of the Eucharist, Carmel of Lisieux.
Paul (October 16, 1871), delivered stillborn.

The Martin Family

Louis Martin married Marie-Azélie Guérin in Alençon on July 13, 1858.
They had nine children:
Marie-Louise (February 22, 1860-January 19, 1940),
known as Marie, godmother of Thérèse,
became Sister Marie of the Sacred Heart,
Carmel of Lisieux.
Marie-Pauline (September 7, 1861-July 28, 1951),
known as Pauline, became Mother Agnès
of Jesus, Carmel of Lisieux.
Marie-Léonie (June 3, 1863-June 16, 1941),
known as Léonie,
became Sister Françoise Thérèse, entered
the Visitation Monastery, in Caen, in 1899.
Marie-Hélène (October 13, 1864-February 22, 1870),
known as Hélène.
Marie-Joseph-Louis (September 20, 1866-February 14,1867),
known as Joseph.
Marie-Joseph-Jean-Baptiste (December 19, 1867-August 24, 1868),
known as Joseph.
Marie-Céline (April 28, 1869-February 25, 1959),
known as Céline, became Sister Geneviève
of the Holy Face, Carmel of Lisieux.
Marie-Mélanie-Thérèse (August 16, 1870-October 8, 1870),
known as Thérèse.
Marie-Françoise-Thérèse (January 2, 1873-September 30, 1897),
known as Thérèse,
became Sister Thérèse of the Child Jesus
and of the Holy Face, Carmel of Lisieux.
She was canonized on May 17, 1925.

APPENDIX FOUR: The Martin and Guérin Family Tree

Pierre-Francois MARTIN (1777-1865) m. Marie-Anne-Fanie BOUREAU (1800-1883)

Isidore GUÉRIN, Sr. (1789-1868) m. Louise-Jeanne MACÉ (1805-1859)

Marie-Louise GUÉRIN (1829-1877) ——→ Sister Marie-Dosithée at the Visitation Monastery in Le Mans (1858)

Marie-Azélie GUÉRIN (1831-1877)

Isidore GUÉRIN (1841-1909) Pharmacist in Lisieux — married in Lisieux on September 11, 1866 — Élisa-Céline FOURNET (1847-1900)

Jeanne GUÉRIN (1868-1938) — married — Doctor Francis LA NÉELE

Marie GUÉRIN (1870-1905) ——→ Sister Marie of the Eucharist in the Carmelite Monastery in Lisieux (1895-1905)

Paul GUÉRIN (stillborn, 1871)

Louis MARTIN (1823-1894) — married in Alençon on July 13, 1858

Marie-Louise (1860-1940) Thérèse's godmother ——→ Sister Marie of the Sacred Heart in the Carmelite Monastery in Lisieux (1886-1940)

Marie-Pauline (1861-1951) ——→ Sister Agnès, then Mother Agnès, in the Carmelite Monastery in Lisieux (1882-1951)

Marie-Léonie (1863-1941) ——→ Sister Françoise-Thérèse in the Visitation Monastery in Caen (1899-1941)

Marie-Hélène (1864-1870)

Marie-Joseph-Louis (1866-1867)

Marie-Joseph-Jean-Baptiste (1867-1868)

Marie-Céline (1869-1959) ——→ Sister Geneviève of the Holy Face in the Carmelite Monastery in Lisieux (1894-1959)

Marie-Mélanie-Thérèse (1870)

Marie-Françoise-Thérèse (January 2, 1873–September 30, 1897) ——→ Sister Thérèse of the Child Jesus and of the Holy Face in the Carmelite Monastery in Lisieux (1888-1897)

APPENDIX FIVE

Biographical Guide of Proper Names

BOUREAU, Marie-Anne-Fanie (January 12, 1800-April 8, 1883)
Known as Fanie, Louis Martin's mother and Thérèse's paternal grandmother. Born in Blois (Loir-et-Cher). She married Pierre-François Martin in Lyon on April 4, 1818. They had five children (three girls and two boys). She died in Valframbert (Orne).

GUÉRIN, Céline (March 15, 1847-February 13, 1900)
Élisa-Céline, née Fournet, Zélie Martin's sister-in law and Thérèse's aunt. Born in Lisieux to Pierre-Célestin Fournet and Élisa-Ernestine Petit. She married Isidore Guérin, Zélie's brother, on September 11, 1866, and had three children, two of whom were daughters: Jeanne (1868-1938) and Marie (1870-1905). A son, Paul, was delivered stillborn on October 16, 1871. After the arrival of the Martin family in Lisieux, she played a maternal role for her nieces, who visited her house each week. Léonie lived in her home from 1895 to 1899.

GUÉRIN, Sr., Isidore (July 6, 1789-September 3, 1868)
Zélie Martin's father and Thérèse's maternal grandfather. Born in Saint-Martin-l'Aguillon (Orne). In 1809, he was drafted into the Army and was a soldier in the 96th Infantry Regiment. He took part in the Battle of Wagram and the Napoleonic Wars. In 1816, he joined the police force first on foot patrol and then on mounted patrol in Saint-Denis-sur-Sarthon. On September 5, 1828, he married Louise-Jeanne Macé. They had three children: Marie-Louise, called Élise (Sister Marie-Dosithée); Marie-Azélie, called Zélie (wife of Louis Martin); and Marie-Victor-Isidore, called Isidore. In 1844, he retired and moved to Alençon, having bought the house on the rue Saint-Blaise in 1843.

GUÉRIN, Isidore (January 2, 1841-September 28, 1909)
Marie-Victor-Isidore, Zélie Martin's brother and Thérèse's

uncle. Born in Saint-Denis-sur-Sarthon (Orne) to Isidore Guérin, Sr., and Louise-Jeanne Macé. He studied to be a pharmacist in Paris (1862) and received a Bachelor of Science degree in 1863. In 1864, he was named an intern at the *Hospice de Bicêtre* (Bicêtre Hospital), then known as the *Hospice de la Vieillesse hommes* (Home for Old Men), in the psychiatric department. In May 1866, he graduated as a Pharmacist 1st Class. He moved to Lisieux and purchased a pharmacy on the Place Saint-Pierre from the Fournets, whose daughter, Céline, he married on September 11, 1866. They had three children: Jeanne (1868-1938), Marie (Sister Marie of the Eucharist) (1870-1905), and Paul, who was delivered stillborn on October 16, 1871.

He was named surrogate guardian to his nieces on September 16, 1877, after the death of their mother. He arranged for the Martin family to move into Les Buissonnets in Lisieux. In August 1888, he inherited the Château de la Musse and sold his pharmacy to Victor La-haye at the end of 1888. He lived in Lisieux at 16 rue Condorcet, then at 19 rue Paul Banaston (at that time, known as rue de la Chaussée). He took the place of a father for his nieces when Louis Martin fell ill (Louis lived the last years of his life with the Guérins). A militant Christian, he founded the Work of Nocturnal Adoration in Lisieux in 1885. From October 1891 to 1896, he actively contributed to the monarchist Catholic newspaper *Le Normand*, crossing swords with his former employee, the founder of *Progrès lexovian* [The Progress of Lisieux], Henri Chéron, a future minister. Monsieur Guérin played an important role in the publication of *Story of a Soul* (1898). His old age was darkened by the death of his wife (1900) and his daughter, Sister Marie of the Eucharist (1905).

GUÉRIN, Jeanne (February 24, 1868-April 25, 1938)

Jeanne-Marie-Élisa was Thérèse's first cousin. She was born in Lisieux and died in Nogent-le-Rotrou (Eure-et-Loir). She was the oldest daughter of Isidore Guérin and Céline Fournet. She married Dr. Francis La Néele on October 1, 1890, and lived in Caen until her mother's death in 1900. The La Néeles then returned to Lisieux to live in the home of her father. Her correspondence with Thérèse often mentioned her sadness over not having a child. After the death of her husband in 1916, she adopted a great-niece of her husband. She was a witness at the Processes for the Beatification and Canonization of Thérèse.

GUÉRIN, Marie-Louise-Pétronille (May 31, 1829-February 24, 1877)
Known as Élise, Zélie Martin's sister. Born in Gandelain (Orne). She established a lace making business with Zélie. She entered the Visitation Monastery of Le Mans on April 7, 1858, and was given the name Sister Marie-Dosithée. Her clothing was on February 24, 1859, and her profession on March 12, 1860. She watched over the education of her nieces Marie and Pauline, who were boarding school students at the Visitation Monastery beginning in 1868, and, on occasion, Léonie, who attended the school sporadically. She died of slow developing tuberculosis.

GUÉRIN, Marie (August 22, 1870-April 14, 1905)
Marie-Louise-Hélène was Thérèse's first cousin. She was born in Lisieux, the second child of Isidore and Céline Guérin. She studied at the Benedictine Abbey of Notre Dame du Pré in Lisieux with Thérèse. She entered the Carmelite Monastery on August 15, 1895, and was given the name Sister Marie of the Eucharist. She was given the habit on March 17, 1896, and her profession was on March 25, 1897. Thérèse, her Novice Mistress, helped her free herself of her scruples. Marie's correspondence with her family remains a valuable source of information regarding Thérèse's last months. She herself died of tuberculosis at the age of thirty-four, despite the care of her brother-in-law, Dr. La Néele, and the use of treatments new for that time.

MACÉ, Louise-Jeanne (July 11, 1805-September 9, 1859)
Zélie Martin's mother and Thérèse's maternal grandmother. Born in Pré-en-Pail (Mayenne). She married Isidore Guérin, Sr., on September 5, 1828. She had three children: Marie-Louise, called Élise (Sister Marie-Dosithée), Marie-Azélie (called Zélie) and Marie-Victor-Isidore (called Isidore). She died in Alençon, in the house on the rue Saint-Blaise.

MARTIN, Céline (April 28, 1869-February 25, 1959)
Marie-Céline was born in Alençon, the seventh child of Louis and Zélie Martin. She attended school at the Convent School of l'Abbaye Notre-Dame-du-Pré in Lisieux (1878-1885). In the years 1887 to 1888, she shared a great intimacy with Thérèse which continued from 1888 to 1894 through a spiritual correspondence of the greatest value. From 1889 to 1894, she helped Louis Martin during his illness. Her father died on July 29, 1894, and Céline entered the

Carmelite Monastery on September 14, 1894, and was given the name Sister Marie of the Holy Face. Her clothing was on February 5, 1895, and she received the name Sister Geneviève of Saint Teresa; her profession was on February 24, 1896. Her novitiate was under the direction of Thérèse. She nursed her during the last months of her life. She played an important role in the spreading of Thérèse's message through books, painting and photography. She was a key witness during the Processes for the Beatification and Canonization of Thérèse. In 1916, she received the name Sister Geneviève of the Holy Face.

MARTIN, Léonie (June 3, 1863-June 16, 1941)

Marie-Léonie was born in Alençon, the third child of Louis and Zélie Martin. Sickly and with an unmanageable character, she was a major worry for her parents. She was Thérèse's sponsor at her Confirmation (June 14, 1884). She only became settled at the Visitation Monastery in Caen, being given the name Sister Françoise-Thérèse, after three previous attempts at religious life: she entered the Monastery of the Poor Clares in Alençon in 1886 and left after less than two months, then entered the Visitation Monastery in Caen in 1887 and left in 1888, and entered the same monastery a second time (1893-1895), being given the name Thérèse-Dosithée. After she left the second time, she lived with the Guérins for four years (1895-1899). She entered the Visitation Monastery in Caen again on January 28, 1899, and made her profession on July 2, 1900. She was a witness at the Processes for the Beatification and Canonization of Thérèse.

MARTIN, Louis (August 22, 1823-July 29, 1894)

Louis-Joseph-Aloys-Stanislas Martin was born in Bordeaux (Gironde). He spent his childhood in Avignon and Strasbourg, and then, in 1830, his family moved to Alençon. He considered entering religious life and visited the Great Saint Bernard Monastery in 1843, returning in 1845 to request admission, but was refused because he did not know Latin. In 1850, he bought a watchmaking business in Alençon and married Zélie Guérin on July 13, 1858. He and Zélie had nine children, four of whom died while very young. Zélie died on August 28, 1877, and he moved to Lisieux on November 30, 1877, into the house known as Les Buissonnets. He had his first attack of paralysis in 1887, and dementia caused by cerebral arteriosclerosis required that he be admitted to Bon Sauveur Hospital in Caen, a hospital for the mentally ill, on February 12, 1889. He remained there three years and returned to Lisieux on May 10, 1892, where he was taken care of by Céline. He died at La Musse (Eure), at the home of his brother-in-law, Isidore Guérin, during their summer vacation.

MARTIN, Marie (February 22, 1860-January 19, 1940)

Marie-Louise-Joséphine, born in Alençon, was Louis and Zélie's first child. She attended the boarding school at the Visitation Monastery in Le Mans from 1868 to 1875. After the death of Zélie, Céline chose Marie to be her second mother. She managed the household at Les Buissonnets. She was Thérèse's godmother. She took care of Thérèse during her illness in 1883, when she was suffering from a nervous disorder, and was her confidant when she was suffering from scruples (1885-1886). She entered the Carmelite Monastery in Lisieux on October 15, 1886, and was given the name Sister Marie of the Sacred Heart. Her clothing was on March 19, 1887, and her profession on May 22, 1888. For three years (1888-1891), she was in the novitiate at the same time as Thérèse. She was responsible for Thérèse writing her childhood memories (Manuscript A, 1895) and the secrets of her "doctrine" (Manuscript B, 1896). She testified at the Processes for the Beatification and Canonization of Thérèse.

MARTIN, Pauline (September 7, 1861-July 28, 1951)

Marie-Pauline, born in Alençon, was the second child of Louis and Zélie. She attended the boarding school at the Visitation Monastery in Le Mans from 1868 to 1877. She took charge of Thérèse's education after Zélie's death and gave her lessons at Les Buissonnets. On October 2, 1882, she entered the Carmelite Monastery of Lisieux and was given the name Sister Agnès of Jesus. Her clothing was on April 6, 1883, and her profession on May 8, 1884, the day of Thérèse's First Communion. She obtained, through intervention, Thérèse's entrance into Carmel at age fifteen. Prioress from February 20, 1893, to March 21, 1896, she ordered her sister to write her childhood memories (*Story of a Soul*). She was the bursar from 1896 to 1899, sub-prioress from 1899 to 1902, and Prioress from 1902 to 1908. She was named Prioress again after the death of Mother Marie-Ange (November 11, 1909) and remained in this office until her death, having been appointed Prioress for life by Pope Pius XI in 1923. She was a witness at the Processes for the Beatification and Canonization of Thérèse.

MARTIN, Pierre-François (April 16, 1777-June 26, 1865)

Louis Martin's father and Thérèse's paternal grandfather. Born in Athis-de-l'Orne (Orne). He enlisted in the Army and participated in the expeditions of Napoleon. In 1816, he was a captain in the 19th Light Infantry Regiment. On April 4, 1818, he married Marie-Anne-Fanie Boureau in Lyon. They had five children: Pierre, who died young in a shipwreck; Marie, who died in 1846 at age 26; Louis, who married Zélie Guérin; Fanny, who died in 1853 at age 27, leaving a son; and Sophie, who died in 1842 at age nine. In 1823, he participated in the expedition to Spain. In 1828, he was the warrant officer to the staff in Strasbourg. In 1830, he retired after more than thirty-one years of service and moved to Alençon.

MARTIN, Zélie (December 23, 1831-August 28, 1877)

Marie-Azélie Guérin, born in Gandelain (Orne). Her family moved to Alençon in 1844. She was a day student at the School of the Religious of the Sacred Hearts of Jesus and Mary of Perpetual Adoration. She felt she had a vocation to religious life and asked to be accepted by the Daughters of St. Vincent de Paul, but she was told by the Superior that it was not the will of God. She asked the Blessed Mother for guidance regarding her future, and on December 8, 1851, the Feast of the Immaculate Conception, she heard an inner voice say, "See to the making of Alençon lace." She understood this to be a directive from God and learned the lace-making profession. She made lace for a Parisian company and then, around 1863, she went into business for herself. She married Louis Martin on July 13, 1858, and they had nine children, four of whom died at a young age. She died of breast cancer in their home on the rue Saint-Blaise in Alençon.

MAUDELONDE, Céline (February 25, 1873-June 1, 1949)

The fourth child of Céline Guérin's sister, Marie-Rosalie Fournet and her husband, Césard Maudelonde. She was born in Lisieux and died at La Flèche (Sarthe). She was a childhood companion of Thérèse. On June 19, 1894, she married Gaston Pottier, a notary. They had two children. She was the recipient of significant correspondence from Sister Marie of the Eucharist (Marie Guérin), her cousin and close friend.

MAUDELONDE, Ernest (September 17, 1862-January 25, 1941)

The oldest child of Céline Guérin's sister, Marie-Rosalie Fournet and her husband, Césard Maudelonde. He was born in Lisieux and died in Caen. He was a notary. In June 1888, he accompanied Isidore Guérin and Céline Martin to Le Havre to look for Louis Martin, who, suffering from dementia, had run away from home. He married Jeanne Massonie on January 21, 1896, with whom he had two daughters.

MAUDELONDE, Hélène (May 9, 1876-June 6, 1944)

The fifth child of Céline Guérin's sister, Marie-Rosalie Fournet and her husband, Césard Maudelonde. She was born in Lisieux. On August 4, 1896, she married Jules Houdayer, a lawyer in Lisieux; they had two children. She disappeared during the bombing of Caen in World War II.

MAUDELONDE, Henry (September 4, 1864-September 19, 1937)

The second child of Céline Guérin's sister, Marie-Rosalie Fournet and her husband, Césard Maudelonde. He was born in Lisieux and died in Bernières-sur-Mer. He was an attorney. In 1890-1891 he attempted to marry Céline Martin, who declined his advances. He married Marie Asseline on April 20, 1892, and they had two children. She died on December 5, 1895, and he married Hélène Meynaerts on October 12, 1899, with whom he had three children.

MAUDELONDE, Marguerite-Marie (February 24, 1867-April 30, 1966)

The third child of Céline Guérin's sister, Marie-Rosalie Fournet and her husband, Césard Maudelonde. She was born in Lisieux and died in La Délivrande. On October 14, 1889, she married René Tostain, deputy public prosecutor in Lisieux, a nonbeliever for whom Thérèse prayed especially in 1897. She died childless.

MAUDELONDE, Marie (June 29, 1843-November 11, 1926)

Marie-Rosalie Fournet, Céline Guérin's sister, was born and died in Lisieux. She was the daughter of Pierre-Celestin Fournet and Élisa-Ernestine Petit. She married Césard Maudelonde on July 7, 1861, and they had five children: Ernest (1862), Henry (1864), Marguerite-Marie (1867), Céline (1873), and Hélène (1876). The Martin and Maudelonde children were frequent visitors to the Guérin's home in Lisieux and while they were on vacation, particularly in Trouville.

ROMET, Hortense-Scholastique (1825-July 6, 1898)

Born in Alençon and died in Caen. She was the sister of Vital, Pauline, Pierre, Adrien and Augustin-Adrien Romet. She married Auguste Benoît in 1857, and they had three daughters: Marie, Amélie, and Pauline, who were childhood friends of Marie and Pauline Martin. Later the Benoîts settled in Caen. It was Auguste Benoît whom Isidore Guérin asked to take Louis Martin from Les Buissonnets to Bon Sauveur Hospital in Caen on February 12, 1889.

ROMET, Pauline (1829-September 15, 1889)

Pauline-Rose-Marie was born and died in Alençon. She was the sister of Vital, Hortense, Pierre, Adrien and Augustin-Adrien Romet. As a young girl, she would have liked to marry Louis Martin. She was Pauline Martin's godmother. She lived with her brother, Vital, and devoted herself to charitable works.

ROMET, Pierre (1819-September 17, 1904)

Born in Alençon. He was the brother of Vital, Pauline, Hortense, Adrien, and Augustin-Adrien Romet. A successful businessman, in 1844, he founded a store in Alençon, Gagne-Petit, that sold clothing, fabrics, etc., establishing branches in Le Mans and Caen. He asked his brother Vital to give up his pharmacy business in order to manage his store in Le Mans. He was a member of the administrative commission of the Hospice in Alençon.

ROMET, Vital (1830-July 21, 1916)

Born and died in Alençon. He was one of eight children, the brother of Pauline, Hortense, Pierre, Adrien and Augustin-Adrien Romet. He was a pharmacist. Isidore Guérin, as a student, did professional training in his pharmacy. He founded the "Vital Romet Catholic Circle" where young people met each week at his home on the rue du Mans, near the Chapel of Notre-Dame-de-Lorette. He was Céline Martin's godfather. He never married. Vital Romet devoted himself to social works. His brother Pierre asked him to take a leave of absence from his pharmacy business to manage his store, Gagne-Petit, in Le Mans. He returned to his pharmacy business in 1877 and eventually sold it to Jacques Tifenne, pharmacist and friend of Isidore Guérin and Louis Martin and the husband of Léonie Tifenne, Léonie Martin's godmother.

Chronology of the Martin and Guérin Families

1777-1849

April 16, 1777 The birth of Pierre-François Martin in Athis-de-l'Orne (Orne). He was the father of Louis Martin. His baptismal godfather was his maternal uncle, François Bohard.

July 6, 1789 The birth of Isidore Guérin, Sr. in St. Martin-l'Aiguillon (Orne). He was the father of Zélie Guérin Martin.

January 12, 1800 The birth of Marie-Anne-Fanie Boureau in Blois (Loir-et-Cher). She was the mother of Louis Martin.

July 11, 1805 The birth of Louise-Jeanne Macé in Pré-en-Pail (Mayenne). She was the mother of Marie-Louise Guérin (Élise) known in religion as Sister Marie-Dosithée, Zélie Guérin Martin and Isidore.

April 4, 1818 Pierre-François Martin and Marie-Anne-Fanie Boureau were married in a civil ceremony in Lyon.

April 7, 1818 Pierre-François Martin and Marie-Anne-Fanie Boureau were married in Lyon in the Church of Saint-Martin-d'Ainay by Abbé Bourganel. They lived at 4 rue Vaubecourt. They were the parents of Louis Martin.

July 29, 1819 The birth of Pierre Martin in Nantes. He was the oldest brother of Louis Martin. He died in a shipwreck when still very young.

September 18, 1820 The birth of Marie-Anne Martin in Nantes. She was the oldest sister of Louis Martin.

August 22, 1823 The birth of Louis-Joseph-Aloys-Stanislaus Martin on the rue Servandoni in Bordeaux (Gironde). He was the son of Pierre-François Martin and Marie-Anne-Fanie Boureau. He was the brother of Pierre, Marie-Anne, Anne-Françoise-Fanny and Anne-Sophie Martin. He was the husband of Zélie Guérin Martin and the father of Marie, Pauline, Léonie, Céline and Thérèse (St. Thérèse of the Child Jesus).

October 28, 1823 Louis was given the Complementary Rites of Baptism by l'Abbé Martegoutte in the Church of Sainte-Eulalie in Bordeaux. His godparents were Monsieur Leonce de Lamothe and Madame Ernestine Beyssac.

March 10, 1826	**The birth of Anne-Françoise-Fanny Martin in Alençon (Orne). She was the younger sister of Louis Martin.**
1827-1830	Louis attended school as a member of the *Enfants de Troupe* (Children of the Regiment) in the French Army in Strasbourg.
September 5, 1828	Isidore Guérin, Sr. and Louise-Jeanne Macé were married in the church in Pré-en-Pail (Mayenne) by l'Abbé Nourry. They were the parents of Élise, Isidore and Zélie Guérin Martin.
May 31, 1829	**The birth of Marie-Louise-Pétronille Guérin (Élise) in Gandelain, outside of Alençon (Orne). She was known in religion as Sister Marie-Dosithée. She was the daughter of Isidore Guérin, Sr. and Louise-Jeanne Macé, and the older sister of Zélie Guérin Martin and Isidore Guérin.**
July 18-19, 1830	The first apparition of Our Lady to Sister Catherine Labouré, later St. Catherine Labouré, in the convent chapel of the Daughters of Charity in Paris.
July 27-29, 1830	The Revolution of 1830.
November 27, 1830	The second apparition of Our Lady to Sister Catherine, later St. Catherine Labouré. Our Lady revealed her request to Sister Catherine to have the Miraculous Medal made and venerated.
December 12, 1830	Pierre-François Martin, Louis Martin's father, retired from the military.
1831	The Martin family left Strasbourg and moved to a house on the rue des Tisons in Alençon.
December 23, 1831	**The birth of Marie-Azélie Guérin (Zélie) in Gandelain, outside of Alençon (Orne). She was the daughter of Isidore Guérin, Sr., and Louise-Jeanne Macé. She was the sister of Élise Guérin (Sr. Marie-Dosithée) and Isidore Guérin, the wife of Louis Martin and the mother of Marie, Pauline, Léonie, Céline and Thérèse (St. Thérèse of the Child Jesus).**
December 24, 1831	Marie-Azélie Guérin was baptized in the Church of Saint-Denis-sur-Sarthon (Orne) by the Vicar Père M. Hubert.
November 7, 1833	**The birth of Anne-Sophie Martin in Alençon (Orne). She was the youngest sister of Louis Martin. He was her baptismal godfather.**
December 3, 1836	During the celebration of Mass, Père Charles-Eléonore Dufriche-Desgenettes heard an injunction from the Blessed Mother to consecrate the *Basilique de Notre Dame des Victoires* (the Basilica of Our Lady of Victories) to the Immaculate Heart of Mary.
October 8, 1838	Marie-Anne Martin, Louis Martin's older sister, married François-Marie Burin.
January 2, 1841	**The birth of Marie-Victor-Isidore Guérin (known as Isidore) in Saint-Denis-sur-Sarthon, outside of Alençon (Orne). He was the son of Isidore Guérin, Sr., and Louise-Jeanne Macé. He was the**

	brother of Élise Guérin (Sister Marie-Dosithée) and Zélie Guérin Martin. Later he married Élisa-Céline Fournet and became the father of Jeanne and Marie Guérin.
March 11, 1842	Anne-Françoise-Fanny Martin married François-Adolphe Leriche. She was the mother of Adolphe Leriche.
September 23, 1842	Anne-Sophie Martin, Louis Martin's youngest sister, died in Alençon at the age of 9 years old.
1842-1843	Louis lived in Rennes with his cousins and studied clock and watch making.
May 25, 1843	François-Adolphe Leriche died. He was the husband of Louis Martin's sister, Anne-Françoise-Fanny Martin, and the father of Adolphe Leriche, who was born seven months after his father's death.
January 7, 1844	The birth of Adolphe Leriche, son of Louis Martin's sister, Anne-Françoise-Fanny Martin and François-Adolphe Leriche (now deceased).
February 9, 1844	Isidore Guérin, Sr., bought a house in Alençon on the rue Saint-Blaise.
September 10, 1844	The Guérin family moved from Gandelain to their new home on the rue Saint-Blaise in Alençon.
September 1844	Zélie and her sister Élise were enrolled as day students in the School of the Religious of the Sacred Hearts of Jesus and Mary of Perpetual Adoration.
July 20, 1845	Zélie and her sister Élise were enrolled in the Confraternity of the Scapular of Our Lady of Mount Carmel.
September 1845	Louis Martin was refused entrance to the Monastery of the Great Saint Bernard in the Swiss Alps. He was told that knowledge of Latin was needed as an entrance requirement.
October 1845-August 1846	Louis studied Latin, completing 120 lessons, under the guidance of the priest at the Church of St. Leonard in Alençon, M. Jamot. No reason was given for the termination of his Latin studies in 1846.
February 19, 1846	Louis Martin's older sister Marie-Anne Martin Burin died in Argentan at the age of 26.
September 19, 1846	The Blessed Mother appeared in La Salette, France.
1847-1850	Louis completed his apprenticeship in Paris while living with his maternal grandmother, Madame Boureau-Nay and his uncle by marriage, Louis-Henri de Lacauve. Upon completion of his apprenticeship, he became a master watch and clock maker.
March 15, 1847	The birth of Élisa-Céline Fournet (known as Céline) in Lisieux. She was the daughter of Pierre-Célestin Fournet and Élisa Ernestine Petit. She was the sister of Marie-Rosalie Fournet Maudelonde. She later married Isidore Guérin, Zélie's brother. She was the mother of Jeanne, Marie and Paul Guérin (her infant that was

delivered stillborn) and the sister-in-law of Louis and Zélie Guérin Martin. She was the aunt of Marie, Pauline, Léonie, Céline and Thérèse Martin.

Spring 1847 — The Conferences of St. Vincent de Paul was founded in Alençon.

1848 — Due to financial difficulties, Zélie's parents opened a café and billiards room, and wood working business on the ground floor of their home on the rue Saint-Blaise.

1848 — The Revolution of 1848.

June 27, 1848 — **Archbishop Denis-Auguste Affre, Archbishop of Paris (1840-1848), was shot to death at the entrance to the Faubourg Saint-Antoine while attempting to restore peace between the workers and government troops during the Revolution of 1848.**

February 26, 1849 — Anne-Françoise-Fanny Martin Leriche married for a second time after her husband, François-Adolphe Leriche, died on May 25, 1843. She then married her brother-in-law, a widower, François-Marie Burin, the former husband of her sister, Marie-Anne Martin, who had died on February 19, 1846.

1850 - 1869

1850 — The Congregation of the Daughters of Charity refused Zélie's request for admission to the community in Alençon. No reason was given for this refusal.

November 9, 1850 — Louis Martin bought his house in Alençon on 15 rue du Pont-Neuf for 6,000 francs. He set up his business as a clock and watch maker on the ground floor of his home.

December 8, 1851 — Zélie prayed to Our Lady of the Immaculate Conception and heard an interior locution reveal that she was to "see to the making of Alençon lace."

April 25, 1852 — Zélie, Élise and their mother were enrolled in the Association of Prayers for the Salvation of France.

July 18, 1852 — Zélie, Élise and their mother were enrolled in the Confraternity of the Sacred Heart of Jesus.

1853 — Zélie opened her business as a "maker of *Point d'Alençon*" (Alençon lace) on the ground floor of her family home on the rue Saint-Blaise in Alençon. She was assisted by her sister, Élise.

1853 — The railroad in Alençon was built.

1853-1863 — Zélie worked for Maison Pigache, the famous House of Parisian lace.

October 9, 1853 — **Louis' sister Anne-Françoise-Fanny Martin Leriche Burin died in Fécamp (Normandy) at the age of 27. She was the mother of Adolphe Leriche.**

1854 — Pope Pius IX proclaimed the Doctrine of the Immaculate Conception.

396

1854-1861	The Sisters of Providence owned La Maison d'Ozé on the Place de la Magdeleine in Alençon.and taught the making of Point d'Alençon lace. It was here in a lace-making class that Zélie met Marie-Anne-Fanie Boureau Martin, Louis Martin's mother.
January 3, 1857	**Archbishop Marie-Dominique-Auguste Sibour, Archbishop of Paris (1848-1857), was assassinated in Paris by Jean Louis Verger, a priest who had been suspended because of his outspoken views against Church dogma.**
April 24, 1857	Louis bought the property known as the "Pavillon" on the south side of Alençon, now the rue du Pavillon Ste. Thérèse.
February 11, 1858	First apparition in Lourdes – the Blessed Mother appeared to Bernadette Soubirous, later known as Saint Bernadette Soubirous.
April 1858	Zélie Guérin passed Louis Martin on the Bridge of St. Leonard over the River Sarthe in Alençon and heard an interior voice saying, "This is the man I have prepared for you."
April 7, 1858	Zélie's sister Élise entered the Visitation Monastery in Le Mans and received the name Sister Marie-Dosithée.
June 20, 1858	Zélie received a silver medal for the quality of her lace-making by the judges at the Industrial Exposition at the Halle aux Toiles in Alençon. She worked for the House of Pigache in Paris.
July 12, 1858	Louis and Zélie were married on Monday, at 10 p.m. in a civil ceremony in the Town Hall in Alençon.
July 13, 1858	Two hours later, Louis and Zélie Martin were married on Tuesday at midnight in the Church of Notre Dame d'Alençon. L'Abbe Frédéric Hurel witnessed their vows. Louis was 35 years old and Zélie was 27 years old. They moved into Louis' home on 15 rue du Pont-Neuf where Louis had his watch and clock making business. Zélie opened her lace-making business on the ground floor.
July 16, 1858	The eighteenth and final apparition of Our Lady in Lourdes.
October 7, 1858	Louis became a member of the Society of the Most Blessed Sacrament in Alençon.
October 18, 1858	**The birth of Francis La Néele. He later married Jeanne Guérin, the daughter of Isidore and Céline Guérin, on October 1, 1890.**
February 24, 1859	Élise Guérin received the Habit of the Visitation and was given the name Sister Marie-Dosithée.
1859	Zélie's first pregnancy.
September 9, 1859	**Louise-Jeanne Macé Guérin died in Alençon at 50 rue Saint-Blaise at the age of 54. She was the wife of Isidore Guérin, Sr. and the mother of Élise Guérin (Sister Marie-Dosithée), Zélie Guérin Martin and Isidore Guérin.**
February 22, 1860	**The birth of Marie-Louise, in Alençon. She was Louis' and Zélie's first child. She was called Marie.**

February 23, 1860	The baptism of Marie-Louise in the parish Church of St. Pierre de Montsort in Alençon by Father Lebouc. Her godfather was her maternal grandfather, Isidore Guérin, Sr., and her godmother was her paternal grandmother, Marie-Anne-Fanie Boureau Martin.
March 12, 1860	Sister Marie-Dosithée made her religious profession at the Visitation Monastery in Le Mans.
1861	Zélie's second pregnancy.
1861-1867	Sister Marie-Dosithée was the assistant Novice Mistress of the Visitation Monastery in Le Mans.
February 2, 1861	Father Théophane Vénard, now St. Théophane Vénard, was martyred in Kecho Tong-King, Vietnam, at the age of 32. Thérèse had a great devotion to him.
July 7, 1861	Césard Maudelonde married Marie-Rosalie Fournet (Céline Fournet Guérin's sister). They had five children who were playmates of the Martin and Guérin children.
September 7, 1861	**The birth of Marie-Pauline in Alençon. She was Louis and Zélie's second child. She was called Pauline. She was baptized in the parish Church of St. Pierre de Montsort in Alençon by Father Lebouc. Her godfather was her uncle, Isidore Guérin, and her godmother was Pauline Romet, the sister of Vital Romet, both friends of Louis Martin.**
1862	Isidore, Zélie's brother, left Alençon to study medicine in Paris.
1862-1863	Zélie's third pregnancy.
June 3, 1863	**The birth of Marie-Léonie in Alençon. She was Louis and Zélie's third child. She was called Léonie.**
June 4, 1863	The baptism of Léonie on the feast of Corpus Christi in the parish Church of St. Pierre de Montsort in Alençon by Father Lebouc. Her godmother was Madame Léonie Gilbert Tifenne, a friend of Louis Martin. Her godfather was Adolphe Leriche, Louis Martin's nephew.
1864	Zélie's fourth pregnancy.
October 13, 1864	**The birth of Marie-Hélène in Alençon. She was Louis and Zélie's fourth child. She was called Hélène. Marie-Hélène was baptized in the parish Church of St. Pierre de Montsort in Alençon. Her godmother was her sister Marie and her godfather was "Mr. J."**
1864 -1865	Marie-Hélène was sent to a wet nurse.
1865	Léonie was gravely ill. Louis went on a pilgrimage by foot to Sées to pray to Our Lady for Léonie to be cured. Her health was restored soon after.
1865	Isidore withdrew from his medical studies and decided to become a pharmacist.
April 23, 1865	Zélie shared for the first time with her brother, Isidore, her worry about the pain in her breast.

April 23, 1865	Zélie feared her father would suffer a stroke.
June 26, 1865	**Pierre-François Martin died at 15 rue du Pont Neuf in Alençon at 1:00 pm at the age of 88. He was the father of Louis Martin.**
1866	Zélie's fifth pregnancy.
April 1866	Isidore moved to Lisieux and purchased a pharmacy from Pierre Fournet. Zélie experienced Isidore's move to Lisieux as a profound loss.
September 11, 1866	Isidore Guérin and Élisa-Céline Fournet were married in the Cathedral of Saint Pierre in Lisieux.
September 20, 1866	**The birth of Marie-Joseph-Louis in Alençon. He was Louis and Zélie's fifth child. He was called Joseph. He was baptized in the parish Church of St. Pierre de Montsort in Alençon. He was sent to Rose Taillé, the wet nurse in Semallé.**
December 1866	Isidore Guérin, Sr. (Zélie's father), moved back to his home on the rue Saint-Blaise.
1866-1867	After the birth of Marie-Joseph-Louis, Louis and Zélie were very worried about the baby's health.
February 14, 1867	**Marie-Joseph-Louis died from erysipelas and enteritis in Alençon. He was five months old.**
March 1867	Through the intercession of her infant brother, Marie-Joseph-Louis, who had died five weeks earlier, Marie-Hélène recovered from otitis, an ear infection.
1867	Zélie's sixth pregnancy.
December 19, 1867	**The birth of Marie-Joseph-Jean-Baptiste in Alençon. He was Louis and Zélie's sixth child. He was called Joseph. He was baptized in the parish Church of St. Pierre de Montsort in Alençon (Orne). His godmother was his sister, Pauline.**
December 21, 1867	Marie-Joseph-Jean-Baptiste was sent to Rose Taillé, the wet nurse in Semallé.
January 1868	Zélie complained of severe eye pain. She called it "nerve pain."
February 24, 1868	**The birth of Jeanne-Marie-Élisa Guérin in Lisieux. She was the daughter of Isidore and Céline Fournet Guérin. She later married Dr. Francis La Néele. She was the sister of Marie Guérin (Sister Marie of the Eucharist, of the Carmelite Monastery in Lisieux).**
Spring 1868	Louis and Zélie were very worried about the health of their infant, Marie-Joseph-Jean-Baptiste.
July 1868	Marie-Joseph-Jean-Baptiste was gravely ill.
August 24, 1868	**Marie-Joseph-Jean-Baptiste died from enteritis and bronchitis in Alençon. He was eight months old.**
1868	Zélie's father's health began to decline and she took charge of nursing him.
1868	Zélie's seventh pregnancy.

September 3, 1868	Isidore Guérin, Sr., (Zélie's father) died in Alençon (Orne) at the age of 79.
October 1868	Pauline and Marie were enrolled in the Visitation Monastery boarding school in Le Mans.
October 1868	Zélie suffered from "violent" toothaches. Overwhelmed with work, Zélie discovered the maid was stealing from them and dismissed her.
April 28, 1869	The birth of Marie-Céline in Alençon. She was Louis and Zélie's seventh child. She was called Céline.
Summer 1869	Céline was sent to three wet nurses and almost died of starvation due to the second wet nurse being an alcoholic and not feeding her. Finally, Céline was sent to Madame Georges, the third wet nurse, who lived in Semallé.
July 2, 1869	Marie received her First Holy Communion at the Visitation Monastery in Le Mans.
July 1869	Sister Marie-Dosithée's tuberculosis went into remission.
September 5, 1869	Céline was given the Complementary Rites of Baptism in the parish Church of St. Pierre de Montsort in Alençon. Her godmother was Céline Guérin, the wife of Zélie's brother, Isidore, and her godfather was Louis' friend, Vital Romet.
Winter 1869	Sister Marie-Dosithée's health worsened due to tuberculosis.
1869-1870	Zélie's eighth pregnancy.

1870-1899

February 22, 1870	Marie-Hélène died in Alençon. The cause of death was unknown. She was five years, four months old.
May 1870	Isidore Guérin opened a wholesale drug business in Lisieux. This was in addition to his pharmacy in Lisieux.
May 21, 1870	Céline returned to her parents' home from the wet nurse.
July 2, 1870	Marie received her Second Solemn Communion.
July 19, 1870 – May 10 1871	The Franco-Prussian War was fought between France and Prussia.
August 16, 1870	The birth of Marie-Mélanie-Thérèse in Alençon. She was Louis and Zélie's eighth child. She was called Thérèse. Four days later she was sent to a wet nurse in Alençon.
August 22, 1870	The birth of Marie-Louise-Hélène Guérin in Lisieux. She was known as Marie and in religion known as Sister Marie of the Eucharist. She was the daughter of Isidore and Céline Fournet Guérin and the sister of Jeanne Guérin. She was the niece of Louis and Zélie Martin, and the cousin of the Martin and Maudelonde children.
September 1, 1870	Napoleon III and 83,000 French troops surrendered to the Prussians.

400

September 3, 1870	The French Empire fell and the Third Republic was installed as the Franco-Prussian War continued.
September 5, 1870	Marie-Mélanie-Thérèse was given the Complementary Rites of Baptism at the parish Church of St. Pierre de Montsort in Alençon. Her godmother was her sister Pauline.
September 14, 1870	Marie-Louise-Hélène Guérin was given the Complementary Rites of Baptism at the parish Church of the Cathedral of St. Pierre in Lisieux. Her godfather was her uncle, Louis Martin.
October 1870	In a visit to see her baby sister Marie-Mélanie-Thérèse, Marie realized that the wet nurse was abusing and neglecting her sister by starving her. She informed her parents, and immediately Louis rescued Marie-Mélanie-Thérèse in the middle of the night but it was too late. The baby was dying of malnutrition.
October 8, 1870	**Marie-Mélanie-Thérèse died in Alençon. She was seven weeks old. The cause of death was neglect and starvation by the wet nurse who was found to be an alcoholic.**
December 30, 1870	Zélie rescued Marie and Pauline from the Visitation Monastery boarding school in Le Mans as war raged in the city.
January 10-12, 1871	The Battle of Le Mans – the French were defeated.
January 15, 1871	The Prussians occupied Alençon until March 7, 1871.
January 16, 1871	Nine Prussian soldiers were lodged in the Martin's home on 15 rue du Pont-Neuf and a soldier stole jewelry from Louis' shop. Louis and Zélie Martin provided food and lodging for the nine soldiers.
January 17, 1871	The Blessed Mother appeared in Pontmain, France.
January 28, 1871	France and Germany signed the Armistice after the defeat of the French Army.
March 26- May 28, 1871	The population of Paris was defiant in the face of defeat. The local authority seized control calling themselves "The Paris Commune."
May 10, 1871	The Treaty of Frankfurt formally ended the war between France and Germany.
May 21-28, 1871	The French National Assembly crushed "The Paris Commune" during the "Bloody Week" in Paris. Over 20,000 people were executed.
May 27, 1871	**Archbishop Georges Darboy, Archbishop of Paris (1863-1871), along with 64 clerics, were shot to death by the Paris Communard.**
1871	Louis and Zélie incurred substantial financial losses in their stock holdings due to the collapse of the French economy as a result of the Franco-Prussian War.
July 1871	Louis sold his home and watch making business on 15 rue du Pont Neuf to his nephew, Adolphe Leriche. The Martin family moved to the rue Saint-Blaise in Alençon. Zélie had inherited

this property from her father upon his death. Louis closed his business and focused his full attention on supporting his wife in her lace-making business.

October 16, 1871	**Paul Guérin, the son of Isidore and Céline Fournet Guérin, was delivered stillborn in Lisieux.**
1872	Zélie's ninth pregnancy.
May 1872	Louis joined a pilgrimage to Chartres of 20,000 men to pray to the Blessed Mother regarding the religious hostility that was spreading throughout France.
July 2, 1872	Pauline received her First Holy Communion at the Visitation Monastery in Le Mans. Zélie became a member of the Pious Union of Our Lady of Good Counsel.
January 2, 1873	**The birth of Marie-Françoise-Thérèse (St. Thérèse of the Child Jesus). She was born on a Tuesday in Alençon. She was Louis and Zélie's ninth child. She was called Thérèse.**
January 4, 1873	Marie-Françoise-Thérèse was baptized in the parish Church of Notre Dame d'Alençon by l'Abbé Lucien Dumaine. Her godmother was her oldest sister Marie and her godfather was Paul Albert Boul, the son of a friend of Louis Martin. L'Abbé Lucien Dumaine later gave testimony regarding Thérèse during the Process of her Beatification.
February 15, 1873	Isidore Guérin entered into a business partnership with his brother-in-law, Césard Maudelonde, in the wholesale drug business in Lisieux.
March 11, 1873	Thérèse was suffering from enteritis and was entrusted to Rose Taillé, the wet nurse in Semallé.
March 27, 1873	Isidore Guérin's wholesale drug business in Lisieux was destroyed by fire. It was later reopened.
April 1873	The Martin's oldest daughter, Marie, was diagnosed with typhoid fever, a potentially fatal disease at that time.
May 5, 1873	Louis went on a pilgrimage to the Butte Chaumont to pray for Marie to be cured.
May 27-28, 1873	Louis went on a second pilgrimage to Chartres.
July 1873	Pauline received her Second Solemn Communion.
July 23, 1873	By decree, the French National Assembly approved the construction of the *Basilique du Sacré-Coeur* (Basilica of the Sacred Heart) in Montmartre, Paris.
October 1873	Louis went on a pilgrimage to the Grotto in Lourdes.
April 2, 1874	Thérèse returned home from the wet nurse on Holy Thursday.
December 8, 1874	Zélie took Léonie to the *Basilique de l'Immaculée Conception* in Sées (Basilica of the Immaculate Conception) to obtain the grace to make a good First Holy Communion.
March 25, 1875	Zélie was enrolled in the Archconfraternity of the Agonizing Heart of Jesus.

May 23, 1875	Léonie received her First Holy Communion on the feast of the Most Holy Trinity in the Church of Notre Dame d'Alençon.
1875	The Pope was confined within the limits of the Vatican.
July 7, 1875	A serious flood in Lisieux left the Carmelite Monastery with severe damage. Zélie Martin sent financial assistance to Lisieux.
August 2, 1875	Marie completed her studies at the Visitation Monastery boarding school and returned to Alençon.
August 20–23, 1875	Louis went on a three day retreat to l'Abbaye de la Trappe in Soligny, France.
November 25, 1875	Louis Martin was one of the founders of the Albert de Mun Catholic Circle in the parish of Notre Dame d'Alençon. He was one of the first pioneers of social action in Alençon.
1875 or 1876	Louis was stung behind the left ear by a poisonous fly. He suffered a great deal from this and it would affect him until his death.
May 21, 1876	Léonie received her Second Solemn Communion.
May 22, 1876	Léonie received the Sacrament of Confirmation.
October 20, 1876	After eleven years of silence, Zélie told her sister-in-law, Céline Guérin, that she was very worried about the pain in her breast.
December 17, 1876	Zélie was diagnosed with inoperable breast cancer.
February 24, 1877	**Sister Marie-Dosithée (Zélie's sister Élise) died on Saturday at the Visitation Monastery in Le Mans from tuberculosis at the age of 48.**
March 10, 1877	Marie, the oldest daughter of Louis and Zélie Martin, brought to Zélie's attention that Louise Marais, the servant, was emotionally and physically abusing Léonie. After Zélie became aware of this abuse, Léonie's behavior changed significantly. Sister Marie-Dosithée was credited with this miracle.
June 17-23, 1877	Zélie, Marie, Pauline and Léonie went on a pilgrimage to Lourdes to pray for Zélie to be cured.
August 26, 1877	Zélie received Extreme Unction.
August 28, 1877	**Zélie Guérin Martin died on Tuesday at 12:30 a.m. in Alençon from breast cancer at the age of 45. She was surrounded by her husband Louis, her brother Isidore, her daughter Marie, and a nursing Sister.**
August 29, 1877	The Funeral Mass for Zélie was held in the Church of Notre Dame d'Alençon and the burial took place in the Cemetery of Notre Dame d'Alençon. Thérèse chose Pauline, and Céline chose Marie as their "second mother."
September 1877	Pauline Martin withdrew from the Visitation Monastery boarding school in Le Mans due to her mother's death.
November 15-16,1877	The Martin children moved to Lisieux and settled in the newly leased family home they called Les Buissonnets.
November 30, 1877	Louis Martin was reunited with his children in Lisieux after selling

	the lace-making business in Alençon for 3,000 francs payable within five years.
1878	Louis Martin and Isidore Guérin established the Nocturnal Eucharistic Adoration in Lisieux.
January 1878	Léonie and Céline were enrolled in the Convent School of l'Abbaye Notre-Dame-du-Pré in Lisieux.
June 17-July 2,1878	Louis, Marie and Pauline went to Paris for the 1878 Exposition Universelle (1878 Paris World's Fair). They also visited Versailles, the Comédie Française and the Bidel Circus.
Summer 1879 or 1880	Thérèse had a prophetic vision of her father's trial.
May 13, 1880	Céline received her First Holy Communion.
June 4, 1880	Céline received the Sacrament of Confirmation in Lisieux.
July 15, 1880	Louis Martin sold the house on the rue Saint-Blaise for 12,000 francs to Jean-Achille Isambart.
1880	Thérèse made her First Confession to l'Abbé Ducellier in Saint Pierre's Cathedral in Lisieux.
October 3, 1881	Thérèse was enrolled in the Convent School of l'Abbaye Notre-Dame-du-Pré in Lisieux where she would continue her studies until March of 1886.
October 2, 1882	Pauline entered the Carmelite Monastery in Lisieux.
March 25, 1883	Louis Martin took Marie and Léonie to Paris to spend Holy Week. On the evening of Easter Sunday Thérèse became ill. Louis was notified and returned home immediately.
April 6, 1883	On Friday Pauline received the Habit of Carmel and the name Soeur Agnès de Jésus (Sister Agnès of Jesus).
April 8, 1883	**Marie-Anne-Fanie Boureau Martin died on Sunday in Valframbert (Orne) at the age of 83. She was Louis Martin's mother.**
May 13, 1883	Thérèse was cured when she saw the statue of Our Lady smile at her. The statue is now called the Virgin of the Smile and rests above the reliquary of St. Thérèse in the chapel of the Carmelite Monastery in Lisieux.
Aug. 20-Sept.3,1883	The Martin family made their first trip back to Alençon to pray at Zélie's grave, to celebrate Thérèse's recovery and to visit family friends. It was the sixth anniversary of Zélie's death.
April 26, 1884	Louis was enrolled in the Archconfraternity of the Holy Face.
May 8, 1884	Thérèse received her First Holy Communion in the chapel of the Convent School of l'Abbaye Notre-Dame-du-Pré in Lisieux.
May 8, 1884	Pauline Martin (Sister Agnès of Jesus) made her Solemn Religious Profession.
May 22, 1884	Thérèse received her Second Solemn Communion.
June 14, 1884	Thérèse received Confirmation from Bishop Flavien Hugonin in Lisieux. Her godmother was her sister, Léonie Martin.

June 26, 1884	Louis gave Thérèse a dog, a spaniel named Tom.
April 26, 1885	Thérèse was enrolled in the Archconfraternity of the Holy Face of Tours.
Aug. 22-Oct.17, 1885	Louis went on a pilgrimage to Central Europe and Turkey.
February 1886	Louis Martin withdrew Thérèse from the Convent School of l'Abbaye Notre-Dame-du-Pré in Lisieux.
March 1886	Madame Papinau became Thérèse's private tutor.
October 1886	The Martin family visited Alençon for the second time to pray at Zélie's grave and to visit family friends. It was the ninth anniversary of Zélie's death. This occurred right before Marie entered the Carmel in Lisieux.
October 7, 1886	Léonie abruptly entered the Monastery of the Poor Clares in Alençon.
October 15, 1886	Marie entered the Carmelite Monastery in Lisieux.
December 1, 1886	Léonie returned home from the Monastery of the Poor Clares in Alençon due to poor health.
December 25, 1886	After Midnight Mass, Thérèse received the grace of conversion at Les Buissonnets. This is known as the Christmas conversion.
1887	Louis Martin lost 50,000 francs on his Panama Canal stock holdings.
March 19, 1887	Marie received the Habit of Carmel and the name Soeur Marie du Sacré-Coeur (Sister Marie of the Sacred Heart).
May 1, 1887	Louis Martin had his first stroke. It temporarily affected his whole left side and his speech. He had two additional strokes in 1887.
May 29, 1887	Thérèse received permission from her father to enter the Carmelite Monastery in Lisieux.
June 1887	Louis, Léonie, Céline and Thérèse attended the International Maritime Exposition in Le Havre.
July 1887	A picture of Jesus bleeding on the cross revealed to Thérèse her apostolic vocation.
July 16, 1887	Léonie entered the Visitation Monastery in Caen for the first time.
August 31, 1887	Thérèse prayed for Pranzini the night before he was sent to the guillotine.
September 1, 1887	Thérèse read in the newspaper *La Croix* the account of Pranzini's execution. Through this account she understood that her prayers were answered. The sign she received affirmed her understanding of Jesus' merciful love. She called Pranzini her "first child," and this confirmed her vocation to pray for sinners.
October 31, 1887	Thérèse went to Bayeux to ask Bishop Flavien Hugonin for permission to enter Carmel.
Oct.1887-April,1888	Thérèse encountered multiple obstacles in her attempt to enter the Carmelite Monastery in Lisieux.

Nov. 4-Dec. 2, 1887	Louis Martin, Thérèse and Céline left for a pilgrimage to Italy (Rome, Milan, Padua, Venice, Loretto, Naples, Pompeii, Assisi, Florence, Pisa and Genoa). On their return trip they visited Marseilles and Lyon.
November 20, 1887	In an audience with Pope Leo XIII, Thérèse asked him for permission to enter the Carmelite Monastery in Lisieux.
1888	Louis Martin offered a gift of a new High Altar to the Cathedral of Saint Pierre in Lisieux. He donated 10,000 francs for the purchase of the altar.
January 6, 1888	Léonie left the Visitation Monastery in Caen and returned home to her family in Lisieux.
April 9, 1888	Thérèse entered the Carmelite Monastery in Lisieux.
May 1888	Louis Martin received a special grace in the Church of Notre Dame d'Alençon, an inspiration to offer his life to God.
May 22, 1888	Marie Martin (Sister Marie of the Sacred Heart) made her Solemn Profession.
June 16, 1888	Céline revealed to her father her wish to enter the Carmelite Monastery in Lisieux.
June 23, 1888	Louis Martin's mental state was seriously deteriorating from dementia and he ran away to Le Havre.
August 12, 1888	Louis Martin had another stroke.
October 31, 1888	Louis Martin had a serious relapse in Le Havre.
January 10, 1889	Thérèse received the Habit of Carmel and the name Soeur Thérèse de l'Enfant-Jésus (Sister Thérèse of the Child Jesus). Later she added the title "of the Holy Face" to her name.
February 12, 1889	Louis Martin was admitted to the Hospital of Bon Sauveur in Caen. This hospital served the mentally ill.
Feb. 19-May 5, 1889	Céline and Léonie became boarders with the Sisters of Saint Vincent de Paul to be near their father at the Hospital of Bon Sauveur in Caen.
April 20, 1889	Isidore Guérin sold the pharmacy to Victor Lahaye and bought a house on the rue de la Chausée in Lisieux, later renamed 19 rue Paul Banaston.
1889	Léonie and Céline went with the Guérin family to Paris for the *1889 Exposition Universelle* (the 1889 Paris World's Fair) for the official opening of the Eiffel Tower.
December 25,1889	The lease on Les Buissonnets expired.
1890	Louis Martin gave an offering of 10,000 francs to the Carmelite Monastery in Lisieux for Thérèse's dowry.
Spring 1890	Céline and Léonie traveled with the Guérin family throughout southern and western France and northern Spain.
September 8, 1890	Thérèse made her Profession of Vows at the Carmelite Monastery in Lisieux.

406

October 1, 1890	Jeanne Guérin and Dr. Francis La Néele were married in Lisieux.
1891-1892	Several sisters in the Lisieux Carmel died as a result of an epidemic of influenza in France. Thérèse nursed the sisters during this crisis.
December 5, 1891	**Mother Geneviève died at the age of 86 in Lisieux. She was the founder of the Carmelite Monastery in Lisieux. She was born in Poitiers on July 19, 1805.**
May 10, 1892	Louis Martin was discharged from the Hospital of Bon Sauveur in Caen and returned to Lisieux. Isidore and Céline Guérin brought Louis, Léonie and Céline to live in their home.
May 12, 1892	Louis Martin visited Carmel for the last time.
June 1892	On Corpus Christi Sunday, in a procession of the Blessed Sacrament through the town, the procession stopped in front of the Guérin home where an Altar of Repose was set up. The priest touched the Monstrance containing the Blessed Sacrament to Louis' head for a prolonged time and Louis' eyes filled with tears.
July 1892	Louis, Léonie and Céline moved to a house they rented across from the Guérin family on 7 rue Labbey in Alençon.
February 20, 1893	Pauline Martin (Mother Agnès of Jesus) was elected Prioress of the Lisieux Carmel until March 21, 1896.
June 24, 1893	Léonie entered the Visitation Monastery in Caen for the second time.
May 27, 1894	Louis suffered a severe stroke affecting his left side. Later that day he received Extreme Unction for the first time.
June 5, 1894	Louis had a serious heart attack.
July 4, 1894	Louis, Léonie and Céline went to La Musse for a few days of rest.
July 28, 1894	Louis had another serious heart attack and received Extreme Unction for the second time from l'Abbé Chillard, the pastor of the village Church of St. Sebastien-de-Morsent.
July 29, 1894	**Louis Martin died on Sunday at 8:15 a.m. at the age of 71 in the presence of his daughter, Céline. Also at his side were Isidore and Céline Guérin. He died at the Château de La Musse in St. Sebastien-de-Morsent (Eure).**
August 2, 1894	The Funeral Mass for Louis was held on Thursday in the Cathedral of Saint Pierre in Lisieux and the burial took place in the cemetery in Lisieux.
August 1894	Céline, the Guérin family, Jeanne and Francis La Néele spent a week in Caen and on the coast of Nacre.
September 14, 1894	Céline entered the Carmelite Monastery in Lisieux and was given the name Soeur Marie de la Sainte-Face (Sister Marie of the Holy Face).

October 11, 1894	After Louis' death, Isidore Guérin made arrangements for Zélie and her four children that died, Zélie's father, Louis' mother and other family members to be exhumed in Alençon and buried in a family tomb in the cemetery in Lisieux.
December 1894	Mother Agnès of Jesus requested that Thérèse write her childhood memories.
December 7, 1894	**Adolphe Leriche died on Friday at the age of 50. He was the son of Louis Martin's sister, Anne-Françoise-Fanny Martin Leriche Burin. He was the husband of Marie Nanteau and the father of their two children. He bought the clock and watch making business from Louis Martin. After Louis Martin moved to Lisieux, his mother Marie-Anne-Fannie Boureau Martin remained in her apartment at 15 rue du Pont Neuf, the home of Adolphe Leriche, her grandson, who took care of her. Later, Louis moved his mother to a home in Valframbert and she was cared for by Rose Taillé, the former wet nurse of three of the Martin children.**
1895	During this year Thérèse wrote Manuscript A at the request of her sister, Mother Agnès of Jesus.
February 5, 1895	Céline received the Habit of Carmel and the name Soeur Geneviève de Sainte Thérèse, in memory of the foundress of Carmel. In 1916 her name was changed to Soeur Geneviève de la Sainte-Face (Sister Geneviève of the Holy Face).
June 9, 1895	Thérèse was inspired to offer herself to Merciful Love.
June 11, 1895	Thérèse and Céline made the Oblation to Merciful Love.
July 20, 1895	Léonie left the Visitation Monastery for the second time.
August 15, 1895	Marie Guérin entered the Carmelite Monastery in Lisieux.
1896-1899	Pauline Martin (Sister Agnès of Jesus) was elected bursar of the Carmelite Monastery in Lisieux.
February 24, 1896	Céline made her religious profession at the Carmelite Monastery in Lisieux.
March 17, 1896	Marie Guérin received the Habit of Carmel and the name Soeur Marie de l'Eucharistie (Sister Marie of the Eucharist).
April 2-3, 1896	Thérèse experienced the first hemoptysis.
April 3, 1896	Thérèse experienced the second hemoptysis.
September 8, 1896	Thérèse wrote Manuscript B (addressed to Jesus) at the request of her sister, Sister Marie of the Sacred Heart.
Sept. 13-16, 1896	Thérèse wrote a letter to Sister Marie of the Sacred Heart. This became the first part of Manuscript B.
March 25, 1897	Marie Guérin (Sister Marie of the Eucharist) made her religious profession at the Carmelite Monastery in Lisieux.
April 1897	Thérèse fell gravely ill.
June-Sept. 1897	Thérèse wrote Manuscript C at the request of her Prioress, Mother Marie de Gonzague.

July 30, 1897	Thérèse received Extreme Unction.
September 30, 1897	**On Thursday around 7:20 p.m., Thérèse Martin (Sister Thérèse of the Child Jesus) died at the age of 24 in the Carmelite Monastery in Lisieux. Her final words were, "Oh My God, I Love You."**
October 4, 1897	Thérèse was buried in the cemetery in Lisieux. Léonie Martin led the funeral procession with Mr. Césard Maudelonde (Isidore and Céline Guérin's brother-in-law), from the Chapel in the Carmelite Monastery to the cemetery in Lisieux. Isidore Guérin was unable to attend due to his suffering from gout.
September 30, 1898	*Story of a Soul*, a 475 page book, was published. Isidore Guérin financed the publication of the First Edition and 2,000 copies were printed.
1899-1902	Pauline Martin (Sister Agnès of Jesus) was elected sub-prioress of the Carmelite Monastery in Lisieux.
January 28, 1899	Léonie definitively entered the Visitation Monastery in Caen.
May 11, 1899	The Guérin and Maudelonde families agreed to sell Château de La Musse. In 1932, after passing through many hands, it became a large sanatorium for tuberculosis patients.
June 30, 1899	Léonie received the Habit of the Visitation and the name Soeur Françoise-Thérèse.

1900 - 2008

February 13, 1900	**Élise-Céline Fournet Guérin died on Tuesday in Lisieux of influenza one month before she was 53. On her death bed her last words were "My Jesus I love You – I offer my life for priests like my little Thérèse of the Child Jesus." She was the wife of Isidore Guérin, the mother of Jeanne Guérin La Néele, Marie Guérin (Sister Marie of the Eucharist) and Paul Guérin (delivered stillborn). She was also the sister-in-law of Louis and Zélie Martin and the aunt of Marie, Pauline, Léonie, Céline and Thérèse.**
July 2, 1900	Léonie made her solemn religious profession. Her cousin, Dr. Francis La Néele, represented the family at the ceremony. Jeanne Guérin La Néele and her father, Isidore Guérin were unable to attend due to illness and her aunt, Madame Céline Guérin, had died on February 13, 1900.
1902-1908	Pauline Martin (Mother Agnès of Jesus) was elected Prioress of the Carmelite Monastery in Lisieux.
December 17, 1904	**Mother Marie de Gonzague died at the age of 70 of cancer on Saturday in the Carmelite Monastery in Lisieux, where she had been the former Prioress. She was born in Caen on February 21, 1834.**
April 14, 1905	**Marie Guérin (Sister Marie of the Eucharist) died on Friday at 10:15 a.m. of tuberculosis at the age of 34 in the Carmelite Monastery in Lisieux. She was the daughter of Isidore and Céline Fournet**

Guérin and the sister of Jeanne Guérin La Néele. She was the niece of Louis and Zélie Martin and the cousin of Marie, Pauline, Léonie, Céline and Thérèse.

September 28, 1909   Isidore Guérin died in Lisieux on Tuesday at 10:45 a.m. at the age of 68 after suffering from chronic liver ailments and arthritis. He was the brother of Élise Guérin (Sr. Marie-Dosithée) and Zélie Guérin Martin. He was the husband of Élisa-Céline Fournet Guérin and the father of Jeanne Guérin La Néele, Marie Guérin (Sister Marie of the Eucharist) and Paul Guérin (delivered stillborn). He was also the brother-in-law of Louis Martin and the uncle of Marie, Pauline, Léonie, Céline and Thérèse. He was a member of the Carmelite Third Order and as a Carmelite he was known as Brother Elijah of the Blessed Sacrament.

October 1, 1909   The Funeral Mass for Isidore Guérin was held on Friday in the Cathedral of Saint Pierre in Lisieux.

November 1909   Pauline Martin (Mother Agnès of Jesus) was elected Prioress of the Carmelite Monastery in Lisieux after the death on November 11, 1909, of Mother Marie-Ange, and remained Prioress until her death.

1910   The Martin home on the rue Saint-Blaise was purchased by the Carmelite Monastery in Lisieux.

August 1910   The opening of the Bishop's Process for the Beatification of Sister Thérèse of the Child Jesus.

June 10, 1914   The Cause for the Beatification of Sister Thérèse of the Child Jesus was introduced by Pope Pius X.

March 17, 1915   The Apostolic Process for the Beatification of Sister Thérèse of the Child Jesus was opened in Bayeux.

1916   The name of Sister Geneviève of St. Teresa (Céline Martin) was changed to Sister Geneviève of the Holy Face.

March 19, 1916   Dr. Francis La Néele died on Sunday at the age of 57. He married Jeanne Guérin on October 1, 1890. In 1894, he treated Louis Martin in his final days. In 1897, he treated Thérèse several times for her illness. He was extremely dissatisfied with the medical care she was receiving. In 1908, a major miracle occurred at the grave of Sister Thérèse of the Child Jesus. A four-year old blind child was instantaneously cured and Dr. La Néele, not in favor of the Beatification of Thérèse, was obliged to validate the cure. He signed the medical certificate on May 7, 1908. On September 6, 1910, he was present at the exhumation of Sister Thérèse at the Lisieux Cemetery with several hundred people present. He made the customary statement of a medical doctor. In December 1909, he bought Les Buissonnets and by 1913 the house was opened for pilgrim visits. In 1922, Jeanne Guérin La Néele sold Les Buissonnets to the Building Society for Pilgrims. In the early 1900's Dr. La Néele also acquired property in Belgium for the Lisieux Carmel in the event that the French Republic closed the monasteries and expelled the nuns from France.

November 15, 1919   Father Almire Pichon died in Paris at the age of 76. He was a missionary to Canada and had been the spiritual director to the Martin family.

August 14, 1921   Pope Benedict XV promulgated the Decree on the Heroicity of the Virtues of the Venerable Servant of God, Sister Thérèse of the Child Jesus.

1923   Pope Pius XI appointed Mother Agnès of Jesus Prioress for life at the Carmelite Monastery in Lisieux.

March 26, 1923   Thérèse's relics were taken from the cemetery to the Carmelite Monastery in Lisieux where 50,000 pilgrims lined the route. Her relics remain there today.

April 29, 1923   The Beatification of Sister Thérèse of the Child Jesus at St. Peter's Basilica in Rome by Pope Pius XI.

December 23, 1923   Louise Marais, the Martin's family servant, died. In marriage she was known as Madame Legendre. She was the mother of several children.

May 17, 1925   The Solemn Canonization of Blessed Thérèse of the Child Jesus at St. Peter's Basilica in Rome by Pope Pius XI.

December 14, 1927   Pope Pius XI proclaimed St. Thérèse of the Child Jesus Principal Patroness, equal to Saint Francis Xavier, of all missionaries, men and women, and of the missions of the whole world.

April 25, 1938   Jeanne-Marie-Élisa Guérin La Néele died on Monday in Nogent-le-Rotrou (Eure-et-Loir) at the age of 70. She was the daughter of Isidore and Élisa-Céline Fournet Guérin, the sister of Marie Guérin (Sister Marie of the Eucharist) and the wife of Dr. Francis La Néele. She was also the niece of Louis and Zélie Martin and the cousin of Marie, Pauline, Léonie, Céline and Thérèse. After her husband died in 1916, she adopted her husband's great-niece.

January 19, 1940   Marie Martin (Sister Marie of the Sacred Heart) died on Friday at the age of 79 in the Carmelite Monastery in Lisieux.

June 16, 1941   Léonie Martin (Sister Françoise-Thérèse) died on Monday at the age of 78 in the Visitation Monastery in Caen.

May 1941-Nov.1954   Fragments of Zélie Martin's letters are published in the *Annales de sainte Thérèse de Lisieux*.

May 3, 1944   Pope Pius XII named Saint Thérèse of the Child Jesus Secondary Patroness of France, equal to Saint Joan of Arc.

June 6-Aug. 26, 1944   The nuns of the Carmelite Monastery of Lisieux hid in the crypt of the Basilica of Saint Thérèse during the bombing of Lisieux during World War II.

1946   The publication of *Story of a Family* by Father Stéphane-Joseph Piat, O.F.M.

July 28, 1951	**Pauline Martin (Mother Agnès of Jesus) died on Saturday at the age of 89 in the Carmelite Monastery in Lisieux.**
March 22, 1957	The opening of the Bishop's Process to explore the Cause for the Canonization of Louis Martin.
October 10, 1957	The opening of the Bishop's Process to explore the Cause for the Canonization of Zélie Guérin Martin.
1958	The exhumation of Louis and Zélie Martin and their transferal to the Basilica of Saint Thérèse in Lisieux.
February 25, 1959	**Céline Martin (Sister Geneviève of the Holy Face) died on Wednesday at the age of 89 in the Carmelite Monastery in Lisieux.**
1971	The Beatification Process of Louis and Zélie Martin proceeded as a single cause.
1973	The celebration of the Centenary of the birth of Saint Thérèse.
March 15, 1994	The Congregation for the Causes of Saints recognized the heroic virtues of Louis and Zélie Martin.
March 26, 1994	Pope John Paul II promulgated the Decree on the Heroicity of the Virtues of the Venerable Servants of God, Louis and Zélie Martin.
1997	The celebration of the Centenary of the death of Saint Thérèse of the Child Jesus.
October 19, 1997	Pope John Paul II proclaimed Saint Thérèse of the Child Jesus and of the Holy Face a "Doctor of the Church."
May 25, 2002	Pietro Schilirò was born in Monza, Italy, and taken immediately to the intensive care unit with a serious respiratory insufficiency.
June 3, 2002	Doctors declared Pietro in mortal danger.
June 2002	Father Antonio Sangalli, O.C.D., a friend of Pietro's parents, suggested they say a novena to the Servants of God Louis and Zélie Martin for Pietro to be cured.
June 29, 2002	An inexplicable medical recovery of little Pietro Schilirò, as a result of his parents, family and friends praying to the Servants of God Louis and Zélie Martin.
July 2, 2002	Pietro taken off the respirator.
July 27, 2002	Pietro discharged from the hospital completely recovered. He was 63 days old.
June 10, 2003	Cardinal Dionigi Tettamanzi, Archbishop of Milan, officially recognized the miracle and complete recovery of Pietro Schilirò.
October 19, 2008	The Beatification of Louis and Zélie Martin in the Basilica of St. Thérèse in Lisieux, France.

The Summary of the Cause of Beatification of Louis and Zélie Martin

It is very clear that Louis and Zélie were beatified on October 19, 2008, not because they were the parents of a saint, their daughter Thérèse, canonized by Pope Pius XI on May 17, 1925, in Rome, but because their lives – each of them – were recognized by the Church, after a meticulous and long investigation, to be in accordance with Christian life.

Of course, this investigation applied to their personal lives. The one concerning Louis Martin was conducted by a tribunal in the Diocese of Bayeux and Lisieux and Zélie's by a tribunal in the Diocese of Séez, since she died in Alençon.

There's only one distinctive feature that is important, it's true: beginning in 1971, their cause advanced as that of a couple. Up until then, in the history of sainthood in the Catholic Church, there's been only one other case like this.[612]

The main steps of the process were as follows:[613]

In 1925, during the celebrations in Lisieux of Thérèse Martin's canonization, Cardinal Antonio Vico, Prefect of the Sacred Congregation of Rites (which then dealt with the causes of saints), exclaimed, "Well, Rome now asks that we take care of Papa!"

Because of *Story of a Soul* (1898), written by Thérèse, Louis was much better known than Zélie Martin.

In 1941, the publication of her mother's letters began in the

---

[612] Luigi and Maria Beltrame Quattrocchi died respectively in 1951 and 1965. They had four children. Pope John Paul II beatified them on October 21, 2001.

[613] For this summary, we have greatly benefited from the work of Marie-Béatrice de Cérou, Doctor of Law, Director of Research at The Law School of Aix-en-Provence, published in *Vie Thérésienne*, No. 160, 2000. *"Louis et Zélie en route vers la béatification"* ["Louis and Zélie On the Way Towards Beatification"], pp. 7-23.

journal *Annales de sainte Thérèse de Lisieux* and, in 1946, *Histoire d'une famille* [Story of a Family] by Father Stéphane-Joseph Piat, O.F.M., was published. Its success was considerable. Its reprinting continues today and has exceeded more than one hundred thousand copies. It's been translated into numerous languages with particular success in the United States and Canada.

On February 6, 1946, during the golden jubilee of Sister Geneviève of the Holy Face (Céline Martin,) Bishop François-Marie Picaud, the Bishop of Bayeux and Lisieux, while making a toast, expressed a wish in front of the Apostolic Nuncio of France, Archbishop Angelo Roncalli (the future Pope John XXIII) that the cause of the Martin parents be opened.

In 1953, Sister Geneviève published *Le Père de sainte Thérèse de l'Enfant-Jésus* [The Father of Saint Thérèse of the Child Jesus] (Carmelite Monastery of Lisieux) with sixteen letters by Louis Martin in the appendix.[614]

In 1954, *La Mère de sainte Thérèse de l'Enfant-Jésus* [The Mother of Saint Thérèse of the Child Jesus] was published (same publishers), also written by Céline Martin.[615]

All over the world petitions suddenly appeared asking for the opening of their cause. Thus a bishop in the United States (in Paterson) received thirty thousand seven hundred signatures.

It was then, in a letter dated February 2, 1956, that Mother Françoise-Thérèse, the Prioress of the Carmelite Monastery in Lisieux, asked the Bishop of Bayeux and Lisieux, Bishop André Jacquemin, to open the two causes.

On February 24, 1956, for the sixtieth anniversary of Céline's religious profession, the bishop announced the forthcoming opening of the informative process for Louis Martin. It's true that, according to Canon Law, it should have been prepared in the Diocese of Evreux

---

[614] This book was initially published in English in 1955 under the title *The Father of the Little Flower*, by M.H. Gill and Son, Ltd., Dublin, as well as The Newman Press, Westminster, Maryland, and reissued in 2005 by TAN Books and Publishers, Inc., Charlotte, North Carolina, by permission of Office Central de Lisieux.

[615] This book was initially published in English in 1957 under the title *The Mother of the Little Flower* by M.H. Gill and Son, Ltd., Dublin, and reissued in 2005 by TAN Books and Publishers, Inc., Charlotte, North Carolina, by permission of Office Central de Lisieux.

since he died in La Musse, but Bishop Alphonse-Paul-Désiré Gaudron, the Bishop of Evreux, relinquished the cause for the benefit of the Diocese of Bayeux and Lisieux.

Two Processes for Canonization

At first they were prepared separately from 1957 to 1960.

The process for Louis Martin began in Lisieux on March 22, 1957. Twenty-three witnesses were questioned in Sées, one in Vannes and one in Le Mans for a healing attributed to Louis.

On February 12, 1960, the Bayeux process was closed in the chapel of the Carmelite Monastery in Lisieux. Taken to Rome, it was recognized as valid on June 8, 1990, by the Congregation for the Causes of Saints.

In parallel, *the process for Zélie Martin* took place from October 10, 1957, to January 7, 1959, in Sées. Thirteen witnesses were heard, one in Chartres, one in Vannes and two in Paris. Eight were questioned in Lisieux for a total of twenty-five witnesses.

The validity of this process was recognized by Rome on February 15, 1991.

On June 9, 1964, the writings of Louis and Zélie Martin were examined and approved by Pope Paul VI and the Sacred Congregation for Rites.

In 1971 the cause became "historical" because of the small number of living witnesses.

The Joining of the Causes of the Two Spouses

Mgr Giovanni Papa, Vice General Rapporteur in Rome, and Madame Marie Perrier (of the secular institute *Notre Dame de Vie*) worked on the presentation of the cause "as a couple."

Forty-nine libraries or archives were consulted, including those of the Carmelite Monastery in Lisieux, which has 9,700 letters essentially evoking veneration of the Martin parents.

This considerable work, after several unforeseen events (various deaths, reorganization of the Roman Curia, etc.) led to a *Positio* in two volumes of 690 and 1,340 pages. Father Simeon of the Holy Family, the Postulator General of the Carmelites, appointed since

1973, brought to a successful conclusion all the work begun thirty-four years earlier.

On March 19, 1991, Father Simeon asked Rome to examine the *Positio* and to recognize "the heroic virtues" of the Martin parents.

Joining him were the Carmelite Monastery in Lisieux, the Diocese of Bayeux and Lisieux, the bishops of France, associations of lay people and Catholic families the world over, the Pontifical Council for the Laity and that of the Family.

On December 20, 1993, the theological consultants gave a favorable opinion.

On March 15, 1994, under a proposal put forth by the Canadian Cardinal Edouard Gagnon, the bishops and cardinals of the Roman Congregations recognized Louis and Zélie Martin as heroic in the practice of their virtues.

On March 26, 1994, in the Year of the Family, Pope John Paul II signed the decrees of heroic virtues of Louis and Zélie Martin and declared them "Venerables."

Thus one could venerate them while awaiting the recognition of a miracle for them to be beatified.

That miracle just took place.

The Healing of the Baby Pietro Schilirò

Pietro Schilirò, the fifth child of Valter and Adèle Leo, was born on May 25, 2002, at Saint Gerard Hospital (Ospedale San Gerardo) in Monza, Italy. He was immediately transported from the delivery room to the intensive care unit due to serious respiratory insufficiency. He was intubated and hooked up to a respirator. On June 3rd, the doctors declared him to be in mortal danger. His parents called Father Antonio Sangalli, O.C.D., a Carmelite priest in Monza, to baptize Pietro immediately as a matter of urgency, which he did. On June 6th, with the consent of his parents, a biopsy was done to help make a diagnosis.

Father Sangalli then suggested to the parents, whom he'd known for years, that they say a novena to Louis and Zélie Martin, which they agreed to do, asking many friends and family members to join them. They gave them the text of the novena. A picture of the Martin parents was attached to Pietro's crib. The results of the biopsy weren't good,[616] and yet the doctors were surprised to notice that the child was tolerating the ventilation of his lungs without succumbing.

Doctor d'Allessio, a surgeon at the Hospital of Legnano (Milan), declared that the results of the macroscopic examination indicated the worst conditions, and, in his opinion, Pietro's condition was hopeless.

Doctor Capellini of the hospital in Monza, based on a histological examination, spoke of a congenital malformation due to an insufficiency in lung maturation. Doctor Zorloni warned the Schilirò family that the fatal outcome was approaching and that some postmortem specimens would be taken on the newborn for future examination.

The family and their friends began a second novena. On June 13th, after the recitation of the rosary, Father Sangalli repeated the request to Louis and Zélie Martin to make known the will of God and cure the child.

The doctors noticed some unexpected improvements to the point that on June 29th, Pietro's feast day, a noticeable improvement became apparent. On July 2nd, the child was taken off the respirator, and on the 27th, he left the hospital. He was sixty-three days old.

On September 14th, Pietro was brought to the parish of Monza to receive the Complementary Rites of Baptism in the presence of 400 people who gave thanks.

A number of doctors advised the parents to have their son's case reviewed by a committee of the Church.

From December 31, 2002, to January 3, 2003, the Schilirò family, with seven-month old Pietro, Father Sangalli and some Italian pilgrims, went to give thanks in Lisieux.

The Cardinal Archbishop of Milan, Cardinal Dionigi Tettamanzi, opened the process to examine this inexplicable healing.

On June 10, 2003 (after an interrogation of dozens of witnesses, including seven doctors), in the chapel of the Archbishop of Milan

---

[616] Examination number I 10107.2002 on June 6, 2002 of Pietro Schilirò, born May 25, 2002, hospitalization number 2002021927, Codes T-28000 M74000. Ospedale San Gerardo in Monza, Italy. V.O. of anatomy and pathological histology. Director: Professor R. Buffa.

and in the presence of the Carmelite Postulator for the Cause of the Martin parents, Father Simeon of the Holy Family; Bishop Angelo Amadeo, Instructor of the Process; Bishop Guy Gaucher, Auxiliary Bishop of Bayeux and Lisieux; the Schilirò family; Pietro (thirteen months old) and about a hundred other people, the Cardinal recognized the miraculous origin of this healing and announced it to the Congregation for the Causes of Saints. On July 7, 2003, Pope John Paul II was informed about it.

Louis and Zélie Martin were beatified on October 19, 2008, in Lisieux, France at the Basilica of St. Thérèse.

Bibliography

For any additional research done for the English edition of this book, the source(s) have been documented in the footnotes. Below is the bibliography for the French edition of the book.

Regarding the Martin family, one can refer to the *Nouvelle Édition du centenaire: Œuvres complètes de Thérèse de Lisieux* [New Centenary Edition: The Complete Works of Thérèse of Lisieux], Éditions du Cerf-Desclée de Brouwer, 1992, comprising eight volumes. (Not translated.)

MARTIN, ZÉLIE, the mother of St. Thérèse of the Child Jesus, *Correspondance familiale (fragments), 1863-1877* [Family Correspondence (fragments), 1863-1877], Lisieux, France: Office Central de Lisieux, 1958.

PIAT, STÉPHANE-JOSEPH, O.F.M., *Histoire d'une famille*, Lisieux, France: Office Central de Lisieux, 1946. *Story of a Family*, Charlotte, North Carolina: TAN Books and Publishers, Inc., 1994.

_____ *Céline, soeur et témoin de sainte Thérèse de l'Enfant-Jésus*, Lisieux: Office Central de Lisieux, 1964. *Céline, Sister and Witness to St. Thérèse of the Child Jesus*, San Francisco, California: Ignatius Press, 1997.

_____ *Marie, soeur aînée et marraine de sainte Thérèse de l'Enfant Jésus* [Marie, Oldest Sister and Godmother of St. Thérèse of the Child Jesus], Lisieux: Office Central de Lisieux, 1966. (Not translated.)

_____ *Léonie (une soeur de sainte Thérèse à la Visitation)* [Léonie, A Sister of St. Thérèse at the Visitation Monastery], Lisieux: Office Central de Lisieux, 1966. (Not translated.)

SISTER GENEVIÈVE OF THE HOLY FACE (CÉLINE MARTIN), *Le Père de sainte Thérèse de l'Enfant Jésus (1823-1894) Témoignages et documents* [The Father of St. Thérèse of the Child Jesus, Testimony and Documents], Lisieux, France: Office Central de Lisieux, 1966, with 16 letters by Louis Martin in the appendix. *The Father of the Little Flower, Louis Martin 1823-1894*, tr. Fr. Michael Collins, S.M.A. Charlotte, North Carolina: TAN Books and Publishers, 2005.

_____ *La Mère de sainte Thérèse de l'Enfant Jésus (1831-1877), souvenir filial* [The Mother of St. Thérèse of the Child Jesus, Filial Memories], Lisieux, France: Office Central de Lisieux, 1966. *The Mother of the Little Flower, Zélie Martin 1823-1894*, tr. Fr. Michael Collins, S.M.A. Charlotte, North Carolina: TAN Books and Publishers, 2005.

CADÉOT, DR. ROBERT, *Louis Martin, «père incomparable» de sainte Thérèse de l'Enfant Jésus, un témoin pour notre temps* [Louis Martin, "Incomparable Father" of St. Thérèse of the Child Jesus, a Witness for Our Times], Preface by René Laurentin, V.A.L., 1985. (Not translated.)

_____ *Zélie Martin, «mère incomparable» de sainte Thérèse de l'Enfant Jésus, une «femme forte» pour notre temps* [Zélie Martin, Incomparable Mother of St. Thérèse of the Child Jesus, a "Strong Woman" for Our Times], Preface by Marie-Baudouin-Croix, V.A.L., 1990. (Not translated.)

COLLOQUE INTERNATIONAL DE LISIEUX, *«Thérèse et sa famille»* [Thérèse and Her Family], *Vie Thérésienne*. Nos. 157, 158, 159, 160, 2000. 13 lectures (released on audio cassette). (Not translated.)

CONGREGATIO DE CAUSIS SANCTORUM, *Canonizationis servorum Dei Ludovici Martin et Mariae Azeliae Guerin coniugum († 1894, 1877): Positio super virtutibus*, Vol. I, *Roma*, 1991, 679 p., plus 12 p.; Vol. II, *ibid.*, 1252 p., plus 60 p.

Regarding the textual problems, see *Correspondance familiale*, pp. 551-562.

Unpublished works on "Little Thérèse": copies of Zélie Martin's letters by Sister Marie of the Trinity published in *Vie Thérésienne*, No. 88, October 1982, pp. 310-318; No. 89, January 1983, p. 66 (letter dated March 10, 1926); No. 93, January 1984, pp. 70-80.

One can also refer to the *Archives de famille* [Family Archives], published in *Vie Thérésienne, Nos. 33 to 56, October 1969 to January 1974.